The A–Z of
BRADMAN

Every fact you ever wanted
to know about the Don,
and many you had never imagined

ALAN EASON

ABC
Books

Published by ABC Books for the
AUSTRALIAN BROADCASTING CORPORATION
GPO Box 9994 Sydney NSW 2001

First published by the author in June 2002
This revised edition published by ABC Books in December 2004

National Library of Australia
Cataloguing-in-Publication data:
   Eason, Alan.
   The A-Z of Bradman.

   ISBN 0 7333 1517 8.

   1. Bradman, Donald, Sir, 1908-2001.
   2. Cricket players – Australia – Biography.
   I. Australian Broadcasting Corporation.
   II. Title.
796.358092

Cover design by Christabella Designs
Cover image from a painting in the ABC collection by Paul Newton
Internals set in 11/14pt Times
Colour reproduction by Griffin Press, Adelaide
Printed and bound in Australia by Griffin Press, Adelaide

5 4 3 2 1

About the author

Alan Eason was born in Sydney in 1947. He studied accounting but when he found words were more interesting than figures he tried his hand at compiling cryptic crosswords and published his first, in the *Sydney Morning Herald*, in 1977. Soon after, he branched out into theme crosswords, becoming a regular contributor to newspapers and magazines of puzzles on a wide range of subjects, including cricket, as well as large general knowledge crosswords.

Eason is the author of two books on crosswords and has contributed articles on crosswords to the *Herald*. In 1988 he started Australia's first national crossword club and edited and produced a monthly magazine for members until 1991. Also a trivia buff, he wrote and edited multiple-choice trivia games for interactive television from 1994 to 1998.

Away from the desk, Alan Eason is a keen tennis and soccer player but was stumped in a backyard Test in 1968 by the realisation that his cricket career was effectively over before it had started.

To my wife, Mary, for her patient endurance,
and my brother, Steve, who endured the unendurable

Foreword

No Australian, surely, has ever attracted so much curiosity and so many words of eulogy and analysis as Don Bradman – not Nellie Melba, or R.G. Menzies, or Howard Florey, or Barry Humphries; not even Keith Miller, or Dennis Lillee, or Shane Warne or Steve Waugh. And not even Ned Kelly.

The longer he lived (and he reached 92) the more the almost holy aura around Bradman seemed to grow. The paradox, of course, is that in so many ways he was not the typical Australian: at least not by today's modified standards. He valued his English ancestry almost as keenly as he guarded his privacy. He was conservative. He was the antithesis of the irreverent larrikin, and was certainly anything but the tall, suntanned Digger. Perhaps, as Wendy Frew suggests in this collection, Sir Donald Bradman remains a manifestation of Australia's quest for identity, a quest which has become something of a national obsession. As potent as any sentence in this book is the one which postulates that "The Bradman myth is also as much about nostalgia for a lost Australia as it is about how Australia is defined today." I go along with that. The British equivalent would be Winston Churchill.

Alan Eason's net has stretched far and scooped at great depth. There are already enough biographies of Bradman to prop up the car, with a volume or two to spare, while you change a wheel. The chronology of a conventional life story – especially one recapitulated so many times as this one – can have a leadening effect, but this A to Z is not afflicted in that way.

Nor is it just an A to Z. It is also a 0 to 99.94 – or 334 – or 452 – or 974 – or even 28,067. All but the youngest reader, probably, will know what I mean.

There is trivia aplenty (and doesn't trivia just calm the soul?), and there is also some beguiling, obscure material that generates wonder at its discovery. In the avalanche of tributes following the death of the Don in 2001, how many of us took on board the significance of the elegantly worded condolences from United Nations secretary general Kofi Annan? How many had heard about young Bradman's touching gesture in helping an unemployed miner (wife and eight kids) who stood looking wistfully through the gates into the Trent Bridge ground in 1934?

Page after page is dotted with fascinating data; facts that would otherwise take ages to retrieve. Don hit 2,586 fours in first-class cricket. Why, that's got to be more than I his with that old ball in Mum's stocking dangling from the clothes-line. Just as Billy Bigelow (Gordon MacRae) sang in *Carousel* that his son wouldn't be president unless he wanted to be, so Bradman hit sixes only when he felt like it, and then somewhat reluctantly, briefly suspending his burning belief that the ball was best kept on the turf. He hit 45 balls over the pickets; but naturally it could have been more, had he so chosen.

Sometimes belief is stretched, as in Dickie Bird's claim that his father walked from Barnsley to Leeds to watch Bradman bat. The distance, some 35km, must have taken the best part of seven hours to cover, even for a fit young man, and as soon as he got there it must have been nearly time to start the return journey. Maybe he hitched a ride part of the way. This, though, was the sort of thing people did in order to see Bradman bat. And the lucky ones are bragging about it to this day.

For the statistically minded (and don't ever believe any man who says that stats don't interest him), here is a feast. Consider some of the revelations that follow: if Bradman's 117 centuries are removed from his record, he would still have averaged 58. Even the most cynical, worn-out cricket reader must surely gasp at that. And what was his worst run of innings without a century? A mere thirteen. Had he not had a serious illness brewing within him at that time in 1934, the longest sequence throughout his career would have been even shorter. Time and again the reader is shown how far ahead Don Bradman stood not only of all contemporary batsmen but of all who have ever played the game.

It is important that this should not have become a biased word sculpture of Don Bradman. Alan Eason has incorporated items which pinpoint some of the man's fallibilities. This has long been a bone of contention. Was he – and should he be depicted as – the perfect human being? He was always great company, alert and always ready for a chuckle. Some of us believe that he becomes more interesting and credible when his peccadillos are exposed. This process reduces the gap between him and the rest of us; friends, admirers, and even worshippers. Ah, so he got angry sometimes? He occasionally made wrong decisions? He cared about his image? Look at the entry for "Aestheticization" for a start. And his skipper, Bill Woodfull, "never forgave him for a couple of things" (never identified – one may have been the leak of Woodfull's angry but private remarks during the Adelaide Bodyline Test, and the other the unorthodox batting technique Bradman employed against Larwood and Voce during that red-hot summer, which displeased some of his teammates who themselves were repeatedly hit by bouncers). Nor does the compiler shirk from mentioning the whiff of scandal surrounding the Hodgetts stockbroking-business affair in 1945, a story which angered family and close friends when it made print in 2001.

These squirm-inducing blips serve as important reminders that Bradman was human and vulnerable, though across the years many a toiling bowler must have had serious doubts. The best reminders of his normalness emerge from the cameos of Don, the tyro champion, which pop up in this A to Z from time to time, none more graphic than Banjo Paterson's description of the boy wonder from the bush, employed then (1929) in a Sydney sport shop: "a wiry sunburnt young bush chap ... a hard-looking young fellow and he's very light on his feet."

You need look no further than a remarkable statement made by Bradman when he was 90: "In all my life, I have never had self-confidence in anything I did off the cricket field." The interviewer, Frank Devine, concluded that the iron will exercised by the Don in overcoming that lack of confidence in so many spheres of life was "a marvel of courage sustained."

Don, of course, rejoiced in acknowledging how much he owed to the unwavering support of Jessie, the utterly charming and lovable wife whom he knew for almost the entire duration of his life. The most touching entry here is for Lady Jessie.

This is an astounding pot-pourri of Bradmania. Who souvenired his speech notes after his induction into the Australian Sports Hall of Fame in 1988? What was his only recorded risque remark? Which were the slowest and fastest of his 117 first-class centuries? Who called the doctor when he collapsed with peritonitis during the 1934 tour? How many catches did he miss in his 37 Test matches against England? Who gave him a 21st birthday party at Sans Souci?

The answers to these and hundreds of other questions are here. Read, digest, then apply to go on a television quiz show. You'd be a strong best to take first prize.

David Frith
October 2004

Introduction

Yes, the Bradman story has been told umpteen times (and you can get anything you want on him at the click of a mouse), but this is the first book on the Don in the A–Z format.

The truth is that I wrote this tome for myself. Apart from the fact that (like anyone else old enough to walk) I am fascinated by the achievements and the legend of the Don, one of my favourite idle diversions is to dip into any good reference book and browse at leisure. But I'm gambling that I'm not on my own. And this book is probably *the* quintessential dipper. Such is the density of the detail, it would be a brave soul who tried to read it from cover to cover.

But there were decisions I had to make. The first and most fundamental was what to put in and what to leave out. Charles Dolling gets an entry because it was his death when a Test selector which occasioned Bradman's first appointment to the panel in 1936, but the other two selectors at the time, though they are mentioned in the entry on Clarrie Grimmett, do not score a headword. Of the many "ordinary" cricketers who played with and against the Don, I've included only those with a connection to him through an incident, a quote, or the like. Similarly with non-players. But I was also on the lookout for useless information which would be of interest only to trivia freaks: like the movie which was in production when Bradman visited MGM Studios in Hollywood with Arthur Mailey's tourists in 1932, and the name of the ABC publicist who accompanied mouth-organ legend Larry Adler to the Don's home in 1957.

I agonised over whether or not to cross-reference entries, either with the (*q.v.*) or with a footnote, and eventually decided against it – firstly because it was impracticable (about half of the 260 statistical entries alone each have at least another five related entries), and secondly, because I believed (and now hope) that most readers will prefer to search for (or serendipitously fall upon) entries with related or deeper detail for themselves.

Where I have considered a "fact" about Bradman in another source to be doubtful I have left it out. An example is the reference on a television travel show in early 2001 to the Hydro Majestic Hotel at Medlow Bath in the Blue Mountains of New South Wales, "where Don Bradman once stayed". My enquiries with the Hydro have failed to confirm this, and in fact it is news to the writers of a history of the hotel. There may have been confusion with the Hydora Hotel in Blackheath, a few kilometres from Medlow

Bath. When the Don and a NSW teammate, Wendell Bill, travelled by train to Blackheath for Bradman's now famous appearance in a social match in November 1931, they were taken to the Norwood Guesthouse for lunch before the game. I believe the pair stayed overnight after the match and the dance which followed at either the Hydora (now Gardiners Inn) or the Norwood (now a motel). The Don and Jessie drove to the Blue Mountains soon after they were married in Sydney on April 30, 1932 and stayed at least one night before going on to Melbourne, but *where* is a mystery.

Another example is the anecdote about Bradman being invited by the Liberal and Country League on October 17, 1948 to nominate for endorsement for the "new Bonython division" in the House of Representatives. This seems highly unlikely, at least in 1948, because the Adelaide seat of Bonython (created out of a redistribution) was not proclaimed until 1955. The date might well be when, as the Don related in his *Farewell to Cricket*, he was cabled at sea on his way home from England asking if (as reported in the Australian media) it was true that he had decided to enter politics. He was certainly approached several times by more than one party to stand for pre-selection, but it could not have been in Bonython in 1948.

Some more experienced Bradmaniacs will notice that a couple of my facts are different from the traditional versions. According to a NSW Railways timetable dated October 1926, the second-class return excursion fare from Bowral to Sydney on Saturdays was nine shillings and fivepence, not four and sixpence or eight and sixpence. And the Don's move from Bowral to Sydney was early in 1928, not in September of that year (when he relocated from Concord West to Rockdale).

More than one of Bradman's biographers have been accused of writing a hagiography, but I have striven for balance. While I believe that, from all accounts, much of the criticism of him was ill-informed or coloured by jealousy, he was also human, with human frailties. In writing about controversial events, I have sought simply to record the known facts, and what was written and/or said about them.

The book is self-indexing, with entries in strict A–Z order (ignoring word divisions). Entries starting with a number are filed from the smallest to the largest and appear before alphabetical entries after each letter.

No doubt there will be something in or about the book which will not please everyone – it could not be otherwise – but writing and publishing the first edition and then working on this revised edition for the ABC have been deeply satisfying.

My thanks to the following people for their generous assistance with research and other contributions in the writing of this book:

Nancy Alcorn, Peter Allen, Charlie Ball, Scott Ball, Garry Barnsley, Peter Binns, Bill Brown, Jack Burrows, Kevan Carroll, Colin Clowes, Bruce Collins, Deirdre Cott, Mike Coward, Neville Cush, Bradman Don, Ross Dundas, Jack Egan, John Fahey, Ric Finlay, David Fitzgerald, Warwick Franks, Wendy Frew, Richard Froggatt, Jill Gauvin, Alison Grellis, Barbara Grey, Peter Griffiths, Gideon Haigh, Ron Hamence, Neil Harvey, Brett Hutchins, Ken Inglis, Jon Jobson, Bill Johnston, John Kohler, Bernie Lamerton, Victoria Logue, John Low, Sam Loxton, Steven Lynch, Ron Maslin, Roy Masters, Jim Maxwell, Norman May, Kersi Meher-Homji, Doris Menzies, Roxanne Minchin, Arthur Morris, John Owen, David Parkinson, Michael Parkinson, Rodger Penman, Peter Reynolds, Warren Saunders, Ric Sissons, Jim Smith, Audrey Snell, Carolyn Spooner, David Studham, Tom Thompson, Eric Tindill, Molly Tindill, Warwick Torrens, Ernie Toshack, Kathleen Toshack, John Trainer, Lincoln Tyner, Graeme Vimpani, David Wells, Ken Williams.

Special thanks to David Frith for his foreword and his help with research; Matthew Gibbs, who read every word (and number) of the first edition and made many excellent suggestions (and whose faith in the project never waned); and Gordon Whatman, who filled in many gaps for me on Bowral and the Bradman family.

Every attempt has been made to contact copyright holders prior to publication but I hope any omission will be excused. In my Introduction to the first edition, I neglected to acknowledge Tom Thompson for his kind permission to use extracts from Sir Donald's books *Farewell to Cricket* and *The Art of Cricket*. I am happy to correct that omission now.

I am grateful to Stuart Neal, publisher of ABC Books, for supporting this revised edition of *The A–Z of Bradman*. His offer to publish has given me the opportunity to expand a number of entries and write several new ones. Thanks also to Brigitta Doyle and other members of Stuart's team who worked with me on the project.

Alan Eason
October 2004

A

Aberdeen

Seaport in north-eastern Scotland where the Don played his last game in Britain, his final appearance of the tour in 1948. He considered that his 123 not out (with 17 fours and two sixes) in 89 minutes before a record crowd of 10,000 in the second-class match against Scotland on the Mannofield ground was probably his most crowd-pleasing innings of the tour.

"Abide With Me"

Jessie Bradman's favourite hymn, which was sung at the memorial services in St Peter's Cathedral, Adelaide, for her on September 28, 1997 and for the Don on March 25, 2001.

Accrington

Cricket club in the Lancashire League which tried to entice the Don to England with an offer in August 1931 of a lucrative player's contract worth 600 pounds sterling. The Depression by then had well-and-truly started to bite and Bradman at the time was not happy with his employment with the sports retailer Mick Simmons, because it depended entirely on his success at cricket. Although he made it clear from the outset that he had no desire to leave Australia, he was the target of much criticism when he enquired into the details of the offer. But he also received letters urging him to accept, including one from a senior member of Federal Parliament. The issue was the subject of a raging newspaper debate but the Don remained silent for weeks throughout the controversy, believing it would be improper to comment while negotiations were still going on. It was scathing criticism in the British press (one writer accusing him of "selling his birthright") which eventually prompted him to make a public statement: "I certainly do not appreciate some of the caustic comments which have been made in England about my accepting the Accrington offer, for I have not done so. Should I accept the contract that will be the time for comment. They are pulling me to pieces before I have done anything." In the end he accepted a joint counter offer of a two-year contract at 1,500 pounds a year from three organisations in Australia: Associated Newspapers, FJ Palmer & Son and radio station 2UE. The decision to stay in Australia represented a financial sacrifice for the Don. As a leading player in the Lancashire League he could have earned much more than what he was paid under his contract. Top League professionals were paid bonuses for exceptional performances and earned money from newspaper work and many other sources.

Adelaide Oval

Where the Don played his first and last first-class matches: when he scored 118 batting at number seven for New South Wales against South Australia in a Sheffield Shield match on December 16 and 17, 1927 (becoming the 17th Australian to score a century on first-class debut), and when he made 30 for SA against Victoria in a shield game (which doubled as a testimonial match for SA former Test player Arthur Richardson) ending on March 8, 1949. The Don batted 60 times in 40 first-class matches at Adelaide Oval, making 4,840 runs at an average of 89.62, with 18 centuries (including eight double centuries and one triple century) and 15 fifties. He also took 31 catches. His highest score, 369 (in 253 minutes) for SA against Tasmania at the end of the 1935–36 season, broke Clem Hill's record of 365 for the highest score ever made at Adelaide Oval and the highest ever for SA (and Hill sent the Don a telegram of congratulations). Bradman considered his 251 not out and 90 not out in Adelaide against NSW with Bill O'Reilly in top form in 1939–40 to be his best performance in a shield match.

In 11 innings in seven Tests at Adelaide Oval he made 970 runs at 107.78, with three centuries (all double hundreds, including his highest Test score in Australia of 299 not out against South Africa in 1931–32) and three fifties. But it was also where he was sent packing for a duck by England medium-pacer Alec Bedser in 1946–47 when he was bowled by a ball which the Don considered was the best ever to take his wicket. It was on Adelaide Oval that Bradman the bowler took his only two wickets in Test cricket: the first in the First Test of the 1930–31 series against the West Indies (Ivan Barrow, lbw) and the second in the explosive Third Bodyline Test in 1932–33 (Wally Hammond, bowled). The picturesque facility was where the Don stood as an umpire for the only time when he teamed up with SA Premier Thomas Playford in a game between the Chamber of Manufacturers and Trades Hall in 1949. Bradman ranked the ground as the world's most beautiful first-class arena but he believed that from a player's point of view it was too long and narrow and the pitch kept a little too low for attractive strokeplay.

In December 1984, when every living Test captain who skippered at Adelaide Oval was invited to return to the ground to celebrate its centenary

A

of Test cricket, the Don did a lap of honour in an open car with longtime friend and former adversary Gubby Allen. The dining room at Adelaide Oval has carried the Don's name since 1986, and the John Creswell Stand was demolished in 1989 and replaced the next year by the Sir Donald Bradman Stand. The ground was the venue for the Don's last major television interview, recorded with Ray Martin on April 9, 1996 (Martin turning up in a limousine and his subject arriving in his Holden Nova) and shown on May 29, 1996, for which the Nine Network's owner Kerry Packer paid the Bradman Museum $1.2 million. The Don continued to visit the ground regularly to sign memorabilia for fans until late 1998. On the day after his death, the Adelaide Oval's scoreboard read: "Farewell Sir Donald Bradman, 27 August 1908 to 25 February 2001. Rest in Peace." A month later, on March 25, 2001, a candlelight vigil was held at the ground and a large television screen set up so members of the public could watch a live broadcast of the memorial service from St Peter's Cathedral.

Adler, Larry (Lawrence Cecil)

Mouth-organ player who joined the Don (on piano) in a jam session when the celebrated American called on Bradman at his Adelaide home during a visit to Australia in 1957.

Administration

Before he was old enough to play, the Don acted as scorer for the Bowral Town Cricket Club, and just after his 12th birthday, in September 1920, he attended the annual general meeting to see for himself what happened when the men assembled in committee to plan the coming season. He was fascinated by committee politics and the logistics of operating a cricket club. Before he was eligible to join, he was made an honorary member, and as soon as he was eligible, elected to the Social Committee. Like his father, George, the Don became assistant secretary and treasurer, and a month after his 17th birthday he was elected honorary secretary. His first administrative position in first-class cricket came when he was appointed a South Australian selector in 1935, just after transferring from New South Wales. He was made a Test selector in September the following year on the death of an incumbent, Charles Dolling, just before getting the nod as captain for the 1936–37 Ashes series in Australia. Except for two years in 1952–54, when he took time out to help to care for his polio-stricken son, John, he remained an Australian selector until 1971.

Bradman was appointed to the South Australian Cricket Association's cricket committee in 1938 and, in 1945, at the unusually young age of 37, was elected (as a replacement for his former boss, Harry Hodgetts) as one of the SACA's three delegates to the Australian Board of Control, serving in that capacity until 1980. He was also SACA treasurer in 1949–50 and vice-president from 1950 to 1965. When the Don started a three-year term as chairman of the Board of Control in September 1960, he became only the second former Test cricketer (after Tasmanian Charles Eady in 1910–11) to occupy the chair. Earlier that year he travelled to London with then chairman Bill Dowling for a conference on the throwing controversy, a problem he described at the time as "the most complex I have known in cricket, because it was not a matter of fact but of opinion". He went along with the decision at the conference that for the tour of England by the Australians in 1961 there should be a moratorium for the first few weeks on throwing, but he returned to Australia with a personal solution in mind. He obtained from the state captains a confidential list of suspects and saw to it that none of them were selected.

His second three-year stint as chairman, from 1969, coincided with the ostracism of South Africa from the international cricket community because of its government's apartheid policy. The board under Bradman's chairmanship cancelled the scheduled 1971–72 tour of Australia by the South Africans because of fears over demonstrations after violent protests during the Springbok rugby tour a few months before. A World XI tour was organised as a stand-in. The Don later had input as a member of the board's Emergency Committee which was formed to deal with the World Series Cricket crisis in 1977–79. Tim Caldwell, who succeeded Bradman as board chairman in 1972, described him as a man who was "incisive in thought, who does his homework thoroughly ... and is an outstanding administrator because of his aggressive attitude in those matters in which he believes". Another subsequent chairman, Bob Parish, wrote of the Don: "A man of great integrity, his greatness as an administrator lay principally in his vision and in his encyclopaedic knowledge of the game and its rich history. And, whatever his age, he always came to the table with the ideas and energy of the young and progressive. This is why he has remained a vibrant and relevant figure half a century after the end of his playing career."

In the words of journalist Mike Coward: "Bradman was more than a cricket player nonpareil. He was an eminent cricket person; an insightful and intuitive captain, an astute and progressive administrator; an expansive thinker, philosopher and writer on the game. Indeed, in some respects, he was as powerful, persuasive and influential a figure off the ground as he was on it." In a foreword to the 1998 book *Sir Donald Bradman A.C.*, former Australian captain Richie Benaud said that Bradman "had the most incisive and brilliant mind of any cricketer and administrator the cricket world has known". The Don's last administrative position was on the SACA's Ground and Finance Committee, a role he occupied from 1943 to 1986. In his letter advising the SACA of his attention to retire, he wrote: "There is always a feeling of sadness when you end an association with a game that has been such a big part of your life, but against that is the joy and happiness that I have derived from it over a long period."

"Aestheticization of The Don, The"

Major paper presented to the South Australian State History Conference in Adelaide on May 25, 2002 by Dr Bernard Whimpress, South Australian Cricket Association historian and curator of the Adelaide Oval Museum. Bernard's abstract of his paper: "One of Don Bradman's favourite cricket photographs of himself was a cover drive he made as part of his world record innings of 452 not out. Although he scored many runs with the stroke it was not his signature stroke. Primarily a back foot player he destroyed bowlers more often with violent pull shots and deft late cuts. Bradman was a master batsman who imposed his will on bowlers but was also a cricket functionalist. He was never a pretty player in the sense that Victor Trumper had been before him, of his contemporaries Alan Kippax and Archie Jackson, or of someone like Mark Waugh in recent years. Bradman grew to cricket prominence in the shadow of Trumper and the famous posed picture of Trumper jumping out to drive is the hallmark of Australian cricket aesthetics. Bradman in his early years laboured by comparison with the great Victor no matter how many runs he made, and it was only many years after his own retirement in 1948 that more aesthetic images of him began to appear. Bradman was always careful about his own image and how he would be viewed in Australian and cricket history. In the 1990s a revival of interest, which almost amounted to idolatory, turned The Don into an iconic figure. It is my contention that Bradman himself encouraged a more aesthetic representation of his batting in sculptures, paintings and various reproduced images, than had previously existed. By the use of slides and other illustrative material I will show how the process of aestheticization unfolded."

Allen, (Sir) George Oswald Browning ("Gubby") CBE

Though defying his captain Douglas Jardine by refusing to bowl bodyline, Allen still took 21 wickets in that explosive series of 1932–33. He was a fast-medium-pacer with a classic side-on action, a useful batsman and a good close-in field. In a letter to England just after the Bodyline series, Gubby Allen wrote: "Don Bradman made some incredible shots, but he is a terrible little coward of fast bowling." But Allen later enjoyed a good relationship with the Don. His letter was one of 60 purchased by Sydney's Mitchell Library for about $25,000 at auction in England in 1992, but after being read it was sealed until after Bradman's passing. Allen was born in Australia and had an uncle, Reg Allen, who played a Test for Australia against England in 1886–87. As an amateur, Gubby did not play cricket full-time but appeared in the first of his 25 Tests in England against Australia in 1930 and first captained his country, once again at home, against India in 1936. His Ashes team in Australia in 1936–37 performed moderately against the states in the run-up to the big games but won the first two Tests at the 'Gabba and the SCG when Bradman's men had to bat on rain-affected pitches.

The two captains disagreed on the possible outcomes of these matches had the wickets not turned sticky. The skipper of the home side claimed in *Bradman: The Don Declares*, a radio biography recorded with the ABC in 1987, that the Australians could have won the first Test and saved the second, but this was rejected by Allen, who contended that his side had already effectively won both matches before the heavens opened. In any event, Gubby's men were overrun by the home side to lose the rubber 2–3.

A staunch defender of the traditional virtues of the game, Allen served as an influential administrator for many years after his retirement. At one point he was the youngest man to sit on the MCC Committee, and later served as England chairman of selectors, and MCC president and treasurer. Gubby Allen was awarded a CBE in 1962 and a knighthood in 1986. In December 1984, when every living Test captain who skippered at Adelaide Oval was invited to return to the ground to celebrate its centenary of Test cricket, he did a lap of honour in an open car with Bradman, who by then had become a longtime friend and correspondent. Gubby Allen died in 1989, aged 87. In 1995 the Don gave a collection of letters written between himself and Allen to the Bradman Foundation, stipulating they should not be opened until after his death.

Allsopp, Arthur Henry

New South Wales batsman who impressed the Don in Allsopp's first game at the SCG with his "phenomenal cover driving". In his initial first-class match, against Arthur Gilligan's unofficial MCC side in 1929–30, Allsopp made 117 and 63 not out, but his form fell away soon after.

A

All Stars Memorabilia and Collectibles

Sydney enterprise which released a limited number of 2,000 autographed photo plaques of the Don in association with the Bradman Museum in 1997. The plaque features an action shot of the Don accompanied by engraved brass plates showing details of his Test and first-class careers. Royalties from sales of the plaques, which were priced at $450 each, benefited the Bradman Foundation.

Altham, H(arry) S(urtees) ("Teddy") CBE

Eminent cricket historian who wrote what the Don said was the most moving paragraph about him that he had ever read. In an article for the *Cricketer Spring Annual* in 1941, Altham said: "In the many pictures I have stored in my mind from the burnt-out Junes of forty years, there is none more dramatic or compelling than that of Bradman's small, serenely-moving figure in its big-peaked green cap coming out of the pavilion shadows into the sunshine, with the concentration, ardour and apprehension of surrounding thousands centred upon him, and the destiny of a Test match in his hands."

Amarnath, Lala (Nanik Amarnath Bharadwaj)

India's captain who could not be persuaded by the Don to agree to have the wickets covered during the first series between Australia and India in 1947–48. Bradman considered the tourists would be severely disadvantaged if caught on wet wickets, and his worst fears were realised when the home side won the rubber 4–0. Writing in India's *Sportstar* magazine in September 1998, Amarnath said: "On that tour to Australia, he wanted me to agree to cover the pitches. I did not agree for the simple reason that Australia would have scored two thousand runs in one Test. I dread to think how many he would have." And: "A very pleasant and humble human being. Even though I met him just once, in 1984, after that series, we stayed in touch by writing to each other. It was a very memorable tour for me and I enjoyed it despite the battering from Bradman." Amarnath died in August 2000, one month short of his 89th birthday. In a message conveyed through the website indya.com, the Don wrote: "I was very sad to hear the news that my old cricketing foe, Lala Amarnath, died over the weekend. I remember first meeting Lala on the first tour between our two countries in 1947. I found him absolutely charming and a wonderful amabassador for the game … Throughout his life I know Lala made a significant contribution to Indian cricket. I extend my sympathies to his family."

Andrews, William Harry Russell

Somerset all-rounder who called his 1973 memoirs *The Hand That Bowled Bradman*, so named because he bowled the Don (for 202) in a tour match in 1938. "Hence the light-hearted greeting I've used ever since when meeting someone for the first time, 'Shake the hand that bowled Bradman.'"

Annan, Kofi Atta

United Nations secretary-general (a keen cricketer in his youth in Ghana) who released a tribute to the Don soon after his death in February 2001: "One of the greatest sportsmen the world has ever known, Sir Donald matched his extraordinary record of accomplishment on the field with grace and honour off it. Bradman stood for the values of fair play and international co-operation that are at the heart of the United Nations. I join cricket lovers around the world in expressing my condolences to his family, the Government and people of Australia, and the game of cricket, which have all suffered an irreparable loss."

Annie Get Your Gun

Musical which the Don and his men saw as guests of the management at the Coliseum Theatre in London before the start of the 1948 tour.

"An Old Fashioned Locket"

Dance tune recorded in Sydney by the Don in 1930 for Columbia Records. He recorded another piece, "Our Bungalow of Dreams", in the same year on the same label.

"Antipodean Slugger"

How the Don was labelled by a local newspaper after he and Keith Tolhurst put on 168 runs in 34 minutes in a game in San Francisco during the 1932 tour of Canada and the US organised by Arthur Mailey.

Argo Investments

Company with which the Don served 30 years as a director, including a period in the early 1980s as chairman. Just after Bradman's death in 2001, Argo's managing director Robert Patterson said the hallmark of Sir Donald's directorship was "thoroughness – he was a stickler for doing the right thing; he had great integrity." Mr Patterson, who was company secretary when the Don was chairman, added: "His business achievements were overshadowed but they were considerable.'

A

Arlott, (Leslie Thomas) John OBE

Gravel-voiced English commentator and journalist who wrote in a contribution to Jack Fingleton's 1949 book *Brightly Fades the Don*: "I do not think cricket is under Bradman's skin but I believe it is under his skull, in close control. Therefore he has missed something of cricket that less gifted and less memorable men have gained. How, I wonder, would Don Bradman define happiness?" In an appreciation of the Don which appeared in *Wisden Cricket Monthly* in August 1988, Arlott wrote of the time when he and Bradman were dining and his companion was in the act of drinking soup when a man came up and asked the Don if he would sign his autograph in his book. "Without heat", Arlott said, "but with more than justifiable irritation, Don said, 'Can't you see I am eating?' The man swung on his heel and walked away muttering, and not pleasantly either. Bradman put down his spoon and said: 'Now I suppose he will go away and tell his friends what a rude man I am.'"

Art of Bradman, The

A collection of paintings and drawings by noted artist Brian Clinton featuring the cricketing achievements of the Don. The book of 240 pages was published in 2003 by Funtastic Ltd. The text was written by Richard Mulvaney, director of the Bradman Museum.

Art of Cricket, The

A technical manual by the Don originally published by Hodder & Stoughton in 1958, 239pp. It was fully revised by Bradman in 1969 and by 1982 had gone through eight impressions. Sydney company ETT Imprint published a new edition of the book (with many new photos approved by the Don) in 1998 and followed with the release of a CD-ROM version in August 2000. In the latest edition of the book, its author made only a slight change to his own foreword but in the light of the current laws of the game decided to remove the section on leg theory (bodyline). In one of two prefaces (the other is by English journalist Jim Swanton) to the 1998 edition of the print version, former Australian captain Richie Benaud wrote: "Almost 40 years ago when first produced, *The Art of Cricket* was acclaimed as the most brilliant coaching book ever written and illustrated. Although the finest batsman the world has ever seen, he played his cricket with the creed of keeping it simple, and that line of thinking has continued throughout this book. Despite the passage of time, the book holds the same position as was the case way back in 1958. It is brilliant." The 65 minutes of video on the CD utilises the Don's original demonstration films, interviews, and footage from his Test career to create the world's first personalised electronic coaching clinic. The book and the CD are available from ETT Imprint at the website, www.bradmancopyrightmaterials.com.au.

Associated Newspapers

One of three organisations in Australia which made a joint offer of employment to the Don to counter the offer of a professional cricket contract from the Accrington club in England's Lancashire League in August 1931. The deal with the three organisations (the others were radio station 2UE and men's outfitters FJ Palmer & Son), signed on October 31, was for two years at a total of 1,500 pounds a year. When Bradman returned from North America in September 1932, he applied to the chairman of the Board of Control for permission to continue writing for Associated Newspapers' *Sun* newspaper while playing in the upcoming series against England. He knew the chairman had the power to allow a Test player to write on the game, but what he didn't know was that permission could be granted only if the player's sole occupation was journalism. When the Don's application was refused, he advised the board that he would honour his contract with his employer and stand down from the Ashes series. The issue became a public wrangle, but finally the head of Associated Newspapers, Robert Packer, excused him from writing his articles so he could play in the Tests. Packer knew he would bear the brunt of the public's displeasure if he held Bradman to his contract, thereby preventing him from playing in the Tests.

Aussie Sports

An Australian Sports Commission program of modified sports (e.g., kanga cricket, mini league, T ball, etc.) for primary-school children which was initiated by then federal sports minister John Brown in 1987. The first approach to the Don to launch the program was made by an Invincibles teammate, Ray Lindwall, but negotiations were then taken over by journalist Roy Masters. In a letter to Masters in May 1988, Bradman wrote of his attitude to coaching, referring to "certain reservations I have in regard to coaching (simply because it can, if badly used, hinder the development of a potential champion just as much as it can improve an ordinary player and make him a better one)". But, said Masters, when the Don began to appreciate that Aussie Sports was designed to improve disturbing health and fitness levels of many primary-age children, he embraced the program. Bradman declined to do a television message to launch the initiative but did agree to a radio broadcast, "providing the recording is done in my home or an Adelaide studio". He insisted on minor alterations to a prepared script but his message was eventually received by Australia's primary-school children in June 1988.

A

Australian Confederation of Sport
Body which in 1988 voted the Don the greatest male athlete of the past 200 years.

"Australian Legends"
A series of postage stamps issued by Australia Post each year on Australia Day. The Don was the first living Australian to feature on an Australia Post stamp when he appeared on the two stamps in the first series released in 1997. The two Bradman stamps, one with a portrait shot and the other depicting a free-flowing cover drive, were launched by Prime Minister John Howard at the SCG when he unveiled a plaque with a likeness of the stamps on the Sir Donald Bradman Gate. In launching the stamps, Mr Howard declared the Don to be the "greatest living Australian". In a statement from Adelaide, Sir Donald said: "The real significance was that cricket had been identified as the outstanding sport in Australia's national and international history. It is a tribute to the way in which sport is embedded in the fabric of Australian cultural life. I am merely the symbol through which this is expressed."

Australian Sports Hall of Fame
Into which the Don was the first of 100 great athletes inducted on Australia Day in the Bicentennial Year: January 26, 1988. The swimmer Shane Gould was seated next to Bradman at the luncheon, and she still has his speech notes which he gave Gould at her request.

Australian Sports Medal
An initiative of the Centenary of Federation to acknowledge Australia's greatest sportsmen and women. The Don received his from Prime Minister John Howard on a visit to Bradman's home just a week before his death in February 2001.

Australia Post
The Don was the first living Australian to feature on an Australia Post stamp when he appeared on the first two in the Australian Legends series released in 1997. The two Bradman stamps, one with a portrait shot and the other depicting a free-flowing cover drive, were launched by Prime Minister John Howard at the SCG when he unveiled a plaque with a likeness of the stamps on the Sir Donald Bradman Gate. On March 1, 2001, four days after the Don's passing, condolence books were placed in all of Australia Post's outlets, where they were available for signature by mem-

bers of the public. The books were later formed into leather-bound volumes and lodged at the Bradman Museum in Bowral. A Bradman Memorial stamp was issued by Australia Post on March 30, 2001 and withdrawn in February 2002. The 45-cent stamp, which features an image of the Don in his flannels, could be purchased individually or in sheets of 10. Also available was a special pack containing 10 stamps plus information on the issue for $4.95. Australia Post accepts tax-deductible donations to the Bradman Memorial Fund.

Austrian Airlines

Airline (formerly known as Lauda Air) which named one of its B777s after the Don in a ceremony at Sydney International Terminal in July 2002. The jetliner, which services the Vienna–Sydney–Melbourne route, was christened *Donald Bradman* with fire-truck hoses on the tarmac after landing from Europe. The christening coincided with a function in the Kingsford Smith Suite, where former Australian captain Mark Taylor unveiled a special plaque commemorating the feats of cricket's greatest batsman which was later placed permanently on board the plane. Among other guests were former Test players Bill Brown, Neil Harvey, Max Walker, Geoff Lawson and Dean Jones. Ian Craig and Richard Mulvaney represented the Bradman Museum. All were welcomed by Richard Froggatt, Austrian Airlines' general manager Australia and New Zealand. The carrier's other two B777s are named *Ernest Hemingway* and *Pablo Picasso*. A B737 which services short-haul routes within Europe carries the name *Elvis Presley*.

"Awful"

How the Don described the cables sent by the Australian Board of Control to the MCC protesting England's tactics during the Bodyline series of 1932–33. Bradman was against what Jardine and Larwood called fast leg-theory but was not happy with the way Australia's administration handled the issue. He felt the board should have sought a conference between England manager Plum Warner and captain Douglas Jardine, board chairman Allen Robertson and Australian captain Bill Woodfull.

Aylestone Road

Ground in Leicester where the Don recorded his best average of any arena in which he played in England, but he only batted twice in two matches there (in 1930 and '34) for 250 runs for once out. Of grounds on which he made more that 500 runs, his best average was 201.75 at Worcester, where he scored three double centuries and a century.

B

"Babe and Don, The"
An article by Australian writer Ric Sissons about the meeting between baseball legend Babe Ruth and the Don in the stands at Yankee Stadium on July 20, 1932 which appeared in the anthology *Carlton and United Breweries Best Australian Sports Writing and Photography*, published in 1996 by Heinemann. The account was taken from a book by Sissons about Arthur Mailey's tour of North America.

"Babe Ruth of Cricket, The"
How Arthur Mailey billed the Don to promote the games on the 1932 goodwill tour of North America. The locals might have been confused by cricket, but they certainly knew the name of their living legend of baseball.

Bach, Johann Sebastian
German composer who figured in a blue story once told by the Don. In the chapter on Bradman in his 1975 book *On Top Down Under*, about Australia's Test captains, Ray Robinson wrote: "The only time I heard him tell a story with permissive tinge was to emphasise the importance of practice. He quoted the hard work of the great composer J.S. Bach, father of twenty-three, said by a schoolboy to have 'practised on an old spinster in the abbey'."

Bacigalupo, Don Bradman
A descendant of Italian traders who came to Australia from Genoa in 1853, Bertie Bacigalupo was a bookmaker in the New South Wales country town of Coonamble. He had a passion for horses but was also a mad cricket fan. When he saw the Don (then only 20) play early in the 1928–29 season, he said: "That bloke is going to be the greatest cricketer in the world one day." So when Bertie's wife had a son on November 25, 1928, it was only natural he should name him Don Bradman. Mr Don Bradman Bacigalupo, then 72, told the *Sydney Morning Herald* in March 2001 that he was just eight when he saw his famous namesake play for the only time, at the SCG in 1937. "I remember we sat on the Hill and then this small bloke comes out twirling his bat, and gosh, it was magic, just the way he walked. Of course he was out two balls later. But he was still the Don. That day I still remember."

Badcock, Clayvel Lindsay ("Jack")

Badcock was a right-handed batsman from Tasmania who made his first-class debut in 1929–30 at the age of 15 against Victoria. In 1933–34 he made a Tasmanian-record 274 among a series of big innings but moved to Adelaide in 1934 and threw his lot in with South Australia. When Bradman joined the same side in 1935–36, he felt that Badcock's style was similar to his own and became something of a mentor to him. The Don's assistance may have been a factor in Jack's score of 325 against Victoria in SA's second-last game of the season. The 22-year-old got the nod for the First Test against England in 1936–37 but he failed and was dropped before being reinstated for the last Test of the series, when he made 118, an innings Bradman rated as Badcock's best. Jack went to England with the Don's side in 1938 but although he scored heavily in the county matches he blamed faulty footwork for his dismal failures in the Tests. He took a camera to England and made a film of the tour. Jack Badcock was 68 when he died in Exton, Tasmania, the place of his birth, in 1982.

Balmoral

Where the Don and his men were hosted by King George VI and the Queen after travelling to Scotland for two second-class games at the end of the 1948 tour. Bradman attracted criticism from some quarters when he was photographed with his hands in his pockets when walking with the King in the castle grounds. The Don later suggested that his host would probably have done likewise during their relaxed conversation had he not been wearing a kilt. And an official with the Australian party also had his hands in his pockets but was missing from the photo when it appeared in the press. Bradman was defended by a country newspaper in Scotland in a humorous editorial headed "Idle Hands".

Bannerman, Charles

First man to score a century in Test cricket (opening for Australia in the first-ever Test, against England at the MCG in 1877) who was photographed with the Don when they met at the SCG nets during the 1927–28 season, Bradman's first in first-class cricket.

Bannon, John Charles

Former premier of South Australia who met the Don as a child in the 1950s when the legendary batsman called regularly on Bannon's next-door neighbour, Tim Wall, a former Test teammate and a good friend of Bradman's. John contributed an essay to Pan Macmillan's 1998 book on the Don in the

Ironbark Legends series. His grandmother was a keen cricket fan who travelled to the MCG from Bendigo for about 40 years to watch Test matches.

Bardsley, Warren

New South Wales left-handed opener who at the time of the Don's retirement in 1949 was the only Australian apart from Bradman to have scored more than 50 centuries in first-class cricket, though several others have done it since. Bardsley, who was a great-uncle of tennis player John Newcombe's wife Angie, became the first batsman from any country to score a century in each innings of a Test when he made 136 and 130 at the Oval in 1909. When the Don made over 2,000 runs (2,960) on his first tour of England in 1930, Bardsley was the only other Australian to have achieved the same feat, having compiled 2,072 runs in 1909. And before Bradman came on the scene, Warren Bardsley was the only batsman to make 2,000 runs on three consecutive tours of England. The Don did it a fourth time in 1948. Bardsley's record of 27 hundreds in England (in 175 innings) was broken by Bradman in his 84th innings in England against Nottinghamshire in 1938. The Don made 212 in 202 minutes in a testimonial for Warren Bardsley and Jack Gregory at the SCG in October 1936. Bardsley died in Sydney in 1954, aged 71.

Barnes, Sidney George

A colourful New South Wales right-handed opening batsman, Barnes was renowned for his glorious off-side strokes, but when he shared a world-record fifth-wicket partnership with the Don of 405 (each man ultimately making 234) in the Second Ashes Test at the SCG in 1946–47, his 200 was the slowest double-century in the history of Anglo-Australian Tests. Bradman had been dismissed before him, and when Barnes draw level with his captain's score, he was heard by England fieldsmen to say: "I can't stick it any longer," soon after hitting a catch to Jack Ikin off Bedser. A reader later wrote to the Sydney *Daily Telegraph* commending Barnes for not taking the SCG Test record away from Bradman, but sharing it instead.

As a 21-year-old, Sid Barnes had won a berth in the Don's side to England in 1938, but a broken wrist he sustained in a fall on the ship at Gibraltar spoiled his tour (a request cabled by the Don to Australia for a replacement reserve player was refused). He was fit to take his place in the side for the last Test of the series, the gruelling fifth match at the Oval won by the home side, in which he made 41 and 33. The injury to his wrist was to develop his off-side play amazingly. Barnes played in four of the five Tests against England in 1946–47 and in three of the five Tests against India under the

Don the following summer. During the series against the Indians, Barnes asked the Don (whom he always called "George", Bradman's second given name) if he was going to captain the side leaving for England in a couple of months. Bradman replied that he had not made up his mind and asked why Barnes wanted to know, and Sid said (seriously): "Well, because if you go, I'm available, and if you don't, I'm not."

The Don thought so much of Barnes as a batsman that on arriving in England he ruled that either he or the opener had to play in every match. Barnes had a very successful tour, finishing second in the Test averages behind Arthur Morris, but he spent time in hospital and missed the Headingley Test after a full-blooded blow from Dick Pollard broke his ribs when fielding five yards from the bat in the preceding Test at Old Trafford. A few weeks before, a journalist with the *Daily Express* newspaper had written an open letter to the Don complaining that in fielding so close, at times even with a foot on the pitch, Barnes was intimidating batsmen. Of Sid's performance on that trip, his captain wrote: "Tremendous power in his wrists and forearms. Great fighter, as he showed at Manchester, where despite injury, he insisted on batting, only to collapse in the middle of the pitch … the best short-leg fieldsman in the world".

But Australian administrators were sick of Barnes's eccentric behaviour on the field (in the Don's testimonial game in Melbourne in December 1948 he attempted to play a ball with a toy bat he produced from under his sweater) and he was not to be selected for his country again. Legal action taken by Barnes to force his reinstatement was unsuccessful, and he became a controversial writer on the game. In his 1963 book *It Isn't Cricket*, Barnes wrote of the Don: "I worshipped him. He could do nothing wrong as far as I was concerned." Of all Australians who played as many Tests as Barnes (13), only Bradman has a better average. Sid Barnes left a widow and three children when he took his own life in Sydney in 1973 at the age of 57.

Barnsley

South Yorkshire town from where former umpire Harold ("Dickie") Bird's father is reputed to have walked the 35 kilometres to Leeds to see the Don bat in the 1934 Test at Headingley. Similarly, the journalist and broadcaster Michael Parkinson has written of how his father, before Michael was born, also hoofed it from Barnsley to Leeds to see Bradman in action.

Barnsley, Garry OAM

Bowral solicitor who bashfully "ambushed" the Don at Moss Vale Golf Club in 1983 about the concept of a Bradman Museum. Barnsley told the

Southern Highland News soon after Sir Donald's death in February 2001 that he greeted the batting legend "with sweaty palm" when he broached the possibility of his support for a permanent Bradman memorial in Bowral. But Bradman said to him: "In the last 50 years I've been the subject of the most intense publicity imaginable. Now that I'm retired, I really would prefer to lead a quiet life." But Barnsley persevered with his "Bradman Project", initiating publicity and fundraising which culminated in a proposal for a museum in the former Bradman home in Glebe Street, Bowral, opposite Bradman Oval. With the announcement of a grant from the New South Wales Bicentennial Council in 1985, a committee of Wingecarribee Shire Council was formed to oversee the project, with Barnsley in the chair and Sydney barrister Bruce Collins a leading contributor. The Bradman Museum Trust was formed in 1987. It was then that Sir Donald became formally interested in the project and he agreed to sign over the intellectual property rights associated with his name, likeness and image. Garry Barnsley was chairman of the Bradman Foundation (established in 1993) from 1998 to 2000 and retired from the board in 2001. Of the future, he said: "The work the foundation has undertaken can only continue to grow, and Sir Donald has given us the tools to do the job, not only through his inspiration but also through licensing activities and the deployment of his intellectual property. I think the legend will become even greater as time goes by."

Barrow, Ivan
West Indian wicketkeeper who was the Don's first Test wicket as a bowler. Bradman trapped him lbw for 27 in the last over of the third day of the First Test at Adelaide Oval in 1930–31.

Bartlett, Tanya Kathryn
Sculptor who was commissioned by the Bradman Foundation in July 2001 to create a life-size bronze statue of the Don. The figure was unveiled outside the Bradman Museum in Bowral on February 24, 2002 to mark the first anniversary of his death. Tanya was asked to base the figure on the photo of Bradman acknowledging the applause of the crowd on reaching 200 during his classic innings of 254 in the Second Test at Lord's in 1930. The Don was not wearing a sweater but the sculptor added one to give the work more texture. And she made him older than his 21 years to add character to the face. Bartlett had done a figurine of the same pose as part of a collection of great Australian athletes before the Don passed away, and it earned his approval. The 33-year-old artist from Newcastle, New South Wales, said: "I love the pose that was selected for the life-size because of

find that the man behind the desk who was about to interview him was every boy's hero, Don Bradman. He won the job, and though useless as a clerk, he was liked by the Don and his children and was given a month off by the boss to see the Second, Third and Fourth Tests in Melbourne, Sydney and Adelaide. After the series and just before returning to England, Biles writes, he was invited to the Bradman home for dinner, and Shirley made a present to him of the cap and a Test blazer "which I stuffed in my rucksack". The hitch in Biles's story is that Bradman closed his stock-broking business, Don Bradman & Co., and handed over the premises to his 2IC, Len Bullock, in 1954, four years before the tour by Peter May's side. But Biles sold the cap in London in 1995 for £3,375. Its West Australian owner, Cam Tinley, was to offer it at auction through Lawson-Menzies in Sydney on September 30, 2004.

Bill, (Oscar) Wendell

New South Wales teammate who was batting with Bradman when the Don scored his celebrated century in three eight-ball overs in a semi-social game for Blackheath against a team from Lithgow at Blackheath Oval on November 2, 1931. Bradman plundered 100 off 22 balls faced and Bill scored two singles off the other two. When the Don was invited by Mayor Peter Sutton to join the Blackheath team for the game to open a new malthoid pitch, he was asked if he would like to bring someone along. Bill and Bradman had set a record for a fifth wicket Sheffield Shield partner-ship of 234 (in 135 minutes) against Victoria in 1930–31. In an unpub-lished account of the incident written in 1986, Bill said: "So in three overs Don went from 150 to 250 and I went from 77 to 79. The funny thing is that of all the runs I scored in my career, all the centuries, those two singles are the ones people remember best today." Wendell Bill died in Sydney in 1988, aged 78.

Billiards

When legendary billiards player Walter Lindrum invited the Don to step up to the table at the Adelaide home of Bradman's boss Harry Hodgetts in July 1935, the master batsman started with a respectable break of 56. But when Lindrum replied with his customary century break, his 26-year-old opponent was not happy. Such was his competitive nature, the Don hated not being able to perform at Lindrum's level, so he had a billiards room built in his new home (a couple of blocks away from Hodgetts's mansion), and practised nearly every day for a year until he was able to make a break of 100.

B

Birkett, (William) Norman (1st Baron Birkett of Ulverston) KC
English politician and jurist who presided at the Nuremburg Trials. A great
fan of Bradman, he said at a London dinner at the start of the 1948 tour
after the Don reiterated his intention to make the tour his last: "Never,
never have I heard more tragic words from the lips of any man." Norman
Birkett wrote a foreword to Jack Fingleton's 1949 book *Brightly Fades the
Don*, an account of the Invincibles tour. He was president of the
Lancashire County Cricket Club and represented Wallis Simpson when she
was granted a divorce before marrying King Edward VIII.

Blackheath

Town in the Blue Mountains of New South Wales where the Don scored a
whirlwind century off three eight-ball overs in an innings of 256 for a
Blackheath side against nearby Lithgow on November 2, 1931. Bradman
was invited by Blackheath Mayor Peter Sutton to join the town's team in a
semi-social game to open a new malthoid pitch (called MA Noble wicket)
at Blackheath Oval. His side having passed the opposition's total of 228, the
Don said to batting partner Wendell Bill, a fellow NSW player: "Wendell,
we've passed their score, I think I'll have a go." Bradman faced 22 of the
next 24 balls and took his score from 150 to 250. The sequence of his shots
was 6, 6, 4, 2, 4, 4, 6, 1 (first over, 33 runs), 6, 4, 4, 6, 6, 4, 6, 4 (second over,
40 runs) and 6, 6, 1, 4, 4, 6 (third over, 27 runs). Bill scored two singles off
the other two balls in the third over. The two hapless bowlers in the Lithgow
Pottery Club side were Bill Black (later mayor of Lithgow) and Horrie
Baker (later the town clerk). Black had bowled the Don (playing for a NSW
side) for 42 in an exhibition match against a local combined side at Lithgow
a few weeks before (later having the ball mounted) and had been boasting
about it since. Bradman took 33 off Black's first over and 27 off his second.
He hit 14 sixes and 29 fours (exactly 200 in boundaries) in his innings of
256 before being caught by Lithgow's Alf Reynolds at mid-off.

Bradman later played down the significance of his 100 in three overs, saying it was of "no significance", and not comparable with any first-class
innings because it was achieved in a social match on a ground with a small
boundary. One of the Lithgow bowlers, Bob Nicholson, was to sing at Don
and Jessie's wedding in Sydney six months later. John Boyd, a member of
the Blackheath team, wrote in a privately published account of the Bradman
innings: "I said to my young brother Dick on the day before, something like
this: 'You ought to come down tomorrow and watch the game. You might-
n't ever see anything like it again all your life.' How right I was. Dick did-
n't come down, but, in my opinion, nobody in the world had ever seen such

an exhibition of controlled hitting and probably never will in the future." The innings was not timed, but Bradman believed the century probably bettered the 18 minutes taken by Lorry Quinlan in scoring the then fastest officially recorded century in Australia in Cairns in 1910.

When Mayor Sutton asked the Don after the match for his Sykes bat as a souvenir for Blackheath, the star batsman said it was still new and he wanted to get more use out of it. He did promise, however, that when and if he split the bat, he would make sure that Sutton got it. True to his word, Bradman sent it to him after he damaged it in a charity match at Callan Park in Sydney a few weeks later. Sutton kept the bat (with a notice under it) in the chambers of Blackheath Council for years but took it home when the municipality was merged with the Blue Mountains Council in 1947. After Sutton's death in 1970 it remained in the care of his daughter, Nance Smith. When Richard Mulvaney, head of the Bradman Museum, made the journey to Blackheath in 1990 to ask Mrs Smith for the bat, she was unwilling to part with it. But when Richard noticed it was infested with borers, she accepted his offer to take it to Sydney for restoration and return it to her.

In a letter dated October 25, 1991, Nance wrote to Jack Burrows, the president of Blackheath Bowling Club: "It is time for me to ensure that the cricket bat is in some safe keeping. Would the Blackheath Bowling Club like to have it to put on display in the club-house? It seems an appropriate place being next to the Sports Ground. My father was a founding member of the Club and a green is named after him. The alternative is for me to pass the bat to the Bradman Museum at Bowral. In any case, if you do accept the bat, I ask that if ever it is passed to someone else, it goes to that Museum." The offer was accepted and the bat remained in the trophy cabinet at the club until it was moved recently to a vault. In 2004 the club was taken over by Katoomba RSL Club and renamed Blackheath Sports Club. At the time of writing, the Bradman Museum was negotiating to acquire the bat.

Bodyline

England captain Douglas Jardine and his spearhead Harold Larwood were both to claim in their respective books that their bowling tactic which became known as bodyline was concocted because (unlike his batting partner Archie Jackson) Bradman "flinched" when hit repeatedly by Larwood's leg-side bouncers on a lively rain-affected wicket in the Fifth Test at the Oval in 1930. The claim – made also by Gubby Allen, Jack Fingleton and others – that the Don was afraid of fast bowling was repudiated passionately by him in his autobiography, *Farewell to Cricket*. Bodyline – or what Jardine and Larwood insisted was "fast leg-theory" –

B

was first used against the Australians before the start of that infamous series of 1932–33. In late November, a Melbourne weekly, the *Australasian*, carried an article by Jack Worrall on the game between the MCC and an Australian XI. Part of Worrall's report was the comment: "Voce's half-pitched slingers on the body line provided about the poorest attempt at what should be Test bowling it is possible to conceive." Bradman expressed the view privately to administrators after that match that trouble would develop if the matter was not dealt with quickly. The controversy was already in full swing by the time Australia went in to bat on the first day of the First Test in Sydney. Later that day, the Melbourne *Herald* carried a piece on the game that had been telegraphed from Sydney at lunchtime by its reporter Hugh Buggy. Echoing the phrase used earlier by Worrall, Buggy's article included the expression "bodyline bowling", and this was the first use of the term. It is unlikely that Buggy's intentions were malicious (although Harold Larwood wrote later that he believed the term was "meant to damn me"), and his subeditor Ray Robinson kept the phrase intact. It was quickly taken up by the rest of the press.

The method of bowling fast, short-pitched deliveries directed at the batsman's body (as the Australians claimed) with a ring of fielders (usually five) in short-leg positions and another two men on the boundary was defended by captain Douglas Jardine and Larwood, his spearhead, during and after the tour, as a "fast" version of leg-theory, a recognised tactic of the game at least since the late 19th century. Larwood rejected the term bodyline, insisting that he bowled at leg stump and not at the batsman. Bradman again raised his concerns, privately, after Australia won the Second Test in Melbourne to level the series 1–1. He felt it was the right time to let the England camp know the home side's opposition to the practice lest it be thought the Australians were complaining only because they were being beaten. The controversy reached a peak in the Third Test in Adelaide. In Australia's first innings, skipper Bill Woodfull was struck a bad blow over the heart by a short-pitched ball from Larwood to an orthodox field, but he recovered and indicated he would continue his innings. Gubby Allen (who always refused to bowl bodyline during the series) then bowled a maiden to the Don, but when Woodfull took strike for the next over, Jardine switched to a bodyline field and Larwood bowled the Australian captain another bumper. The huge Saturday crowd of 50,962 (still the record for a cricket match at Adelaide Oval) was enraged, and mass hooting accompanied every ball of the over. Bradman was dismissed soon after for 8, and Woodfull went for 22. Australian player Leo O'Brien told ABC radio many years later how his captain had only just stepped out of the shower in the dressing room when England joint-managers Pelham Warner and Richard Palairet walked in and Warner said: "We've called in to see how you are, Mr Woodfull." The Australian skipper's response was to wave them away with the immortal words: "Mr Warner, there are two teams out there on the field, and one is playing cricket and the other's not. That's all I'll have to say. Good afternoon." O'Brien, who was 12th man for the match, was the only other player in the room at the time of the incident (the only other witness being the Australian team's elderly masseur who, according to O'Brien, was "stone deaf"). Warner and Palairet departed and O'Brien went out to his teammates watching the game and told them of the exchange.

(Warner was ropable when the rebuke from Woodfull was published in the next day's newspapers and created a diplomatic sensation, and he always held Australian batsman Jack Fingleton, a full-time journalist who was playing in the match, responsible for the leak. Fourteen years later in his book *Cricket Crisis*, Fingleton alleged that the culprit was another member of the team but did not name him. In his 1978 book *The Immortal Victor Trumper*, he identified the leaker as the Don. He claimed that he had been told by a Sydney *Sun* newspaper reporter, Claude Corbett, a colleague of Fingleton's, that Bradman had given Corbett the scoop in a secret meeting on the night of the incident, January 14, 1933, in the Don's car in Adelaide's North Terrace. Fingleton wrote that he had long held it against Bradman that he had not cleared him by owning up. He repeated the charge in his last book, *Batting From Memory*, in 1981. In a quote published in a 1983 biography by Michael Page, the Don called Fingleton's claim "a lie", and in *Bradman: The Don Declares*, a series of interviews with ABC radio in 1987, Bradman again rejected the allegation, asserting that Fingleton in fact was the leaker and he had concocted the "fictitious" story of the clandestine meeting between the Don and Corbett as a "smokescreen for himself".)

The Sunday being a rest day, play in the Adelaide Test resumed on the Monday, and there was more drama. Larwood was bowling to a conventional field when Bert Oldfield tried to hook a legitimate bumper and he deflected the ball onto his forehead. Oldfield dropped his bat as he staggered towards slips grasping his head. Mounted police lined up in readiness as the crowd's fury reached white heat. Umpire George Hele said later he believed that had the incident occurred at the MCG, the crowd would have leapt the fence. As it was, they came perilously close. A policeman in front of the Giffen Stand asked an Adelaide barrister why he hadn't jumped the fence. "I won't stop you, sir," he declared. Woodfull came onto the ground to assist Oldfield off, and the game continued in uproar. The diminutive gloveman said later it was his own fault. In Australia's second innings, the Don scored 66 and Woodfull carried his bat for 73 but England won by 338 runs. Bradman took the second of his only two career Test wickets in this match when he bowled the great Wally Hammond in England's second innings for 85.

After the Adelaide Test, the first of several cables of complaint (later described by the Don as "awful") was sent by the Australian Board of Control to the MCC in London. It pointed out the dangers of Jardine's bowling tactics, both for the players and the future of the game, and decried the "unsportsmanlike" behaviour of the England team. The response was clinical and cold, throwing the onus back on the Australian Board by backing Jardine and suggesting that if the Australians really felt it was all that bad, they would reluctantly agree to end the tour there and then. Jardine himself demanded an apology from the Australian Board to him and his players, and said they would refuse to take part in the Fourth Test unless it was forthcoming. The Board did retract the word "unsportsmanlike" and bodyline bowling was immediately back in play in the following Test.

Bradman had decided before the Second Test in Melbourne (he had missed the first match in Sydney because of illness) that he would counter the ploy by stepping away from his wicket to the leg side and playing the ball to the near-vacant off-side. He hoped that it would put the bowler off-balance and force him to revert to a conventional field, that is to weaken the leg field and strengthen the off field. Then he could revert to normal batting style. It was an unorthodox tactic which exposed him to a graver risk of injury than the orthodox method of defending, because as the right-handed batsman moved across to leg, a fast delivery aimed at the leg stump from Larwood and Voce bowling over the wicket would follow him. Bradman had ruled out hooking (though in the first innings in Melbourne he was out first ball when he couldn't resist trying to hook Bowes), and predicted that the crowds would not be content for him to dodge and let the short-pitched balls pass; he had to get runs. The Don's approach was attacked by teammate Jack Fingleton (Bradman's most trenchant critic) in his 1946 book *Cricket Crisis*, but the Don's average for the series of 56.57 was the best of the Australians, and Fingleton himself was dropped during the series after scores in three consecutive innings of 1, 0 and 0, after earlier making 26, 40, and 83. In an interview in *Wisden Cricket Monthly* in 1981, bodyline bowler Bill Voce said: "Bradman didn't like bodyline bowling, but he didn't show it the way some of them did ... Bradman had the right idea; he always knew the best defence was attack. He was very quick on his feet, and he could get out of trouble so fast." In rare praise of Bradman, Douglas Jardine told commentator John Arlott years later: "You know, we nearly didn't do it. The little man was bloody good."

Throughout the Bodyline series and for a time after it, the lawmakers in London refused to do anything about the tactic because of a "lack of evidence". In the Second Test of the 1933 series at Old Trafford, West Indians Learie Constantine and Emmanuel Martindale caused a sensation when they bowled a form of bodyline, Martindale splitting open Wally Hammond's chin with one of many short-pitched rising deliveries. Hammond was reported to have said that unless short-pitched bowling was outlawed, he would retire from first-class cricket. The great Jack Hobbs had made a similar threat after his experience with Bowes in 1932. But the practice continued in county cricket until the MCC effectively banned it in November 1934. The tour of England by Australia earlier that year had been confirmed only after an assurance from the MCC that bodyline tactics would be conspicuous by their absence. Douglas Jardine was reported as having said soon after the arrival of Bill Woodfull's men in the Old Dart: "I have neither the intention nor the desire to play cricket against Australia this summer."

The Don believed that if bodyline bowling had not been outlawed, it would have meant the end of Test cricket and seriously jeopardised the future of the game itself. The respected commentator and former New South Wales captain Alan McGilvray, writing in his 1992 book *Captains of the Game*, said that the Bodyline series "probably did as much to break the umbilical between Australia and the Mother country as any single event of our history". JH Thomas, the then British secretary of state for the Dominions, said: "No politics ever caused me so much trouble as this damn bodyline bowling." As for Bradman's courage under fire, Wally Hammond was to write: "He ran to the off or out to leg to get away from those head-high whistling balls, and he played golf shots and overhead lawn tennis shots, and from one after another the ball went crashing to the pickets. That was sheer courage. Those who said Bradman was afraid of bodyline don't know cricket as it was played on that tour." But to the end, the Don remained sensitive to the charge by some that the most infamous episode in the history of Australian sport came about because his prodigious talent was considered by some to be flawed at the Oval in 1930.

Bodyline
Television miniseries of five two-hour episodes made for the Ten Network by Kennedy Miller and first shown in 1984 starting on July 16. It was also shown in Britain. The producers shot the film mainly at their studios at the old Metro Cinema in Kings Cross and at the SCG, but also used archival footage of the Bodyline matches. Directors were Carl Schultz, George Ogilvie, Lex Marinos and Denny Lawrence, and the senior writers were

Robert Caswell, Lex Marinos, Denny Lawrence and Terry Hayes. Cinematographer was Dean Semler. The story was told from the viewpoints of Bradman and England captain Douglas Jardine. The Don was played by Gary Sweet, Jardine by Hugo Weaving and Harold Larwood by Jim Holt. Former Australian Test spinner Peter Philpott played Clarrie Grimmett and also served as consultant. Others in the cast of 47 included Julie Nihill, Max Cullen, Arthur Dignam and Frank Thring. According to cricket writer David Frith, the miniseries contains "many laughable inaccuracies".

Also a BBC television documentary of 1983 made by Alan Patient, a 40-minute program featuring newsreel footage and interviews with many survivors of the series.

Bodyline Autopsy: The Full Story of the Most Sensational Test Cricket Series – England V Australia 1932–33

Book by David Frith, published in hardcover in 2002 by ABC Books, 480pp, touted by the publisher as "the most comprehensive work ever written on the fast-bowling controversy of the 1932–33 Test Series". Jamie Grant's review in *Wisden Cricketers' Almanack Australia* (2003–04):

"For a truly authoritative account of the Bodyline series, one need look no further than David Frith's *Bodyline Autopsy*. This may be the culmination of Frith's already distinguished career as a cricket writer. It is more than just a history of the Bodyline series – though it is by far the most meticulously researched and documented account of that period – as Frith's immense knowledge of cricket history enables him both to place the series in context and to examine its long-lasting consequences. Interestingly, while he deplores England's tactics in 1932–33, Frith feels the West Indian attack of the 1980s vastly exceeded the brutality of Larwood and Voce, which he sees by comparison as 'mild by virtue of its restricted and intermittent usage'. He is splendidly vehement in his condemnation of those 'academics and boring, paranoid windbags' who allowed the West Indians to avoid punishment, or even serious criticism, for fear of being suspected of racism. Frith's book also goes further than other histories of the series because it is not concerned only with the Test matches and their much-publicised political ramifications. Using contemporary newspaper reports, private letters and other documents, Frith supplies a complete account of every stage of England's tour of Australia and New Zealand; every minor match is detailed, as is every off-field incident of any significance. What emerges is a pattern which helps to explain the unprecedented animosity which developed between the English and

Australian teams. It is clear that a certain amount of acrimony existed long before Jardine's novel tactics were deployed, and after reading Frith's book one is tempted to speculate that some form of confrontation might well have developed even without Bodyline. For this revelation alone, Frith's book must be seen as the year's most impressive cricket book."

Frith concludes that it was "probably Bradman" who leaked the famous dressing-room incident to the press, but that the act was good for cricket, since it opened Australia's realisation that even Woodfull deplored this form of bowling. That allowed the public to give full vent to its objections.

Bodyline – It's Just Not Cricket!

Hour-long television documentary made by the ABC and first shown on November 13, 2002, in *The Big Picture* time slot. Executive producer was Margot Phillipson, Lincoln Tyner was the writer/producer, Mike Coward conducted the interviews and Michael Habib was the narrator. The program was made in association with David Frith's book *Bodyline Autopsy*, to mark the 70th anniversary of the infamous series of 1932–33. The documentary boasts the first recorded interview with the eldest daughter of Douglas Jardine, Rev. Fianach Lawry, who made the point that her father told her that the bodyline tactics were all worked out and agreed upon by the MCC before the team left for Australia and that her father felt very let down by the Lord's establishment when he was made to wear the full responsibility for the subsequent furore.

"Bohemians"

Team of former Test bowler Arthur Mailey's which visited New South Wales country centres on promotional tours in the late 1920s. It was as a member of the side on such a tour at the end of the 1927–28 season, the Don's first in first-class cricket, that he played in Cootamundra, the town of his birth, for the only time. Sadly, he could only score 1, saying later: "It was disappointing for me to be run out for 1 the only time I played in my birthplace." The Bohemians wore distinctive, specially tailored striped blazers. James Bancks, the creator of the Ginger Meggs comic strip, is seen (with the Don) in a team photo taken on the 1927–28 tour in Dudauman.

Borwick, George Eric

Australian umpire who controversially gave the Don not out when England players appealed for a catch by Jack Ikin in the slips off Bill Voce when on 28 in the First Test of the 1946–47 series at the 'Gabba in

Brisbane. Bradman thought it was a bump ball and Borwick concurred, but many England players were not impressed. Skipper Wally Hammond thought Borwick was wrong but agreed to the reappointment of the same two umpires for the following Test in Sydney.

Bouncers

During the 1987 radio interview with Norman May, the Don spoke about his attitude to his bowlers serving up short-pitched balls on the 1948 tour of England. He said that he would never encourage the use of bumpers as a deliberate and consistent policy, even with an ordinary field. "An occasional one is all right, but not persistent." Later in the interview, when the discussion turned to the subject of bouncers in the modern game, Bradman said: "Cricket is supposed to be a game and a sport, and it saddens me very much to think there is any necessity for batsmen to wear helmets in self-protection. I also make the observation that I find it hard to believe that a batsman wearing a helmet, with a visor, can have the same unrestricted vision, speed, freedom of movement that he would otherwise possess ... and I think the legislators should grapple with this question of short-pitched bowling and do it quickly."

Boundary

Journal of the Friends of the Bradman Museum, first issued in spring 1990 and published quarterly. Edited by staff members Richard Mulvaney and Allison Hyland, *Boundary* reports on the museum's latest and forthcoming activities and also features regular commentary on past and present cricket matters, news of recent collection acquisitions by the museum, and changes in membership of the current board of directors, etc. The magazine is produced entirely in-house, with all senior staff contributing, and is printed by a contractor.

Bowes, William Eric

The tall bespectacled fast bowler was the first man to bowl what was to become known as "bodyline" when he sent down bumpers to a packed leg-side field in a county game playing for Yorkshire in August 1932. The method of Bowes's was attacked at the time in a newspaper article by Pelham Warner, who said the tactic was "not cricket". Bowes soon after toured Australia with the Ashes team for the Bodyline series and became the first and only man to dismiss the Don first ball in a Test when Bradman played on to him in Australia's first innings in the Second Test at the MCG. Illness had forced the Don out of the first match in Sydney, won decisively by the tourists (despite a superb knock of 187 not out by Stan McCabe), and there was great expectation that Bradman would set things right in Melbourne. When he went in at no. 4, cheers accompanied his every stride to the wicket and continued while he took guard. The noise died but twice it started up again when Bowes started his run-up and twice Bradman turned away. Each time while he waited for the crowd to quieten, Bowes moved a leg fieldsman to a squarer position, more (he would later write) for the sake of something to do. But when Bradman looked at each of the two men changing positions in the field, Bowes sensed that the batsman expected a bouncer, and he decided to do what he could to convince the Don that that was his intention. When he came in to bowl for the third time, the crowd remained quiet and "I pulled a face as if there was to be tremendous effort. I bowled it short but did not dig it into the ground, as you must to bowl a bouncer. Almost as the ball left my hand, Bradman set himself for a pull stroke … All set for the ball at shoulder height, he suddenly realised it was coming to him at the height of the bails or less. He altered his shot and swung down at the ball, got the faintest of edges to it without altering its direction, and the ball crashed into the stumps … A stunned and complete silence came on the crowd as Bradman surveyed his stumps, turned, and walked slowly to the pavilion." The Don atoned with 103 not out in the second innings, and Australia won by 111 runs, thanks in no small part to Bill O'Reilly's 10/129. Bradman was Bowes's only wicket of this match and the Test was the only one of the series in which Bowes played, but he claimed the Don's scalp in three consecutive Test innings at Headingley and the Oval in 1934, though only after Bradman had made 304, 244 and 77. Bill Bowes died in 1987, aged 79.

Bowled
How the Don got out 78 times in his 295 first-class dismissals and another 70 times in 267 second-class dismissals.

Bowling
The Don took plenty of wickets with his leg-breaks early in his career for Bowral on the coir matting but said much later that in big cricket he was happy to "leave the bowling to those who knew what they were doing". In his 52 Tests Bradman bowled 25.2 six-ball overs (15.2 against England, nine against the West Indies, one against South Africa) and one eight-ball over (against India). His best performance was 1/8, against the West Indies in 1930–31, and his career figures were 2 wickets at an average of 36. Both of his Test scalps were taken on Adelaide Oval: West Indian Ivan Barrow (lbw)

in 1930–31 and Englishman Wally Hammond in 1932–33 (bowled). During the gruelling Oval Test in 1938 Bradman put himself on to give his exhausted bowlers a "spell" during England's mammoth first innings total of 903. He had sent down 2.2 overs when he stepped in a hole which had been worn by Bill O'Reilly and fractured a bone in his ankle. In all first-class matches, the Don sent down 2,118 balls for 36 wickets at 37.97, with a strike rate of 58.70. His best figures were 3/35 against Cambridge University in 1930.

Bowral

The town which nestles below Mt Gibraltar in the Southern Highlands of New South Wales, 109km from Sydney, was home to the Don from 1911 to 1928. Bowral was originally part of a property granted to explorer John Oxley in 1825. He erected a prefabricated house, "Wingecarribee", shipped from England. The first known reference to the name Bowral appears in one of Major TL Mitchell's field books, in which he noted on May 13, 1828: "Walked to the top of Gibraltar the hill to the north of Mr. Oxley's station at Wingarribee, called by the natives Bowrel." In 1859, when it was announced that the railway was coming to the area, part of the Oxley estate was subdivided by members of the family. The settlement was first called the Village of Wingecarribee, then the Village of Burradoo and finally, when the railway came in 1867, the Village of Bowral. After the arrival of the railway the town grew rapidly, and well before the turn of the century it became something of a mecca for Sydney's elite, who went there to escape the summer heat. The town still has something of a gentrified feel to it, although it is fast disappearing.

Cricket was played in Bowral at least as early as 1863. A match was played in "Loseby's paddock" at Bong Bong between Mittagong and Sutton Forest in 1865. The earliest reference in print to sport in Bowral was an item in April 1871 in the *Goulburn Herald* which mentions that a team from Wollongong was to play against Mittagong at Bowral. The annual meeting of the Bowral Cricket Club is referred to in the *Scrutineer* in September 1881, from which it may be inferred that the club was in existence at least as early as 1880. In 1884 cricket was being played in "Oxley's paddock". The highlight of cricket the following year was a two-day match between an English eleven and a Moss Vale twenty-two at Moss Vale. England 432 drew with Moss Vale 14 and 4/19. About 1,000 watched the first day's play and 1,200 attended on the second day. English cricketers returned to Bowral in 1887, and again in 1891, when they were led by WG Grace in a match against a local team (which included two of the Don's future uncles) at Loseby Park. The Bowral club moved to its present home ground in Glebe Park soon after and in 1904 joined the Wingecarribee Cricket Union. By 1919 the cricket association was called Berrima District, which included towns within a 50km radius of Bowral.

Bradman was two years and nine months old when his father George moved the family from the small railway settlement of Yeo Yeo, near Cootamundra, where he was struggling as a wheat and sheep farmer, to Bowral for the benefit of the health of the Don's mother, Emily. The Bradmans first lived at 52 Shepherd Street, where for hours on end he famously threw a golf ball against the base of a water tank and tried to hit it on the rebound with a cricket stump, and also threw a golf ball at a rounded fence rail in a nearby paddock and tried to catch it as it returned. When the Don read a book about the history of Bowral a couple of years before his death, he remembered as a boy riding around the town on the back of a horse helping to light gas lamps on the streets. In 1924 the family moved around the corner to 20 Glebe Street, in a house built by George, opposite Glebe Park, later renamed Bradman Oval. He left school in 1922 with his Intermediate Certificate at the age of 14 and his parents arranged employ-ment for him with local real estate agent Percy Westbrook at 276 Bong Bong Street. It was no accident that they chose real estate. A building boom had started just after the Great War and continued through the 1920s. By 1923, local brickmakers could not cope with the demand. In 1927, land in the main street of Bowral was selling at the inflated price of 50 pounds a foot.

When the 18-year-old Bradman started playing grade cricket for St George near the end of 1926, living in Bowral not only meant a three-hour train trip to the city and back each Saturday, but it also meant he could not practise during the week on Sydney's turf wickets, which played quite dif-ferently from the coir matting on concrete pitches he was used to. He com-muted to Sydney to play with St George all through the 1926–27 season and for part of the next. Early in 1928, by which time he was playing for NSW, the Don's employer opened an office in Sydney and offered the 19-year-old the chance to run it. When arrangements were made to board in Sydney with insurance agent Geoffrey Pearce, a friend of the family, the die was cast. The Boy from Bowral went home for a public farewell in March 1930 at the Empire Theatre before he left for England, and was wel-comed back at a reception in the town's Corbett Gardens in November after his record-breaking tour, but his visits after that were infrequent, though he convalesced for three months in 1935 and for nine months in 1941–42 at the property of Jessie's parents in nearby Mittagong.

Lore has it that many of Bradman's contemporaries, before they either died or left the district, were unhappy with the celebrated batsman because he severed most ties with the town when he became a Test cricketer. But Gordon Whatman, a former president of the local cricket association whose grandfather, Mark, was a brother of the Don's mother Emily, says Bradman will always be part of the town. "I knew Don and he always felt he belonged here, even though he very rarely came home. The simple fact is that his memory is embedded here and it always will be." A thanksgiving service for the Don was held at the Church of St Simon and St Jude, followed by a memorial service at Bradman Oval, on March 28, 2001, and the Don's and Jessie's ashes were scattered in the grounds of the Bradman Museum at the oval in a private ceremony on October 18, 2001.

Bowral Boy

A thoroughbred racehorse which was running at Newmarket on the last day of a match between the Don's Australians and Surrey at the Oval in June 1948. The tourists arrived at the ground needing just 122 runs to win the game and were keen to wrap it up so they could get to Wimbledon in time to see the final between Australia's John Bromwich and the American Bob Falkenburg. During the rush for the required runs, which were acquired thanks largely to a quick-fire 73 from Neil Harvey, the Don received a telegram at the ground from the connections of Bowral Boy with a tip for the horse and two others at the same meeting. The team got to the tennis in plenty of time (to see Ray Lindwall's fellow tennis club member at home lose the match after holding three match points), but the punters in the Australian side did not get a chance to have a bet and, true to form, not only was Bowral Boy first to greet the judge (at 25–1!) but so too were the other two tips.

Bowral Pubic School

School in Bendooley Street attended by the Don from September 1913 to December 1922. The school was established by the Anglican Church in 1863 and many of the pupils were children of men employed on the construction of the railway line. The school was taken over by the Council of Education in 1867 and several buildings were added from 1869. The site's oldest remaining building, dating from 1885, is now known as the Old Woodwork Room (where the Don attended kindergarten in 1913). In 1892 Bowral became a Superior Public School with three departments (it was to drop the word Superior when a separate high school was established in Bowral in 1930). The senior classes became an Intermediate High School in 1914 (though it was not gazetted until 1918) and by 1916, as the only high school in the district, had over 100 students enrolled. When the young

Bradman walked to school each day from his home in Shepherd Street he crossed Glebe Park, which many years later was to bear his name. As a 12- and 13-year-old in 1921, he accompanied the year-younger Jessie Menzies, who was staying at the Bradman home for her first year of high school so she would not have to travel the 12km each day from the family property at Glenquarry by herself.

The Don's favourite subject at high school was mathematics. Science ran a close second until an explosion caused by a student carrying out an unauthorised experiment "made me apprehensive". His academic record was better than average, usually finishing third behind a girl named Iris Payne and a boy called "Sooky" Turner. Away from the desk, the Don joined other boys in a crude form of cricket in the main quadrangle with stumps drawn on the bellpost as a wicket and a bat hewn from the branch of a gum tree. Bradman's first organised game was during the summer of 1919–20, when he turned out for his school against another school on the dirt football field at Glebe Park. The Don was still in primary school but his side boasted some players from the high school. He batted at no. 4 and faced a hat-trick ball before making 55 not out. The following summer he scored 115 not out (his first century) and took eight wickets for his high school against Mittagong High at Mittagong (when he was admonished by his headmaster, Amos Lee, for leaving his bat behind). In the return match at Bowral his captain asked him to retire after making 72, and the Mittagong skipper then asked Bowral to leave him out of the team, or his club would forfeit the match. But as well as playing cricket, the Don represented his school in tennis and rugby, and in athletics one year he won all races up to 880 yards for boys of his age. He left school with his Intermediate Certificate (with two A passes and six B passes) at the age of 14 in 1922 and went to work for local real estate agent Percy Westbrook.

One of the school's oldest existing buildings houses a museum in honour of its most famous student. The brainchild of longtime headmaster David Williams, the museum was the school's Bicentennial project in 1988. The Don declined an invitation to attend the opening but assiduously answered the school's letters. Just outside the door of the museum is the bellpost which the young Don and his schoolmates used as a wicket for their lunchtime "Tests". The post has been moved about 50 metres from its original location in the quadrangle and the bell has been adopted by the museum as its symbol. The museum is set up as a classroom of the early 1900s, and the "schoolmarm" is Barbara Grey, who was the school's teacher-librarian from 1967 to 2000. She dresses in a costume of the time and teaches classes to students, who also dress up for the occasion. Barbara takes pupils not just from Bowral Public but also from other schools in the district. Visitors to the museum can see an admissions register enclosed in a glass case which records the five-year-old Bradman's enrolment in his first class.

The Don visited the museum with Jessie at Mr Williams's invitation on October 13, 1989, when they were in town for the opening of the Bradman Pavilion, and the school's most famous old boy was a little miffed to find that when his father George enrolled Don he gave his occupation as "fencer" rather than "carpenter". He was fascinated by the photographs of the Bowral of his childhood and told Barbara many stories associated with them, including one about the time he nearly drowned in the local swimming pool. The Bradmans spent an hour and a half at the school, the Don interacting warmly with the children and posing for many photographs for the school photographer, but he insisted it was a private visit and refused to talk to reporters. He signed about 20 cricket bats and anything else the kids put in front of him. And he faced up in front of the bellpost to demonstrate his famous technique and pass on some of his secrets to the boys of the school cricket team. For Barbara's part, it was a marvellous experience to meet the hero of her father's in the 1930s, when he regaled the family many times with tales of the great man's batting at the SCG.

"Boy from Bowral, The"

Tag which the Don always thought was ridiculous given that he had lived the bulk of his life away from his boyhood home. Nevertheless, it was his dying wish that his ashes be returned to the New South Wales country town where he grew up, where he played his first cricket and where he met Jessie, his beloved wife of 65 years.

Boyle, Gregory

Then 13-year-old Adelaide schoolboy who in 1991 wrote to the Don saying he was doing a school project on him. The legendary batsman phoned him and invited him around. He signed a bat for the boy, posed for photos, told him he would've loved to have played one-day cricket and to keep his eye on the ball.

Bradenham/Bradnam

Sir Donald's son John used the name Bradenham for a period before changing it by deed poll to Bradsen in 1972 to escape the shadow of his famous father. Bradenham is the original family name. Cricket umpire and Bradman researcher Nigel Ward traced Sir Donald's family past back to the 16th century and the rural village of Bradenham that gave him his name. Nigel told the *Sun-Herald*'s Matthew Benns in 1998 that he had found an 89-year-old woman, Annie Smith, who claimed to be the Don's third cousin. "Does he know he has spelt his name wrong?" she asked. Vague details given earlier by the Don in response to Ward's letter from Withersfield in Suffolk set him off on a 10-year trail of discovery which eventually led to Bradman's namesake village in Norfolk. "I was in the village church in Great Saxham near Bury St Edmonds (in Suffolk) when I found the marriage of Sir Donald's earliest-known relative. The records show the marriage between Edmunde from Bradenham and a local woman. He was obviously a poor labourer and had no surname so they called him Bradenham."

Nigel's research proved that most of the Don's ancestors had lived in Bradenham before moving to Withersfield. It was Thomas Bradman, the brother of John Bradman, the Don's great-grandfather, who was Annie Smith's great-grandfather. John Bradman and Lucy Rowlinson, who tied the knot in Withersfield in 1838, unwittingly sparked the confusion over the Bradman name. In their marriage certificate John's surname was recorded as Bradman but he signed his name Bradnam. As their six children were baptised the names varied and the confusion grew. Eventually it proved too much for the vicar, who wrote in the margin: "The family are recorded in the parish records as BRADMAN." Annie Smith told Nigel Ward she remained convinced that Sir Donald should really carry her maiden name and be Sir Donald Bradnam. It took the Don himself to end the confusion. In a letter to Ward he wrote: "The odd switch from Bradman to Bradnam is very strange. On the score of probability I think BRADMAN wins the day."

Bradford
Where the Don's Invincibles came closest to defeat in 1948 in the first of two games on the tour against Yorkshire. But the Australian skipper did not play, and a leg injury prevented Sam Loxton from batting.

Bradman, Charles
The Don's grandfather, a farm labourer who emigrated to New South Wales in 1852 from Suffolk, England, to escape the harsh agricultural recession. He was living at 26 High Noon Lane, Withersfield, during the June 1851 census but by the following summer had emigrated and was playing cricket in Mittagong. Charles Bradman left rumours behind him that he had been deported for sheep stealing, but in 1998 Bradman

researcher Nigel Ward told the *Sun-Herald*'s Matthew Benns that he had finally ended that rumour: "I spent days going through the Bury St Edmunds Quarter Sessions covering a seven-year period and Charles Bradman did not appear." (On reading the news in a letter from Ward, the Don replied: "I guess there is some consolation in finding that I am not descended from a convict.") Charles Bradman married Elizabeth Biffin of Mittagong and soon after moved to a farm at Jindalee, in the Cootamundra district, where they raised a family of six, including the Don's father, George. Charles and Elizabeth Bradman are buried in Cootamundra, the birthplace of their famous grandson.

Bradman, Emily

Emily Whatman of Mittagong was 21 when she tied the knot with 17-year-old George Bradman, of Jindalee, at Cootamundra, on December 16, 1893. It was for the benefit of his wife's health that George moved the family from Yeo Yeo, near Cootamundra, to Bowral in 1911, when the Don was almost three. Emily wanted to be near her family, which had been long-established in Mittagong, near Bowral, before her marriage. In fact she went to school with James Menzies, the father of her son's future wife, Jessie. When Jessie as a girl was boarding with the Bradmans in their Shepherd Street home, and she and Don left for school together, Emily stood on the verandah to make sure her 12-year-old son opened the gate for his 11-year-old companion. The Don's mother played cricket as a girl and she bowled regularly to the budding batsman in the backyard, left-handed with a tennis ball, after the cry: "Come on, Mum, give us a bowl." After her son's rise to fame, Emily said: "If Don breaks any more records I don't know how I will manage to get through the clerical work involved in answering congratulations," and: "Although I am so proud of him – and what mother would not be? – I am not the least afraid of his success turning his head as it might do with most young fellows."

Emily never ventured far from home, and chose not to accompany husband George and son Vic to Goulburn airport to meet her son when he returned from his sensational tour of England in 1930. Tall, thin and shy, she shrank also from the crowds and the cameras. Instead, she allowed herself to be driven to the Bong Bong bridge, a few kilometres out of Bowral on the road to Goulburn. She and her son embraced when they met for the first time in eight months. Emily and other members of the family devoted considerable time to maintaining the scrapbooks which many years later were to form part of the collection of memorabilia donated by the Don to the State Library of South Australia. Emily and George moved from Bowral to Campbelltown, near Sydney, in the 1930s and Emily died aged 72 in Camden Hospital on December 16, 1944, the anniversary of her marriage.

Bradman, George

The Don's father was the son of an English immigrant from Withersfield, in the Haverhill area of Suffolk, a farm labourer who was attracted to New South Wales by the gold strikes near Bathurst in the 1850s. George Bradman, from Jindalee in the Cootamundra district, was only 17 when he married the Don's mother, Emily Whatman, 21, of Mittagong on December 16, 1893. Donald George was their fifth and youngest child, born at mid-wife Eliza Scholz's house at 89 Adams Street, Cootamundra on August 27, 1908, when the family was living on a wheat and sheep farm in the nearby community at Yeo Yeo. When George moved his wife and five children to Bowral in 1911 to benefit Emily's health, he took up carpentry and often worked for local builder Alf Stephens, the captain of Bowral Town Cricket Club, who was to have a big influence on George and his sons Victor and Donald becoming involved in the local cricket scene. George turned out for the Bowral team and after the war became assistant secretary and treasurer of the Bowral club and also honorary secretary of the Berrima District Cricket Association.

The young Don was inspired to play at the SCG by a spectacular century by Australia's Charlie Macartney when his father took the 12-year-old to see two days' play in the Fifth Ashes Test at the famous ground in February 1921. He wrote in his autobiography, *Farewell to Cricket*: "My father must have been amused when I said to him: 'I shall never be satisfied until I play on this ground.'" He added: "In the years that followed it was lovely to reflect upon the fulfilment of those early hopes, and to know that my father saw many of the wonderful matches in which I was privileged to take part on that famous ground. And he was there to see my final appearance in the Kippax-Oldfield Testimonial Match." George Bradman made the trip from Bowral to Sydney with his 18-year-old son in October 1926 when the Don was asked to attend a practice session at the SCG so selectors could run their eye over talented young cricketers from the country.

In a statement issued for the Sir Donald Bradman Oration in Melbourne in August 2000, the Don said of his dad: "My father never made a century in his life but always wore with pride a gold medal on his watch chain for some bowling feat. Whilst my mother was preparing the evening meal I persuaded him to bowl to me in the backyard. In those humble days I was taught the rudiments of the game which consumed so much of my later life." Of his celebrated son, George once said: "All Don's achievements are the result of his own effort." And: "I would describe his batting as practically a freak. There is no other term which adequately describes it." George and Emily Bradman moved from Bowral to Campbelltown, near Sydney, in the 1930s. After Emily's death in 1944, George returned to Bowral, where he died of heart failure in 1961, aged 84.

Bradman, Greta (Marguretta Jessie)

The Don's granddaughter, the daughter of son John, born in 1979. She was in the audience with her father and her brother Tom at the inaugural Sir Donald Bradman Oration which was delivered by Prime Minister John Howard in Melbourne in August 2000. At a press conference she attended with her father and brother soon after the Don's death, she said he was "a fantastic grandpa". At the memorial service in Adelaide, Greta said her grandfather showed her how to be true to herself and to her word. He had had a complete lack of vanity and pretension. After speaking, she sang a duet from Andrew Lloyd Webber's *Requiem* with a friend, Emily Roxburgh, and also sang three pieces as a member of the Adelaide Chamber Singers. Greta, who sang at her grandmother Jessie's memorial service in 1997, is also an accomplished pianist.

Bradman, Islet Natalie

The oldest of Emily and George's five children and three daughters, born in 1894. Not long after the family moved from Yeo Yeo to Bowral in 1911, she wrote to a friend: "Lily and I don't like Bowral half as well as we did Yeo Yeo." Islet married Lloyd Whatman and lived in Mittagong.

Bradman, (Lady) Jessie Martha (nee Menzies)

Born in Bowral on June 11, 1909, Jessie was one of four girls and two boys (one sister died at the age of 12) of Lilian (nee Kell) and James Menzies of Glenquarry, a farming village 12km east of Bowral. She attended Glenquarry Primary School but when she was 11, her father, who had known the Don's mother Emily since their school days in the late 1870s (and their families had known each other before that), arranged for Jessie to board with the Bradmans in town for her first year of high school through the week so she would not have to make the daily trek to Bowral by herself. The Don told Ray Martin in the 1996 television interview about how he was besotted by Jessie when she came to live in the same house. "I remember the day very well, because I had been sent down the street by my mother to buy some groceries, and I ran into the doctor's car on my bike and had an accident. He had to take me home. I had my nose all cut and scratches all over my face. And when I got home she was there at the door, having just been delivered by her father, because she was going to stay with us for 12 months and go to school. And we went to school together every day for the rest of the year. That was when I fell in love with her, that very first day. I don't think she fell in love with me until much later, because I was a terrible sight the day she saw me."

In 1926, Jessie moved from Bowral to the Sydney suburb of Burwood with her mother and two sisters for education and employment opportunities for the girls. They lived in a large house at 73 Liverpool Road, on the corner of Burwood Road (a short walk from the church where Jessie was to marry). The Don, who had been travelling from Bowral each week to play with the St George club since November 1926, shifted to Sydney early in 1928 to board with insurance traveller Geoffrey Pearce in the adjacent suburb of Concord West. When Jessie accepted the Don's proposal of marriage in early 1930, he wanted to become engaged immediately, but Jessie put him off because she wanted him to go to England as a "free man". When the couple were engaged the following year, Jessie had graduated from business college and was working for the Commonwealth Bank in Sydney. At their wedding at St Paul's Anglican Church in Burwood on April 30, 1932, the church was filled to capacity and outside hundreds of women and children continually broke through police barriers to be close to the couple when they emerged. The Don had been living at 172 Frederick Street, Rockdale, since moving from Concord in September 1928 to board with St George administrator and Board of Control member Frank Cush, whose wife's name, coincidentally, was also Jessie.

The newly married couple rented half of a two-storey house in McMahons Point, at the northern end of the then brand new Sydney Harbour Bridge. Before tying the knot with Jessie, the Don had been asked by former Test player Arthur Mailey to join an Australian team on his private goodwill tour of North America, and he accepted only on the condition that Jessie could also go. She was the only player's wife in the party and the trip served as an extended honeymoon. When Bradman was offered a contract of employment by Adelaide stockbroker and cricket administrator Harry Hodgetts early in 1934, Jessie was most reluctant to leave New South Wales. But when her husband accepted the offer and moved to Adelaide in February 1934 for a few weeks before leaving for England so as to gain qualification for South Australia on his expected return in October, Jessie remained in Sydney. When the Don became critically ill with peritonitis in England at the end of the tour, the great aviator Charles Kingsford-Smith offered to fly Jessie to London, but Australian aviation authorities would not allow it. Instead, she took a train from Sydney to Melbourne, intending to travel overland to Perth and then board the *Maloja*, which had sailed from Sydney several days before. When Jessie heard a rumour in Melbourne that her husband had died, she phoned the hospital in London. On being told the report was somewhat premature, she continued her journey. Jessie was hosted by India's first great Test batsman (to be), Vijay Merchant, when her ship stopped over in Bombay (now Mumbai). (In a foreword to *Some Indian Cricketers*, a book by another Indian batsman, Rusi Modi, the Don wrote of his affection for Merchant, whom he'd never met: "Such a kindness portrayed the man, and for that she and I remain eternally thankful.")

The Don was released from hospital only the day before Jessie arrived in England, and the couple holidayed in Scotland before returning to London for sightseeing (escorted by Cabinet Minister John Burns) and then heading off to the Continent. They spent Christmas in the south of France and arrived back in Australia in February 1935. The Don rested up at the property of Jessie's family's new property at Mittagong, and the pair arrived in Adelaide on Anzac Day. Soon after, they built the red-brick double-storey house at 2 Holden Street, Kensington Park, which was to remain the family home for the next 60 years.

In *Farewell to Cricket*, the Don wrote of the effect on Jessie of the death of their two-day-old son, Ross, in October 1936: "The hopes and ambitions of a father for his son, fine and noble though they may be, are as nought alongside the natural love of a mother." Jessie was allowed to join her husband near the end of the tour of England in 1938 only when an earlier decision by the Board of Control not to allow her to join the team was reversed after the Don's players sent a cable of protest. But not only did Jessie get permission to go, the wives of the other players were also allowed to join their husbands if they wished. The Bradmans had a second son, John, in 1939, but there was more misfortune when their daughter, Shirley, was born two years later with cerebral palsy. John's polio as a young teenager was a trying time for the family. Jessie rose night after night to go to her son (who was in splints) and turn him in his bed to ensure he was comfortable. He eventually made a full recovery and even excelled at athletics. Jessie herself had been a fine sportswoman in her own right; in her youth she was an accomplished horsewoman and tennis player and later played excellent lawn bowls and golf. Of her concern for her famous husband in the heat of the battle, she once said: "I have never been more than a little apprehensive. His calmness always inspired me with confidence." But Jessie was widely recognised as her husband's constant source of support, comfort and encouragement.

Jessie had a hip replacement and heart surgery in her 60s and 70s but had periodic relapses in the years that followed. Nevertheless, she was a tireless charity and community worker well into her 80s. She derived great enjoyment from her garden, and in the weeks before her death from leukaemia on September 14, 1997 it gave her great pleasure that the perfume of freesias (her favourite flowers) permeated the house. Soon after her passing, the Bradman Foundation's executive officer, Richard Mulvaney, said: "She was a figure something akin to the Queen Mother, a woman who would embrace you and take an interest in you. She was a wonderful woman and I think her warmth, support, level-headedness and matter-of-factness helped Sir Donald maintain a sense of equilibrium when his career was at its height and the publicity greatest." In his autobiography, the Don wrote of the "comfort and encouragement" and "sound judgement and counsel" he received from his wife. He later said: "I would never have achieved what I achieved without Jessie."

Lady Jessie Bradman was cremated in a private funeral in Adelaide and a public memorial service followed at St Peter's Cathedral on September 28. In his eulogy at the memorial service for his father in the same church three-and-a-half years later, John told of his mother's courage in the face of death, recalling her words near the end: "I don't know what all the fuss is about, I'm only dying." Charles Williams, the Don's most recent biographer, dedicated his 1996 work to Jessie, calling her an "Australian heroine in her own right".

Bradman, John Russell

The Don's only living son, born on July 10, 1939, three years after the death of the Bradmans' first child, Ross, just two days after he was born. When John contracted polio as a 13-year-old his father gave up all his administrative duties associated with cricket to help Jessie care for him. He made a complete recovery and excelled at athletics, at one point holding the South Australian title in the 120 yards hurdles. John was also a capable cricketer, in his last year at school scoring a century and taking a swag of wickets to help defeat another school team which included Ian Chappell. He studied law and became a barrister, along the way marrying Judith Young. In the early 1970s he played the tuba in a revivalist jazz band in Adelaide led by Dave Dallwitz. John changed his surname to Bradsen in 1972 to escape what he called the "metaphysical glass cage" of being the son of a legend. Writing in a newspaper article in the same year he said: "I'm tired of people discovering who I am; I'm an individual, not a social souvenir." His famous father wanted to know why he had not chosen a

B

name like Smith or Jones, but John had not wanted a complete break. (Bradman senior was not too keen on the name Bradsen, because it was almost Scandinavian, and he was not enamoured of Scandinavian morals.) From then on, though not estranged, the pair inhabited different worlds.

When Jessie died in 1997 her son took all his leave then resigned his post as a lecturer in law at Adelaide University so he could spend more time with the Don. He learned to play bridge so he could join in sessions with his father. The two spoke, often for hours, almost daily and had become close before the Don's passing in February 2001. John has told of how they were together on one occasion at his father's home in 1998 when a leading author said something on a television program which was less than complimentary about his dad, and it was then that he decided to go back to his original name and speak publicly in defence of his father at every opportunity. The day after the Don's death, John said he was "a wonderful father, grandfather and friend and we feel many will share our loss. His love, generosity, humour and strong good sense will be very much missed." At a press conference at Adelaide Oval two days later, he said: "I really hope that people won't enshrine my dad too much. This iconic stuff is a little bit troubling. I don't think he should become a religious figure. I don't think they should see him and just genuflect. I think they should see him and reflect on the qualities that make people feel as they do." And soon after: "He clearly has touched people's lives, and has really touched the community, and it's not his achievements … his achievements were astonishing, but it is his qualities, not his achievements … and how we understand those and what they say to the community will unfold over time as we re-explore these questions."

Greta and Tom were present with their father at the press conference at Adelaide Oval, and the three were joined by John's partner, Megan Webster, at the public memorial service in Adelaide's St Peter's Cathedral on March 25, 2001, when John, Greta and Tom spoke and Greta also sang. Two-year-old Nicholas joined other members of the family at the thanksgiving and memorial services at Bowral three days later. When, in November 2001, the *Australian* newspaper published two negative articles about the Don, the Bradman family and the Bradman Foundation soon after issued a statement expressing disappointment at the publication of the material, saying it "had caused a considerable amount of distress and sadness amongst members of the family and the Foundation". John said: "My dad was a decent person and scrupulously honest. He was a man who made an enormous contribution to the welfare of the community. It is unfair that the material has been published when my dad is not able to defend himself." In 2004, John

Bradman gave his first extended television interview when he appeared on the ABC documentary *Bradman: Reflections on the Legend*. Among other things, he spoke of his ordeal when he had polio and about his namechange.

Bradman, Lilian Mabel

The second of the Don's three sisters, born in 1897. She was an accomplished pianist (and taught her younger brother how to play) and became a music teacher. Lilian married Charles Sproule and lived at Campbelltown, near Sydney.

Bradman, (Elizabeth) May

The youngest of the Don's three sisters, born in 1902. She married Eric Glover in 1922 in Bowral and lived for most of her life in Mittagong. May spent her last few years at Harbison Retirement Village at Burradoo, just south of Bowral.

Bradman, Nicholas

The Don's youngest grandchild, John's younger son, born in 1998. Not long before his death, his grandfather wrote to Nicholas: "I'll always be with you in spirit; try hard but with integrity, and have lots of fun."

Bradman, (Victor) Paul

The only son of the Don's brother, Victor, born in 1943. In an interview with the *Australian* newspaper's David Nason, published on November 16, 2001, Paul characterised the Don as a snob who forgot his family and his Bowral connection after his rise to fame. "Don Bradman was only ever worried about Don Bradman. He thought he was above everyone in the family and he didn't want to know anyone ... He had very little to do with any of his family." Paul told of how his aunties (the Don's sisters) were astonished when their brother did not turn up for his mother Emily's funeral in 1944 (when he happened to be in Sydney) or for his father George's funeral in 1961. And, according to Paul, he was also a no-show at the funerals of his three sisters and his brother. Two days after the publication of the interview, Mike Gibson, writing in another News Limited paper, the *Sunday Telegraph*, was scathing of Paul's putdown, slamming the "bile that emanates from his tirade" and the "dishonouring of the dead". When asked to comment on Paul's remarks, family relative and longtime Bowral resident Gordon Whatman said: "That's Paul. He's like that with everyone, although I get on with him all right. But I feel sorry for him. He had a pretty hard life, what with his parents breaking up and his father being the subject of local gossip."

Bradman, Ross Moyes

Jessie and the Don's son, their first child, who died in Adelaide on October 29, 1936, just 36 hours after his birth. Bradman had accepted congratulations on the birth from the recently arrived England players at a function on the morning after the delivery but he had been told by the attending doctor to fear the worst. Because of the bereavement the Don withdrew from the match between South Australia and the MCC which started the following day.

Bradman, Shirley June

The Don and Jessie's daughter, born on April 17, 1941, with mild cerebral palsy. With her parents' support she has devoted much of her adult life to voluntary service to handicapped children and the blind. She married Ian Samuels in Adelaide in 1975. In an interview with Margaret Geddes for the 2002 book *Remembering Bradman*, the Don's friend Jill Gauvin said: "Shirley copes very well, and she copes very well because Don has enabled her to cope well. He's been a wonderful father. They've allowed her to live independently, and I think he tried to make up for what she couldn't have." Shirley's brother John sent a cheerio call to his sister during his remarks at their father's memorial service in St Peter's Cathedral in Adelaide, saying "she has not been well."

Bradman, Thomas Alexander

The Don's grandson, John's son, born in 1981. Tom was in the audience with his father and his sister Greta at the inaugural Sir Donald Bradman Oration delivered by Prime Minister John Howard in Melbourne in August 2000. At a press conference he attended with his father and his sister soon after the Don's death, he described his grandfather as "wonderful". At the memorial service at St Peter's Cathedral in Adelaide, he read a poem, "Lulla and Grandpa" (by an unknown author), which his father had found among Sir Donald's possessions. Tom, a law student, said his grandfather's life could not be celebrated without his grandmother, Jessie. He attended the thanksgiving and memorial services in Bowral with other members of the family in March 2001.

Bradman, Victor Charles

The Don's only brother, born in 1904. He played in the Bowral Town cricket team with his father George and Don and served on the club committee with his younger brother. The two were out shooting rabbits near Bowral when the team for the 1930 tour of England was announced on radio. Vic was best man at the Don's wedding in Sydney in 1932. On leaving school, Victor Bradman studied accountancy and ran his own practice in Bowral for a few years before buying a menswear business two doors from the post office. The venture was so successful (and his SP bookmaking activities also proving so lucrative) that he was able in the 1930s to build a palatial home at Mittagong. It was while clearing land around the house that he injured a leg in an accident while using a rotary hoe, thereafter walking with a pronounced limp. Victor's son, Paul, told the *Australian* newspaper in November 2001 that his father was a ladies' man who served with the local hospital board and tennis association only because of the opportunity to meet women. Victor's 1935 marriage to Lorraine Webb failed in 1949 and his de facto relationship (at a time when living in sin was regarded as just that) with another woman for the next 10 years was apparently the subject of local gossip. Paul said that after his rise to fame, the Don sought to distance himself from all his family at Bowral, but particularly his brother. Victor once said: "I was a mug cricketer compared to Don." He died of a heart attack in a picture theatre in Sydney's Rose Bay in 1960.

Bradman

The first substantial biography of the Don, written by AG "Johnny" Moyes and published in May 1948 by Harrap, 222pp. The book has a foreword by former England captain and commentator Arthur Gilligan and the text is interspersed with photographs. Since the work was published before the end of Bradman's career, the statistical supplement at the back of the book is incomplete. Moyes had the closest relationship with the Don of any of his biographers. One of the three New South Wales selectors who cast an eye over Bradman when the 18-year-old trialled at the SCG in October 1926, he helped him into first-class cricket and became a close confidant over the next few years. Moyes's introduction to his book starts: "One day in 1926 a quiet knock sounded on the door of my office in Sydney. It opened to admit a fair-haired, keen-eyed, intelligent-looking youth of lithe physique. 'I'm Don Bradman,' he said, with a shy grin, as he entered the room and sat down. Then began the first of those many talks on cricket which have been such a joy to me over the years." Of his biography, Moyes said: "When my book was published some critics suggested hero-worship. Nonsense. Admiration? Yes. Doesn't he deserve that? I think so." **Also** the title of a television documentary produced and directed by Jack Egan. Executive producer was David Salter. Originally shown on the ABC in 1990, the film features the Don's first extensive interview on camera. His insights are interspersed with archival footage of his major innings and off-the-field scenes during his English tours, as well as series-by-series coverage of his Test statistics and interviews with teammates.

Egan, who interviewed Bradman for the program, had been collecting archival film of Australian cricket for several years and wrote to Sir Donald a couple of times asking him for an interview to go with the collection, but he politely declined. Jack takes up the story: "Then I met him through Bruce Collins (a key figure in the establishment of the Bradman Museum and the first chairman of the Bradman Museum Trust) in connection with work I was doing for the museum, and when Sir Donald realised the extent of the collection and saw that he could make a significant contribution by identifying and commenting on the old film, he readily agreed. Although a stickler for getting things right, I found him friendly, outgoing, helpful and humorous. Once he was committed to the job, he couldn't do enough to help. I was really impressed at how bright and quick-witted he was. I was also struck by the warmth and wisdom of Jessie Bradman." The video is available from the ABC and the Bradman Museum.

Also the title of a song written and recorded in 1987 by Paul Kelly.

Bradman Albums, The

Compilations of letters, telegrams, diary entries, photographs, press clippings and other memorabilia selected from the Bradman scrapbooks which were held in Adelaide's Mortlock Library in the State Library of South Australia. The two-volume, 800-page albums were published by Rigby and launched by then prime minister Bob Hawke at a black-tie dinner at Adelaide Oval in October 1987 in the presence of the Don and Jessie and nine of the other 12 survivors of the 1948 Invincibles. Speakers included Richie Benaud and then Australian rugby union coach Alan Jones, and MC was Ken Cunningham. Of the guest of honour, Mr Hawke said: "It was not merely his extraordinary run-scoring feats but his manner of achieving them which made Bradman a hero in his own country and a household word wherever cricket is played. His demeanour, and that of the teams which played under him, was unfailingly sportsmanlike and professional. In an era when communications were much less developed than they have become since, and in which the old British Empire played a bigger part in Australia's external interests than it now does, the international image of Australia was very much that of Bradman." And, "The superb *Bradman Albums* were vividly brought to life by a priceless collection of personal memorabilia that only add lustre to the brilliant Bradman legend." Proceeds from sales of the albums go to the Crippled Children's Association, the Don's favourite charity.

Bradman: An Australian Hero

The eleventh and (at the time of writing) last biography of the Don, written by Welsh banker Lord Williams of Elvel, a Labour life peer in the House of Lords, published in 1996 by Little, Brown, 336pp. In his book, Williams proposes that many of Bradman's illnesses during his career were psychosomatic – that is, real and physical in their symptoms but originated or influenced by emotional stress – and that Bradman may have suffered bouts of clinical depression, during, for example, the Bodyline series. The author had a four-hour session with the Don, and his subject read the manuscript and commented on it in great detail. Lord Williams told ABC radio that the only time Bradman became bitter during the interview was when he talked about the clique of Irish Catholics among the Australian players, referring pointedly to the time when the team arrived by train in Melbourne and were met by "priests in cassocks". The Don told Williams of Bill O'Reilly's and Jack Fingleton's "disloyalty based on jealousy and religion", and said that Fingleton, as the ringleader, "carried on a vendetta against me all his life". Of his work, Lord Williams said: "It is not a 'cricket book' in the normally accepted sense, it is almost as much about Australia as it is about Bradman, aiming to explain the importance of his career in the whole sociology of Australia." Lord Williams dedicated his work to "Jessie Bradman, an Australian heroine".

Bradman and the Bodyline Series

Book by Edward Wybergh Docker, published in hardback in 1978 by Angus & Robertson (UK), 165pp, including 16 pages of photographs. The publisher's blurb in the book:

"It is an open secret that 'bodyline' in its most developed form was devised primarily to deal with Don Bradman, the geatest batsman of modern times. Jardine, the English captain, planned the use of formidable fast bowlers, particularly Larwood, with meticulous care before the 1932–33 test series, and stirred up a whirlwind of controversy and bitterness that still has its reverberations in cricket today.

"This book, which also gives a perspective of Bradman's career before and after bodyline, concentrates on the great Australian batsman's role in meeting the challenge posed by the English team and vividly recreates with ball by ball accounts of the crucial matches the turbulent and rancorous atmosphere of these controversial tests.

"Somewhat unbending and an intensely private person, Bradman's enigmatic character and utter dedication to cricket emerge more clearly than ever before in Ted Docker's authoritative text which has been approved by Sir Donald Bradman himself."

The author's father was Wybergh Docker, a former NSW player, who took his son to the SCG to watch Don Bradman in action in the Second Ashes Test in 1946–47. Bradman obliged by scoring 234.

Bradman, Benaud and Goddard's Cinderellas
Book by RS Whitington published in 1964 by Howard Timms, Cape Town, 237pp. An account of the South African tourists in Australia and New Zealand in 1963–64, with chapters on the Don and Richie Benaud.

Bradman Bitter Ale
Ale whose unauthorised manufacture by Queensland's Power Brewing in 1993 was smartly quashed by the Bradman Foundation after the discovery of an empty stubby during a match between a Bradman XI and a South African XI at Bradman Oval.

"Bradman Collection, The"
Collection held by the State Library of South Australia which reflects the life and achievements of the Don through material gathered by or presented to him from around the world. In the 1960s an informal agreement was reached between Bradman and the then state librarian, Hedley Brideson, a personal acquaintance through Rotary Club, by which the Don would give the library a significant portion of his very valuable collection of memorabilia. It included trophies, bats and balls, stumps, clothing, artworks, scorecards, photographs, posters, newspaper banners and other mementos. A project undertaken in conjunction with assembling the collection was the creation of 52 volumes of scrapbooks compiled from material collected by the Don and his family throughout his playing career. The scrapbooks were developed between 1967 and 1972 by library staffer Jill Gauvin, with advice from Bradman, and bound in green leather by the library's bindery. A duplicate set was presented to the National Library of Australia. In 1983 the collection was legally transferred to the State Library in perpetuity, and the Don later transferred more of the collection to the library.

In 1986, the year of South Australia's sesquicentenary, the high-profile Mortlock Library of South Australiana was established, bringing together published material from the South Australian Collection and the non-government unpublished material in the Archives. "The Bradman Collection" was one of the jewels in the crown of the Mortlock collections, catalogued as

Private Record Group 682 of the Archival Collection. It boasted 23 motion picture films and 48 sound recordings, the latter being catalogued as part of the JD Somerville Oral History Collection at OH 29. The collection has been expertly catalogued and received dedicated curatorial and conservation attention from archivist curator Neil Thomas; the then oral history officer, Beth Robertson; library conservation staff; and the state conservation agency, ARTLAB. The scrapbooks and some of the more important other objects in the collection had always been on public display in the Mortlock Library, but most of the collection was housed in a storage area, and the challenge of creating a venue to publicly display the collection was not taken up by the State Library for some years.

In 1997, associate director Elizabeth Ho, whose responsibility included the Mortlock Library, realised the significance of the items in storage and determined to create a permanent exhibition for the full collection. The newly formed State Library Foundation mounted a public campaign which raised $1.5 million from government, business sponsors and the community to create a first-class venue. A major fundraising event was a $125-per-head Grand Bradman Dinner held in 1998 at the Adelaide Convention Centre to celebrate the Don's 90th birthday. It was attended by over 1,200 guests from around the world, including Sachin Tendulkar, the star Indian batsman whose style Bradman considered was most like his own. The "Bradman Collection" exhibition was opened by Prime Minister John Howard on January 29, 1998 in its new home in Adelaide's historic Institute Building, part of the State Library precinct. It is open seven days a week. Since February 26, 2001, when the $3 admission charge was abolished (in accordance with the Don's wishes), attendance figures have tripled. Of the many objects on display, one of the most popular is the Royal Worcester Vase presented to Bradman in 1938 by the Royal Worcester Porcelain Works to commemorate his three consecutive double centuries on the Worcester ground. The front panel features a painting by ceramic artist Harry Davis which depicts the Don batting with Worcester Cathedral in the background. Another highlight is the replica of a Roman marble vase at Warwick Castle, a gift from 'cricket lovers of Britain' in 1948. Continuous audio and video footage includes film of Bradman at the crease.

Fans from around the world can see the collection on the State Library website, the Bradman Digital Library (formerly known as the Bradman Legend), at www.slsa.sa.gov.au/bradman/index.html. The site has digitised images and descriptions of all the objects and photographs in the collection. It also features 800 digitised pages from the scrapbooks, 160 digital images donated by Adelaide's *Advertiser* newspaper, biographical material, audio and video clips, an interactive component and activity sheets for school visits.

Bradman Corporation Pty Ltd

Group of developers against which the Bradman Foundation took legal action in 2000 under the Trade Practices Act for passing off and misleading the public to believe its business was connected to the Don and the foundation. Under the terms of a settlement reached just two days before the Don's death on February 25, 2001, the group agreed to change its name (to Bradcorp Holdings Pty Ltd) within two years and also to transfer the website name "bradman.com.au" to the foundation.

"Bradman Cottage"

The house in which the Don lived at Yeo Yeo, near Cootamundra, until he was two years and nine months old. In the 1970s, the owner of the Yeo Yeo property, Bob Caldwell, was concerned about the safety of the deteriorating cottage (transients were "camping" in it and lighting fires), and so offered it to Cootamundra Shire Council for dismantling and re-erection in one of the town's parks. When the committees set up by the council to consider the matter could not come to a decision, Mr Caldwell was approached by a Queanbeyan businessman about moving the cottage south. But the owner wanted it to remain in the district where the Don was born, so he offered it to the Temora Historical Society, which gladly accepted. A voluntary work party, which included members of the Temora District Cricket Association, was organised by the then president of the society, Ron Maslin, to dismantle the cottage, in doing so preserving as much as possible of the original material. The building was moved to Temora in August 1980. Incredibly, the 100-year-old hardwood slabs which formed the outer walls were in excellent condition, as were the multi-pane windows, but the rough-sawn floorboards and much of the other original material had to be replaced. Subsequent occupants of the house were consulted in an attempt to establish details of the original structure before their alterations were made. After much hard work by members of the historical society and local cricketers, the cottage was opened to the public at the Temora Rural Museum on March 12, 1983. The Don declined an invitation to open the exhibit and the honours instead were done by Reg Miles, a legendary local cricketer, by then living in Canberra, who in the 1930s was dubbed "the Bradman of the Bush". Mr Maslin, now vice-president of the society, published an article soon after about the project for the organisation's magazine, *Wirrimbirra*.

B

Bradman: The Don Declares

Eight-part radio biography which the Don recorded in interviews with Norman May in the Adelaide studios of the ABC in 1987. The program was rounded out with interviews with many of Bradman's contemporaries. The voices for contributions from those no longer alive were supplied by Paul Jennings. The series was produced in conjunction with the Australian Bicentennial Authority. Research was by Bill McGowan and Robyn Campbell and executive producer was Alan Marks. The eight 55-minute programs originally aired on ABC radio over eight weeks at 9am on Saturday between January and March 1988. They were published in Australia by ABC Enterprises that year and an edited version was released in the UK in 1990. Originally offered as eight audio cassettes in a plastic folder, they were re-issued in a smaller boxed set of six tapes in 2000. A set of eight compact discs was released in 2001.

Veteran broadcaster (now retired) Norman May recently recounted his involvement in the project and his memories of Sir Donald:

"It started off in 1986, when we wrote to Bradman from ABC Sport suggesting that he should do something for the Bicentennial. He wrote back saying he didn't want to do television but he'd do radio – and picked me to do it, because at the time Alan McGilvray had retired, and he wouldn't have anything to do with Channel Nine, because of the World Series Cricket. There was still a lot of bitterness there, and he wouldn't have Benaud or any of those, so he had to do it with the ABC, and I was the only one still there who was a long-term broadcaster of cricket. So I was the only one left. I went to see him in Adelaide early in 1987, and he said that he would do it. We worked out that each of us would do some research, and I went to the Australian Bicentennial Authority and the fellow in charge there said we'd like him to do it and we'll give him $25,000, which was a good fee. But the thing was he was doing almost six months' work for it, and when you equate that to about $50,000 a year, it wasn't all that much money.

"But he agreed to do it, and I went away and worked out 15 typewritten pages of questions I would ask him, right through his career. I gave him the questions, and at the next meeting we decided that in the interview we were not going to jump ahead. If we're talking about 1928 for instance, we wouldn't refer to 1934, or 1936, or whatever, because we had to stick within the timeframe of what we were talking about. And he was fantastic, because he could stick to that. He was 78 at the time, and he had a terrific memory. And what he did … anything to do with the technique of cricket, he ad-libbed; anything to do with fact, he researched it. He had an old Grundig typewriter on which he would type out his answers if it had to do with material fact.

"A day or two before we started the interview I went to his house for lunch with Don and Lady Bradman, and surprisingly, he offered me a Scotch before we had lunch. All those stories of him being a non-drinker weren't quite right. He would drink, but he would drink good stuff. Max Schubert, the winemaker for Penfolds, was a good friend of his. He wouldn't drink much, but he was not a teetotaller. We arranged to use the ABC's stereo studio in Adelaide and recorded the program over three weekday mornings, from 9 until about 1. After breaks to change tapes and so on, we had something like nine hours of material. But out of the nine hours, we used almost everything he said, because we took out the seasons that had no importance in those days. For example, 1933–34 in Australia was a nothing season; there was no Test cricket, no nothing. The Bodyline series was followed by a domestic season, and the tour to England was next, so it was just natural to jump from Bodyline to the tour of England.

"After we took out the off-seasons we finished up with eight 55-minute programs, so we used about 80 per cent of the material. We listened to the whole lot, and we found eight small mistakes of fact. For example, when he made his world-record 452 not out in 1930, he thought he was out for a duck in the first innings but he actually got 3. And we corrected a few other little mistakes like that. They were the only mistakes in seven hours 20 minutes of recording. His recall of fact and information was just amazing. And I found him to be a very strong character; if he said he'd do something, he did it. He would not let you down. I was later asked by Ray Martin on television whether I was overawed going to visit him. I said that I wasn't, because if you do a lot of interviews, no matter who the person is, you treat them like a normal person – you don't treat them any differently. And that's how I treated him, and he was quite courteous, and open to suggestions. But we agreed it was going to be about his cricket life, not his personal life. He said he'd got a lot of pleasure out of doing it, but he really did it for the Bicentennial. He owed it to Australia to tell his story – not as any special favour to me or the ABC, but just to the people of Australia. To tell his story in his own words, in his own way."

Bradman Era, The
Video of the Don's career, recalled by Bill O'Reilly, made in 1983. It shows many of Bradman's great innings but also has profiles of other players of the era, as well as controversial incidents during the Bodyline series. Directed and produced by Albie Thoms and written by Jack Egan, who was the executive producer.

Also the book version of the preceding, recalled by O'Reilly and compiled by Egan. Published by ABC/Fontana in 1983, 207pp.

Bradman Foundation

A Bradman museum (which would house mainly memorabilia of the local cricket clubs) at Bradman Oval was the idea of two Bowral cricket officials, Gordon Whatman and Keith Moore, but the local council told Gordon in 1975 that part of the necessary funds would have to be provided by the local cricket clubs. When the clubs showed very little enthusiasm for raising the money, the project stalled. It was Garry Barnsley, a Bowral solicitor, who bashfully "ambushed" the Don at Moss Vale Golf Club in 1983 about the concept of a Bradman Museum (although it was intended that it would be established in the former Bradman home in Glebe Street, opposite the oval). Barnsley told the *Southern Highland News* soon after Sir Donald's death in February 2001 that he greeted the batting legend "with sweaty palm" and broached the possibility of his support for a permanent Bradman memorial in Bowral. But Bradman said to him: "In the last 50 years I've been the subject of the most intense publicity imaginable. Now that I'm retired, I really would prefer to lead a quiet life." But although the Don told Garry that he would not support the concept, he did not disapprove of it, so Barnsley went back to the drawing board and became a one-man fundraiser. With the announcement in 1985 of a grant from the New South Wales Bicentennial Council, a committee of Wingecarribee Shire Council was formed to oversee the "Bradman Project", with Barnsley in the chair and Sydney barrister Bruce Collins a notable contributor. The Bradman Museum Trust was established in 1987. It was then that Sir Donald became formally interested in the project and he agreed to sign over the intellectual property rights associated with his name, likeness and image. In a restructure, the Bradman Museum Trust effectively became the Bradman Foundation in 1993.

Headed by Richard Mulvaney, the foundation is a non-profit charitable trust whose objective was to build a cricket museum to commemorate the achievements of the Don, and also to strengthen the growth and development of cricket in Australia. The foundation helps young cricketers by sponsoring a scholarship scheme to Australian universities and by conducting coaching clinics for boys and girls. The International Outreach Program brings young overseas players to Australia to play in matches at Bradman Oval. In recent years the foundation has taken legal action to stop commercial entities from using the Bradman name to suggest a connection that does not exist. One such action, against Bradman Corporation, a development company, was settled in 2001 when the directors of the company agreed to stop trading under the name Bradman within two years. Of the future, Garry Barnsley said before his retirement from the board at the end of 2001: "The work the foundation has undertaken can only continue to grow, and Sir Donald has given us the tools to do the job, not only through his inspiration but also through licensing activities and the deployment of his intellectual property. I think the legend will become even greater as time goes by." The foundation has a staff of about 20 but also has several contractors and more than 60 volunteers.

Patron of the Bradman Foundation is Mr Richie Benaud OBE, and the members of the board are:

Mr John Fahey AC, Chairman
Mr Bob Horsell, Deputy Chairman
Mr Michael Ball AM
Ms Rina Hore
Mr Andrew McMaster
Mr Basil Sellers AM
Mr Mark Taylor AO
Mr Richard Sheppard (Alternate Director)
Mr Ian Craig OAM (Immediate Past Chairman)

Bradman the Great

BJ Wakley's book is the definitive statistical account of the Don's first-class career. The first part of the work boasts a description of every one of Bradman's 234 matches and the second analyses every aspect of his batting performances and features reviews of the Don as captain, bowler, fielder and selector. The monumental project was started for Wakley's spare-time amusement. In his preface, he acknowledged the kindness of his subject in reading through his manuscript. The main source of information was the original scorebooks of the Australian scorer, Bill Ferguson (made available by Bill's widow), who recorded 201 of Bradman's 338 first-class innings and 16,020 of his 28,067 runs. Wakley also consulted scorebooks in the MCC Library and the records of County Clubs, as well as the files of many newspapers in England and Australia. He also acknowledged *Wisden Cricketers' Almanack* among many books on cricket. Wakley's work was originally published by Nicholas Kaye of London in 1959 (315pp) in an edition of only 500 copies. A second edition, published by Mainstream Publishing of Edinburgh, did not appear until 40 years later. A note on the sleeve of Mainstream's edition claims that "Original copies of the book are so rare that it has legendary status among collectors." In fact they changed hands for as much as 5,000 pounds.

Bradman: The Illustrated Biography

Written by Michael Page, published in 1983 by Macmillan, 368pp. Bradman was on the board of Rigby in Adelaide and Michael Page had recently retired as the company's publishing manager when Macmillan approached Page early in 1983 to write a biography of Bradman. Although to that point Page had written about 15 books (both fiction and non-fiction), he had little interest in cricket, but agreed to take on the job. Time was short though – the publisher wanted the book out before Bradman's 75th birthday in August 1983. The Don co-operated fully, granting the author a number of interviews and lending him many books and newspaper cuttings. Page worked for 12 hours a day on the project, and Bradman read and approved every chapter as he wrote it. The book was quite successful both in Australia and Britain. Michael still lives in Adelaide and his book credits now total 37.

Bradman Memorial Fund

Fund set up after the Don's death in February 2001 and administered through the Bradman Foundation by a committee made up of representatives of the foundation, Cricket Australia and the Bradman family. The fund is being used entirely for the promotion and encouragement of cricket among disadvantaged groups, including indigenous Australians. The Don's decision to include a reference to indigenous children in his instructions for the conduct of the fund was largely influenced by the fact his son, John, had formed a strong friendship with an Aboriginal boy at school in Adelaide. Prior to his death Bradman also specified that no "bronzes" or monuments should be built from proceeds of the fund. Australia Post accepts tax-deductible donations.

Bradman Memorial Issue

Stamp issued by Australia Post on March 30, 2001 and withdrawn in February 2002. The 45-cent stamp, which features an image of the Don in his flannels, could be purchased individually or in sheets of 10. Also available was a special pack containing 10 stamps plus information on the issue for $4.95.

Bradman Museum

Soon after the Bradman Pavilion was completed in 1989, the Bradman Museum Trust sought approval from the local council to build a museum behind the pavilion in Glebe Park. The council supported the proposal but there was strong opposition from some in the Bowral community, who objected to the loss of public parkland. After an extremely tough battle in the Land and Environment Court, the trust was granted a 99-year lease on the site. The museum was opened by Prime Minister John Howard on August 27, 1996, the Don's 88th birthday. Bradman did not make the trip from Adelaide. The dedication reads: "The Bradman Museum was commissioned by the Bradman Foundation. It is dedicated to Sir Donald Bradman, AC, whose distinguished career and contribution to the development of cricket will for ever stand as an inspiration to all those who seek to emulate the achievements of this truly great Australian." A cricket museum at Bradman Oval was the idea of Gordon Whatman, then president of the local cricket association, and Keith Moore, who was the secretary. Though it would be known as the Bradman Museum, it was intended that it would house mainly memorabilia of the local cricket clubs. When Gordon approached the council during a refurbishment of Bradman Oval in 1975 (also Gordon's project), he was told he would have to raise part of the necessary funds through the local cricket clubs. But the clubs were less than excited by the idea and the project lapsed. Eventually the campaign was taken up by local solicitor Garry Barnsley, who asked Bradman for his imprimatur at Moss Vale Golf Club in 1983. Although the Don told Garry that he would not support the concept, he did not disapprove of it. Barnsley then became a one-man fundraiser, printing shirts proclaiming "He's Our Don Bradman – Bowral, New South Wales, Australia." With the announcement in 1985 of a grant from the New South Wales Bicentennial Council, a committee of Wingecarribee Shire Council was formed to oversee the "Bradman Project", with Barnsley in the chair and Sydney barrister Bruce Collins a leading contributor. The Bradman Museum Trust was established in 1987. It was then that the Don became formally interested in the project and subsequently signed over the intellectual property rights in his name, likeness and image.

Although the museum was established to commemorate his career, its aim is also to preserve and document the history of cricket. Several exhibition themes highlight the origins of the game and its growth in Australia. There are five major permanent display galleries: the Bradman Gallery; the Origins of Cricket; the Golden Age; Cricket in Australia; and A Perfect Ten. Much of the museum's recent work has centred on improved documentation and digitisation of the collection. The display galleries are supplemented by a special exhibition gallery with changing displays, a 100-seat theatre, a library, a children's area, a tea room and a souvenir shop. There are daily screenings in the theatre of newsreel footage of the Bradman era and a feature on Bodyline. The museum has hosted three major temporary exhibitions since mid 2002: The Ashes, which showcased the rich history of contests between Australia and England; The Art of Bradman, which used the artwork of Brian Clinton to trace the cricket highlights of Sir Donald Bradman in a "hyper-realistic" style; and Trophies and Toastracks, which features some of the treasures from the Melbourne Cricket Club Museum. Trophies and Toastracks is on display until the end of 2005. A full-size statue of the Don by Newcastle sculptor Tanya Bartlett was unveiled outside the museum by Bill Brown and Ian Craig on February 24, 2002 to mark the first anniversary of his death.

Richard Mulvaney has been director of the museum since its inception. The Bradman Museum Trust purchased the Don's former family home at 20 Glebe Street, opposite Bradman Oval, in 1987 and restored the exterior to its original state. The house is now part of the Bradman Walk, a self-guided tour which starts at the museum and visits some of the sites associated with the Don's early life in Bowral. In May 2003 the museum's administrative staff moved into another nearby house purchased by the foundation and converted into an office. The vacated museum space will be used for a new permanent exhibition focusing on contemporary cricket at the elite level. Planning for this exhibition is well advanced and it is scheduled to open in 2005. The Friends of the Bradman Museum was established to bring together supporters of the Don and cricket enthusiasts who want to be actively involved in the museum and its programs. Various levels of membership start at $50 a year, and funds raised from membership go towards acquiring objects for the museum collection, special events such as international matches and running the various Friends activities. The museum's website is at www.bradman.com.au.

Patron of the Bradman Foundation is Mr Richie Benaud OBE, and the members of the board are:

Mr John Fahey AC, Chairman
Mr Bob Horsell, Deputy Chairman
Mr Michael Ball AM
Ms Rina Hore
Mr Andrew McMaster
Mr Basil Sellers AM
Mr Mark Taylor AO
Mr Richard Sheppard (Alternate Director)
Mr Ian Craig OAM (Immediate Past Chairman)

Bradman 1927–1941: New South Wales, South Australia, Australia

Book by EL Roberts published by Hudson in 1944, 64pp.

B

"Bradman 99"

Bronze bust of the Don created by Melbourne artist Stanley Hammond. The bust, which is 360mm high and set on a base with an identifying plaque, was commissioned by the State Library of South Australia Foundation in January 1998 to commemorate the establishment of the Bradman Collection exhibition at the library and Sir Donald's 90th year. Ninety-nine of the busts were cast, celebrating Bradman's Test batting average of 99.94. A limited number of the busts are available from the State Library of SA Foundation for $4,500 plus GST.

Bradman Oval

The oval at Bowral formerly known as Glebe Park is the home ground of two cricket clubs: Bowral and the Bowral Blues, each fielding three teams in the district competition. The land on which the oval stands was part of a 4,200-acre grant to Henry Molesworth Oxley and John Norton Oxley, the sons of the explorer. It was subsequently part of a glebe attached to the Church of England and was included in an area of 24 acres leased from the church by the local council for recreation purposes. The council later acquired the area and opened the cricket oval in 1909. The original cricket wicket, of ant-bed construction, was situated almost on the Glebe Street roadway but later moved to its present site and made into a concrete pitch. But it was a little on the rough side and the ball wore quickly, so it was covered with coir matting. When coir was believed to favour the spin bowlers, it was decided to lay a canvas cover known as Kippax matting. This material didn't stand up to wear over long periods and was replaced by a glazed wicket. But this wicket put batsmen in danger of serious injury so, finally, it was replaced in 1946 by a turf wicket. It was the first turf strip in the district and remained the only one for several years. The surface was very successful, though it required (as it still does) considerable maintenance. The change of name to Bradman Oval was first mooted by Bowral Cricket Club in 1938 but was not to come about until 1947.

It was at Glebe Park (not on the cricket ground but on the dirt football field) in the summer of 1919–20 that the 11-year-old Bradman played in his first organised game of cricket. He went in at no. 4 and survived a hat-trick ball before carrying his bat for 55. The following season he made 29 not out (on the cricket pitch) when opening the innings for the Bowral Town team on the second Saturday of a game against Moss Vale. In the same summer, playing for Bowral Intermediate High School in a return school match against Mittagong High, his captain asked him to retire when he had made 72. Bradman's most famous innings on the ground was during the 1925–26 season when, as a 17-year-old, he scored 234 in one afternoon (on the coir) for Bowral against Wingello after twice being spilled early off Bill O'Reilly.

In 1972, Gordon Whatman, then president of the Moss Vale and Southern Districts Cricket Association, asked then Bowral Municipal Council to carry out improvements to the ground. The council agreed to level the playing surface (which fell away from St Jude's Street towards Glebe Street), improve the drainage system and replace the steel mesh fence with a picket fence. The project required about 1,200 cubic metres of fill, plus top soil, and the removal and replacement of 7,000 square metres of turf. The work did not exactly proceed apace, but in the meantime, in April 1974, Gordon proposed that the Don and Bill O'Reilly be invited to the re-opening of the oval (with Tiger bowling the first ball to the maestro) and that a match be played between a team of top players from Sydney and a local side. Gordon's idea got the nod from the council and on the big day, September 4, 1976, everything went according to plan. Further significant improvements were made to the ground in the early '90s to bring it up to international standard. These included a complete new centre wicket square; a new purpose-built and -designed scoreboard; two new purpose-designed and -built sightscreens; four new full-length concrete enclosed practice wickets with synthetic tops; new outfield drainage; and a new picket fence. Many of the improvements were funded by the Bradman Museum Trust and by private donation, but much was achieved with the aid of equipment and labour provided by Wingecarribee Shire Council. The Don returned to the oval for the opening of the Bradman Pavilion, the first stage of the Bradman Museum Project, on October 14, 1989, but did not attend the opening of the Bradman Museum, next to the pavilion, on August 27, 1996, his 88th birthday. A hastily arranged tribute match was played on the ground by teams from Bowral High School on the day after the Don's death on February 25, 2001. A memorial service was held at the oval on March 28, 2001, and the Don's and wife Jessie's ashes were scattered in the gardens at the ground and on the oval itself on October 18 of the same year.

Bradman Pavilion

The first stage of the Bradman Museum Project was opened on Saturday, October 14, 1989 by the then NSW minister for Industrial Relations and Employment and member for Southern Highlands, John Fahey (standing-in for Premier Nick Greiner, who had been hospitalised with gallstones), in the presence of Sir Donald and Lady Bradman, who was invited by Mr Fahey to unveil the plaque. Bill O'Reilly also made an appearance. The pavilion, which was designed on gracious turn-of-the-century lines, has a players' club room, change rooms, a meeting room and a library. The old "pavilion", built in 1954, was a limestone and brick building with a few wooden seats, two dressing sheds and two toilets. The Bradman Pavilion had its genesis in the mind of Gordon Whatman, then president of the Moss Vale and Southern Districts Cricket Association. In 1975, while refurbishment of Bradman Oval (also his project) was in progress, he proposed to Bowral Municipal Council that another floor be added on top of the existing building. The extensions would contain a kitchen, a meeting room, a cricket museum and a viewing terrace.

The council costed the job at $20,000 but told Gordon he would have to raise part of the funds through the two Bowral cricket clubs. But the clubs were not overly excited by the task and the plan stalled. The cause was taken up a few years later by local solicitor Garry Barnsley, who saw the project as a means of providing a first-class facility while at the same honouring the achievements of the great batsman. When he approached the Don with the proposal at Moss Vale Golf Club in 1983, Bradman said he would not support the project, although he did not disapprove of it. Barnsley then became a one-man fundraiser, printing shirts proclaiming "He's Our Don Bradman – Bowral, New South Wales, Australia." With the announcement of a grant from the New South Wales Bicentennial Council, a committee of Wingecarribee Shire Council was formed to oversee the "Bradman Project", with Barnsley in the chair and Sydney barrister Bruce Collins a leading contributor. The Bradman Museum Trust was formed in 1987. It was then that Sir Donald became formally interested in the project and he agreed to sign over the intellectual property rights associated with his name, likeness and image. Two years later, when the pavilion was completed, Gordon Whatman said to Collins, who had since become the trust's first chairman, that it was "a dream come true".

Bradman: Reflections on the Legend

A 2 x 1 hour television program made by the ABC and first shown in September 2004 in *The Big Picture* time slot on consecutive Sundays at 7.30 pm. Margot Phillipson was executive producer, Lincoln Tyner was the writer/producer, Mike Coward conducted the interviews and Don Barker was the narrator. The documentary is a retrospective on the life and achievements of Sir Donald Bradman as seen through the eyes of a cross-section of cricket luminaries from all over the world, including some of the game's greatest players: Arthur Morris, Neil Harvey, Bill Brown, Sam

Loxton, Bill Johnston, Sir Alec Bedser, Sachin Tendulkar and Steve Waugh. The documentary also features the first extended television interview given by Sir Donald's only son, John, who shares intimate memories of his famous father and, in particular, the role he played in helping John overcome his childhood battle with polio. For the first time, John speaks candidly about how living with the pressure of the Bradman name forced him to change his name in the early 1970s.

Bradman Revisited – The Legacy of Sir Donald Bradman

Book by AL (Tony) Shillinglaw (co-written by Brian Hale) with a foreword by Geoffrey Boycott, published in hardback in 2003 by The Parrs Wood Press, 212pp. The work is an examination of everything about the style and technique which made the Don unique.

Part of Philip Derriman's review in the *Sydney Morning Herald* in July 2003:

"If Tiger Woods had a grip, stance and backswing that were different from everyone else's, the chances are that half the world's golfers would be doing their best to copy him. So why haven't batsmen tried to copy Don Bradman? He had a grip, stance and backlift that were unique and, statistically, his superiority in his sport was greater than Woods's, yet few if any cricketers have sought to model themselves on Bradman. Why has the great man's example been ignored? The question has inspired a new book, *Bradman Revisited*, written by, of all people, an Englishman. It argues Bradman's batting methods should be accepted as mainstream and orthodox and that young batsmen around the world would do well to hold the bat with his unusual grip, place it between their toes, lift it towards gully and, finally, bring it around in a smooth, rotary motion into the shot.

"The book's author, Tony Shillinglaw, a coach and former Cheshire player, has spent much of his cricketing life trying to discover the key to Bradman's success. He decided early on that there had to be one, that Bradman must have enjoyed some special advantage, since, in his opinion, no amount of natural talent, practice and mental toughness could have made Bradman so much better than everyone else. It is the something else that Shillinglaw believes he has identified; the way Bradman held his bat, lifted it and prepared for each stroke. Shillinglaw believes this gave Bradman an important advantage in terms of balance and ensured he was always ideally positioned to play his shot. In other words, it was what Bradman did before a shot that set him apart, not the stroke itself. For years Shillinglaw tried to persuade other coaches in England that Bradman wasn't a one-off and that his technique deserved serious consideration, but they were not willing to listen. Today, Shillinglaw is dismayed to find a national junior coaching program in England developed by the MCC still pushes the old pendulum idea that the bat should be lifted back towards the stumps and swung forward in roughly the same plane. 'Up and down the country youngsters are being taught to take their bats straight back,' he writes. 'The indications are they are being given a handicap from the very beginning.'

"But can anyone be sure the batting method which worked for Bradman, including, in particular, the rotary motion of his bat as he lifted it and swung into a stroke, would work for others? Shillinglaw convinced himself they would when he tried batting Bradman-style in the nets near the end of his own career. He writes: 'Batting was not just different. With practice it suddenly became a thrilling new experience. As long as the speed of the bowling on the indoor surface was within my capacity, the sight of the ball did, in Bradman's words, trigger a corresponding reaction. Never before in my cricketing experience had I timed the ball so consistently well, nor hit it so fast all around the wicket and with so little mental and physical effort. When Bradman's aggressive intent and determination is considered, together with the additional freedom and scope of his method, it becomes possible to come to terms with his remarkable record.'"

Bradman's Band

Book by former Test spinner Ashley Mallett, published in 2000 by UQP, 223pp; mainly a collection of anecdotes and reminiscences about Bradman and those who played with and against him.

An excerpt from a review by Tasmanian academic Brett Hutchins which was published in *JAS Review of Books* in October 2001:

"Ashley Mallett's *Bradman's Band* can be reviewed on a couple of levels. If you are a casual reader looking to acquire general knowledge of Australian cricket history and in particular the Bradman era, it is adequate. Alternatively, if you are an avid reader of cricket literature or social history and possess a proficient grasp of the events and personalities of the Bradman years, Mallett will not add much to what you already know.

"The idea behind the book is a good one. The past seventy years or so have seen a plethora of biographies, celebratory volumes, anniversary publications, cricket histories and videos detailing the playing career of Australia's greatest cricketer, Sir Donald Bradman, from the late 1920s into the 1940s. In the wake of these texts, many talented cricketers who played alongside the Don have been neglected. Mallett attempts to right this imbalance ...

"Overall, *Bradman's Band* is a competent book on a period of Australian cricket that has already been well traversed. Given its limited focus, it is a satisfactory cricket history, but falls short of qualifying as thought provoking Australian social history."

Bradman's Best: Sir Donald Bradman's Selection of the Best Team in Cricket History

Book by Roland Perry, published by Random House Australia in 2001, which reveals the Don's World XI. Bradman agreed to name his all-time best team only on the condition that it not be published until after his death so he would not have to weather the expected avalanche of argument about his team. The side is Arthur Morris, Barry Richards, Don Bradman, Sachin Tendulkar, Garry Sobers, Don Tallon, Ray Lindwall, Dennis Lillee, Alec Bedser, Bill O'Reilly, Clarrie Grimett, and 12th man Wally Hammond. The Don asked Perry to choose the captain. No prizes for guessing who. Part of the proceeds from the book go to the Bradman Memorial Fund.

Bradman's Best Ashes Teams

Follow-up book by Roland Perry, published by Random House Australia in 2002. Features portraits of each member of the Don's Ashes dream teams, chosen from all Australian and English Test players over the last 125 years. The Australian team is Bill Ponsford, Arthur Morris, Don Bradman, Neil Harvey, Charlie Macartney, Keith Miller, Don Tallon, Ray Lindwall, Dennis Lillee, Bill O'Reilly, Clarrie Grimmett and 12th man Richie Benaud. The England side is Jack Hobbs, Len Hutton, Denis Compton, Peter May, Wally Hammond, WG Grace, Godfrey Evans, Fred Trueman, Alec Bedser, SF Barnes, Hedley Verity and 12th man Ian Botham. The book also includes Bradman's nominations of the top five batting and bowling Ashes performances he ever witnessed and his assessment of what he considered his own five best innings in Ashes competition. As with Perry's *Bradman's Best*, some of the royalties from the sale of this book go to the Bradman Memorial Fund.

"Bradman's Birthplace"

The house at 89 Adams Street, Cootamundra, New South Wales, where the Don was delivered by midwife Eliza Scholz on August 27, 1908. The cottage was purchased in 1989 by Cootamundra Shire Council from the Catholic Church, to whom it was left as part of the deceased estate of Polly

O'Dare, and restored and converted to a museum. "Bradman's Birthplace" was opened by the president of the NSW Cricket Association, Alan Davidson, AM, MBE, in 1992. Visitors pay $3 admission to see portraits, scorecards and photos and watch a 10-minute video. The council also owns an adjoining property which houses a collection of memorabilia on loan from local couple Peter and Jenny Cash. A dispute between the council and the Bradman Foundation over the use of the name "Bradman's Birthplace" was resolved in 2001 and it now also has approval to sell Bradman memorabilia. The museum is on the Web at www.cootamundra.nsw.gov.au/bradman.html. A life-size bronze statue of the Don wielding his bat is prominent in Jubilee Park, a couple of hundred metres from the museum.

Bradman Scholar

The Bradman Foundation's Bradman Scholarship program started in 1990 with a student funded to study at Exeter College, Oxford, but was later suspended. It was re-established in 1996 with the current focus on Australian scholars only. One of the central aims of the foundation is the development of cricket particularly among the young, a principle which was one of the central pillars upon which Sir Donald signed over his naming rights. In the role of a non-profitable trust, the foundation sponsors a scholarship-winner for three years.

The foundation currently has three Scholars. The Bradman Scholar for 2004 is Thomas Barratt, of Western Australia. He graduated from high school in 2003 and is now studying law and economics at the University of Western Australia. A top-order batsman and a medium-pace outswing bowler, Thomas was selected last year in the state U17 team. He was also one of 10 students chosen to represent Western Australia at the United Nations Youth Association National Youth Conference. Thomas wrote on being named a Bradman Scholar:

"... upholding in my sport and in my life, the values, beliefs, good sportsmanship and morals that make the name Bradman held in such esteem by the Australian, and the wider cricket community. I feel that the way the late Sir Donald was able to be an inspiration, through both his on and off field achievements and his devotion to Australian cricket and society, would need to be upheld by the scholar, which I do believe I have the attributes both within sport and the other aspects of my life, to do."

The other two current Bradman Scholars are Mark Faraday, who plays for Manly and NSW 2nd XI (studying Bachelor of Law/Bachelor of

Communications at the University of NSW), and Alexandra Blackwell, who plays for the NSW Breakers and Australia (studying Medicine at the University of NSW).

Bradman's First Tour
A scrapbook of newspaper accounts of the 1930 tour of England, published by Rigby in 1981.

"Bradman v. England"
An *Evening News* poster in England in 1934.

Bradman: What They Said About Him
A book which is a collection of comments spoken and written about the Don. Edited by Barry Morris and published in 1995 by ABC Books, with a foreword by the director of the Bradman Museum, Richard Mulvaney.

"Bradman Will be Batting Tomorrow"
Code with which Allied troops were told of a forthcoming assault on Monte Cassino Monastery in Italy in March 1944.

Bradman Years, The: Australian Cricket 1918–1948
Book by Jack Pollard, published in 1988 by Angus & Robertson, 411pp. The Don wrote a foreword to another of Pollard's books, *Australian Cricket: The Game and the Players*, published in 1982 by Hodder & Stoughton in association with the ABC, 1,162pp.

Bradman Young Cricketer of the Year
Each year the Bradman Foundation and Cricket Australia award a cricket bat autographed by the Don to an outstanding young player of the season. The maestro signed just 99 of these bats for the award. The program started in 1989 and will continue for the lifetime of the bats. All contracted first-class players are given one vote to select the best player under the age of 24. The player must not have appeared in more than 10 first-class matches before the start of the voting period in early January, and players are not permitted to vote for their state teammates. The Bradman Young Cricketer of the Year for 2004 was Shaun Tait, a fast-medium bowler who made an immediate impact when he debuted for South Australia against Western Australia in December 2002.

B

Bradsen

The surname adopted by deed poll by the Don's son John in 1972 to escape the glare of publicity. He had used the name Bradenham briefly before the official change. He resumed using his original name in 1999.

Bramall Lane

The Don considered the crowds in Yorkshire knew more about cricket than people anywhere else in England, and he believed the Bramall Lane crowds were the most knowledgeable in Yorkshire. The Sheffield ground hosted its last first-class match in 1973, and hosted a Test only once: a contest in 1902 between England, led by Archie MacLaren, and an Australia combination under Joe Darling.

Bribes

The Don told Ray Martin in 1996: "I can assure you that nobody spoke to me about a bribe in any way, shape or form."

Brideson, Hedley

Then director of the State Library of South Australia and friend of the Don's who suggested to him that he entrust his Royal Worcester porcelain vase to the library for safekeeping after an earthquake in Adelaide in the early 1950s. The precious vase, presented to Bradman by the Worcester Cricket Club after his three consecutive double centuries on their ground in the 1930s, got a case of the wobbles on Bradman's mantelpiece in the quake, and his family persuaded him to hand it over to the library for security. In the 1960s Brideson persuaded the Don to donate the bulk of his personal collection of memorabilia, a contribution which was to form the basis of the library's "Bradman Collection".

Brightly Fades the Don

Book by Jack Fingleton, with a foreword by Sir Norman Birkett, published by Collins in 1949, 256pp, reprinted (with the addition of an introduction by Michael Parkinson) by Pavilion Books in 1985. The work is mostly an account of the 1948 tour of England, which the author covered for the Sydney press. Fingleton by then was no longer playing first-class cricket, but in the '30s (when he was a teammate of the Don's) he combined his cricket career with his work as a full-time journalist. He and Bill O'Reilly were Bradman's greatest critics.

Brinsmead
The Don's grand piano in his drawing-room at 2 Holden Street, Kensington Park, in Adelaide.

Bristol
Where the Australians made a tour-best (and best-ever by an Australian side against a county) 774 runs in an innings against Gloucestershire before a record crowd in 1948. The visitors were led by tour vice-captain Lindsay Hassett, the Don having decided to remain in London after the previous game at the Oval against Surrey. The total (of which Arthur Morris made 290) exceeded the previous best of 721 by the Invincibles a few weeks before in Southend against Essex, but it occupied the first day of the match and about three hours of the second, whereas the innings score at Southend (when the Don made 187 in 130 minutes) was compiled in a day.

Brockton Park
Ground in Vancouver where the Australians played three one-day matches early in Arthur Mailey's 1932 tour of Canada and the US. The Don considered it was the most beautiful cricket venue he had seen.

Broken Hill
Famous mining town (known as Silver City) in far-western New South Wales where the Don played his first game with a Sheffield Shield side in December 1927. The NSW team stopped off for a match on the way from Sydney to Adelaide and Melbourne for shield fixtures. The match was played on a concrete pitch (with a concrete run-up for the bowler) on a ground of deep-red-coloured soil with not a blade of grass. Playing in his street shoes, the Don scored 46 and managed to souvenir the ball.

Brown, William Alfred OAM
The New South Wales and Queensland opener toured England three times with the Don: in 1934, '38 and '48. He made 73 in his Test debut in 1934 at Trent Bridge and followed up with a century in the following Test at Lord's. But Brown's best tour was 1938 under Bradman when he carried his bat for 206, again at Lord's, and his tour average was bettered only by his captain. Of Bradman and Brown's partnership of 170 on that tour (when Bill made 133 and his captain 144 not out) which staved off defeat in the First Test at Trent Bridge, the Don was to write: "I do not think either of us played a more valuable innings for the side."

Brown led an Australian team to a win over New Zealand in Wellington in a Test (the first between the two countries) in 1946, a trip Bradman passed up because he had not fully recovered from the fibrositis which forced his discharge from the Army in 1941. Bill, who was appointed Queensland captain in 1937–38 after moving from NSW back to his home state in 1936, said he was honoured to get the nod in the Don's absence over Lindsay Hassett, who had recently skippered the Australian Services team. In England in 1948, the strong opening combination of Sid Barnes and Arthur Morris restricted Brown to two Test appearances, but after the tour his skipper wrote of him: "[He] Was still the perfect copy-book model in cricket. All his shots were made with delightful orthodoxy and he played every one in the book when the right ball came along."

Of Bradman, Bill has said: "The effect that Don had on the crowd was amazing. It is hard to describe to people who weren't born in that era. When word got around that Bradman was to bat, the crowd would increase from 10,000 to 30,000, and he never disappointed them. A single off the first ball and then away he went. Shots all around the wicket, played with power and certainty. Without a doubt, the finest run-getting machine I have ever seen." And: "When I was opening with Jack Fingleton for NSW and we were still out there at lunch-time, we were batting in 'Bradman time'. After the resumption, if there was a rap on the pads, not only would the opposing players appeal, the whole crowd would go up as well." When asked recently about the reputed resentment by Jack Fingleton of Bradman because of his support of Brown over Fingleton for the third opener's spot on the 1934 tour of England, Bill said it was merely "hearsay", adding that nothing was said to him about it at the time.

On February 24, 2002, Bill and then Bradman Museum chairman Ian Craig unveiled a life-size bronze statue of the Don outside the museum in front of 200 invited guests. After the ceremony, Bill said it was a privilege and an honour to be associated with the event. Now a well-preserved 92, Bill Brown lives in suburban Brisbane. He is the only surviving member of Australia's Test teams from before World War II – and he could be for a while yet. When Bill asked his doctor a couple of years ago how long he thought he had left, the medico gave him five. Years, that is. But in June 2004, Bill had a pacemaker fitted to correct a dangerously slow heart-rate. He claims that he now changes traffic lights at will and can turn his air conditioning on and off without leaving his chair.

Bull, W(illiam) C(harles)

Longtime honorary secretary and president of the Balmain club in Sydney who served as the Australian team's treasurer on the 1934 tour of England, when the Don was vice-captain to Bill Woodfull. As a member of the Australian Board of Control, Bull attended the Imperial Cricket Conference while in London.

Bunt, Oscar William

Southern Highlands table tennis champion who was beaten by the 17-year-old Don at a social get-together between Bradman's Bowral club and Bunt's Kangaloon club in Kangaloon Hall, near Bowral, in 1925. But the four-months-older Kangaloon youth had beaten the Don earlier in the night. Not long before this encounter, Bunt won a tournament in Bowral after Bradman was eliminated in an early round. Some time later, Bunt was placed on a handicap of 25 (meaning he had to score 25 points before he got on the board), and under these conditions was never beaten! Oscar moved from Kangaloon to Sydney in 1939. He died in Nepean Hospital in September 2004, aged 96. Don Bradman's maternal grandfather and Oscar Bunt's maternal grandmother were brother and sister.

Burns, John

A former British Labour politician who spent a day showing the Don and Jessie the less well-known sights of London when Bradman was convalescing after his illness in 1934. Burns was elected MP for Battersea in 1892, became president of the Local Government Board in 1905 and of the Board of Trade in 1914, but resigned soon after because of his opposition to the war. Burns was the first working-man cabinet minister in Britain.

Burton, James

Brisbane hotelier who, with his nephew Bob Burton, promised to pay the Don 10 shillings for each run he scored in the Fifth Test against India at the MCG in 1947–48. Bradman retired hurt with a torn rib cartilage in Australia's first innings when he was on 57, but after the match Jim said he and Bob would give the Don 100 pounds because they considered he would have scored 200 had he completed his innings.

Bushby, C(harles) H(arold)

Manager of the 1934 tour of England, when the Don was vice-captain.

C

Calcutta

Where the Don and wife Jessie's plane made a brief refuelling stop in June 1953 during the flight to England where Bradman was to report on the Ashes series of that year for the London *Daily Mail*. It was the first time the Don had trodden Indian soil. Hundreds of fans waiting at Dum Dum airport swarmed onto the runway when the plane landed and the Bradmans had to be escorted in an army car. The Don spoke to the press from a divan in a hut on the outskirts of the airport and thanked his Calcutta admirers for their reception, but later complained to the airline BOAC for not keeping secret his presence on the plane as he had requested.

Cambridge University

Side against which the Don scored his first duck in England, on his second tour in 1934, when he was bowled by off-spinner Jack (JGW) Davies with the fourth ball he faced. But it was against the same side four years earlier in the students' first innings that Bradman took 3/35 with his leg-breaks, the best bowling figures of his first-class career. And he followed with 3/68 in the second innings.

Campbell, Reginald

Artist Bill Leak tells the story of when he visited the Don in 1989 to paint his portrait, he noticed on his wall a painting of Bradman which Leak knew to have been done in the 1950s by Reg Campbell. But he asked the Don if there was a reason it was not signed. There was. Shortly after the painting was completed, the subject was showing it to his friends, one of whom fancied he "knew a thing or two about art" and opined that while it was "a pretty good effort", it was a bit ordinary in terms of its composition because it was "about three inches too long". Bradman's response was to lop about 5cm off the bottom. Years later, when the Don visited Campbell at his Blue Mountains home and asked Campbell to re-sign the portrait, he was told in no uncertain terms where to put it.

Captain

The first indication that Australian Board members saw the Don as a future Test captain was when they gave the 25-year-old the nod as Bill Woodfull's vice-captain on the 1934 tour of England ahead of Bradman's New South Wales skipper Alan Kippax. The first time the Don captained a state side was South Australia's first match of the 1935–36 season, his first game for his new state. Bradman's first Test as captain was the opening match of the Ashes series at the 'Gabba in December 1936, a contest the home side lost by 322 runs, and his last was the Fifth Test at the Oval in 1948, which the tourists won by an innings and 149 runs. In all, Bradman skippered Australia in 24 Tests in five series, winning 15 matches, losing three and drawing six. In 19 Tests in four series against England, he won 11, lost three and drew five. He had a run of 15 consecutive Tests over three series (two against England and one against India) without a loss, starting with the First Test at the 'Gabba in December 1946 and ending with the Fifth Test at the Oval in August 1948. The nearest he came to losing a rubber was the level series in England in 1938. At Test level, the Don averaged 101.51 (with 14 centuries) in his 38 innings in 24 appearances when captain, and 98.69 (with 15 centuries) in 42 innings in 28 appearances when not captain. In all first-class cricket, he averaged 98.78 (with 66 centuries) in 167 innings in 120 matches when captain, and 91.57 (with 51 centuries) in 171 innings in 114 matches when not captain. Of the 120 games in which he was skipper, his side won 61, lost 13, draw 45 and tied one.

Cardus, (Sir) Neville

Legendary British journalist who was asked by his editor at the *Manchester Guardian* to write an obituary when the Don became ill with peritonitis at the end of the 1934 tour of England. Cardus, whose other area of speciality was classical music, had written a particularly melodramatic piece in the *Guardian* a few weeks before about the Don's innings of 36 in the Test at Lord's, and four years later was to write a preposterously romantic account of Stan McCabe's great 232 at Trent Bridge, the innings which Bradman considered was the best he'd seen. Cardus was commissioned by Wisden in 1963 to write an appreciation of the cricketers he considered were the six greatest players of the last century for the 100th annual edition of the *Cricketers' Almanack*. In his piece on the Don he wrote: "Bradman's achievements stagger the imagination. No writer of boys fiction would dare to invent a hero who performed with Bradman's continual consistency." He said that when he once asked the Don in

C

Melbourne to give him some idea of "how he did it all", Bradman replied: "Every ball for me is the first ball, and I never think there's a possibility of anybody getting me out." The other five players nominated by Cardus were SF Barnes, WG Grace, Jack Hobbs, Tom Richardson and Victor Trumper. Neville Cardus published three volumes of autobiography (the first of them written in a Kings Cross flat in Sydney during World War II) and was knighted in 1967 for his services to journalism. He died in 1975 at the age of 86.

Casino Theatre
Where the Don and his teammates took in a performance of the musical *Show Boat*, featuring Paul Robeson, during the private tour of North America in 1932.

Caught
How the Don lost his wicket 174 times in his 295 first-class dismissals and 340 times in 562 dismissals in all recorded matches.

Caught and Bowled
How the Don lost his wicket 13 times in his 295 first-class dismissals.

Caught by a Fieldsman Other than the Bowler
How the Don lost his wicket on 124 occasions in his 295 first-class dismissals.

Caught by Wicketkeeper
How the Don lost his wicket 37 times in his 295 first-class dismissals.

Centenary Test
In March 1977 the Don gave the major address at the official luncheon in Melbourne to celebrate the Test at the MCG.

Centennial Bakery Museum
Museum operated by Hurstville (the home of the Don's first Sydney club, St George) City Council which had an exhibition for several weeks in September–October 2000 devoted to the master batsman's early career.

Centennial Park Cemetery
Adelaide cemetery where a private funeral for the Don was held on the evening of March 1, 2001. His son, John, walked at the front of the pro-

cession for the first few hundred metres of the 18-kilometre journey from the funeral home to the cemetery, where his father was cremated. He acknowledged the crowd's applause with an appreciative nod. Though John respected his father's wish for a private funeral, he also recognised the people's desire to say goodbye by making public the route of the procession. A large crowd had gathered outside the funeral home and hundreds more took up strategic positions along the way. When the hearse arrived at the funeral home it was covered with red roses, blue irises, white snapdragons and white lilies. Inside, a smaller mixed bouquet of mainly blue and white flowers lay ready to be placed upon the Tasmanian blackwood coffin – Sir Donald's personal choice. With a police motorcycle escort and traffic lights co-ordinated to green along the route, the entourage slowly wound its way through the streets of Adelaide before entering the cemetery, which was opened expressly for the funeral. The 100 or so people who attended were much the same group as attended Jessie's funeral in 1997.

Central Cumberland
Sydney grade club (now Parramatta) which invited the Don on board after Harold Cranney, one of three New South Wales selectors and a Cumberland official, ran his eye over the 18-year-old at a trial at the SCG in October 1926. But the offer was withdrawn when the committee decided they could not afford to pay Bradman's rail fare of nine shillings and fivepence each Saturday from Bowral to Sydney and back.

Chairman
Position the Don first held with the Australian Board of Control for International Cricket from September 1960 to September 1963. He had another stint from 1969 to 1972. Bradman was only the second former Test player to occupy the chair. He also served as chairman of several public companies, including Argo Investments, Wakefield Investments and Rigby Publishers.

Chapman, (Arthur) Percy (Frank)
England captain in four of the five Tests in the 1930 series in England who took what Bradman considered was the best catch ever to dismiss him. He held the Don at short extra cover off left-arm spinner John White to bring to an end what, coincidentally, Bradman believed was his best Test innings in a technical sense: his chance-free 254 in the Second Test at Lord's.

C

Chappell, Gregory Stephen MBE

The stylish and prolific Test batsman and captain of the 1970s and '80s has the next-best Test average (of players who scored a minimum 3,000 runs) on the list of Australians after the Don. A grandson of Victor Richardson, another Test captain and a teammate of Bradman's, Chappell was the first player to overtake the great man's record by an Australian of 6,996 Test runs. Greg believes that quite a few of the world's top batsmen over the years were capable of doing in the nets everything that the Don did in the middle. What set Bradman apart, Chappell said, was his ability to take to the middle that freedom of mind, body and spirit that other batsmen, himself included, have felt only in the nets. "I'd say he had very little in the way of self-doubts. There was nothing anyone could bowl at him he didn't feel capable of mastering. He was obviously unique. He was a package of physical and mental talents that apparently have never been found together in another individual." Greg owes something of his own success to a fortuitous meeting with the Don when Bradman was a selector with South Australia in 1968: "I was fortunate to be exposed to Sir Donald early in my first-class career with South Australia. The good fortune was multiplied when he offered me some advice on my grip in my second season with the state. That piece of advice turned me from a leg-side player into one who could play shots all-round the wicket and allowed me to develop a stroke range that would not have been possible with my original grip. It was the single most important technical change that I made as a mature-age cricketer."

Chappell has taken a special interest in the Don's "unorthodox" backlift, and has become convinced that it had a lot to do with his phenomenal success. "Basically, Bradman didn't lift the bat at all – he levered it up ... the bat virtually weighed nothing because it was pointing straight up ... Once he'd levered the bat up, Bradman's hands were in the middle of his body, and his balance was perfect. The reason he's the best player ever is that he was the best-balanced player ever." On August 27, 1998, Chappell officiated at the cutting of the Don's 90th-birthday cake on the steps of the building of the State Library of South Australia which houses the Bradman Collection. In July 2001, he auctioned through Christie's in Melbourne five letters which Bradman had written to him between the 1970s and the '90s. The letters were bought for $16,000 by, it was later revealed, an anonymous group of businesspeople calling themselves Some Australians Value Ethics (SAVE), whose intention it was to donate them to the Bradman Foundation. The letters were handed over by 12-year-old cricketer Tim Wilson on behalf of the group to the foundation's executive officer, Richard Mulvaney, at a lunch at the Melbourne Cricket Club on August 27, 2001.

Chester, Frank

Englishman who was ranked by the Don as the greatest umpire he played under. His opinion was based partly on Chester's "miraculous judgement" in the First Test at Trent Bridge in 1938 when he correctly gave Bradman out caught behind by Les Ames off Reg Sinfield. Chester told Bill O'Reilly in England in 1948, when O'Reilly was covering the Australians' tour for the Sydney *Sun*, that he thought "Tiger" was the best bowler he had stood behind. Frank Chester was a promising batsman with Worcestershire who took to umpiring when his playing career was cut short by the loss of an arm in World War I. He officiated in many of the matches on the Don's four tours of England. Of the Australian run-machine, Chester once said: "I left the Lord's Test in 1930, after watching Bradman, firmly convinced that he was the greatest batsman of all time."

Chipp, (The Hon.) Donald Leslie AO

The last man to partner Bradman at the crease. A then federal Liberal politician who was later to found the Australian Democrats, Chipp was at the other end when his namesake and captain was dismissed for 4 by Brian Statham when the pair were playing for Robert Menzies's Prime Minister's XI against an MCC XI at Manuka Oval, Canberra, in February 1963.

Chipperfield, Arthur Gordon

A right-handed batsman from New South Wales who toured England twice with the Don: in 1934 and 1938. Chipperfield had the unfortunate distinction of being the only Australian and the first batsman from any country to make 99 on Test debut. On the second day of the First Test at Trent Bridge in 1934, he was one short of his ton when he went into lunch and was caught behind off the third ball after the break. This match was notable also as the only Test in six Ashes series between 1928 and 1938 that Australia won without Bradman scoring a hundred. Australia's vice-captain could only manage 29 and 25, the first two in a run of five ordinary scores in the first three Tests of the series. It was Chipperfield who called in Dr Lee when the Don took ill with peritonitis in the team's London hotel at the end of the tour. Arthur got his Test century in South Africa in 1935–36. He died in Sydney in 1987 at the age of 81.

Chopin, Frederic Francois

The Don's favourite composer for the piano. He played Chopin's works until he was at an age when his fingers were no longer able to move well enough for him to perform at the standard he required. He had to be satis-

C

fied with playing music which was more manageable but his granddaughter, Greta, played Chopin for him.

Christ, Charles Percival ("Chilla")
Queensland left-arm leg-spinner who had the Don caught for 225 in a Sheffield Shield game at Adelaide Oval in December 1938. Bradman gave a chance earlier off Christ's bowling when he was 147 but was "saved" when the catch was grassed. Bill Brown (his state captain), considers Christ (with another Queenslander, Don Tallon) was unlucky not to go to England with the Don's side in 1938. And Bradman told the ABC's Norman May in 1987 that he believed Christ would have done well had he gone.

Churchill, (The Rt Hon. Sir) Winston Leonard Spencer KG, OM, CH, TD, PC, FRS
British politician and statesman who once said to an unknown companion of the Don's: "Isn't that Bradman you are with? I would like to be introduced."

Clark, Donald
Twelve-year-old boy who shook hands with Bradman at the farewell luncheon at the end of the 1948 tour organised by *People* newspaper. Clark, who was named after the great man, was one of 12 youngsters who represented the thousands of British fans who subscribed to the Bradman Fund, a shilling fund set up by the newspaper. Part of the fund was used to buy a replica of the famous Warwick Vase, which was presented to the Don at the luncheon, and the rest used to lay concrete pitches in parkland throughout the British Isles.

Clarkson Ltd
Company whose board the Don joined in the mid-1940s.

Coalport
English company which produced a commemorative plate to recognise the Don's 100 centuries in first-class cricket. Issued in 1979 and limited to 500 pieces, it has an imprint of the scores and the opposition against which he made each of his hundreds.

Collins, Bruce Wilkie QC
Bruce Collins became a member of the Bradman Museum Project Committee in 1985 under the chairmanship of Bowral solicitor Garry

Barnsley. He formed the Bradman Museum Trust in 1987 and was its founding chairman until 1993. Although the concept of a new pavilion with a museum at Bradman Oval was the idea of two local cricket officials, Gordon Whatman and Keith Moore, in the early 1970s, it was Collins, a Sydney barrister, who was the driving force behind the realisation of the first stage, the Bradman Pavilion, completed in 1989. Two floors of exhibits in this building constituted the Bradman Museum pending the completion of the main museum building in 1996. Bruce worked through many of the issues of the Museum Project with Sir Donald during several visits to his Adelaide home both before and after the trust was established. He collaborated closely with the architects Devine Erby and Mazlin, the firm engaged to design both Stage I and Stage II of the museum complex, and spent many hours on domestic and international flights in a quest to raise funds. Collins said recently that his three most satisfying achievements while chairman were all related to the game: the complete redevelopment of Bradman Oval to bring it up to the standard to host first-class and international matches; the institution of scholarships for young Australian sportsmen and women to Australian universities and to Oxford University; and the launching of the highly successful Bradman Trust coaching clinics for young cricketers. But Bruce was at pains to stress that nothing could have been achieved without the time and effort of many other people.

In a speech at the museum's inaugural Spring Dinner in Sydney held in October 1989, just prior to the opening of the pavilion, Sir Donald said:

"... I have purposely refrained this evening from commenting on the many people who have been very generous to the trust both with their donations and with the work they have put in for it, but nobody has been in a position to pay a proper compliment to the chairman, Bruce Collins. Only those who have worked with Bruce in this matter have any idea of the volume of time and effort that he put into this project over a period now of the last two or three years. Knowing what the fees of barristers are, I should think if we worked out the value of the time it would be a colossal contribution, but in addition to that is the enthusiasm and integrity that he has put into the work ..."

In October 1993, the then chairman of the Bradman Museum Trust, Bob Radford, published an article in the museum's magazine, *Boundary*:

"The Trust, at its meeting held on 14 October 1993, received the resig-nation of its Chairman, Bruce Collins, with regret. Bruce was instrumental in the affairs of the Trust since becoming a Committee Member in October 1985, of its forerunner the Bradman Museum Project Committee, under

C

the chairmanship of Mr. Garry Barnsley. In September 1987, when Garry stood down as Chairman of the Museum Project (the Trust had been formed in the preceding month), Bruce Collins became the Trust Chairman. Garry remains a most valued Trustee. The next six years were memorable indeed as the Trust and its achievements took shape to the point where today the project has taken on both national and international significance.

"Friends of the Museum and other readers of Boundary will be aware of the achievements to date, and of the fact that despite the recent decision to defer temporarily the turning of the first sod for Stage II (or as the architects term it, 'our second innings'), what has been created thus far is immense. What they will not be fully aware of, however, is the input of Bruce Collins to every single facet of the Trust's operations throughout the whole period. His indefatigable approach to the affairs of the Bradman Museum Trust has amazed his closest friends and fellow Trustees. His hours devoted have been countless: his generosity boundless.

"Bruce personally oversaw and expanded the scholarship scheme; the coaching clinic; the building design (for both Stages I and II); the purchase – through the generosity of Sir Ron Brierley and Industrial Equity Limited – of most valuable display items at the Lord's auction; an important legal case in Bowral which threatened our very existence; the Ashes exhibition in 1988, brilliantly supported by the State Bank; the appointment of the Curator, Mr. Richard Mulvaney; the raising of substantial amounts of money; and improvements to Bradman Oval in conjunction with the Wingecarribee Shire Council. These historic and meaningful accomplishments reflect only in part the dedication and character which Bruce Collins displayed to a cause which, to him, amounted to far more than a labour of love. It has been, in reality, a driving spirit and ambition to devise and create a pleasant place in our country which will, for current and future generations, honour the greatest living Australian.

"The inaugural Spring Dinner held on 13 October 1989 and the opening of the Bradman Pavilion in Bowral the following day, were happy and memorable events. It is no exaggeration to state that every fellow Trustee in attendance at those functions were acutely aware that, without Bruce Collins, his drive, energy and splendid vision, we would not have been there. Whilst we hope, as time permits, Bruce may continue to share his many gifts with the Trust, it behoves, in the time honoured tradition of cricket, the remaining Trustees and Curator to carry on with the very real dream of the completion of our 'second innings' – Stage II of the Bradman Museum, Bowral.

"Every now and then, in the life of any such project, a true leader emerges. We thank Bruce for his hands-on leadership. Every person associated with this exciting project is in Bruce Collins' debt. We owe it to him, therefore, to succeed. And we will. Thanks Bruce – we'll see you at the Grand Opening!"

In November 1993, the then deputy chairman of the Bradman Museum Trust, Garry Barnsley, wrote to Collins:

"... Your contribution to this project has been simply magnificent. I have never seen anything to match your energy, resolve and talents as an advocate and visionary. Without these qualities and their selfless application to the task the Bradman Museum would not have achieved the splendid form it takes today ..."

Just after the opening of the second stage of the project in August 1996, then Wingecarribee Shire president Peter Reynolds said in a note to Collins:

"... I would like to thank you for the enormous effort that you put in to the project at great personal cost. I believe that most would say that it wouldn't have happened without you. I guess you must be pleased that it has finally come to fruition ..."

Bruce Collins is a Queen's Counsel practising in Sydney. He is chairman of the Sydney Cricket Association, a member of the boards of Cricket New South Wales and Cricket Australia, president of the Sydney University Cricket club and president of the Primary Club of Australia.

Collins, Herbert Leslie

Herbie Collins was a patient right-handed batsman who captained Australia in 11 Tests from 1921 to 1926. After his retirement from the game, he returned to his chosen profession of bookmaking, but he also wrote for newspapers. Jack Fingleton told of how Collins saw the Don after the Ashes Test at Adelaide in 1946–47 when Bradman's side had obviously played for a draw. Collins told the Australian captain that he had written an article for a paper about him. "In case they don't print it in full I'll tell you the theme of it," he said. "I've suggested that cricket would be a better game now if you had got out of it."

Colombo, Sri Lanka (formerly Ceylon)

Where the Australians traditionally played a second-class match against a team of locals on the way to England. In 1948, the Don and his men were suspicious about the length of the pitch, and after rain put an early end to proceedings it was found to be about two yards short. But Bradman noted that the scoreboard gave more information than any board he had seen: "A tribute to local enthusiasm." Before the heavens opened, the game was played in great heat. Sid Barnes became violently ill while batting and had to retire, and the skipper was so sick that he was confined to his bed until the ship reached Bombay, where he got up to attend a small on-board function and waved to fans on the dock.

"Column 8"

Column in the *Sydney Morning Herald* which featured the Don in the first item on its first appearance, on January 11, 1947, four days after the Don had scored 79 and 49 in leading his side to a draw against England in the Third Test at the MCG, the first drawn Test in Australia since 1881–82. The item read: "Don Bradman, Test cricketer, can't remember the number of autographs he's signed – 'Must run into many thousands.' Marcus Oliphant, atom expert, can. He's never been asked for one."

Commemorative Gateway

Gateway at Bradman Oval built to honour the Don on his 90th birthday. It was opened by Invincibles teammate Arthur Morris on August 27, 1998.

Commonwealth Club

Adelaide club of which the Don was elected president in 1944. Notable people to address the club during Bradman's tenure included Enid Lyons, John Curtin, Anthony Eden and Lord Montgomery.

Companion General Division Order of Australia (AC)

Honour for the Don which was announced in the Queen's Birthday Honours on June 16, 1979 and conferred by Governor-General Sir Zelman Cowen.

Compton, Denis Charles Scott CBE

Just as the Don was "our Don Bradman" to a nation of adoring Australians in the Depression of the 1930s, Compton was "our Denis" to the average Briton in post-war-weary England. The brilliant batsman, who played football for Arsenal and England and was featured as the original "Brylcreem Boy" in hair cream advertisements, was at the centre of a controversial decision in the Third Test of the 1946–47 Ashes series in Melbourne. When Ernie Toshack was bowling to Compton and appealed for an lbw, the Don was fielding almost directly behind the bowler's wicket and believed the dashing right-hander was clearly out, as adjudged. But when hit on the pad, Denis quickly moved his right foot away to the leg side and photos showed his leg clear of the stumps. English journalists wrote that the decision was wrong but Compton's batting partner Cyril Washbrook agreed with Bradman that the decision was the correct one. England captain Wally Hammond, though not happy with umpiring in the match, did not ask for a change of officials for the remaining two Tests. This match was the first Test drawn in Australia since 1882, contests down under before 1946–47 having been played to a finish. The debonair Compton rewrote the record books in the English summer of 1947 when he rattled up 3,816 first-class runs at an average of 90.86, with 18 centuries.

After seeing Bradman for the first time in eight years on arriving in Australia in 1946, looking so ill, Compton said: "Some of us wondered whether or not he was due for a nursing home rather than a cricket pitch." But in his 1980 book *Compton on Cricketers Past and Present*, he wrote of the Don: "He was unique, a batsman appearing not just once in a lifetime but once in the life of a game." In the same book, he said he shared the view of England spin bowler Hedley Verity that Bradman's relatively poor record on sticky wickets was not because he could not master such wickets, but that, because he was very much against uncovered pitches, he refused to overcome them on principle. In his *Farewell to Cricket*, the Don described Compton as "a glorious natural cricketer", but, curiously in light of Bradman's view of the incident in Melbourne, also dubbed him "a grand sportsman". Denis Compton was 78 when he died in 1997.

Constantine, Learie Nicholas (Baron Constantine)

West Indian cricketer whom the Don considered was the best all-round fieldsman he had seen. Constantine toured Australia in 1930–31 and starred with the Nelson club in the Lancashire League in England. It was his recommendation on his return from Australia that led to Lancashire League club Accrington offering the Don a player's contract in August 1931. Learie Constantine later wrote books, became a broadcaster and was appointed Trinidad and Tobago's high commissioner in England. He was awarded an MBE, knighted and created a Life Peer. Trinidad awarded him the Trinity Cross, the country's highest honour.

Cootamundra

Farming town in the Riverina district of New South Wales where the Don was delivered by midwife Eliza Scholz at her house at 89 Adams Street on August 27, 1908. The building is now a museum, having been purchased in 1989 by Cootamundra Council from the Catholic Church, to whom it was left as part of a deceased estate. Visitors pay $3 admission to see portraits, scorecards and photos and watch a 10-minute video. The council also owns an adjoining property which houses a collection of memorabilia on loan from local couple Peter and Jenny Cash. A dispute between the council and the Bradman Foundation over the use of the name "Bradman's Birthplace" was resolved in 2001 and it now also has approval to sell Bradman memorabilia. The museum is on the Web at www.cootamundra.nsw.gov.au/bradman.html. A life-size bronze statue of the Don wielding his bat is prominent in Jubilee Park, a couple of hundred metres from the museum. Cootamundra's favourite son played in the town of his birth only once: when he went on a country tour with Arthur Mailey's Bohemians at the end of the 1927–28 season. He was dismissed for 1, later saying: "It was disappointing for me to be run out for 1 the only time I played in my birthplace." None of the great man's relatives remain in town but it is the resting place of his paternal grandparents, Charles and Elizabeth. A special match was played at the local oval a few days after the Don's death in February 2001.

Cowichan
Ground in Victoria, Canada, where Arthur Mailey's Australians played their first match of the 1932 tour on June 17. The local team of 18 men made 194 and the tourists replied with 8 for 503, the Don and his skipper Victor Richardson at one stage adding 50 runs in 7 minutes. Six different balls were lost during the day in nearby woods.

Craig, Ian David OAM
A former New South Wales and Australian captain who was once hailed as "the new Bradman", Ian Craig is immediate past chairman of the Bradman Foundation and the Bradman Museum. In the early 1950s, he became the youngest man to appear in Sheffield Shield cricket and the youngest Australian Test player. At the Don's memorial service at Bradman Oval, Ian said that anyone present in Bowral on this day would recall having witnessed "this very final occasion".

Cranney, Harold ("Mudgee")
New South Wales selector who took a shine to the Don's batting style when Bradman was invited to attend a trial for country players at the SCG in October 1926 and asked the boy from Bowral to join Cranney's Central Cumberland club. The Don agreed but the club decided it could not afford to pay the train fare of nine shillings and fivepence for his trip each Saturday from Bowral to Sydney and back. He was signed up soon after by the St George club.

Crawford Casting Pty Ltd

Sydney company which did the casting work on Tanya Bartlett's full-size statue of the Don which was unveiled at the Bradman Museum at Bowral on February 24, 2002 to mark the first anniversary of his death. When Tanya finished work on her sculpture in October 2001, men from Crawford's travelled to her studio in Newcastle and made a master mould of silicone rubber in three pieces. The mould was brought to Sydney where a wax impression was taken and a shell mould formed around the wax. Once the mould was set, the wax was burned out of the shell to produce a negative of the sculpture. The shell mould was then fired in a kiln and molten metal poured into it. When the metal was set, the mould was chipped off the bronze. The whole thing was then reassembled and welded together. Chemicals were applied to form a black coating and the statue was then polished to bring out the high-lights in the colour. Tanya and Alan Crawford, the principal of Crawford's, each drove to Bowral in a convoy with the truck which transported the statue from the foundry in Sydney to Bowral two days before the unveiling. The Don was fixed to a sandstone base with stain-less steel pins under each of the feet and another in the bottom of his bat.

"Cricketer of the Year"

Title accorded the Don in 1931 by cricket bible Wisden for his perform-ances the previous year in England.

CricketWorld

A company which produces statistical database computer programs, CricketWorld has proposed that a perpetual trophy known as the Sir Donald Bradman Trophy be awarded each year (on the Don's birthday, August 27) to the World Champion Test Cricket nation. The suggested annual title, based on results over the previous three years, would supple-ment the ICC Test Series Championship, which is calculated on results of the previous five years. The luminaries of CricketWorld claim their pro-posed points system is more realistic than the ICC's version, which is based on a method formulated by *Wisden Cricket Monthly*. There has been support for the initiative, though mainly from past players. Former Australian Cricket Board chairman Denis Rogers said before his retire-ment that he thought the idea had "much merit". Details of CricketWorld's scheme are on their website at www.cricketworld.com.au.

Crippled Children's Association

The Don's and Jessie's favourite charity. Their son John had polio as a child and their daughter Shirley was born with mild cerebral palsy. The great bulk of the couple's work for the charity was carried on in Adelaide, but the Don visited the Crippled Children's Hospital in Perth just after a game against Western Australia and before boarding the ship for England in March 1948.

Cuff Links

What the Don had made to present to each player and official who participated in his testimonial match in Melbourne in December 1948. A little cricket ball was linked by a chain to a bat on the other side.

Cupitt, Sidney

A member of the Bowral team in 1920–21 when the 12-year-old Don was acting as scorer for the side in a game at Moss Vale. When one of the team failed to show, the boy was given his chance in the middle. He had to use a man's bat ("almost as tall as I") but made 37 not out when he went in at no. 10, and afterwards Cupitt gave the lad one of his old bats. It was cracked but nevertheless the young Don was proud to take possession of his first blade. His father George sawed three inches (eight centimetres) off the bottom and he used it to score 29 not out when he opened the second innings at Bowral the following Saturday.

Cush, Frank Maitland OBE

Secretary (and later president) of the St George District Cricket Club at whose house at 172 Frederick Street, Rockdale, the Don boarded from September 1928 (when it became necessary for him to live in the area to remain eligible to play for St George under the new residential rules) until his marriage to Jessie in April 1932. He had been playing with the club since November 1926 and boarding with Geoffrey Pearce a few kilometres away in the suburb of Concord West since his move from Bowral to Sydney early in 1928. At the reception at Bowral for the Don before he left for the 1930 tour of England, Frank said: "To me, Don is more than a member of the Australian XI, having lived in my house for the last 12 to 18 months, and I describe him as one of the finest characters that ever graced a cricket field." Frank Cush served on the Australian Board of Control (including a stint as chairman), was honorary treasurer and a life member of the New South Wales Cricket Association, and at one point was the only non-Englishman not to have played first-class cricket to be made a life member of the MCC. Frank's son, Neville, was 11 when the Don made his world-record 452 not out at the SCG in January 1930. The maestro was 205 not out at the close of play on the Saturday, and Neville can recall him saying at the lunch table on the Sunday: "I'm going to break the record tomorrow." Frank Cush was 92 when he died in 1984.

Cutler, (Sir Arthur) Roden VC, AK, KCMG, KCVO, CBE

War hero and a former governor of New South Wales who was patron of the Bradman Foundation and the Bradman Museum from 1994 until his death in February 2002. In February 1979, when governor, he and Lady Cutler hosted a reception at Government House in Sydney and later a reunion dinner at the Hilton Hotel for the Don's 1948 Invincibles. Fifteen of the famous team attended, including the captain. It was the first time they had been together since the tour. Sir Roden recalled how as a student in the 1930s at Sydney Boys High School, in Moore Park, next to the SCG, he always knew when the Don had gone in to bat watching the empty trams going down Anzac Parade outside the school. "As soon as the trams filled up we knew Bradman was in and it was a signal for us to wag school to watch him." Sir Roden Cutler attended the memorial service for the Don at Bradman Oval on March 28, 2001.

Cutten and Pentelow

Adelaide sharebroking firm for whom the Don did consultancy work in retirement.

D

Dahle, Thelma
Sydney sculptor who created a wax cast of the Don as he was in 1930. The bust is in the Bradman Museum.

Daily Telegraph, The
London newspaper whose readers selected the Don as the best-ever athlete in a poll in April 2001. He finished ahead "by some considerable margin" of contenders like Muhammad Ali, Pele and Tiger Woods.

Dalton, Eric Londesbrough
South African cricketer who inflicted the Don's only defeat during the Test series in Australia in 1931–32 when he beat him at table tennis. Not long after, Dalton had his jaw broken in two places by the first ball he faced from Laurie Nash in the match against Tasmania in Hobart.

Davies, Douglas
Welsh club cricketer and music-loving teacher whose long relationship with the Don started in 1982 when he heard on radio a 1930 piano recording of him playing the songs "Old Fashioned Locket" and "Our Bungalow of Dreams". He sent Bradman a cassette and asked him to record the songs for him on his own piano. They corresponded regularly for the next 18 years, and the Don invited Davies to his home twice when he was in Australia, in 1997 and 1999.

Davies, J(ack) G(ale) W(ilmot) OBE
Off-spinner for Cambridge University who bowled the Don in the third tour match in 1934 when Bradman registered his first duck in England. Davies became a director of the Bank of England and president of the MCC.

Davis, Charles Norman
Victorian biochemist and cricket aficionado who argued in an article in the *Sydney Morning Herald* in 1995 that the Don was the greatest sportsman of all time. By using a statistical technique known as the bell curve, Davis calculated that Bradman was a one-in-a-million batsman. He fur-

ther developed his analysis of the Don's career in a book, *The Best of the Best: A New Look at the Great Cricketers and their Changing Times*, published in 2000, in which he calculated that we cannot expect to see another cricketer of Bradman's calibre for at least 6,000 years. The work generated debate, and was generally praised by reviewers in Australia and overseas.

Davis, Joe OBE
The world's then greatest snooker player who took on the Don in a game in London one night during the 1938 tour.

Davis & Westbrook
Bowral real estate firm for which the Don went to work as a clerk on leaving school as a 14-year-old in 1922, an arrangement made by Bradman's parents. When the principal, Percy Westbrook, opened an office in Sydney in early 1928, he installed the 19-year-old Bradman as secretary. The Don, who had been travelling from Bowral to Sydney and back each Saturday by train since early in the 1926–27 season to play with his grade club St George, moved to the city to board with insurance agent Geoffrey Pearce in the suburb of Concord West.

Dawson, Peter Smith
Australian baritone (and composer of many ballads under the name JP McCall) who entertained the Don's team and other guests with a song at a Lord Mayor's Dinner in London at the start of the 1948 tour.

Deakin, James
One-time Australian amateur middleweight wrestling champion who is held by the Don in a reverse headlock in a photograph in the book *Images of Bradman*.

Deane, (The Hon. Sir) William Patrick AC, KBE, QC
Former governor-general of Australia and friend of the Bradman family who described the Don at the Adelaide memorial service as "a cherished elder of our nation ... the best known and most admired Australian of our times". Sir William represented the public at the ceremony at Bradman Oval on October 18, 2001 when the Don's and wife Jessie's ashes were scattered on the oval and in the gardens.

D

De Mello, Anthony

A former president of the Board of Control for Cricket in India who bemoaned in a treatise on Indian sport: "One of the sorrows of my life was that I was not able to bring Sir Donald Bradman to India before his days of Test cricket were over." De Mello officiated at a rather hurried presentation to Bradman and his players when their ship docked briefly in Bombay on their way to England in 1948.

Diverticulitis

Inflammation of an intestine, an ailment which troubled the Don late in life.

Dolling, (Dr) C(harles) E(dward)

Test selector from South Australia upon whose death in June 1936 the Don was appointed to the panel as a replacement three months later, before he got the nod as captain for the 1936–37 Ashes series in Australia. Bradman was serving with Dolling as a state selector in South Australia at the time of his death. Charles Dolling made 20 appearances as a batsman with South Australia between 1905–06 and 1922–23 and toured New Zealand with an Australian team in 1913–14. He was only 49 when he died.

Don, The: A Biography of Sir Donald Bradman

Biography by Australian author Roland Perry, published in 1995 by Macmillan, 645pp. Some of the royalties earned by the book benefit the Bradman Museum. Perry, whose earlier books covered a range of subjects, interviewed Bradman for the work and quoted him at length. They had agreed it was to be an unauthorised biography, but Perry said that his celebrated subject never once said: "You can't put that in." When the book was finished, the Don asked to see the manuscript, "to look at it for factual errors". He received the work of 250,000 words in the mail about lunchtime on a Tuesday and on the Wednesday rang Perry. "Roland, I've read your book. I've taken four pages of notes. There are about 80 points I want to discuss with you." The corrections were mostly to do with spellings and statistics. The biography was summarised by Philip Derriman in a review in the *Sydney Morning Herald* as "well researched, well illustrated and well written", but Gideon Haigh, writing in the *Australian* newspaper, expressed a slightly different opinion. He said the "text itself stinks", and described Perry as "an appalling writer". And Haigh criticised the author for glossing over or ignoring anything to Bradman's discredit.

D

Don, The – A Photographic Essay of a Legendary Life

Book published by Sun-Macmillan in 1988, 97pp. Authors Michael Page and Des Fregan reproduced much of the illustrative material in Page's 1983 book and added a biographical sketch.

Don, Bradman Windsor

Retired insurance consultant from Kenthurst, on the outskirts of Sydney, who was named after his celebrated namesake by his cricket-mad father, Richard H. Don, when he was born in Colombo, Sri Lanka, on June 2 (the same birthdate as the Waugh brothers) in 1937. Don played grade cricket and for the British High Commission in Colombo before migrating in 1964 to Melbourne, where he played grade for Elsternwick and also won the Southern Districts Tennis Championship with Toorak Park. He was at a Test at the MCG between Australia and England in 1965–66 when he heard that his reverse namesake was visiting the players in the dressing room. But when he presented himself at the door and gave his name, Bradman Don got no further. He says he could have produced his driver's licence had he been given a chance.

Don moved to Sydney in 1969 and in July 1972 made an appearance in court in Kilmore, Victoria, to appeal a conviction for speeding. When he lost and was ordered to pay the grand sum of $2, the case was written up in the Melbourne *Herald* under the headline: "An appeal, and 'the Don' is out for two." Soon after, Don's boss at a large insurance company in Sydney, who as it happened was a friend of the "real" Don's, received a phone call from him wanting to know about his namesake. It was not until many years later though – in 1997 – that Bradman Don wrote to the other Don seeking an audience. In fact he wrote three times in 1997–98 but did not receive an acknowledgement. Mr Don was the subject of a potted pro-file with a photo in the August 2000 issue of *Wisden Cricket Monthly*. And, in March 2001, the *Sydney Morning Herald*'s "Column 8" reported that our would-be hero happened to be in a bottle shop in Russell in New Zealand's North Island on February 26, 2001, when the news of Sir Donald's death came over the radio. "That's a pity," said the shop owner. The tourist did-n't say a word – he just handed over his credit card.

Don Bradman

Biography by Philip Lindsay, son of the artist Norman Lindsay, published in 1951 by Phoenix House, 64pp.

Also a biography written by G.N. Natu in the western Indian language of Marathi and published by R.B. Samurda in 1936, 96pp.

D

Don Bradman & Co.
The Don's stockbroking firm in Adelaide which he started when his employer Harold Hodgetts declared himself bankrupt (and was shortly after convicted of fraud) in 1945. In 1946, though he owned a car, Bradman travelled the five kilometres from his home in suburban Kensington Park to his office and back by tram, arriving at 9 and leaving at 5.30. The takeover by the Don of his former boss's premises and client list was the subject of a negative article by David Nason in the *Weekend Australian Magazine* in November 2001. Don Bradman & Co. ceased trading on June 28, 1954, when the principal retired from stockbroking to concentrate on his company directorships.

"Don Bradman Dahlia"
The grower named it "because of its strength and vigorous growth. In colour it is toned from a deep orange to chrome yellow with a blush of pink."

Don Bradman – How to Play Cricket
Video produced by Festival Records in association with the Bradman Museum and released in 1993.

Don Bradman Limited
Company established by the Don with JT Smith in September 1933 to sell clothing and sporting goods. He licensed the company the right to use his name, image and signature for promotional purposes.

Don Bradman's Book
Subtitled "The Story of My Cricketing Life with Hints on Batting, Bowling and Fielding," written by the Don and published by Hutchinson in December 1930 with a foreword by Pelham Warner, 256pp. Reprinted in 1938 with additional chapters by Bruce Harris. It was this book which got Bradman in hot water with the Board of Control on his return to Australia after the 1930 tour of England. The tour manager reported that the book had been serialised in a British newspaper during the tour, and that therefore its author was in violation of a clause in his player's contract which provided that a member of the team should not publicly express his views on the cricket while the tour was in progress. The Don had made it clear to the newspaper that nothing he wrote about the tour was to be published until it was over, but he was nevertheless found guilty as charged and fined 50 pounds. It could have been as much as 150 pounds though, because that was the amount the board had withheld from each player's tour payment until the manager's report had been received.

Don's Last Innings, The

One-act play by Timothy Daly, first performed in 1986. Synopsis: "At John and Marjorie's house it is still 1948 and after tea every evening Don Bradman goes in to bat for Australia. Beneath its quirky humour, this play examines how a woman is coerced into a lifetime of indulging her husband's fantasies."

Duck

Score which the Don made more often than any other in his Test career: seven times (five times in Australia and twice in England) in 70 dismissals. It was also his most common score in his overall first-class career: 16 times (12 in Australia and four in England) in 295 dismissals. Of the 16 ducks, six were "first balls" (including four in a row from 1936–37 to 1940–41) and three were "second balls". He never scored a pair in the same match (though he only batted seven times in the second innings after failing to score in the first) but was twice dismissed for nought in successive innings in different matches. Of Bradman's seven ducks in Tests, six were against England and one against the West Indies. The bowlers were (in chronological order) Herman Griffith (WI, SCG in 1930–31, bowled); Bill Bowes (MCG in 1932–33, bowled); Gubby Allen ('Gabba in 1936–37, caught Fagg); Bill Voce (SCG in 1936–37, caught Allen); Alec Bedser (Adelaide Oval in 1946–47, bowled); Alec Bedser (Trent Bridge in 1948, caught Hutton); and Eric Hollies (the Oval in 1948, bowled).

The Don was dismissed 20 times in 22 Test innings in England before registering his first Test duck there in Nottingham in 1948. The only time he was dismissed first ball in a Test was when he played on to Bowes in the first innings of the second match of the Bodyline series at the MCG. Of his nine ducks in 225 first-class dismissals other than in Tests, there were seven in 149 dismissals in Australia and two in 76 dismissals in England. Bradman's first duck in Australia was when he was bowled first ball by Queensland leg-spinner Frank Gough in the 19-year-old Don's third first-class match, for New South Wales in a Sheffield Shield game at the SCG in January 1928. The first time the Don went for nought in England was against Cambridge University in the third tour match in 1934, when he was bowled with the fourth ball he faced. The student prince was off-spinner Jack (JGW) Davies, who was to become a director of the Bank of England and president of the MCC.

Duldig, Lance

Then captain of the first South Australian schoolboys team who was 13 when photographed with the Don during a Sheffield Shield game at the

D

MCG in January 1936 when Bradman was playing his first away match for South Australia. Duldig was to make his first-grade debut on his 19th birthday against New South Wales alongside the great Clarrie Grimmett in his last first-class appearance.

"Dynamite Don"

What an American newspaper dubbed Bradman during Arthur Mailey's tour of Canada and the US in 1932.

Dysentery

Infectious disease which brought about the Don's demise according to a report in the *Cooktown Independent* newspaper in north Queensland in December 1931:

"Don Bradman Dead – Australia today mourns the loss of the greatest batsman the world has ever seen. During the progress of the Test Match in Brisbane (Australia v. South Africa) Don Bradman was attacked with dysentery, to which he succumbed on Saturday."

Of the report, the Don wrote in *Farewell to Cricket*: "Thank goodness it was only in the *Cooktown Independent*, but it just goes to show that things can really happen in this world without our knowledge."

E

8

Most number of consecutive Tests (all against England) in which he batted that the Don made a century in each, starting with his 270 in the Third Test at the MCG in January 1937 and ending with 234 in the Second Test at the SCG in December 1946. In between, he made scores of 212, 169, 144 not out, 102 not out, 103 and 187.

Also the number of fifties in Bradman's 44 innings in 31 Sheffield Shield games for South Australia. By comparison he made 19 centuries.

Also the figure which appears in the Don's score in his first innings in three watershed matches: his initial first-class game, his first Test, and his first Test in England. He made 118 at Adelaide Oval in December 1927, 18 at Brisbane's Exhibition Ground in December 1928, and 8 at Trent Bridge in June 1930.

11

The most number of consecutive Test innings against England that the Don went without making a hundred. The drought started with his 8 in the first innings of the Third Test at Adelaide Oval in January 1933 and ended with his 30 in the Third Test at Old Trafford in July 1934.

Also the number of times Bradman topped the averages in his 14 full seasons in Australia (with eight completed innings as qualification).

Also the number of times the Don was stumped in his 295 dismissals in first-class cricket.

18

Number of Tests the Don played against England in Australia. He batted 33 times and scored 2,354 runs at 78.46, with eight centuries, nine fifties and four ducks. He also took 15 catches.

Also the number of centuries in the Don's 50 innings in 33 Tests in Australia. The total included seven double centuries. He also made 10 fifties.

80

Number of innings played by the Don in 52 Test matches: 50 in 33 Tests in Australia and 30 in 19 Tests in England. Of the 80 times he went in to bat, he scored 50 or more on 42 occasions (52.50%), 29 times going on to make at least 100. Of Bradman's 29 Test hundreds, 18 were in Australia and 11 in England, and they included 10 double hundreds (seven in Australia and three in England) and two triple hundreds (both in England). He made 13 fifties (10 in Australia, three in England) and seven ducks (five in Australia, two in England). The Don compiled a total of 6,996 runs at an average of 99.94. He only had to make 4 in his last Test innings at the Oval in 1948 (when he was out for a duck) to finish with an average of 100. Bradman had 63 innings in 37 Tests against England at an average of 89.78, with 19 centuries, 12 fifties and six ducks; six innings in five Tests against the West Indies (74.50,2,0,1); five innings in five Tests against South Africa (201.50,4,0,0); and six innings in five Tests against India (178.75,4,1,0).

Also the most number of runs the Don made before lunch (in 70 minutes' batting) on the first day of a first-class match in Australia: for South Australia against Queensland in a Sheffield Shield game in 1939–40 when he went on to score 138 in 115 minutes, his fifth century in successive innings against the northern state. He twice made a hundred before lunch in England.

82.35

The Don's average in his 84 innings in 54 first-class matches against all touring teams in Australia, including Tests.

84

Number of innings the Don played in 54 first-class games (including Tests) in Australia against all touring teams. He scored 6,529 runs at 82.35, with 25 centuries, including eight double centuries. His highest score was 299 not out in the Fourth Test against South Africa at Adelaide Oval in 1931–32.

84.80

The Don's average in his 331 second-class innings.

86.82

The Don's average in his 93 innings in grade cricket.

87 *Not Out*

The marketing title of the video of the Don's interview with Ray Martin which was screened on the Nine Network on May 29, 1996, so named because the subject was 87 at the time. Most of the interview took place at Adelaide Oval.

88

Number of the Don's centuries in 258 innings in 182 appearances in first-class cricket other than Tests. They included 21 double hundreds, three triple hundreds and one quadruple hundred. He also scored 56 fifties.

89

The score which was the nearest the Don got to making a Test century without attaining it: in his second innings of the Second Test at Lord's in 1948, when he was caught in the slips by Bill Edrich off Alec Bedser. It was the fifth time in successive innings in Ashes Tests that Bedser had taken Bradman's wicket. The Don said later that he had actually made 90, claiming that a single called a leg-bye came off his bat.

89.79

The Don's average in his 63 innings in 37 Tests against England.

8,926

The Don's aggregate in 96 innings in 62 Sheffield Shield matches: 4,633 in 52 innings in 31 matches for New South Wales, and 4,293 in 44 innings in 31 matches for South Australia. He averaged 110.20 (107.74 for NSW and 112.97 for SA) and made a total of 36 centuries (17 and 19) and 20 fifties (12 and 8).

18,230

Runs scored by the Don in his 218 innings in 142 first-class appearances in Australia, including 4,322 in Tests and 8,926 in Sheffield Shield. He averaged 94.46, with 76 hundreds and 45 fifties.

$80,000

Approximate price paid for the first of the Don's baggy greens to be offered at public auction: the cap he wore during his last series in Australia, the rubber against India in 1947–48. But before it went under the hammer, at Ludgrove's in Melbourne in February 2003, it was sold to a "prominent businessman under 40", who had been actively seeking to buy a cap worn by Bradman for some time. The Don gave the cap to India's team manager Pankaj ("Peter") Gupta after the series to inspire the game on the subcontinent. Gupta left the cap to a relative when he died and it passed through several owners over the years to the vendor in England.

E

Eagle Star Insurance Company

Company whose South Australian board the Don joined in February 1948. Later that year during the tour of England, when his team was playing in London the manager of the West End branch of the company placed his secretary at Bradman's disposal to help him reply to the mountain of mail he received each day. She came to the team's hotel at about 8 each morning and he dictated to her for an hour or two before going to the match. When he returned in the evening, the letters had been typed and delivered to the hotel ready for his signatures.

eBay

Online trader which marked the Don's 92nd birthday in August 2000 with an auction of Bradman memorabilia, including books and pictures autographed by him.

Egan, John Bryan

Author and documentary-maker who produced and directed the television documentary titled *Bradman*, first shown on the ABC in 1990 and later available on video. Jack, who interviewed the Don for the program, had been collecting archival film of Australian cricket for several years and wrote to Sir Donald a couple of times asking him for an interview to go with the collection, but he politely declined. Jack takes up the story: "Then I met him through Bruce Collins (a key figure in the establishment of the Bradman Museum) in connection with work I was doing for the museum, and when Sir Donald realised the extent of the collection and saw that he could make a significant contribution by identifying and commenting on the old film, he readily agreed. Although a stickler for getting things right, I found him friendly, outgoing, helpful and humorous. Once he was committed to the job, he couldn't do enough to help. I was really impressed at how bright and quick-witted he was. I was also struck by the warmth and wisdom of Jessie Bradman."

Elliott, Herbert

Nottinghamshire man whom the Don noticed looking wistfully through the gate at Trent Bridge during the First Test in 1934. Bradman asked him if he would like to come in, and in a matter of seconds the astonished man was inside the ground. Elliott was an unemployed coalminer from Radford with scarcely a penny to his name and no hope of seeing the match. Bradman paid his way, found him a place in the grandstand and gave him a few shillings for expenses. When it was discovered later that Elliott had a wife and eight children, a subscription list was started. The Don opened it with a generous donation.

Empire Theatre

Bowral theatre where the people of the district farewelled the 21-year-old Bradman at a reception and dance on March 5, 1930 before he left on his first tour of England. Speechmakers included Alf Stephens, the president of Bowral Town Cricket Club, and the mayors of Bowral and Moss Vale. The Don's boss, Percy Westbrook, said the people's motto that night might well be: "We are proud of you, Don, and we tell you so." The crowd joined in a rousing rendition of "For He's a Jolly Good Fellow" and Mr Stephens presented the honoured guest with a pair of silver entree dishes and a wallet stuffed with notes. The Don started his reply with: "This is the proudest evening of my life, to be able to return to Bowral to say goodbye to the friends I made when a boy and to see those who helped me a bit along the road." He went on to give special thanks to Mr Westbrook for letting him go to Sydney in 1928. "It was due to him that I got my chance in big cricket." After his speech there was yet another "For He's a Jolly Good Fellow".

England

The man who was the scourge of English cricket for 20 years was revered as much in England as he was in Australia. Thousands of disappointed fans were routinely turned away at grounds whenever Bradman was to play, or when the word got around that he was making runs. Anthony Davis wrote in his 1960 biography: "He made fools of the English bowlers but the English crowds, with national masochism, did not care; they adored him all the more." According to the *Daily Pictorial* newspaper, "Street urchins clambered onto the running board of Bradman's car just to catch a glimpse of him, and to greet him with their shrill tribute." The faces of the boys in the photograph taken near the gate as the Don walked out to bat in the first innings at Headingley in 1938 epitomises the awe in which he was held in the north. Former Test umpire Harold ("Dickie") Bird has told of how his father walked 35 kilometres from his home in Barnsley to Leeds and back every day of the 1934 Headingley Test to see Bradman in the flesh. Similarly, the journalist and broadcaster Michael Parkinson has written of how his father, before Michael was born, also hoofed it from Barnsley to Leeds to see the Don in action. The Parkinsons believed the head of the family had a "slate loose", but in retelling the story many times over the years, the proud man would say: "But I saw HIM bat and they didn't."

E

Michael said that "I still envy my father that memory." But such was the Australian connection with England in the early 1930s that when Bradman announced his decision to take up contracts in Australia rather than accept the offer from Lancashire League club Accrington, he said: "… which I accepted in preference to going home to the Old Country."

The Don played in four Ashes series in Australia: 1928–29, 1932–33, 1936–37 and 1946–47; and four in England: 1930, 1934, 1938 and 1948. In 63 innings in 37 Tests, he scored 5,028 runs at 89.79, with 19 centuries (including six double centuries and two triple centuries), 12 fifties and six ducks. His highest aggregate in a series against England was his record 974 in England in 1930 at an average of 139.14 (also his best). His highest score in an Ashes Test was his then world-record 334 at Headingley in 1930 and he took a total of 20 catches against the Old Enemy. Bradman's only Test wicket against England was that of Wally Hammond (bowled) in the Bodyline Test in Adelaide in 1932–33. In 33 innings in 18 Tests against England in Australia he made 2,354 runs at 78.47, with eight centuries (including three double centuries), nine fifties and four ducks. His highest aggregate in an Ashes series in Australia was 810 in 1936–37 at 90.00, but his best average was in 1946–47, when he made 680 runs at 97.14. His highest score against the Old Enemy in Australia was 270 at the MCG in 1936–37 (his best Test score on the ground) and he held 15 catches. The Don's 30 innings in 19 Tests in England produced 2,674 runs at 102.85, with 11 hundreds (including three double hundreds and two triple hundreds), three fifties and two ducks. He took five catches.

Bradman's first Test as captain against any country was the opening match of the Ashes series at the 'Gabba in December 1936, a contest his side lost by 322 runs, and his last was the Fifth Test at the Oval in 1948, which the tourists won by an innings and 149 runs. As skipper in 19 Tests in four series against England, he won 11, lost three and drew five. In 73 first-class matches in England other than Tests, the Don batted 90 times for 7,163 runs at 94.25, with 30 centuries (including seven double centuries), 21 fifties and two ducks. His highest score was 278 against the MCC at Lord's in 1938 and he took 35 catches. Bradman's performances in and against England are further analysed in several other entries. (On two of his four tours, he played in the match against Glamorgan in Wales, so references to total first-class matches, innings, etc. in England should generally be read as England and Wales. In 1930, a first-class game against Scotland in Edinburgh was washed out after the local side batted for three hours.) But the Don regarded England as more than merely the opposition in the cricket arena. In his radio interviews with the ABC in 1987, he was at pains to point out that England were "enemies on the field, friends off it" (though one can safely assume that a certain single-minded captain of the 1930s was the conspicuous exception).

In fact, such was his empathy with the country and its people that one suspects he would not have been all that put out to have been born an Englishman. In his 1950 autobiography *Farewell to Cricket*, Bradman wrote of his walks through the woods near the home of his surgeon Sir Douglas Shields in Berkshire when recuperating after injuring a leg in the Headingley Test in 1934: "Nothing in this world has appealed to me more than England as nature made her." Again in *Farewell to Cricket*, this time upon his departure for Australia after the 1948 tour: "I love England and its people very dearly. I could live there happily, and have always felt that I see my English friends all too seldom." The Don returned to England to write on the tours of 1953 and 1956 for the *Daily Mail* newspaper. He made the trip again four years later as a member of the Australian Board of Control for the historic ICC conference on throwing and then once more for a charity dinner for the Lord's Taverners Fund in 1974, when he spent a day signing all 900 menus. Bradman declined several offers to become president of the MCC but he was made an honorary life member in 1958 and a life vice-president in 1988.

The flags at the home of cricket were lowered to half-mast soon after news was received on February 26, 2001 of the Don's death the day before. Reports of his passing appeared on the front pages of nearly every major British newspaper. Most of the papers carried stories on more than one page and included the personal reminiscences of old foes and cricket fanatics. The *Times*'s Christopher Martin-Jenkins said Bradman was "the greatest batsman of any generation", and in its obituary, the paper said: "No other batsman, not even the legendary WG Grace, has dominated cricket in quite such a decisive manner." The *Independent*'s Derek Hodgson wrote: "I did get to meet him, in a lift in Sydney in 1978. He was 70 years old and when we shook hands I felt as if I was holding a coiled spring. There will never be another cricketer like him." The *Daily Telegraph*'s Martin Johnson said: "The biggest surprise about the sad news from Adelaide is that the great umpire in the sky chose to raise the finger before Don Bradman had the chance to rack up yet another century." The BBC and independent television networks covered the event with extensive reports, including live interviews with current and former players.

Essex

County against which the Don's Australians posted a world first-class record of 721 in a day at Southend in the sixth game of the 1948 tour. The skipper threw away his wicket after making 187 (his highest score on the tour) in 124 minutes, with 32 fours, including five each in an over from leg-spinners Vigar and Price. It was the fastest innings of Bradman's first-class career, averaging 90 runs an hour. He put on 219 in 90 minutes with Bill Brown and 166 in 65 minutes with Sam Loxton. The team total of 721 took just 350 minutes, the first 500 coming up in 247 minutes. All this despite the fact that the Essex side contained two Test bowlers and another who was on the verge of selection. The Australians bowled out the local side twice in one day, and, though it was a three-day game, the local committee got only two days' gate money.

ETT Imprint

Sydney company which (as ETT) published a new edition of the Don's autobiography, *Farewell to Cricket*, in 1994 and then published a revised edition (with substantial corrections to the original 1950 Hodder text) in 1997. ETT Imprint also published a new version of the Don's coaching manual, *The Art of Cricket*, firstly in book form (1998) then as a CD-ROM (2000). The book version contains a new preface by Richie Benaud as well as many photos not in the original 1958 edition. The CD utilises Bradman's original demonstration films, interviews and footage of his Test career to create the world's first personalised electronic cricket coaching manual. The Don shows and talks about all aspects of the game from batting, bowling and fielding through to the roles of the captain and the umpire. In conjunction with the books and CD, ETT Imprint also offers a range of Bradman memorabilia, including First Day Covers in the "Australian Legend" collection, coins, posters, videos and signed limited-edition copies of the book version of *The Art of Cricket* with an accompanying Bradman Test cap. These products, as well as *Farewell to Cricket* and the CD-ROM of *The Art of Cricket*, are available at the website, www.bradmancopyrightmaterials.com.au. The publication of Bradman's works in electronic form is a joint venture with the Sydney Cricket Ground Trust.

"Every Day is a Rainbow Day for Me"

Song composed by the Don (with words by Jack Lumsdaine), recorded at Columbia Records's studios at Homebush, Sydney, in 1930. When it was introduced by Elsie Hosking during a performance of the pantomime *Beauty and the Beast* at Melbourne's Grand Opera House in February 1931, it was described by a Sydney newspaper as "pleasantly melodious and sentimental, with a refrain in which saxophones and brasses vigorously supported the vocal theme, ere it was taken up smartly by a well-trained ballet".

Exhibition Ground

Brisbane ground where the Don played his first Test, the opening match of the 1928–29 Ashes series, from November 30, 1928. It was also the first time Test cricket was played in the Queensland capital. Bradman made only 18 (lbw Tate) and 1 (c Chapman b White), but his score in the first innings was the third-highest in Australia's total of 122, and the second innings was played on a sticky wicket (the first time the Don had seen one) when the home side were skittled for 66. England amassed 521 and 8/342 dec., and their win by a whopping 675 runs was a record margin of victory in a Test by runs alone. The contest also brought the first declaration in a Test in Australia when skipper Percy Chapman called a halt in England's second innings with eight wickets down. Bradman's 223 in his only other Test on the ground, against the West Indies in 1930–31 (when he was missed in the slips on 4), was then the highest score by an Australian in a home Test. His average in three Test innings at the Exhibition Ground was 80.67, and he took two catches. It was here that the Don scored a century in each innings of a first-class game (131 and 133 not out) for the first time in his career, for New South Wales against Queensland in a Sheffield Shield contest in 1928–29. Bradman made only four appearances at the Exhibition Ground before first-class cricket in Brisbane moved to the 'Gabba in 1931–32. After a slow start his seven innings yielded 620 runs at 103.33, with three hundreds (including his Test double hundred) and one fifty. His only catches were the two he took in his two Tests.

Eyesight

In his 1958 book *The Art of Cricket*, in a chapter titled "The Art of Batting", the Don wrote: "The story was strongly circulated that my ability to make runs was because of exceptional eyesight which enabled me to see the ball earlier than others and react more speedily. The professor of physics at Adelaide University, hearing of this, requested that I submit myself to tests to check up on the theory. I willingly did so. The result was that he discovered my reaction was minutely slower than that of the average university student. So that theory was exploded." When Bradman was suffering a recurrence of muscular trouble in the Army towards the end of 1940, an eye specialist examined him and found signs of further illness. The Don wrote in his *Farewell to Cricket*: "Despite this knowledge I agreed to play in two first-class matches for which leave was obtained. They merely confirmed the doctor's evidence, for I could register but 18 runs in four innings, including two ducks. I just couldn't see the ball." His muscular ailment worsened and he had three spells in a military hospital before being invalided out of the Army in June 1941.

F

4

Number of times the Don scored a hundred in both innings of a first-class match, on the first occasion when he made 131 and 133 not out for New South Wales against Queensland at Brisbane's Exhibition Ground in his side's first Sheffield Shield game of the 1928–29 season, the seventh match of his first-class career. To that point, a century in each innings had been scored on only nine previous occasions in shield cricket. Bradman achieved the feat twice more before doing it for the only time in a Test against India at the MCG in 1947–48.

Also the number of times the Don was run-out in his 295 first-class dismissals. He was an uncertain runner early in his career but developed into a good one. Of his four dismissals by run-out, three were in his first three seasons in first-class cricket.

4.73 Per Cent

Proportion of the Don's ducks to his total first-class innings: 16 in 338, a relatively high number.

5

Number of 300-run partnerships in which the Don figured in his 80 Test innings. All were against England. The best was 451 (in 316 minutes) for the second wicket with Bill Ponsford in the first innings at the Oval in 1934, a world Test record for any wicket that stood for 50 years. The other four were with Sid Barnes (405, SCG, 1946–47), Ponsford (388, Headingley, 1934), Jack Fingleton (346, MCG, 1936–37) and Arthur Morris (301, Headingley, 1948).

Also the number of Bradman's double hundreds in his 17 centuries in 52 innings in 31 Sheffield Shield games for New South Wales. He also made one triple hundred and one quadruple hundred.

Also the number of double hundreds in his 19 centuries in 44 innings in 31 Sheffield Shield games for South Australia. He also scored one triple hundred.

Also the score which the Don made most often apart from nought in his 338 first-class innings. He made a duck 16 times and scored 5 eight times. His next most common scores were 1, 2 and 13 (all seven times) and 18 (six times).

14

Number of successive Tests against England in which he batted that the Don made at least one score of 50 or more, starting with the Second Test at the SCG in 1936–37 and ending with the Second Test at Lord's in 1948.

Also the number of centuries the Don scored in his 24 Tests as captain, one fewer than his 15 in 28 Tests before becoming skipper.

15

Number of Tests the Don won as captain, 11 from 19 against England and four from five against India.

Also the number of wickets he took (at 47.46) in 41 first-class matches for New South Wales from 1927–28 to 1933–34. His best performance was 3/54.

41

Number of centuries the Don scored in 120 innings in 92 appearances in first-class cricket in England. The total included 10 double centuries and two triple centuries.

Also the number of partnerships of 200 or more in which Bradman figured in his 338 first-class innings.

Also the number of his first-class appearances for New South Wales. He had 69 innings and scored 5,813 runs at 98.53, with 21 centuries, 17 fifties and three ducks. He also took 17 catches.

42

Number of scores of 50 or more the Don made in his 80 Test innings (52.50%). Of the 42 times he reached 50, he went on score 100 or more 29 times.

42 Runs an Hour

The Don's average rate of scoring over his first-class career. For his 186 innings of 50 and over, his average was 44 runs an hour, and for his 117 centuries it was 46 runs an hour. In his 37 innings of 200 or more, he scored at the rate of 49 runs an hour.

43

Number of not-outs in the Don's 338 first-class innings.

F

44

Number of the Don's innings in 31 Sheffield Shield matches for South Australia. He made 4,293 runs at 112.97, with 19 centuries (including five double centuries and one triple century), eight fifties and two ducks. His highest score was 357 against Victoria in 1935–36, his first season with SA. **Also** the number of appearances in all first-class cricket for South Australia. He made 5,753 runs in 63 innings at 104.60, with 25 centuries, 12 fifties and three ducks. He also held 36 catches.

45

Number of the Don's fifties in his 218 innings in 142 first-class appearances in Australia. By comparison, he made 76 centuries.

Also the number of sixes he hit in his 28,067 runs in 338 innings in first-class cricket. The total included only six sixes in his 80 innings in Tests. Bradman's ratio of sixes to runs scored is low compared with other top batsmen because, even when hooking and pulling, he usually kept the ball on the ground. Most of his sixes were hit late in a big innings, or when the result of a match had been decided. By comparison, he scored 2,586 fours.

46 Runs an Hour

The Don's average rate of scoring in his 117 innings of 100 runs or more.

49

Number of fours in the Don's then world first-class record 452 not out for New South Wales in a Sheffield Shield game against Queensland in Sydney in 1929–30. It was the most fours he made in a first-class innings.

50

Number of the Don's innings in 33 Tests in Australia. He scored 4,322 runs at 98.23, with 18 centuries (including seven double centuries),10 fifties and five ducks.

50 Pounds

Amount which the Australian Board of Control withheld from the Don's final tour payment of 150 pounds after the 1930 series in England because of an alleged breach of his player's contract. A book he had written on his life, titled *Don Bradman's Book*, had been serialised in a British newspaper during the tour and the matter was reported to the board by the team manager. Bradman considered there had been no breach, firstly because the board had given the nod for Clarrie Grimmett to enter into a similar arrangement, and secondly, because the Don had made it a condition of the serialisation that the newspaper could not publish anything he had written regarding the tour until the team had returned to Australia. But the matter was beaten up by sections of the press in Australia. One paper said that "Don has done things this tour which no lesser player would have dared to attempt". The same journal reported that he signed a contract to appear in a London music hall and had to renege when the team manager found out about it and "nipped the scheme in the bud". It got to the point where the chairman of the board was moved to make it clear publicly that the only cause for disagreement between the board and the Don was the issue of the publication of the book, and that "the press statements are thoroughly unfair and unjust". But Bradman's writings were held by the board to be a breach of contract and he was docked a third of his final payment.

50.23

Average runs per wicket scored by the Don's Invincibles in their 31 first-class matches in England in 1948, as against their opponents' 19.66.

51

Number of innings (and matches, all second-class) played (in 75 days) by Arthur Mailey's team of Australians on their 1932 goodwill tour of Canada and the United States. The Don turned out in every game, scoring 3,782 runs at 102.21. His top score of 260 (to that point the highest ever in Canada) was made on a matting pitch laid over grass in the grounds of a Toronto prison. He also took 189 wickets on the tour with his leg-breaks.
Also the number of wickets (at 7.80) Bradman took as a 17-year-old in 1925–26, his first season as a regular player for Bowral in the Berrima District Competition. He also held 26 catches.

52

Number of Tests played by the Don, 33 in Australia and 19 in England. His first was the First Test against England at the Exhibition Ground, Brisbane, from November 30, 1928, when he scored 18 and 1, and his last was the Fifth Test against England at the Oval from August 14, 1948, when he made his famous duck. He was dropped only once, for the Second Test against England at the SCG in 1928–29 (when as 12th man he substituted in the field for the injured Bill Ponsford and took a catch to dismiss Maurice Tate in England's second innings). Bradman had 80 Test innings, including 10 not-outs, and scored 6,996 runs at 99.94, with 29 centuries (including 10 double centuries and two triple centuries), 13 fifties and seven ducks. He appeared in 37 Tests against England (63 innings, highest score 334, average 89.79), five against India (6, 201, 178.75), five against South Africa (5, 299 not out, 201.50), and five against the West Indies (6, 223, 74.50). Bradman never played Test cricket (or any first-class cricket except for the three hours he fielded in a first-class game against Scotland in Edinburgh in 1930 before it was washed out) anywhere other than in Australia and England. His doctors forbade him to tour South Africa in 1935–36 because they considered it would be too arduous for him even some 12 months after the peritonitis which almost killed him in England, but he did play a full (though relatively short) season of Sheffield Shield for his new state South Australia while the Australian team was in South Africa. He did not accompany the Australian side which travelled to New Zealand in March 1946 and played a first-class international in Wellington, a match which was only granted Test status by the ICC two years later.

Also the number of the Don's innings in 31 Sheffield Shield games for New South Wales. He made 4,633 runs at 107.74, with 17 centuries (including five double centuries, one triple century and one quadruple century), 12 fifties and three ducks. His highest score was his world-record 452 not out against Queensland at the SCG in 1929–30.

54

Number of the Don's first-class appearances (including Tests) in Australia against all touring teams. He batted 84 times for 6,529 runs at 82.35, with 25 centuries,

55

Number of innings the Don played in 32 first-class matches against MCC and England touring teams in Australia. He scored 3,352 runs at 67.04, with 11 centuries, including three double centuries (all three in Tests). His highest score was 270 at the MCG in the Third Test in 1936–37.

Also the number of innings the Don took to make 5,000 runs in Sheffield Shield cricket. He reached the landmark when he got to 17 during his innings of 357 for South Australia against Victoria at the MCG in January 1936. The previous quickest was Bill Ponsford's 62 innings.

Also the Don's score (not out) in his first organised game of cricket, on the football field of Bowral's Glebe Park (now Bradman Oval) in the summer of 1919–20, when he was 11. He carried his bat after coming to the crease at no. 4 and facing a hat-trick ball.

56.57

The Don's lowest average in a Test series, against England in the Bodyline Tests in Australia in 1932–33. But it was the best of the batsmen from either side in the series who played at least eight innings. And his aggregate of 396, Bradman's lowest in a Test series, was the highest of the Australians, though he played in only four of the five matches.

58.20

What the Don averaged in the 221 of his 338 first-class innings in which he did not score a century. This is higher than the lifetime averages of most other great batsmen, including Boycott, Compton, Fry, Hammond, Hobbs, (Barry and Viv) Richards, Sobers, Walcott and Weekes.

59.25

What the Don would have averaged in his Test career had he been compelled to retire at 100 in all his Test innings.

422 Minutes

The longest time it took the Don to reach 200 in a first-class innings: in his dig of 212 in the Fourth Ashes Test at Adelaide Oval in 1936–37.

452 Not Out

The Don's highest first-class score and a new world record (which was to stand for 29 years), registered when he starred for New South Wales in the second innings of a Sheffield Shield game against Queensland at the SCG on January 4 and 6, 1930. Bradman's knock also set records for most fours (49) in a shield game, and the fastest and youngest scorer of 400. The epic innings took just 415 minutes (with only two half-chances), compared with 621 minutes taken by previous record-holder Bill Ponsford for his 437 playing for Victoria, also against Queensland, at the MCG two years before. Bradman made 205 on the first day, and on the second day added 105 before lunch and 142 between lunch and tea, when his skipper Alan Kippax declared. The slowest 50 of the innings occupied just 58 minutes. When he surged past the old mark with a boundary to square leg, Queensland skipper Leo O'Connor led three cheers for the 21-year-old. Later that day, the Don received a congratulatory wire from Ponsford. Of the mammoth innings, he said in his *Don Bradman's Book*, published later that year, that he had "definitely and deliberately" set out to capture the record. "The highest individual score in first-class cricket was the one record I wanted to hold, and the opportunity came my way in this match," he wrote.

F

But 20 years later, in his *Farewell to Cricket*, he said: "It was one of those occasions when everything went right. The wicket was true and firm, the outfield in good condition and the weather warm but not unduly hot. In the early stages of the innings I had no thought of creating a record, but once my score was over the third century I felt so well that the possibility of achieving this record became obvious. Eventually, when Alan Kippax closed our innings with the New South Wales score at 8 for 761, I felt quite fit to go on." Bradman at the time was boarding with Frank Cush at Rockdale in Sydney, and Frank's son Neville can recall Bradman saying at the lunch table on the Sunday (when he was to resume on 205 on the Monday): "I'm going to break the record tomorrow." Remarkably, although 1929–30 was quite a good summer for him (early in the season completing a century and scoring a double century in one day in a Test trial match), the Don's record tally was his only hundred in 10 innings in shield cricket during the season. The bat he used to make the huge score sold for $56,000 in 1999.

458 Minutes

The time occupied by the Don's longest Test innings: his 270 in the third match of the Ashes series at the MCG in 1936–37. It was the highest score by a Test captain in Australia and the best captain's innings and highest second-innings score in an Ashes Test.

488 Minutes

The time occupied by the Don's longest innings in first-class cricket: his 340 not out for New South Wales against Victoria in a Sheffield Shield game in Sydney in 1928–29, when at 20 years 151 days he became the youngest batsman from any country to score a triple century in a first-class innings.

4,293

Number of the Don's runs in 44 innings in 31 Sheffield Shield games for South Australia at an average of 112.97. He made 19 centuries and eight fifties.

4,322

Number of runs made by the Don in 50 innings in 33 Tests in Australia at an average of 98.23. He scored 18 centuries (including seven double centuries) and 10 fifties. He was painfully close to his only Test triple century in Australia when he finished on 299 after running out his last partner, Hugh Thurlow, when attempting the vital single off the final ball of an over against the South Africans in Adelaide in 1931–32.

4,368

Number of runs made by the Don in 1930, more than any other batsman had made in a calendar year before. Wally Hammond broke the record in 1933 with 4,445 runs, but needed 69 innings to do it, against Bradman's 52. Denis Compton improved on Hammond's total in 1947 with 4,962 (also in 69 innings), but Bradman's mark remains a record for an Australian.

4,633

The Don's aggregate in 52 innings in 31 Sheffield Shield appearances for New South Wales. His average was 107.74 and he scored 17 centuries and 12 fifties.

5,000

Number of autographed sheets signed by the Don and his team on their way to the Old Country in 1948. They were all gone within a week of setting foot on English soil.

5,028

Number of runs the Don made against England in 63 innings in 37 Tests at an average of 89.79. He racked up 19 hundreds (including six double centuries and two triple centuries) and 12 fifties, and his highest score was his world-record 334 at Headingley in 1930. Of his 56 dismissals in Ashes Tests, Bradman made six ducks, the first when he was bowled first ball by Bill Bowes in the first innings of the Second Bodyline Test at the MCG.

5,753

The Don's aggregate in 63 innings in 44 first-class matches for South Australia. He averaged 104.60 and scored 25 centuries and 12 fifties.

5,813

The Don's aggregate in his 69 innings in 41 first-class games for New South Wales at an average of 98.53. He made 21 centuries and 17 fifties.

15,120

Number of runs scored by the Don's Invincibles in their 31 first-class matches in England in 1948. Their opponents made 10,932.

$46,000

What a bat used by the Don in the 1936–37 Ashes series sold for in London in 1996. A spokesman for Charles Leski Auctions said in February 2001 that the same bat by then could have brought as much as $100,000.

F

$56,000

What the bat used by the Don to score his then world-record 452 not out at the SCG in January 1930 brought in 1999.

$425,000

Price paid in June 2003 for the baggy green cap which Bradman wore on his last tour of England in 1948. It was the most paid for any baggy green. The deal was done before the cap was offered at auction by Ludgrove's International in Melbourne. The vendor was the Don's English godson, Richard Robins, who was given the cap by Bradman in 1956, and the buyer was Tim Serisier, a New South Welshman who had won $250,000 on a TV quiz show a few weeks before. News Limited had mounted a public campaign in the run-up to the auction to bring the baggy green home, but Cricket Australia chairman Bob Merriman said at the time that he was pleased with the outcome, because the new owner had indicated he would put the cap on public display in Australia. It was shown during matches at cricket grounds in Australia during the summer of 2003–04 and will be on loan to the new MCG Museum from early 2006. Before its sale, the baggy had been on display for three years at the Bradman Museum.

Fahey, (The Hon.) John Joseph Anthony AC

Former premier of New South Wales and federal finance minister who was appointed to the board of the Bradman Foundation in November 2001 and elected chairman at the AGM in December 2003. As NSW minister for Industrial Relations and Employment and the member for Southern Highlands, John opened the Bradman Pavilion, the first stage of the Bradman Museum Project, in 1989. John Fahey said recently that he sees the Bradman Museum as "a national focal point that educates, informs and celebrates the excellence that Bradman personifies, the very best of sporting endeavour and the life values contained in cricket". As NSW premier and chairman of Sydney's bid to host the 2000 Olympics, John's gazelle-like leap into the air on the announcement of Sydney's win in Monte Carlo in 1993 was seen on live television by many millions around the world.

Fairfax, Alan George

All-rounder and brilliant gully fieldsman from New South Wales who shared in a record fifth-wicket stand of 183 with the Don in the Fifth Ashes Test at the MCG in 1928–29. Fairfax toured England in 1930 with

Bradman and returned to the Old Dart two years later to end his career as a professional in the Lancashire League. He wanted it known that Bradman was only one of a team: "The boys in the Australian team feel they are not getting a fair break from the crowd. Bradman, Bradman, all is Bradman. Well, the boys know he is a cricket genius, but that does not mean that the other players should be left right in the void." A serious injury during World War II led to Fairfax's early death in 1955 in London at the age of 48.

"Fancy Doing That"

What the Don said when he returned to the pavilion after being bowled by Eric Hollies second ball for a duck at the Oval in 1948 in Bradman's final Test.

"Farewell My Love"

Haunting melody played by a lone piper at the Don's memorial service at Bradman Oval, Bowral, on March 28, 2001.

Farewell to Bradman: A Final Tribute

Book edited by Peter Allen and published by Pan Macmillan Australia. Produced by Allen & Kemsley Publishing in association with the Bradman Museum. The official Bradman Museum commemorative deluxe edition was released in November 2001 at $2,000. A trade edition, distributed by Pan Macmillan, was released in the same month at $55. The book's 272 pages, 60 of them in colour, summarise the Don's life and achievements, both as a cricketer and as an administrator. It includes world reaction to his passing and contains the full record of both the Adelaide and Bowral memorial services.

Farewell to Cricket

Of the Don's autobiography, first published in hardback in 1950 by Hodder & Stoughton, HS Altham wrote in the *Spectator*: "It is a remarkable book, and by virtue of its range, penetration and authority must rank as one of the classics of the game." Ian Peebles, whose boseys bamboozled Bradman in the Manchester Test in 1930, wrote in the *Sunday Times*: "One of the most comprehensive and absorbing books yet published on an extremely well documented subject." According to a claim on the 1988 hardback edition published by Pavilion Books in London, the book "is probably the most thoughtful and comprehensive cricketing memoir ever published". But in an article on Bradman in Melbourne's *Age* newspaper in 1998, Les Carlyon

F

wrote: "One criticism of his autobiography *Farewell to Cricket* is that he had a logical explanation for everything he did; a hard-headed clerk of facts, fussy and uncompromising, still a loner who works things out his own way." The Don's work is a detailed chronological account of events in his life and his cricket, but he also offers assessments of many other players and discusses all aspects of the game. The book also carries a run-down of his career statistics. In 1994, Sydney publisher Editions Tom Thompson (ETT) brought out a new edition as an Imprint paperback and (as ETT Imprint) reprinted it three years later in a larger C format. The 1994 edition contains no new material by Bradman but substantial corrections were made to the 1950 Hodder text. A large-print (16pt) version was published by Melbourne's Bolinda Press in 1996.

Fearnley, Allan
Artist who painted Bradman playing a stroke in two studies, one known as the Sydney version and the other as the Melbourne version.

Fenton, Peter
Poet who recited one of his works, "Bradman at the Test", at the memorial service at Bradman Oval on March 28, 2001.

Ferguson, William Harold BEM
Legendary New Zealand-born scorer and baggage man who travelled the world with touring sides for 50 years, starting with the Australians who toured England in 1905. During his career he was attached to 14 Australian teams but also did duty for sides from England, South Africa, New Zealand, the West Indies and India. In all, Bill travelled with 41 touring parties, witnessed 204 Test matches, scored in 1207 tour matches and travelled almost a million kilometres. He used a scorebook of his own design which contained at least twice as much information as any other in the world. At the end of each day's play he copied all the important figures into a more orthodox book which was kept as the official record of the tour. Fergie jealously kept the secrets contained in his own book and resisted attempts by managers, skippers and players to commandeer it. He invented the batting chart – now seen routinely on television – which plots the batsman's innings shot-by-shot in a circle. He began drawing charts before World War I to demonstrate the scoring shots of various batsmen to "amuse myself". During the Invincibles tour of 1948, Bill was asked by King George VI: "Tell me, Mr Ferguson, do you use an adding machine when the Don comes in to bat?" Bradman once said of Bill: "There will never be another to com-

pare with him." A few years earlier, Fergie wrote of the Don: "In the summer of 1930 a cricketing machine by the name of Donald Bradman played havoc around the County grounds of England, pulverising the finest bowlers in the land, shattering records left, right and centre and making a tour debut the like of which will surely never be seen again." In a chapter of his life story, *Mr Cricket – An Autobiography of Fergie*, Bill assessed the Test captains he travelled with throughout his career. Of Bradman, he wrote: "Perhaps the most successful captain of all time, yet it is surprising how many people imagine that Don, as a man, did not enjoy the confidence, or the affection, of those who served under him. This legend of Bradman's unpopularity is quite unearned, and having seen every Test match in which he played I can say that not once did I hear him have an altercation with anyone." Bill Ferguson was awarded his British Empire Medal in 1952 and died at his home in Bath, Avon, in 1957, aged 77.

Fibrositis

A debilitating muscular complaint which troubled Bradman on and off over the first few years of his career, but a serious bout occasioned his discharge from the Army in June 1941. He had three spells in a military hospital before a medical board pronounced him unfit for further service. The Don returned to wife Jessie's parents' property at Mittagong to try to regain his health, as he had in 1935, but at one point he could not raise his right arm, and he even lost – permanently – all feeling in the thumb and index finger of his right hand. He and Jessie returned to Adelaide in 1942 and by the end of 1945 his condition had improved sufficiently for him to play two matches: one for South Australia in Adelaide and a Patriotic match in Melbourne. When the fibrositis returned with a vengeance three months later, a visit to a Melbourne masseur, Ernie Saunders, on the recommendation of a fellow selector, brought great relief.

Fielding

At which the Don was superbly skilled. He was inspired by Australian Johnny Taylor's fielding in the Fifth Ashes Test at the SCG in February 1921 which he saw as a 12-year-old, and later regarded fielding on the boundary as "one of the great joys of cricket". In an introduction to *Don Bradman's Book*, written by Bradman in 1930, Englishman Pelham ("Plum") Warner wrote: "So much for his batting – but he was also a long field of the very highest class, quick to start, a fast runner, and the possessor of a return as swift as an arrow from a bow, and full pitch into the wicket-keeper's hands. Australia have had many fine deep fields, but never a finer – judging him on his form here – and those who were at the Test Match at Headingley will never forget the manner in which he threw down Hobb's [sic] wicket, at Oldfield's end, from deep mid-off. Never have I see [sic] anyone move forward faster to a ball, pick it up more quickly, or throw it harder."

In his 1959 book *Bradman the Great*, BJ Wakley wrote of the Don's fielding: "At the start of his career, Bradman normally fielded in the deep, where he established a reputation as high as for his batting; he was in the great tradition of Australian outfielders, very fast and very sure, and with a long, low and accurate throw. Later on, when his duties as captain required his presence nearer the wicket, he normally fielded as mid-off or extra cover, and again was very good indeed in these positions, though after the war, naturally, a good deal slower, and didn't throw himself about as much as in his younger days. Perhaps his abilities as a catcher were not quite on the same plane as his ground fielding and throwing; though possessing a safe pair of hands by normal standards, he did sometimes miss a possible chance. For instance, he dropped some eight possible catches in his 37 Tests against England, including three in 1928–9, his first Test series; as well as two v South Africa in 1931–2. However, in the course of his career as a fieldsman, he took 127 catches altogether (87 in Australia and 40 in England); in addition he held one catch when fielding as a substitute and stumped one and caught four in the two matches in which he kept wicket. In Test matches he caught 32 catches (plus one when substitute); 20 v England, four v West Indies, two v South Africa and six v India."

In his 1975 book *On Top Down Under*, Ray Robinson wrote of the Don: "For rapid interceptions and high-velocity throwing he was in the first flight of outfielders and mid-offs up to the second world war. His catching did not have the same confidence. Playing in 52 Tests, plus one as twelfth man, he held 33 catches, three-quarters of the chances he reached."

"Final Salute, The"

Title of the life-size bronze statue of Sir Donald in the courtyard of the Bradman Museum. Newcastle, New South Wales, sculptor Tanya Bartlett was asked to base the figure on the photo of the Don acknowledging the applause of the crowd on reaching 200 during his classic innings of 254 in the Second Test at Lord's in 1930. Bradman was not wearing a sweater but the sculptor added one to give the work more texture. And she made him older than his 21 years to add character to the face. The statue was unveiled by Bradman teammate Bill Brown and then Bradman Museum chairman Ian Craig on February 24, 2002 to mark the first anniversary of Sir

Donald's passing. Replica statues in two sizes – 11.5cm and 40cm – are available from the museum.

Fine Leg

Where the Don was caught by Len Hutton off Alec Bedser in three consecutive innings in the first two Tests in England in 1948. On the second night of the First Test at Trent Bridge in 1948, when the Don was not out on 130, Bill O'Reilly, who was travelling with the Australian team as a journalist, advised Alec Bedser (who had been attacking leg stump) to move his fieldsman back from leg slip to fine leg, in position for the leg glance. In Bedser's second over the next day, Bradman obliged by leg-glancing and was caught at fine leg by Len Hutton. And the Don was dismissed exactly the same way – caught by Hutton at fine leg off Bedser – in the second innings of this Test for a duck, and also in the the first innings of the next Test at Lord's for 38. He was out the same way later in the tour when caught by Denis Compton off Whitcombe in a match against Middlesex, again at Lord's. When, during the Don's radio interview with Norman May in 1987, the ABC replayed comments from Bedser in which he spoke about his leg trap and mentioned the help he got from O'Reilly, the Don said it was the first he knew of "Tiger's" part in his downfall.

Fingleton, John Henry Webb OBE

The son of a politician in the New South Wales Parliament and son-in-law of the state's chief justice, Fingleton was a sound right-handed opener who found it difficult to secure a permanent place in the Australian side in the early 1930s up against the pair of Woodfull and Ponsford. He played all the Tests in South Africa in 1935–36 (Woodfull and Ponsford having retired), notching up consecutive centuries in the last three innings of the rubber before posting another ton in the first innings of his next Test, the first match of the 1936–37 Ashes series at home. He had performed respectably against the barrage of bumpers in the first two Bodyline Tests – when he was hit repeatedly on the body – with scores of 26, 40, 83 and 1, but was dropped after making a pair in the third. His omission from the side which went to England in 1934 disappointed him greatly and he held the Don largely responsible because Bradman was a supporter of Bill Brown and had openly expressed the view before the side was selected that Brown would be a better batsman in England than Fingleton. The Don was not a selector but it is likely his opinion carried some weight, and he said in *Bradman: The Don Declares*, the radio interview with the ABC in 1987, that this was one of the reasons for Fingleton's dislike of him. Brown said

F

recently that he heard nothing at the time about getting the nod from Bradman over Fingleton, but he had a successful tour in 1934, and when both he and Fingleton toured in 1938, Bill's Test average was vastly superior to Fingleton's.

Jack was a great admirer of Bradman the cricketer (and indeed the chapter on the Don as a batsman in his 1946 book *Cricket Crisis* is generally considered the classic portrait), but he was not a fan of Don Bradman the man. He was far from impressed by the champion batsman's lack of generosity in England 1930 when he received a cheque for 1,000 pounds from Australian-born soap magnate Arthur Whitelaw soon after his record 334 at Leeds. Fingleton was not on that tour but he observed later how the Don did not share the proceeds with his teammates, or even as much as shout them a drink. Fingleton was notably critical of Bradman's ploy against bodyline of stepping away to the leg side and playing to the near-vacant off-side. He wrote that in employing this tactic – adopted, Fingleton alleged, solely to avoid being struck – Bradman was acting against the interests of the Australian team, a claim against which the Don made an impassioned argument in his autobiography, *Farewell to Cricket*.

When the famous words spoken by Australian captain Bill Woodfull to MCC manager Plum Warner during the explosive Adelaide Test appeared in the Australian press, a furious Warner blamed Fingleton, a full-time journalist who was playing in the match, for the leak. Thirteen years later in *Cricket Crisis*, Fingleton alleged that the culprit was another member of the team but did not name him. In his 1978 book *The Immortal Victor Trumper*, he identified the leaker as the Don, claiming that he had been told by a Sydney *Sun* reporter, Claude Corbett, a colleague of Fingleton's, that Bradman had given Corbett the scoop on the night of the incident, January 14, 1933, at a secret meeting in Adelaide's North Terrace. (Bradman was himself contracted to the *Sun* but was not permitted by the Board of Control to write for the paper during the Test series because he was not a full-time journalist.) Fingleton wrote that he had long been dirty on Bradman for not clearing him by owning up. He repeated the charge in his last book, *Batting From Memory*, in 1981.

In a quote in a biography of Bradman by Michael Page (published in 1983, two years after Fingleton's death), the Don called Fingleton's claim "a lie", and again rejected the allegation in his interview with the ABC a few years later, asserting that Fingleton in fact was the leaker and he had "concocted the fictitious story" of the clandestine meeting between the Don and Corbett as a "smokescreen for himself". And he pointed out that Fingleton had only gone public with the claim after Corbett had died. Just over a year before his death, Fingleton told English journalist Ian Wooldridge: "He is still a great hero but in many ways he was a little, churlish man." And a few months later he wrote of the Don in a letter to Harold Evans, editor of London's *Sunday Times*: "No-one doubted his ability but playing under him was different to chaps like Woodfull or [Victor] Richardson. One sensed [they were] playing for Australia; with Bradman it seemed like for his own personal glory. This, perhaps, was not altogether his fault but that is how the players felt."

Although he was in no doubt about the Don's ability with the willow (describing him as the "genius absolute"), Fingleton did qualify his praise by writing that it applied only to his batting on a good wicket. In *Cricket Crisis*, he wrote that when Bradman was confronted by a wet wicket, the Don's "features [were] indistinguishable in the ranks of wet-wicket mediocrities". Fingleton added: "Bradman's repeated failures on wet wickets must remain the mystery of his career. I saw him bat on innumerable occasions on damaged wickets, but only once did I see him succeed."

Fingleton travelled to England as a journalist with the Don's team on the *Strathaird* in 1948. He and Bill O'Reilly were in the press box when the Australian captain walked out to bat to a great reception and then three cheers from the England side around the wicket at the Oval in his last Test. Fifty years later, English journalist Jim Swanton told Bradman's 1996 biographer, Charles Williams, that when the Don was bowled second ball, "I thought they [Fingleton and O'Reilly] were going to have a stroke – they were laughing so much." O'Reilly later admitted to friends that he had laughed, but only at the incongruity of the occasion. In a letter to Williams in 1995, Bradman wrote: "O'Reilly nakedly exposes the disloyalty I had to endure during my early years as Australian captain, a disloyalty based on jealousy and religion. Fingleton was the ringleader. He conducted a vendetta against me all my life." But although the Don, a Protestant, may have believed Fingleton's and O'Reilly's animosity towards him was rooted in the sectarian rift in cricket (and in society) between Protestants and Catholics, neither of the two Catholics ever admitted it.

In 1949, Fingleton published a book about the Invincibles tour, *Brightly Fades the Don*. In it, he wrote: "Much has been said and written of the 'jealousy' of those who played with and against Bradman, but those best qualified to speak are those who played with him; and I have never met a single first-class cricketer of Bradman's age who was not ever ready, indeed eager, to declare that the game of cricket had never known his like before. He had his critics, and will always have, I suppose, for his somewhat indifferent, cold and unfriendly attitude towards most of those with whom he played, but not one, I repeat, has ever denied the greatness which rightly belongs to Bradman. On good pitches, he stood in a class of his own as a scoring machine; and, moreover, the game has never known one to approach, yes, even approach, his miraculous consistency. When you boiled Bradman down, when you analysed his eyesight, his footwork, his judgement, his range of strokes, there was still something left in which he was also superior to all others, and that was consistency."

Fingleton was press secretary to prime ministers Billy Hughes and Ben Chifley and later worked in the press gallery in Canberra. He helped his old foe Harold Larwood to immigrate to Australia in 1950. In 1993 the State Library of New South Wales acquired 30 boxes of Fingleton's correspondence, scrapbooks, notebooks and photographs.

Fingleton, (Dr) James Street

Jim Fingleton, the eldest of three sons of former Australian Test cricketer and journalist Jack Fingleton, is a lawyer who works exclusively for (mainly UN) aid agencies in developing countries. Jim advises governments on policy and legislative reforms (mainly in agriculture and natural resources laws) in Asia, Africa and the South Pacific. He also farms beef cattle on the north coast of NSW. In March 2003, when the *Australian* newspaper published the contents of letters written by the Don to good friend Rohan Rivett which were very critical of Jack, Jim wrote to the paper defending his father. He described Bradman's claim to Rivett that Jack spent "virtually a lifetime of using me as a meal ticket" as "ridiculous", and added: "As for being jealous ... my father was an entertainer and a popular member of the team. Perhaps Bradman envied my father's popularity." He concluded: "One matter my father did not forgive Bradman for was that he allowed my father (the only journalist at the time in the Australian team) to take the blame for leaking the famous 'dressing-room incident' to the press during the Bodyline series. This slur, Jack believed, cost him his place in the subsequent tour to England. Much later it was established that Bradman himself had been the author of the leak – reason enough, one might think, for his attempt to undermine my father's reputation for veracity."

FJ Palmer & Son Ltd

Clothing retailer which was one of three Australian companies that made the Don a joint offer of a contract for two years to keep him in Australia when the Accrington club in Lancashire tried to lure him to England with the offer of a professional cricket contract in August 1931. Part of the arrangement with the men's outfitters was for the Don to conduct coaching clinics under the banner of Palmers Cricket Coaching Club.

Fleetwood-Smith, Leslie O'Brien ("Chuck")

A left-arm spinner from Victoria who often made birdcalls on the field, Fleetwood-Smith twice dismissed nine batsmen in an innings for his state. He spun the ball viciously but was often astray with his line and length. He was severely punished (along with the rest of the Victorian attack) by the Don on his way to 238 in a Sheffield Shield game at the SCG at the start of the 1932–33 season, the day after a leading critic had written that Bradman did not possess the spectacular flair of a Trumper or a Macartney. Chuck was even more notably humiliated by the Don in another shield game at the SCG before a record crowd at the end of the next season, when Bradman hit him for three sixes in an over towards the end of his innings of 128, in all notching up four sixes and 17 fours. When the Don tried to give his wicket away (to Fleetwood-Smith) by skying a ball in the deep, he was dropped, so he had to repeat the dose, this time the catch being held by Len Darling. (Bradman told Jack Egan in a 1990 television interview: "That evening we put things all right because my wife and I invited Fleetwood out to our home for dinner. We had a pleasant meal together.")

Fleetwood-Smith did not gain a Test place when he toured England with the Don in 1934, but played three of the five Tests with Victor Richardson's side in South Africa in 1935–36 and was a spin partner of Bill O'Reilly's in all four Tests with Bradman's side in the Old Dart in 1938, when he notably bowled 87 overs and took 1/298 in the gruelling Fifth Test at the Oval. In domestic cricket, he held a sizzling catch off Frank Thorn to dismiss the Don in a shield game in 1938–39 to deny Bradman a world-record seven consecutive first-class hundreds.

Fleetwood-Smith was one of four Australian Test players, all Irish Catholics, summoned before the Board of Control in a famous incident during the 1936–37 Ashes series at home. Gubby Allen's side had performed moderately in the lead-up games against the states, and after they won the first two Tests (when the Don's Australians were caught on sticky wickets) a newspaper report just before Christmas alleged that some Australian players were not supporting the Don (a Protestant) as captain. Although this was denied by both the players and Bradman, a section of the cricketing public thought the burden of captaincy (his first in a Test series) was undermining the Don's batting (in the first two matches he made 38, 0, 0 and 82). Some of the Australian players believed the job of skipper should have gone to Victor Richardson, the popular leader of the side which put the cleaners through the South Africans in South Africa the previous season, but the difficulty was that the selectors did not consider Richardson's form to be good enough for him to be included in the XI.

When, after the Third Test in Melbourne (won by Australia), Fleetwood-Smith and the other three players, Bill O'Reilly, Stan McCabe and Leo O'Brien, were called before a committee of the board, the proceedings were never made public but the Don believed the quartet were disciplined over their alleged disloyalty to him. Bradman said he had not complained to the board and that he knew nothing of the hearing until it was reported in the press. He complained bitterly to a couple of board members, saying they had placed him in "the most embarrassing and invidious position" by carpeting the four players. He was told that he was kept in the dark because they wanted him to be "completely innocent and at arm's length", but the Don was convinced that under the circumstances the four players would believe that he was responsible.

In his interview with ABC radio in 1987, the Don said it was "a very unfortunate happening, I don't think it was justified, and I was very sad that it happened". But Bradman believed that in the long run the incident actually improved the relationship between the players and himself when they recognised that he had been placed in a very embarrassing position and that it wasn't his fault. The last years of Fleetwood-Smith's life were much tarnished, an alcoholic vagrant living out his post-war years in degradation on the banks of Melbourne's Yarra River, so near the MCG where he had thrilled the crowds through the 1930s. He spent time in Pentridge Gaol in 1969 for stealing a woman's handbag. Chuck Fleetwood-Smith died in 1971 at the age of 62.

Florance, Hugh and Dorothy

Couple who occupied the Bradman house at Yeo Yeo, near Cootamundra, for 10 years during and after World War II. The Don lived in the house until he was two years and nine months old before the family moved to Bowral in 1911. The Florances named the cottage "Andaluka", after an Aboriginal girl they knew. During their time there, they renovated the homestead and oiled the hardwood slabs of the outer walls, actions which were to aid the dismantling and re-erection in Temora many years later. The Florances and subsequent owners were consulted by the Temora Rural Museum to establish details of the original construction before renovations were carried out. Hugh Florance's father was a doctor who was practising in Cootamundra at the time of the Don's birth there in 1908.

Flying Doctor, The

Australian motion picture released in 1936 in which the Don made a much-publicised cameo appearance. The title character, played by James Raglan, is a cricketer who takes Bradman's wicket in a match at the SCG in a scene which features footage of the Sheffield Shield game in 1933–34 in which the Don famously took the long handle to Chuck Fleetwood-Smith. When he is dismissed, Bradman makes a gesture of acknowledgement to the hero before turning and walking off to the pavilion.

Folkestone

English town in Kent near Dover where the Don plundered 30 (three sixes and three fours) off one six-ball over from leg-spinner Alfred "Tich" Freeman on his way to 149 not out (in 105 minutes) in a game against an England XI near the end of the 1934 tour. Bradman survived a chance when only 1 before going on to record his 50th century in first-class cricket. At 26 years eight days, he was the youngest man to do so. His world-record 30 in a six-ball over was equalled by South African batsman-wicketkeeper Jock Cameron the next year in a tour match against Yorkshire at Bramall Lane, Sheffield.

Frankston

Now a Melbourne suburb, Frankston was a coastal resort when Lieutenant Bradman served as a physical training supervisor there at the Army's School of Physical and Recreational Training during the war in 1940–41. He had joined the RAAF in June 1940 as an observer but was transferred to the Army because service chiefs considered they could make better use of his profile and standing in the community as a supervisor in the field of physical training. But the Don suffered from severe muscle spasms associated with fibrositis and, after three spells in a military hospital, was discharged from the Army on medical grounds in June 1941.

Fraser, Harold Edwin

Wicketkeeper and teammate of the Don's at the St George club in Sydney who hosted a 21st birthday party for the star batsman at Fraser's house, "Palmyra", in Sans Souci on August 27, 1929. Fraser was born in Sydney in 1893, learned to play the piano as a child and attended Sydney University. He joined the Army in April 1915 and fought at Gallipoli before being evacuated in December of that year. Harold was later posted to Europe and transferred to the RAAF. He studied aeronautical engineering at Oxford University and also found time to play cricket for the uni-

F

versity. On returning to Australia, Fraser formed Australia's first professional jazz band, "the Syncopas". The group's Dixieland music proved so popular at Sydney's Wentworth Hotel that the hotel built a new ballroom to accommodate the patrons. The band soon after moved to a pavilion in Clifton Gardens and played there for two years.

But despite his musical success, Harold still had the flying bug, and rejoined the RAAF in 1924. Three years later, Squadron-Leader Fraser led the formation of Wapiti aircraft in the fly-past at the opening of Parliament House, Canberra. In 1938 he joined the Department of Civil Aviation at Mascot Airport as a traffic controller and in 1948 was appointed airport manager. He retired in 1958. Harold joined the St George District Cricket Club in 1924–25 and had six seasons with Bradman at the club from 1926–27 to 1931–32. In 1935 Fraser formed the St George Veterans Cricket Club. A sports oval at Blakehurst was opened and named Harold Fraser Oval on August 25, 1979. It is now known as Harold Fraser Reserve.

"Fred"

Alias used by the Don as a cover in the late 1960s when he dined regularly at an Italian restaurant in Adelaide with wife Jessie and friends Jill and Rob Gauvin. He got away with it until the restaurateur twigged one night when the Don asked him if he knew the cricket score.

Freemasonry

In November 2001, the *Weekend Australian Magazine* alleged in an article that the Don's takeover of his employer Harry Hodgetts's stockbroking business in 1945 after Hodgetts's bankruptcy was facilitated partly by Bradman's Freemasonry connections. The writer of the article, David Nason, observed that the Don was a Freemason, and the head of the exchange, Andrew Young, was grand master of the South Australian Grand Lodge of Freemasons. But in fact in 1945 the Don had not been a member of the order for over 10 years. When the subject of Freemasonry came up during a taped conversation with journalist Frank Devine in 1995, Bradman said that after enrolling as a Mason in Sydney (in Lodge Tarbolton) in November 1929, he had attended only one meeting and resigned before moving to Adelaide in 1935.

Freesia

A favourite flower of Jessie Bradman's. There were fresh freesias in the Bradman home in Adelaide when Jessie died on September 14, 1997.

Frew, Wendy Margaret

Financial journalist who wrote a 10,000-word research dissertation on the Don and Australia's identity for a Master of Arts in History degree at the University of Sydney in 2001. The study explores the use of Bradman by some sections of the community – the media and politicians in particular – as an example of Australia's national character. Working on the premise that Australians have long strived to create a national identity, Wendy identifies the characteristics attributed to the Don that were deemed to be "quintessentially Australian". She argues that there is more than one idea about what constitutes the essence of this country called Australia, and asks why Bradman was chosen to represent the nation. The writer sets out to examine how the Don acquired his almost mythical status and how he was used to symbolise a certain idea of Australia. She also examines how the Bradman myth functioned at a particular time in Australian history when there was a continuing debate about the nation's "real history", divisions between the indigenous and non-indigenous communities, and fresh debate about refugees and immigration.

Wendy asserts that the Bradman myth is merely the latest manifestation of the "Australian quest for identity". As historians have pointed out, this search has become a national obsession. The fact that the Don (the myth and the man) represented qualities that were almost the antithesis of those attributed to other national characters such as bushranger Ned Kelly, or the Digger and the Larrikin, points not to his unsuitability as a mythical character but to the inherent instability of Australia's national identity project, which is constantly "fractured, questioned and redefined" by economic, political and social forces. The Bradman myth is also as much about nostalgia for a lost Australia as it is about how Australia is defined today. If we are to talk about myths, Wendy argues, then we must also talk about myth makers. As it was with the so-called Australian bohemian writers of the 1890s, who claimed that the bushman and mateship were central to Australian identity, it was the media who were primarily responsible for creating the Bradman myth.

Friends of the Bradman Museum

Organisation established to bring together cricket enthusiasts who want to be actively involved in the museum and its programs. Funds raised go towards acquiring objects for the museum collection, special events such as international matches, and running the various Friends activities. There are several levels of membership with yearly subscriptions starting at $50 a year. Benefits include a quarterly magazine, *Boundary*, and the right to attend the

F

museum's two formal functions: the Annual Dinner in April and the Bradman Birthday Lunch held each year on Sir Donald's birthday, August 27. Friends are also eligible to attend events such as exhibition openings and guest speakers and enjoy priority seating on match days plus discounts on entry to the museum and on products in the museum shop. They even have an opportunity to play on Bradman Oval with the Friends team.

Frith, David

Resident in both England and Australia, British-born author of 26 cricket books and the founding editor of *Wisden Cricket Monthly* who contributed a foreword to the 1988 Pavilion Books edition of the Don's autobiography, *Farewell to Cricket*. In his piece, David recounts how late one night in Adelaide he almost perished with Bradman when they were nearly hit by a speeding car at an intersection when the Don was driving him back to his hotel. Frith recently suggested that the headline next day might have read "CRICKET WRITER KILLED IN CAR CRASH: Old Cricketer Also Perishes".

In an interview with Margaret Geddes for her 2002 book *Remembering Bradman* Frith told Margaret: "Of course he had plenty of enemies but suggestions have been made that he didn't have many friends. He had friends in a social setting but I think he was very hard to live with on the cricket field. He was so good he was self-enclosed. But as far as I know, there were quite a range of friends, from Archie Jackson through to Ben Barnett, Ron Hamence and Charlie Walker … They were probably the sort of gentle friends that he wanted around him. They knew what to say and when to say it, and they were good fun to be with, and they were nice men. But if there was any suggestion of combat – verbal combat – I think away from the necessities of life, he didn't want any more of that than he had to put up with."

David's cherished friendship of 30 years with Bradman left him with a legacy of 119 letters from the Don, "many of them fairly intimate and revealing". David Frith's collection of cricket memorabilia, possibly the finest in private hands in the world, includes many Bradman items, the first of which was a pair of batting gloves handed to Frith by the man himself at the Lord's Taverners function at London's Hilton Hotel in 1974. Frith says he is regarded as Australian in England and English in Australia. Though he has no letters after his name, David's bride has conferred on him the title of "Professor of Cricket". The professor featured prominently in the ABC television documentary *Bradman: Reflections on the Legend*, first shown in September 2004.

"Frogmore"

Home of Queen Mary, the Queen Mother, just south of Windsor Castle, where Mary posed for a team photo with the Don's Invincibles on June 27, 1948.

Fry, C(harles) B(urgess)

Charismatic England Test player (and long-jump world record-holder, soccer international, author, scholar and parliamentarian!) around the turn of the 19th century whose record of six consecutive first-class hundreds, set in county cricket in 1901, was equalled by the Don in Australia in 1938–39. The feat has since been matched by South Africa's Mike Procter (1970–71). When a critic once said Fry had only one stroke, he replied: "True, but I can send it in twenty-two places." Of Bradman, Fry once said: "Don Bradman is a monopoly. Drama is afield the moment this jaunty dignity and purposeful poise emerge from the pavilion." But he described the shot played by the Don when he was bowled by Hedley Verity for 82 in the Second Test of the 1936–37 Ashes series at the SCG as "the worst stroke in the history of cricket". Fry made a speech greeting Bradman and his men at a luncheon of the Royal Empire Society in London in 1948. He was 84 when he died in 1956.

G

'Gabba, The (Woolloongabba)

The facility which replaced the Exhibition Ground as Brisbane's first-class venue in 1931–32 was to become famous as the site of cricket's historic first tied Test, between Australia and the West Indies in 1960–61. The Don played seven innings in five Tests here: three against England (1932–33, 1936–37, 1946–47) and one each against South Africa (1931–32) and India (1947–48). He compiled 736 runs with three centuries (including one double hundred) and one fifty. He also took four catches. His highest score was 226 against South Africa. His average at the 'Gabba of 105.14 was his third-best of the five Australian grounds on which he played Test cricket, after the MCG and Adelaide Oval. It was here that Bradman first captained Australia in a Test – against the Old Enemy in 1936–37. And the 'Gabba was the scene of a controversial incident in the corresponding match 10 years later when the Don was resuming Test cricket after a wartime of ill-health. After he had taken 75 minutes to reach 28, he appeared to give a catch when he edged a ball from Bill Voce to Jack Ikin at second slip, but Australian umpire George Borwick adjudged it a bump ball. Critics were divided about the decision, but even some Australians thought it was out, and the England camp were not happy, particularly when Bradman went on to make 187 to set up an easy victory.

It was on a green-top wicket in a Sheffield Shield game at the 'Gabba 15 years earlier that Aboriginal paceman Eddie Gilbert dismissed the Don for a duck during a sensational spell of hostile pace bowling. One delivery knocked the bat out of Bradman's hand, and he wrote later that Gilbert's bowling during a short burst when he claimed 3/12 was "the fastest 'bowling' I can remember". (The quotation marks around bowling are the Don's, because he thought Gilbert's action was suspect, a view shared by many in the cricket fraternity, but subsequent slow-motion film of the speedster from several angles was inconclusive.) In 16 first-class innings at the 'Gabba, Bradman made 1,593 runs at 99.56 with eight centuries (including two double centuries) and two fifties. He also took nine catches. His highest Test score at the ground of 226 was also his best first-class score. Of the 'Gabba, the Don wrote in 1950 in his *Farewell to Cricket*: "At the moment it possesses a pitch of even height and pace which batsmen would probably say is the best in Australia. It is always a credit to the curator."

Galle

Where players and officials in a Test between Sri Lanka and England paid a silent tribute to the Don before the start of play on the day after his death was announced on February 26, 2001.

Gauvin, Jillian Claire

Former staff member of the State Library of South Australia who developed a close friendship with the Don and Jessie through working with him on the scrapbooks he presented to the library in 1967 which were to form the centrepiece of the "Bradman Collection". Speaking at the Don's memorial service in Adelaide, Jill said that John Bradman had asked her to talk about his father as a fun-loving and caring friend. She said that "he taught me how to play contract bridge, he taught me how to play golf, he taught me how to appreciate wine, he taught me about humility, and he taught me about unconditional love and loyalty to friends". Jill told of the time when the Don and Jessie joined her and husband Rob at a favourite Italian restaurant of theirs. The Don wanted to remain anonymous, so it was agreed he would be introduced as "Fred". This became the established routine for two or three years whenever the four dined at the restaurant until one night the restaurateur twigged when the Don asked him if he knew the cricket score.

Gavaskar, Sunil Manohar

Indian opening batsman who was the first player to equal then surpass Don's 29 centuries in Test cricket. He made his 30th Test ton on December 28, 1983. Gavaskar retired with 34 Test hundreds in 214 innings, 134 more than Bradman. When he passed the Don's record Test aggregate of 6,996 during an innings of 83 at Lahore in 1982–83, Bradman commented: "… He is a wonderful batsman, a player of rare gifts. But I would point out that while my runs were made in 52 Tests, Sunil's runs were made in a greater number of Tests." When Roland Perry's book *Bradman's Best* was published in 2001, Sunny Gavaskar told the *Hindustan Times*: "I refuse to believe the Bradman Dream XI was actually Sir Don's personal selection for the world's greatest-ever combination. Sir Don was a man who steered away from all controversies in his lifetime. Even when he was the target of bodyline tactics in 1932–33 he never uttered a word. I am sure that he would not have stuck out his neck for something like this which is bound to give rise to a huge debate …" In Gavaskar's book *Idols*, he described Bradman as "Idol of Idols".

G

General Motors

Car makers who presented the Don with a red Chevrolet sports car in Sydney on his return from his triumphant tour of England in 1930. It became something of a talking point among the neighbours when Bradman parked it outside Frank Cush's home at 172 Frederick Street in the Sydney suburb of Rockdale, where he was boarding.

George, (Dr Most Rev.) Ian

Anglican Archbishop of Adelaide who conducted the memorial service at St Peter's Cathedral for Jessie Bradman on September 28, 1997 and for the Don on March 25, 2001.

Gibbons, Carroll

Renowned pianist of the time with whom the Don played a duet in London's Savoy Hotel where Gibbons was performing in 1948.

Gibraltar

Where Bradman drew criticism from a reporter for saluting troops with his hat off in 1938 on the way to England.

Also where film of his team on board *Strathaird* was sent ashore by launch to be flown ahead to London in 1948.

Also, at one point when Harold Larwood was being punished by Bradman during his world-record knock at Headingley in 1930, Pelham Warner turned to Lord Hawke in the pavilion and said: "This is like throwing stones at Gibraltar."

Gilbert, Eddie

Queensland Aboriginal cricketer who enjoyed enduring fame as "the man who bowled the Don for a duck" (although he actually had him caught behind) when he claimed 3/12 in a particularly fast burst of bowling in a Sheffield Shield game against New South Wales in Brisbane at the start of the 1931–32 season. But Bradman was to have his revenge when South Australia played Queensland in the Don's second shield game for his new state early in the 1935–36 season. He made 233, and Gilbert finished with 2/121. Although considered by some to be a "chucker", the Aboriginal speedster was "called" only once by an umpire – in a shield game at the MCG soon after the sensational match in Brisbane. When Andrew Barlow no-balled five deliveries in Gilbert's first over, the largely Victorian crowd hooted and jeered, calling for Barlow to get off the field. Although Barlow had his supporters, slow-motion film of Gilbert's bowling from various angles was inconclusive, and it was widely believed by the cricketing public that the accusation of "chucker" was a ploy by administrators to keep him out of the Test side because of his race. Eddie Gilbert died in 1978, aged about 73, in a mental hospital at Goodna, south-west of Brisbane, where he had been confined for 30 years with syphilis. He was honoured posthumously in 1999 as a "Black Opal", a sporting hero and role model for Aboriginal people.

Gilligan, Arthur Edward Robert

When one English writer, seeing the ball fly on a sticky wicket at the 'Gabba during the Ashes series in 1946–47, accused the Don's Australians of bowling bodyline, Gilligan wrote in a newspaper piece: "Utter nonsense, utter rubbish. The man who wrote it should be in a lunatic asylum." Arthur Gilligan was a fast bowler who led the beaten English tourists in Australia in 1924–25 and later became an administrator and author. He was also a respected radio commentator, especially in partnership with Australia's Victor Richardson, whose question "What do you think, Arthur?" became something of a catchphrase. In a foreword to AG Moyes's 1948 biography *Bradman*, Gilligan wrote of the Don: "Future generations will regard him not only as a very great batsman, but also as a brilliant captain and, above all, as one of the truest gentlemen who has ever worn flannels." Arthur Gilligan died in 1976, aged 81.

Giltinan, James John

Prominent Sydney sportsman and rugby league pioneer who presented the Don with a special cap to commemorate his 340 not out, then an SCG record, for New South Wales in a Sheffield Shield match against Victoria in 1928–29.

Girardi, Ramon

Artist who painted the Don scoring the run which brought up his 100th first-class century in a game between an Australian XI and the Indian tourists at the SCG in November 1947. A limited edition of 1,500 prints were numbered and signed by Girardi and his subject, image size 57cm x 42cm.

Glebe Park

Former name of the home ground of the Bowral Cricket Club. It was renamed Bradman Oval in 1947 but the park on which the Bradman Museum was built, just south of the oval, is still known as Glebe Park.

G

Glebe Street

Street in Bowral to which the Bradman family moved (at no. 20) from 52 Shepherd Street, Bowral, in 1924, when the Don was 15. His bedroom was a verandah lean-to built by his father, George. The street runs along the eastern boundary of Bradman Oval, formerly Glebe Park.

Gloucestershire

County against which the 1930 tourists played the only tie in history between an Australian side and an English county side. The Don made 42 and 14. Gloucester spinners Parker and Goddard bowled superbly on a horror wicket for batsmen. When Bradman had made 7 in the first innings, he carried his tour aggregate to 2,571, surpassing Victor Trumper's record tally of 2,570 for an Australian on tour in England, made in 1902.

"Goldie"

A nickname of the Don's early in his career because of the colour of his hair.

Golf

A game which the Don took up in earnest when recuperating after his serious illness in England in 1934. He joined the Mount Osmond club near Adelaide in the winter of 1935 to get his muscles back into condition for cricket, taking his handicap from 14 to 5 before winning the club championship a couple of months later. Bradman welcomed the opportunity to get out on the course during the hectic cricket schedules in England (he told Jack Egan in an interview in 1990 that when the Australians played a round at Gleneagles in 1930, Bill Woodfull exclaimed that when he (Woodfull) played, it was not a matter of replacing the turf, but of returfing the place). In his autobiography, *Farewell to Cricket*, the Don wrote: "These occasional golfing jaunts throughout the summer are one of the cricketer's joys. It is such a relief to get away from the incessant strain – to be envious of some other's ability, but above all to get the mental relaxation which golf so peculiarly affords."

Bradman believed that golf does not affect one's cricket, but conversely cricket seriously affects golf. "There is the tendency to bend the left arm and slice the ball over the 'covers', which is a splendid method of getting in the rough." He was forced to use the baseball grip, because the pounding of bat on ball enlarged the muscle between his right thumb and forefinger to the extent that the interlocking grip became impossible. Golf became the Don's sporting passion after his retirement from cricket. By 1960, at 51, he had reduced his handicap to scratch and was still good enough in 1988 at the age of 79 to win the A-grade medal at Kooyonga with a 76 off the championship tees. He was still shooting around 90 off the stick in his late 80s. On his way home from a golf game in April 1996, the Don was pinched for speeding on Adelaide's Formula One grand prix circuit next to Victoria Park racecourse. When the gobsmacked police officer realised who it was he had pulled up, he gushed: "It's a great pleasure to meet you." The Don replied: "I wish I could say the same."

Golja, Dean

Photographer from the ACT who accompanied Roland Perry to Adelaide in 1995 for Perry's interview with the subject for his biography, *The Don*. Dean takes up the story: "I agreed to join Roland on the strength of his work and character, but recall being curious that he should ask a photographer who knew absolutely nothing about cricket. There were no contracts or monies involved in my participation. It was totally speculative, as were my chances of getting any pictures; the subject was renowned for his dislike of being photographed, and I was resigned to coming away with little or no material. On arrival at Sir Donald's home, we were escorted by Lady Jessie to the living room, where the man of the house soon joined us. He asked about my preference for seating position so as best to suit the pictures. I indicated that the photography would remain casual and that any place chosen for the interview would be fine. There followed in the dimly lit room over five hours of conversation: questions and answers so engrossing that I had to remind myself to take a picture every now and then. When the dialogue ended, Sir Donald asked me whether I would like to continue with more pictures. I took this as an invitation to proceed with some more formal portraits, which I did for the next hour or so.

"This was a day successful beyond all expectation, yielding an astounding quantity of imagery and sorting out much detail for the forthcoming biography. It was not my normal practice to do so, but I sent the proofs of the photos to Sir Donald to be edited. This seemed like the right thing to do with consideration to the many intrusions and misrepresentations that he had endured as a consequence of his fame. After a short time I received a letter from him thanking me for the gesture. He enclosed a list of the 'worst' shots, but said that it would be up to me which pictures to use. Many of the 'better' photographs have since been published in magazines throughout the world. Roland Perry wrote of the session with Sir Donald on page 592 of his biography: 'The Don was oblivious of the ubiquitous camera, capturing him in the longest portrait session ever given. The aim was to portray him as he approached 90 – intellectually vigorous, humorous, pensive, thoughtful and with powers of concentration that would put a monk to shame. Add a refreshing directness and integrity and you have much of the Bradman character and demeanour. Dean secured what was required.'"

Goodhart, Joseph Christian
Adelaide artist who painted a large (120cm x 75cm) Bradman oil on canvas in 1940. The Don is depicted in batting stance at the crease at Kensington District Cricket Club.

Gough, Francis Joseph
Leg-spinner who bowled the Don first ball in the 19-year-old Bradman's third first-class game, for New South Wales against Queensland at the SCG in January 1928. In his *Farewell to Cricket*, the Don wrote of his faux pas: "Instead of the ball coming slowly and turning as I anticipated, it went straight through and fast, taking with it my middle stump. Since that day I have never made up my mind what to do with the ball before it was bowled."

Gould, Shane Elizabeth MBE
Former champion swimmer who was seated next to the Don at the luncheon when 100 top athletes were inducted into the Australian Sports Hall of Fame on January 26, 1988. She asked for (and received) her table companion's speech notes as a keepsake.

Gowrie, (The Rt Hon.) Earl of VC, GCMG, CB, DSO
A distinguished soldier who won a VC in the Sudan in 1899 and served in France and Gallipoli in 1914–18. As Brigadier-General Sir Alexander Hore-Ruthven he was governor of South Australia from 1928 to 1934 and governor of New South Wales in 1935–36. As Lord Gowrie he served as governor-general of Australia from 1936 to 1945, a record term. When the Don was offered a transfer from the RAAF reserve to the Army as a physical training instructor in 1940, he sought the advice of Lord Gowrie, who advised him to accept. In the mid-'40s, the Don acted as honorary secretary and organiser of the Gowrie Scholarship Trust Fund, which financed scholarships to members of the Services or their children. The Earl was president of the MCC when Bradman's Invincibles toured England in 1948 and officiated at many functions for Don and his men. On the Sunday of the Lord's Test he escorted the team on an inspection of Windsor Castle. The Earl of Gowrie sent the Don his congratulations soon after the announcement of his knighthood on New Year's Day 1949. He died in 1955, aged 83.

G

Grace, (Dr) W(illiam) G(ilbert)

Legendary English cricketer who was the payee on a cheque which a local
enthusiast sent to the Don as a souvenir during the 1934 tour of England.
The cheque was endorsed by the doctor and had been presented to the
bank in 1907. In his *Farewell to Cricket*, Bradman wrote of a visit on the
1948 tour to the London Stock Exchange: "True to tradition, I was greeted on the floor by an enthusiastic audience. They had left a small space in
the middle where a cricket pitch had been rigged up – all implements provided and one of the members bedecked as W.G. to do battle with me.
Perhaps the most amusing thing was the whisky and soda provided at the
bowler's end. That may have been in accordance with the tradition of the
Grace era – I don't know – it certainly doesn't exist today." Later, in a discussion of the evolution of cricket, he wrote: "W.G. was a disciple of forward play and the 'firm right foot'. Grace advised against moving the
back foot across in front of the stumps. Practically all modern coaches do
the reverse – as they must if batsmen are to learn correct back-defensive
methods."

Grace's tall, broad, bearded figure became the symbol of Britain's passion
for sport and the spirit of the Empire. He was rated by former *Wisden
Cricketers' Almanack* editor John Woodcock in the 1998 edition above the
Don as the greatest-ever cricketer but few would disagree, even in England,
that Bradman was the greater batsman. In a first-class career which extended from 1865 to 1908, Grace made 54,896 runs with 126 centuries, but his
averages of 39.55 in first-class cricket and 32.29 in Tests are far inferior to
the Don's, although allowances must be made for the different standards in
pitches and the changes in the psychology and technique of the game. When
the doctor's side toured Australia in 1891, they played a match against a
local side at Loseby Park, Bowral. His last year in first-class cricket was the
year Bradman was born. WG Grace died in 1915 and has had by far the
biggest entry in *Wisden Book of Obituaries*.

Grade Cricket

The Don played 16 seasons in first grade with three clubs. He had seven
seasons with St George (1926–27 to 1932–33), one (short) season with
North Sydney (1933–34), and eight with Kensington (1935–36 to
1947–48). He did not play any cricket in 1934–35. Bradman had a total of
93 innings and accumulated 6,599 runs at 86.82, with 28 centuries. His
best score was 303 for Kensington against Glenelg in 1939–40. When
comparing his relatively low average in grade cricket with his Test and
overall first-class averages, it should be remembered that grade matches

were played only over two afternoons, and he threw his wicket away many more times than he did at the higher levels.

Grant, George Copeland ("Jackie")

Cambridge and Trinidad batsman who was only 23 when he led the first West Indies team to visit Australia, in 1930–31. In the First Test at Adelaide Oval he became the first man to score a not-out fifty (53 and 71) in each innings of any Test. He headed the averages for his side in the series and twice took a catch to dismiss the Don.

Grasshoppers

Insects which invaded the ground in plague proportions during a match in Winnipeg between the Australian tourists and a combined Canadian team in 1932. The Don observed that on more than one occasion a ball landed on a grasshopper on the pitch and did the unexpected.

Greats of '48, The

Television documentary of 30 minutes which was written and presented by Norman May and first shown on the ABC in February 1979 to mark the 30th anniversary of Bradman's Invincibles. May interviewed several of the players from the team, including the Don, whose two-minute chat on camera was a condition set by the sponsors of a reunion dinner at Sydney's Hilton Hotel held to celebrate the anniversary. The interviews were augmented by footage of two of the Tests. The producer of the program was Brian Harvey.

Gregory, Jack Morrison

The withdrawal of Gregory and Hampden Love from the New South Wales Sheffield Shield team for the trip to Adelaide and Melbourne in 1927–28 provided places for the Don and Albert Scanes. It was the first time Bradman had been outside NSW. He was named 12th man for the game against South Australia but got his chance when Archie Jackson was scratched because of a boil on his knee. In that game at Adelaide Oval the Don made 118 in his first-class debut. Bradman played against Jack Gregory earlier that season in a grade game in Sydney. As a member of the AIF team which played a match against NSW in 1920, the great all-rounder opened the batting and scored a century in each innings, opened the bowling and took eight wickets, and held three catches. His last Test, when he broke down with a bad knee, was the Don's first, the opening match of the 1928–29 Ashes series at Brisbane's Exhibition Ground. In his *Farewell to Cricket*, Bradman wrote glowingly of Gregory and his attitude to the game and to other players. He described him as "possibly the most magnetic personality that Australian cricket has known". The Don made 212 in 202 minutes in a Bardsley-Gregory testimonial match at the SCG in October 1936. Jack Gregory died in 1973, aged 77.

Gregory, Ross Gerald

First chosen for his state when still a schoolboy, the 20-year-old Gregory made 128 for Victoria against the MCC in 1936–37 and was chosen for the last two Ashes Tests, when he scored 23, 50 and a brilliant 80. In a reference to Gregory in *Farewell to Cricket*, the Don wrote of "an untimely accident" (after the 1936–37 series) which "temporarily retarded his advancement". Gregory's omission from the touring side to England in 1938 infuriated many, and Bradman, as captain and a selector, copped much of the blame, as he did for the non-selection of Clarrie Grimmett in the same party. Bradman always stuck to protocol by never revealing selectors' discussions, but in a section on "Selectorship" in his 1958 book *The Art of Cricket*, he effectively owned up to Gregory's omission: "The worst experience I ever had in that regard was in helping to choose an Australian team for England prior to World War II. It came to a decision between two players from different states ... The boy omitted was a great personal friend of mind and a magnificent character and I was very grieved in casting my vote against him because my conscience so dictated. I scarcely slept a wink for two nights after that decision. However, I consoled myself with the thought that he was young and would go later. Alas, he never did. Instead he lost his life in the service of his country in World War II as a very gallant airman." Ross Gregory was killed while on active service with the RAAF in India in 1942. He is the subject of a recent book by David Frith.

Griffith, Herman Clarence

Fast bowler who was responsible for the Don's first duck in Test cricket when he bowled him with a slower ball in the Fifth Test on the first West Indian tour of Australia in 1930–31. Thirty-seven-year-old Griffith had dismissed Bradman earlier in the series for 4, and was fond of referring to the Don as his "rabbit". Griffith had missed out on a tour of England several years before because he was rumoured to be a communist.

Grimmett, Clarence Victor

Small, prematurely bald and wizened in the face, "the Gnome" was a great leg-break bowler for Australia who was born in New Zealand and made his first-class debut for Wellington in 1911–12, before moving to Sydney in

G

1914, then to Melbourne in 1917. When he could not cement a place in the Victorian team he went to South Australia and made his debut for that state in 1924–25, playing his first Test in the same season (at the age of 33) when he took 5/45 and 6/37 against England in Sydney. Of his first encounter with Grimmett (in the Don's first-class debut in a Sheffield Shield game for New South Wales against SA at Adelaide Oval in December 1927), Bradman wrote in his 1950 autobiography: "In our second innings against SA, Clarrie Grimmett bowled marvelously well on a turning wicket to take 8/57, and in scoring 33 out of our total of 150, I faced leg-break bowling of a higher calibre than any I had met before … Apart from the cricket itself, I treasured the opportunity of meeting Clarrie Grimmett and watching the way he could spin a soft rubber ball on a table. I have not seen anybody who can make the ball perform such tricks. At that time I thought Grimmett the best slow leg-break bowler I had played against. With the passing of the years I see no reason to alter my opinion. No other leg spinner since 1918 has possessed his phenomenal accuracy … Grimmett was a theorist. He liked to adopt a stereotyped field and stick to it, basing his success upon the law of averages. The field he set was sound, and he bowled to it as no other slow bowler in history could do. I have seen Grimmett take the ball, and immediately drop into a perfect length to bowl three or four maidens in succession. He rarely sent down a truly bad ball, and thus could be used for long periods without being inordinately expensive."

Grimmett had successful tours of England with the Don in 1930, when he captured 29 wickets in the Tests (and took all 10 wickets in an innings for 37 against Yorkshire), and in 1934, when he and Bill O'Reilly formed the spearhead of Australia's attack and took 28 and 25 scalps respectively. The other bowlers between them finished with 18. Clarrie had routed the West Indians (in 1930–31) and South Africa (with O'Reilly's help the following season) in Australia but his tour de force was in South Africa in 1935–36, when he finished the series with 44 wickets at 14.59! But the last Test in South Africa was to be the last of Grimmett's career. He was dropped for the Ashes series in Australia in 1936–37 and again overlooked for the tour of England in 1938, on both occasions in favour of his South Australian leggie partner, Frank Ward. Many Australian players (notably Bill O'Reilly) and observers of the time were rocked by the Gnome's omission from both teams, but particularly his absence from the touring party, and were convinced that the Don, as captain and a selector, was responsible for Grimmett's dumping. (Bradman's co-selectors were WJ (Bill) Johnson and EA ("Chappie") Dwyer, two men who had played first-class cricket in Australia but had never been to England.) O'Reilly was later to tell commentator Alan McGilvray many times how he would have loved to have had his "old mate" at the other end to help during the gruelling Test at the Oval when the home side scored 7/903 and O'Reilly and Chuck Fleetwood-Smith had to bowl 85 and 87 overs respectively.

Bradman always insisted that selectors' discussions were confidential and so never revealed publicly how he voted, but writing about the lead-up to the 1936–37 Ashes series in his *Farewell to Cricket*, he implied that in fact he went into bat for Grimmett: "A Selector's job is interesting, sometimes exasperating, occasionally heartbreaking. For a captain to sit on a committee which leaves one of your trusted colleagues out of an Australian team, because in their *collective judgement* [this author's italics] he must give way to a better player, is not a pleasant experience." And in a discussion of "Selectorship" in his 1958 book *The Art of Cricket*, he gave the game away: "When I was Australian XI captain and selector, I was castigated more than once for the omission of a certain man when in fact I fought for his inclusion. But those details can't be published. I simply mention them in the hope that the difficulties of selection committees may be fully understood." But it is likely that on both occasions Bradman was referring only to selection for the 1936–37 series in Australia, because in 1987 he told the ABC's Norman May that he did not want Grimmett in the 1938 touring side, because at 46 years of age he was too slow in the field. And he defended to May the decision by selectors to take Grimmett's South Australian teammate Frank Ward as the third slow bowler behind O'Reilly and Fleetwood-Smith.

Grimmett and Bradman were teammates in the Kensington club in the Adelaide grade competition in the second half of the 1930s. They were the subjects of two plaster sculptures (with the Don taking strike and Clarrie bowling to him) originally exhibited on the Farmers Union stand at the Royal Adelaide Show in 1935. The figures, which were made to look as if they were fashioned from butter, were rediscovered and put on permanent display in Adelaide in 1977. (There is a photo of Clarrie and the Don sharing in a joke as they size up their likenesses at the opening.) Clarrie Grimmett was still taking plenty of wickets for SA at the age of 49 when first-class cricket was suspended in 1941. In his Sheffield Shield career, he bowled a mammoth 3,558 overs and collected 513 wickets (at the time more than twice as many as his nearest rival) at 25.29. Grimmett shares with England's Hedley Verity the honour of dismissing Bradman more times than any other bowler: 10 times each. He was 88 when he died in 1980. In December 1988, a boulder of Adelaide bluestone was unveiled in remembrance of Clarrie before dignitaries and invited guests near the

G

northern gates to Adelaide Oval. After the speeches, Bradman heard a voice ring out: "Don!" He turned to see Bill O'Reilly striding toward him with hand outstretched. If there had been any resentment before, there was none that day.

Grip

In his 1948 biography *Bradman*, AG ("Johnny") Moyes wrote of the reaction to the Don's grip when he trialled at the SCG as a 17-year-old in October 1926: "Some noticed this freakish grip and advised a change. Bradman would not hear of it. It had served him well and would, he believed, continue to do so." The grip grew from the lad's use of the cricket stump to learn how to hit a ball. At his home in Shepherd Street, when he faced the base of the water tank off which the ball ricocheted, the off-side was blocked by a wall, but the on-side was open. To hit the ball into space, then, Bradman would have needed a grip that allowed the bottom hand to turn the ball forcibly to the leg side (the stump having no "face" that he could have angled). Thus, he would have had to play his shots with a strong bottom-handled grip. Aiding him was his short-handled, light bat. With his grip, a heavy bat would have required the wrists of a blacksmith. Writing in his *Farewell to Cricket* about the experience of his first season in Sydney, the Don said: "One thing in particular caused me a lot of thought. I noticed that my grip, developed on the concrete wickets, was different from that of most players. It assisted me in pulling a ball, and was much safer for on-side shots, though it handicapped me somewhat in playing the ball between mid-off and point. I experimented – worked out the pros and cons – and eventually decided not to change my natural grip." And in *The Art of Cricket*, he noted that his grip gave the bat "what might be termed, in golfing parlance, a shut face. I think it helps to keep the ball on the ground, especially when playing on-side shots ... I refuse to condemn an unorthodox grip just because it is different. The use of wrists and arms and the method of stroke production cannot be stereotyped."

H

Haigh, Gideon Clifford Jeffrey Davidson

Melbourne-based journalist (and former editor of *Australian Wisden*) who savaged Roland Perry's 1995 biography of the Don in a review in the *Australian* newspaper in December 1995. Gideon wrote a piece on Bradman for the September 1998 issue of *Wisden Cricket Monthly* entitled "Sir Donald Brandname" (republished in the first edition of *Best Australian Essays*) and contributed an essay he called "Beyond the Legend" to the 2002 edition of *Wisden Cricketers' Almanack*. Haigh has published 14 books, most of them on cricket (including biographies of Warwick Armstrong and Jack Iverson) but also a couple on business. His *One Summer, Every Summer: An Ashes Journal* was short-listed for the *Age* Book of the Year Award in 1995, the first sporting book to be so honoured.

Hall, Wesley Winfield

In his interview with ABC radio in 1987, the Don said he considered Wes Hall to be the most exciting of any West Indian pacemen he had seen: "To see him charging in from his enormous run must have been a frightening thing for the batsman ... very exciting for the spectators." Others he included in the top bracket were Andy Roberts, Michael Holding, Joel Garner and Malcolm Marshall. Of the last-mentioned he said: "This boy Marshall was the shortest of them, but my word he was fast."

Hamence, Ronald Arthur

In 1935–36, also the Don's first season with his new state, Hamence made 121 for South Australia in his first-class debut when he figured in a record stand of 356 with his captain against Tasmania at Adelaide Oval. Ron made one Test appearance under the Don against England in 1946–47 and another two against India the following season, and got a berth on the boat to England in 1948. Although he played some valuable innings against the counties (in one match he was on 99 when he fell to what the Don considered was the best ball of the day), he was a familiar figure with the drinks tray in the Tests, unable to force his way into a very strong side. After the tour, Bradman wrote of Hamence: "A fine batsman of the strictly orthodox type. Very sound and reliable with his game based on driving ... Above all, a great tourist who did wonders for the morale of the side." Of the Don, Hamence later said: "I've made the statement a lot of times that if they'd have had televised one-day cricket when Bradman was in his prime I don't think the cameramen would have been quick enough to follow his shots. He was phenomenal. I batted with him quite a few times. He used to do some amazing things. It was a great privilege and an education to play with him. I doubt if we'll ever see another player like him. I also found him to be a good bloke and an excellent captain." Ron Hamence, who in his younger days had a fine tenor voice, is now 89 and lives in Adelaide. He is in pretty good shape aside from failing sight in his left eye.

Hammond, Stanley MBE
Melbourne artist who created a bronze bust of the Don titled "Bradman 99". The bust, which is 360mm high and set on a base with an identifying plaque, was commissioned by the State Library of South Australia Foundation in January 1998 to commemorate the establishment of the Bradman Collection exhibition at the library and Sir Donald's 90th year.

Hammond, Walter Reginald
One of the greatest of all cricketers, Hammond was a brilliant, naturally talented right-handed batsman (particularly strong on the off-side), an outstanding slips fieldsman (rated by the Don as England's best ever) and a useful medium-pace bowler. On his first tour of Australia, in 1928–29, his Ashes-record aggregate of 905 runs at 113 with four centuries (including two double centuries) in the Tests was a major factor in England winning back the urn. He had moderate success in the Bodyline series (his dismissal for 85 by the Don in the explosive Adelaide Test was the second of Bradman's only two wickets in his Test career) but his 336 not out in 318 minutes against New Zealand in Auckland on the way home broke the Don's world Test record of 334 set at Headingley in 1930. Back in England a couple of months later, the West Indian tourists gave Jardine and his men a taste of bodyline bowling, and Hammond's chin was split open by a short-pitched rising ball from Emmanuel Martindale. Hammond was reported to have said soon after that unless short-pitched bowling was outlawed, he would retire from first-class cricket. Wally Hammond first captained England in an Ashes series in 1938, having "turned" amateur just before the Australians arrived. The Don's side hung on to the urn when the rubber was drawn 1–1.

Hammond was often disappointing during his career in Tests in England but his 240 at Lord's during the 1938 series was a tour de force. After serving in the RAF, Hammond returned to Australia as captain for the Ashes series of 1946–47. It was an unhappy time for the 43-year-old from Gloucestershire. There was continuing acrimony between himself and the Don, who captained Australia. Hammond was privately contemptuous of the ability of his own players and was involved in several rows over decisions by the local umpires. One such dispute, in the first match of the rubber at the 'Gabba, involved his opposing captain. When Bradman was on 28, the England players appealed when he appeared to give a catch to Jack Ikin in the slips off Bill Voce, but the Don thought it was a bump ball and referee George Borwick concurred. (Jack Fingleton claimed in his book, *Brightly Fades the Don*, a couple of years later that it was a catch and that the umpire had erred.) At the end of the over, Hammond said to Bradman: "That's a bloody fine way to start the series." The Don went on to make 187. Though the England captain remained unimpressed, he agreed to the reappointment of the same two umpires for the following Test. But Hammond was angered by another decision, later in the series, when Denis Compton was given out lbw to Toshack. Realising he had been caught plumb in front, the Brylcreem Boy quickly moved his leg out of the line of fire, but Bradman, who was fielding close to the bowler, felt there was no doubt about it, and even the batsman at the other end, Cyril Washbrook, later admitted Compton was out.

Hammond had success with the bat in the minor games in 1946–47 but in eight innings in the first four Tests his highest score was 37. Such was his disenchantment (and the pain from his fibrositis), he handed over the captaincy to Norman Yardley for the final Test of the series. Bradman's side won the rubber 3–0. Hammond resumed the captaincy in the one Test in New Zealand on the way home, when he top-scored with 79 in his final international appearance. Wally was to make his respect for the Don clear when he said: "If I were choosing a side out of all cricketers who have ever lived, I would put Bradman's name down first. None of us had the measure of him and that's a plain fact." Like Bradman, Hammond made a century of first-class centuries, but he needed 679 innings to reach the landmark compared with the Don's 295. His 36 scores over 200 was only one less than Bradman's total. He was named by the Don as 12th man in his World XI, published after his death in 2001. In 85 Tests, Wally Hammond compiled 7,249 runs at 58.45 with 22 centuries, including six double centuries and a triple century. He settled in South Africa and died there in poverty at the age of 62.

Hampshire

The opposition at Southampton on the 1930 tour of England when the Don was on the field for an entire match for the only time in his first-class career. The game got under way on May 31 and Bradman needed 46 to complete his 1,000 runs in May, a feat never before achieved by a touring batsman. Things looked grim when the local side won the toss and batted first but good bowling by Clarrie Grimmett saw them all back in the shed by 3.15pm. Bill Woodfull sent the Don in to open with Archie Jackson and by tea he was 28. Rain delayed play but on resuming he took his tally to 39 before more rain started to fall. But two loose deliveries on the leg side from Newman were both dispatched for four to take Bradman to 47 and his aggregate to 1,001 before the players ran for cover in the torrential rain. The next day he was last man out when caught in the slips for 191. In his *Farewell to Cricket*, the Don wrote: "I feel that there was a measure of generosity on the part of the Hampshire captain [Lord Tennyson] in allowing play to continue when the weather might reasonably have caused a cessation. I was not unmindful of this when it fell to my lot in 1938 to close the Australian innings at Lord's [against Middlesex] and thereby give Bill Edrich a chance to score 1,000 runs in May." On that same tour, in 1938, Bradman again brought up his 1,000 runs in May during an innings (of 145 not out) against Hampshire in Southampton.

Hanif Mohammad

Great Pakistani batsman who beat the Don's world record for a first-class innings when he made 499 for Karachi against Bahawalpur in Karachi in 1958–59. On hearing of Bradman's death, Hanif said: "Cricket at this critical juncture couldn't afford to lose Bradman. After hearing all the depressing news of corruption, it was Bradman upon whom people used to look for the brighter side of the game. I sincerely hope that after the Don, cricket continues to flourish and be played the way Bradman liked it to be played."

Hannaford, Robert Lyall

A South Australian artist who is a regular finalist in the Archibald Prize, Hannaford painted a portrait of the Don in 1972 (which is hung in the Long Room at Lord's) and created the statue of Bradman which stands near the eastern gates of Adelaide Oval. The $115,000 project was commissioned by Adelaide City Council in 1999. The 2.5m-tall figure of the great batsman was unveiled by the Governor of South Australia, Marjorie Jackson-Nelson, on February 25, 2002 to mark the first anniversary of the Don's passing. Hannaford said after the unveiling that the work had been extremely difficult and a "life-changing event". According to press reports at the time, Bradman is depicted playing a "classic cover drive", but Bernard Whimpress, in his paper "The Aestheticization of The Don", presented to the South Australian State History Conference in May 2002, claimed that Bradman is playing a straight drive veering towards an on-drive. And Robert confirmed this recently when he said he made a conscious decision to have the Don playing a straight drive. He said that none of the individual photos or video images of Bradman that he viewed were suitable for sculpture, and all aspects of his design were worked out in close consultation with his subject.

Harris, 4th Lord (George Robert Canning)

Legendary English player and administrator who wrote a creed which the Don lived by and commended to all players: "You do well to love cricket, because it is more free from anything sordid, anything dishonourable than any game in the world. To play it keenly, generously, self-sacrificingly is a moral lesson in itself, and the classroom is God's air and sunshine. Foster it, my brothers, so that it may attract all who find the time to play it, protect it from anything that will sully it, so that it may grow in favour with all men."

Harvey, (Robert) Neil MBE

One of the greatest of all left-handed batsmen, and a brilliant fieldsman, Harvey was the youngest member of the Don's 1948 Invincibles and is one of Bradman's most passionate admirers. He scored a century in his first game for Victoria, his first Test hundred as a 19-year-old under the Don against India in 1947–48 (and is still the youngest Australian to make a hundred in a Test), and another ton in his first Test against England in the Headingley match in 1948 (when he hit the winning four in the second innings to bring up a historic victory for Australia). In a game against Surrey earlier in that tour, Harvey held a catch in the outfield which his captain rated as the best of its kind he had seen. In an assessment of his Invincibles after the tour, the Don wrote of Harvey: "Capable of tearing the best bowling to shreds and altering the whole outlook of a match in no time ... Very many critics, and players too, rated him the finest outfield ever seen in England. His catching and throwing were sensational."

And for his part, Harvey once said of Bradman: "There is nothing he doesn't know about cricket and no matter how long a player has been in the game an hour's chat with Sir Donald will teach him more about the intricacies of batting and bowling than he ever dreamed of." Recently Neil said: "I was privileged to be the first young bloke after the war to be selected – and to go away with this magnificent 1948 team was one of the highlights of my cricketing life." Between 1948 and 1963, Neil Harvey played in more Tests than any other Australian, scored more runs in Tests than all but the Don, and was bettered only by Bradman in Australian Test centuries and averages. His 21 Test hundreds were made on 15 different grounds. Neil captained his country in one Test and later served with the Don as a national selector. He published a book, *My World of Cricket*, in 1963. Now 76, he lives on Sydney's North Shore.

Hassett, (Arthur) Lindsay OBE

The small, whimsical man from Victoria toured England with the Don's side in 1938 (when he was the hero of Australia's exciting win at Headingley when he threw caution to the wind to beat the gathering storm clouds) and led the AIF side in the Victory Tests in England in 1945. He was vice-captain to Bradman at home against England in 1946–47 and India in 1947–48 and retained the post on the tour of England in 1948. In the 1946–47 series, he and Bradman added 276 for the third wicket at the 'Gabba, and against the Indians he made his highest Test score of 198 not out in Adelaide. His best performance in the Tests in 1948 was his 137 at Trent Bridge. Bradman wrote of Hassett after that tour: "Was a great player and valuable lieutenant as vice-captain, his knowledge of the game and views on tactics extremely sound. He was a beautiful stroke maker when in the mood." Of his skipper, Lindsay said: "Batting with him was something special. He was always in control. The way in which he manipulated the bowling was an education to watch. The only bowler I ever saw going anywhere near getting on top of him on occasions was Bill O'Reilly, but it was only occasionally and Bradman, in the end, always finished on top. As a captain, he had no peer in my book." Lindsay Hassett succeeded the Don as Test captain and in five series as leader he never had a bad rubber with the bat. He later became a respected commentator with the ABC and died in 1993 at the age of 79.

Hazare, Vijay Samuel

Indian batsman who played against the Don's Australians in 1947–48, when he became the first Indian to score a century in each innings of a Test, in the fourth match of the series at Adelaide Oval. Bradman described him in *Farewell to Cricket* as "a great player", and in a foreword to Hazare's book, *Long Innings*, wrote: "Hazare was one of the most graceful batsmen it was my pleasure to see and perhaps the best compliment I can pay him is to say that his batting more closely resembled that of the great West Indian star, Sir Frank Worrell, than anyone I can remember." Hazare sent the Don a Christmas card each year for about 50 years, and after the great man's death said: "I'll not stop, because I feel he is still there … like a star in the sky." Now 89, he recalls two treasured moments of the Don on the tour in 1947–48. "When we flew to Sydney … we were surprised that Bradman was waiting to welcome our team at the airport. It was a cherished moment." Hazare also prizes the compliments from the Don after he scored a century in each innings of the Adelaide Test – in one of the rare highlights for India during a 4–0 defeat. "When I scored those centuries, Bradman came along and complimented me. He shook hands and wished me all the best. It was a very happy occasion. He was this sort of a delightful cricketer."

Headingley

The ground in the Yorkshire city of Leeds was the Don's most successful in his four tours of England. In six Test innings he averaged 192.60, with four centuries, one in each of his four Tests, including the world-record 334 in 1930 and 304 in 1934. On the first day of the Third Test in 1930, the 21-year-old Bradman came in during the second over after Archie Jackson was dismissed cheaply, and by lunch was 105, becoming only the third man to that point (after another two Australians, Victor Trumper and Charlie Macartney) to make a hundred before lunch on the first day of a Test. It also represented his fourth century in consecutive Tests. At stumps he was on 309, his double century occupying just 214 minutes and his 300 coming up in 336 minutes. Legend has it that on returning to Queen's Hotel in Leeds at the end of the day the Don shunned celebrations, saying to the girl at the desk: "I'm going to my room. Will you please send me up a pot of tea." After his dismissal on the second day for 334 (which included 46 fours), the British newspaper the *Star* carried a headline which simply said: "HE'S OUT". In 1934, Bradman added 388 with Bill Ponsford in a record Ashes stand for any wicket on his way to 304 (in 430 minutes), an innings which included two sixes (his first in a Test in England) and 43 fours. An article in the autumn 1999 issue of the Bradman Museum's *Boundary* magazine told of how an international umpire who viewed footage of this match concluded that four runs recorded as leg-byes should have been credited to Bradman. In 1935 an Australian writer, DR Hall, reported that Charles Moses's synthetic broadcast of the match on ABC radio had an impact on a federal election campaign back home: "The action of Bradman in making 304 in the Fourth Test match at Leeds destroyed 500 political meetings in Australia which were timed to take place when the detailed description of the innings was coming over the air." In this match, the Don tore a thigh muscle badly when fielding and was not to play first-class cricket again until the next Test at the Oval three weeks later.

H

The Headingley Test in 1938 was rated by Bradman as the best he ever played in. On a good batting wicket Australia dismissed England in their first innings for 223. Bill O'Reilly's pre-lunch figures were 14 overs, 11 maidens, 1 wicket for 4 runs. The marvellous photograph of awe-struck young boys near the gate as the Don walked out to bat in Australia's first innings probably captures the essence of the legend of Bradman as no other image does. He made 103 under gathering storm clouds in atrocious conditions, at one point "the darkest in which I have ever batted", and the Australians established a lead of 19. The Don had not appealed against the light because "I thought we would get more runs in bad light on a dry pitch than in good light on a wet one." When Bradman had made 26 in this innings, he reached 5,000 runs in Test cricket, the first Australian to do so. The only two other batsmen to have achieved the landmark total, Jack Hobbs and Wally Hammond, took nearly twice as many innings. And his century was his 12th of the season, breaking the 36-year-old record of Victor Trumper's (in nearly three times as many innings) for the most hundreds in an English season by any touring batsman. When England were sent packing for 123 in the second innings (due largely to five wickets by Bill O'Reilly at his ferocious best), Australia needed only 105 to win. But both openers, Jack Fingleton and Bill Brown, went for 9 each and then Bradman was dismissed for 16.

Rain looked imminent when the clouds banked up again and the skipper told his batsmen to force the pace. Another wicket fell and, in the words of the Don, "The match became so exciting that for the only time in my life I could not bear to watch the play." But Lindsay Hassett was the hero, opening his shoulders in a race to beat the weather. He was out for 33 and wicketkeeper Ben Barnett soon after hit the winning runs. The victory meant Australia could not lose the rubber, and therefore retained the Ashes. In 1948, the Headingley crowd gave the Don "the most terrific and spontaneous welcome ever accorded me in my long career". When he stepped onto the ground in Australia's first innings, "the applause was amazing". As he walked to the middle, the noise level dropped slightly but when he approached the wicket, the "deafening roar ... raised a lump in my throat". But he made only 33, and, despite fine knocks from Neil Harvey and Sam Loxton, Australia needed 404 in 344 minutes in the second innings to win the match. When Harvey hit the winning runs (Arthur Morris having been dismissed for 182) with 14 minutes to spare to achieve a historic victory, the Don was unbeaten on 173, his fourth hundred (including two triple centuries) in six Test innings at Headingley. When he was on 145, he completed 5,000 runs in Tests between Australia and England, at the time the only man from either country to do so. Australia's 404 for 3 was the highest fourth-innings total to win a Test until 1975–76, when India scored 406 for 4 in about 600 minutes to beat the West Indies in Port-of-Spain, Trinidad. He was presented later in the tour in Scarborough with life membership of Yorkshire County Cricket Club in recognition of his four hundreds in four Tests in Leeds. Bradman did not play any matches at Headingley other than the Tests.

Headley, George Alphonso MBE

The Panamanian-born right-hander known as "the Black Bradman" became the first player to score four Test hundreds before his 21st birthday when he posted four three-figure scores (including two in the same match) for the West Indies in the 1929–30 home series against England. And he made the first hundred by a West Indian against Australia when he scored 102 not out at Brisbane's Exhibition Ground in the Second Test in 1930–31, the same match in which the Don made 223, the highest score to that time by an Australian in a home Test. Headley registered another hundred in the fifth match of the series at the SCG, the game in which paceman Herman Griffith became the first bowler from any country to dismiss Bradman for a Test duck. George Headley was the dominant batsman for his team from 1929 to 1948, and became the first black man to captain the West Indies when he led the home side in the first Test of the 1947–48 series against England. He died in 1983, aged 74.

Heads

What the Don called at the toss for every one of his nine Tests as captain in England. He was wrong on eight occasions.

Hele, George Alfred

Umpire rated by the Don as the best in Australia between the two wars. Hele stood with George Borwick in each of the five Bodyline Tests in 1932–33, and said later he believed that had the incidents which so enraged the crowd in the Adelaide match happened in Melbourne, many of the angry spectators would have jumped the fence. Of Bradman's ability in the field, Hele once said: "He was standing at square leg with the ball in his hand. With three successive throws he hit the one stump visible to him three times ..."

Hele, (Sir) Ivor Henry Thomas

South Australian artist who painted a portrait of the Don in his Australian blazer in 1946. Hele (he pronounced it "heel") was an official war artist

H

during World War II and again in Korea. In the 1950s he won five Archibald Prizes in seven years, but later burned many of his works because he considered them not good enough.

"HE'S OUT"
Banner headline carried by the *Star* newspaper in England on July 12, 1930, when the Don was finally dismissed for his world-record score of 334 in the Third Test at Headingley. The match was drawn.

Heydon, Harold
Heydon was secretary of the New South Wales Cricket Association in 1934 when the Don received an attractive offer of employment from Adelaide stockbroker and Board of Control member Harry Hodgetts. Bradman did not want to leave his home state, but the offer would provide him with a living outside cricket, which he wanted to play purely for pleasure. Bert Kortlang, a friend of Bradman's, went to see Heydon and told him that the champion batsman was considering a move to another state and asked whether the association could do something to keep him in Sydney. Heydon's response was: "The New South Wales Cricket Association has made Bradman what he is, and he can't afford to leave New South Wales." For the Don, this made his mind up, and, despite opposition from wife Jessie, he accepted Mr Hodgetts's offer of 600 pounds a year for a minimum of six years.

Hiawatha
Samuel Coleridge-Taylor's cantata, a performance of which the Don and his teammates attended as special guests in London's Royal Albert Hall in 1930. The young Bradman was photographed after the performance shaking hands with Australian baritone Harold Williams, who sang the leading role.

Hilton, Malcolm Jameson
Nineteen-year-old left-arm spinner who was making only his third first-class appearance (after being added to the team at the last moment) when he claimed the Don's scalp twice (for 11 and 43) when playing for Lancashire against the Australians early in the 1948 tour. Hilton's photograph and his family history appeared on the front page of all English newspapers, and there was a push for his inclusion in the Test team but he was dropped from the county side later in the season. However, he regained his place and went on to play four Tests between 1950 and '52.

Hit Wicket

How the Don lost his wicket once in his 295 first-class dismissals: when he played so far back to Indian captain Lala Amarnath in the First Test at the 'Gabba in 1947–48 that the downswing of his bat broke the wicket from behind. It was the only time Bradman was out hit-wicket in 562 dismissals in first- and second-class cricket.

Hobart

The Don played two first-class matches at the TCA ground on the Domain in the Tasmanian capital, on both occasions en route to Perth to board the ship for England, in 1929–30 and 1937–38. He made 139 and 144 respectively, for an average of 141.50. He also took one catch. The TCA Cricket Museum at Bellerive boasts a large (1200 x 750) Bradman oil on canvas painted by Adelaide artist Joseph Goodhart in 1940. The Don is in batting stance at the crease at Kensington District Cricket Club. The painting was donated by the artist's daughter, Dame Mabel Miller, a former deputy lord mayor of Hobart and member of Tasmania's House of Assembly. In 1989 the TCA arranged for 250 prints of 66 x 43 to be published; all copies were signed by Bradman and were sold framed for $250.

Hobbs, (Sir) John Berry

The great Surrey and England batsman holds the world record of 197 first-class centuries (98 of them made after the age of 40), a mark which will never be beaten. He played his initial first-class game in 1905 at the age of 22 and passed WG Grace's record of 126 hundreds in 1925. Hobbs's tally of 197 is 80 more than the Don's, but the Englishman played 1,315 innings, nearly four times as many as Bradman's 338. Hobbs figured in 66 opening partnerships of more than 100 with Andy Sandham in county matches for Surrey, and eight with Wilfred Rhodes and 15 with Herbert Sutcliffe for England. In his last tour of Australia, in 1928–29, he proved to be prescient in asking the 20-year-old Bradman to pose for a photograph for his personal collection during the Fourth Test at Adelaide Oval. Hobbs's last Test series was the rubber against Bill Woodfull's Australians in 1930, the Don's record-breaking first series in England, but he continued with Surrey for another four years in a (probably ill-advised) attempt to reach 200 tons, and finally retired at the age of 52. The Don did not see Jack Hobbs at this best, but in the radio interview with the ABC in 1987 he bracketed him with Len Hutton as the two best English batsmen he had seen. In a poll conducted by Wisden in 2000 to choose the top five cricketers of the 20th century, Jack came in third behind the Don and Garry

Sobers. As late as 1948, Jack Hobbs was not allowed into the Long Room at Lord's because he had played cricket for money. In 61 Tests he compiled 5,410 runs at 56.94 with 15 centuries. He was knighted in 1953 and died in 1963 at the age of 81.

Hobson, James

English seaman who ran on to the ground at Adelaide Oval to take a photograph of the Don just after lunch on the last day of the Fourth Ashes Test in February 1937. He was ordered off by umpires Borwick and Scott but managed to snap his hero before running from the field. When Hobson appeared in Adelaide Police Court the same afternoon, he claimed that he had become a friend of Bradman's when he "looked after" him as a member of the crew of the *Orford* when the Australians sailed to England in 1934. Despite his insistence that he had "not done anything wrong", the errant sailor was found guilty of entering the playing arena of Adelaide Oval during a cricket match and fined two pounds. It was Hobson's choice not to pay the fine, and in default he was detained in the police cells until 5pm, giving him time to rejoin his ship, the *Ormonde*, before it sailed from Adelaide's Outer Harbour two hours later.

Hodgetts, Henry Warburton

Member of the South Australian Cricket Association and the Australian Board of Control who in early 1934 offered the Don a position in his stockbroking business in Adelaide which it was proposed he would take up later that year on his return from the tour of England. He was guaranteed employment for six years with time off to play cricket, enabling him to play the game as a sport and not for a living. Bradman's cricket-related contract with his three Sydney employers was about to expire and he wanted a career which had nothing to do with the game. He didn't want to leave Sydney but the offer was seriously tempting. When the Don told a friend, Bert Kortlang, that he was considering a move to South Australia, Kortlang went to see Harold Heydon, the secretary of the New South Wales Cricket Association. Kortlang told Heydon that Bradman was considering a move to another state and asked whether the association could do something to keep him in Sydney. Heydon's response was: "The New South Wales Cricket Association has made Bradman what he is, and he can't afford to leave New South Wales." For the Don this sealed the matter, and, despite opposition from wife Jessie, he accepted Mr Hodgetts's offer of 600 pounds a year and a new Chevrolet Roadster motor car.

In order to qualify residentially for South Australia for the 1934–35 season, he took up residence with his new employer in his mansion on the corner of Pembroke Street and High Street in Kensington Park, Adelaide, in February 1934, just before leaving for England. As it turned out, because of his serious illness at the end of the tour, the Don (with Jessie) did not return to Australia until January. He holidayed at Jessie's parents' property at Mittagong, near Bowral, for three months and arrived in the city of churches with Jessie to take up his new job on Anzac Day, 1935. Aside from time off for cricket and 18 months' service in the Army in 1940–41 (and a period of convalescence after his medical discharge), he worked for Harry Hodgetts's firm until 1945, when his boss was declared bankrupt, prompting Bradman to start his own stockbroking business. With Hodgetts awaiting trial for fraud, the Don was elected to his old boss's seat on the Board of Control as one of SA's three delegates. Hodgetts was convicted and sentenced to five years' imprisonment but was released early on health grounds. He died of cancer in an Adelaide hospice in 1949.

In November 2001, the *Weekend Australian* newspaper's *Magazine* published an article by David Nason alleging the Don was complicit in Hodgetts's fraudulent dealings. Nason also claimed that Bradman received special treatment from the official receiver and the Adelaide Stock Exchange in being allowed to take over the business in the Grenfell Street premises complete with Hodgetts's valuable client list, all at no cost to the Don. The article provides an insight into Hodgetts's opinion of Bradman in the wake of the affair from Adelaide lawyer Trevor McFarlane, who said that he was visiting the dying man on New Year's Day 1949 when the news came through on radio of the Don's knighthood. "Hodgetts didn't take very kindly to that. He thought it was most inappropriate." Frank Devine, writing in his column in the *Australian* five days after Nason's story, cited a conversation Devine had had with Bradman on the subject in 1995 and pronounced him innocent on all counts. The day before Devine's column, November 21, the Bradman family and the Bradman Foundation issued a statement expressing disappointment at the publication of the *Australian*'s two articles (another story critical of the Don had been published the day before the article on the Hodgetts affair) which they said "had caused a considerable amount of distress and sadness amongst members of the family and the Foundation". John Bradman said: "My dad was a decent person and scrupulously honest. He was a man who made an enormous contribution to the welfare of the community. It is unfair that the material has been published when my dad is not able to defend himself."

H

Holden Apollo

Bradman's car in his later years which he drove to engagements in the city. He parked inside the grounds of Government House in Adelaide when he attended a reception for his 1948 Invincibles in April 1998. The Don had a routine eye test soon after and was told he did not have to pay for another driver's licence until 2002.

Holden Street

Street in the Adelaide suburb of Kensington Park where the Don and Jessie lived at no. 2 from 1935.

Hollies, (William) Eric

England leg-spinner renowned as the man who bowled the Don for a duck in the last Test innings of Bradman's career at the Oval in 1948. Minutes before, the Australian skipper had walked out to the centre to a stirring ovation from the crowd and received three cheers from Norman Yardley and his team before taking guard. He played the first ball from Hollies with a dead bat, but the second was a perfect-length googly which the Don played on to his off stump. Bradman said many years later that had he known he needed just 4 runs for a Test average of 100, "I might have been more careful." But the shock dismissal was no fluke. The Don's scalp was one of five that Hollies claimed in the innings, and he had bowled Bradman for 31 with a top-spinner a couple of weeks before in Birmingham when he took 8/107 playing for Warwickshire. According to Jack Fingleton, author and one-time teammate of the Don's, Eric Hollies (who took all 10 wickets for 49 in an innings in a county match against Nottinghamshire in 1946) was a reluctant hero, or at least a reluctant Test hero. Writing in his 1949 book *Brightly Fades the Don*, Fingleton said that Hollies (who had played his first Test in 1935 and was to play several more after 1948) actually disliked Test cricket. "When he was chosen in 1948 for the Oval Test, Hollies wanted to withdraw, but the county committee persuaded him to play." Of his famous googly, Hollies was quoted by Arthur Mailey as saying: "I don't think Don saw it properly. He seemed to have tears in his eyes." But though Bradman later admitted to an emotional state of mind after the huge ovation from the crowd and the cheers from the Englishmen at the wicket, he denied that his vision was obscured by tears. Eric Hollies was 68 when he died in 1981.

Hollowood, Bernard

English writer who penned a piece on the Don in his *Punch Book of Cricket*, published in 1985, in which he defended Bradman against critics who claimed he was unsociable: "After a day's play cricketers love to drown their sorrows in beer or gin, but Bradman had no sorrows to drown."

"Home Sweet Home"
Song sung by Lillian Owens, a niece of the Don's, at his memorial service at Bradman Oval on March 28, 2001.

Horbury
Town in West Yorkshire where the Don spent one Sunday in 1930 signing 4,000 Bradman bats in the factory of William Sykes Ltd. The site was later acquired by Slazenger.

Hornibrook, Percival Mitchell
Left-arm spin bowler from Queensland who was the last man out (lbw) when the tour match between Bill Woodfull's Australians and Gloucestershire in 1930 finished in a tie. The Don scored 42 and 14 on a difficult wicket.

House Decorator
Occupation to which the Don once aspired as a boy.

Howard, (The Hon.) John Winston
Australia's prime minister and a "cricket tragic" who opened Stage II of the Bradman Museum at Bowral on August 27, 1996, the Don's 88th birthday. Mr Howard told the assembled crowd they were "paying tribute to the greatest living Australian, the man who had inspired the nation in the depression and continued to inspire young Australians. Sir Donald had enriched the country, and the museum would be a mecca for lovers of cricket everywhere." Mr Howard again proclaimed the Don the greatest living Australian when he launched the two Bradman stamps at the SCG in January the following year as the first of Australia Post's Australian Legends series released each Australia Day. The only time John Howard saw the Don bat was from the Hill as a nine-year-old when Bradman made 53 in his last game at the SCG, a testimonial for Bert Oldfield and Alan Kippax, in February 1949. He has nominated an afternoon he spent with the Don and Jessie in 1997 as his happiest personal memory of the celebrated cricketer.

On August 17, 2000, Mr Howard delivered the inaugural Sir Donald Bradman Oration in Melbourne, and, at the Don's request, in October the same year his government made changes to the Corporations Law Regulations to prevent his name being exploited by companies. A piece by

H

the Prime Minister is one of many writings on the Don in Peter Allen's 2001 book, *Farewell to Bradman: A Final Tribute*. He was the last person outside the Bradman family to visit the Don before he died on February 25, 2001. Soon after his passing, Mr Howard said: "He was a hero to me as a young child and he remained a hero to me all my life. But I'm not alone. There are millions of people around the world. He had a great impact on Australian life, especially during the Depression when his prowess on the cricket field lifted the hopes and the spirits of a people who at times felt they had little else."

Howard, Leslie
British stage and film actor of Hungarian origin who entertained the Australians at his Los Angeles home during the 1932 tour of North America. Howard was to die in 1943 when the Germans shot down his plane when he was returning to the UK after a lecture trip to Lisbon. The enemy believed Winston Churchill to be on board.

Howard, Thomas Harris
Former New South Wales player who served as team treasurer on the Don's first tour of England in 1930.

How to Play Cricket
Film produced in England in 1934, with a script written and spoken by Bradman. It was updated with comments by the Don recorded at his Adelaide home in 1993. An opportunity to study the master's batting technique in detail. Available on video.
Also an instructional booklet written by the Don and published in 1935 by Associated Newspapers, 95pp. Revised editions by various publishers appeared in 1948, 1949, 1953 and 1963.

Hughes, (Rev. Canon) E(rnest) S(elwyn)
Clergyman from St Paul's Cathedral, Melbourne (and a vice-president of the Victorian Cricket Association), who was asked by the Don to officiate at his and Jessie's wedding at St Paul's Anglican Church in Burwood, Sydney, on April 30, 1932. A few days later, the newlyweds were honeymooning in Melbourne at a house lent by a friend when Canon Hughes turned up on the doorstep. After pleasantries had been exchanged over a a cup of tea, he came around to the reason for his visit: "Jessie", he said, "I've got some bad news for you. I haven't been conducting services for some time and when I have, of course, it's been in Victoria, not New South Wales. I'm afraid I didn't get the right papers signed and you're not legal-

ly married – so you can go back on it if you want to." After much merriment all round, the proper papers were duly signed. Canon Hughes was involved in cricket administration from the 1890s, serving as vice-president of East Melbourne for seven years from 1902 and president from 1909 until his death 33 years later. He was a delegate to the VCA for several years and then a vice-president for two years before his election as president in July 1932, three months after his trip to Sydney. He presided over his last meeting on May 11, 1942, on the eve of his 82nd birthday. Two weeks later he died of a heart attack.

Hutchins, Brett

Tasmanian academic who wrote a PhD thesis of 75,000 words titled *Bradman: Representation, Meaning and Australian Culture*, completed at the University of Queensland between 1998 and 2001. Brett's abstract: "This thesis analyses the representation of the nation's greatest cricketer and renowned national hero, Sir Donald Bradman (1908–2001), in Australian culture. Bradman's many cricket records and awards tell us something of how his reputation has been attained and maintained, but they are of limited help in explaining why he is considered an outstanding and uniquely Australian icon. There is a need for explanation in this case due to the overwhelming shortage of critical academic investigation into Bradman in the fields of Australian studies, cultural studies, history and sports studies, which is a surprising omission given the Don's ubiquitousness in Australian popular culture.

"My study has two interrelated aims. Firstly, I seek to examine many of the specific ways that Bradman has been represented in an attempt to explain his heroism. Secondly, via this case study of the Don, it is intended to highlight and analyse some of the cultural discourses and narratives informing Australian iconography and mythologies. It is argued that the interaction between an identifiable combination of representations has constructed Bradman as a uniquely Australian icon, and that, in turn, these representations have both drawn upon and informed dominant formations of Australian iconography and culture. Major issues analysed include heroism, nostalgia, nationalism, mythology, commodification, politics and gender. Attention is also drawn to issues of statistical authority, media, celebrity, scandal, race and class. The objective is to layer different dimensions of Bradman's representation, each dimension affecting and modifying the other, thereby creating an 'ensemble of narratives' that help explain why he is a hero and, in the process, also tell us something about Australian culture."

H

Brett revised his thesis – bringing out the themes of nationalism, politics and commercialisation of the Don – in a book, *Don Bradman: Challenging the Myth*, published by Cambridge University Press in November 2002. He featured prominently in the ABC television documentary *Bradman: Reflections on the Legend*, first shown in September, 2004. Brett Hutchins is a lecturer in Sociology at the University of Tasmania but in 2005 will be taking up the same position at Monash University, Melbourne, in the School of Political and Social Inquiry. He has also published on the social and cultural dimensions of the rugby codes and at the time of writing is researching in the area of media studies.

Hutton, (Sir) Leonard

A dour opening batsman from Yorkshire, Hutton broke the Don's record for Ashes Tests of 334 and the world record of 336 not out held by Wally Hammond when he ground out 364 in 13 hours 17 minutes (more than twice as long as Bradman's innings) on a perfect batting pitch at the Oval in the final match of the 1938 series. It was England's 100th century against Australia. He was later to write: "Don was the first to congratulate me on reaching 335 to beat his score of 334. He was most generous in his praise of my innings." Hutton had a successful series in a well-beaten side against Bradman's combination in 1946–47 (averaging 52 in the Tests) and won back and then retained the Ashes as captain in 1953 and 1954–55. As skipper in 23 Tests from 1952, he did not lose a rubber. In his 1987 interview with ABC radio the Don said he rated Hutton and Jack Hobbs the two best English batsmen he had seen. Len Hutton was the second Englishman (after Hobbs) to be knighted for his services to cricket as a player. He once said of the Don: "... but Bradman was Bradman, unique, a cricketer beyond comparison, and with deep reserves of character to support his talents." Hutton published two volumes of autobiography, *Cricket is My Life* in 1949 and *Fifty Years in Cricket* in 1984. He died in 1990, aged 74.

I

Images of Bradman

Edited by Peter Allen and James Kemsley, a book of photographs published by Allen Kemsley Publishing in association with the Bradman Museum. It contains over 400 pictures (some from the Don's personal collection which had never been published before) and 60,000 words. Launched in October 1994 by Richie Benaud at the SCG, the book was offered simultaneously in three versions: a hardback trade edition which was sold through bookstores for $29.95 rrp, a collector's edition priced at $50 and a leather-bound deluxe limited edition (signed by the Don) at $650. The collector's and deluxe editions were sold directly by the publishers. After Sir Donald's death, they offered remaining copies of the deluxe editions for $1,100 each. A substantial proportion of the profits from the book went towards the building of the museum.

India

When the first Indian side from the newly independent nation toured Australia in 1947–48 they were greatly weakened by the withdrawal of captain Vijay Merchant and several other leading players. Replacement skipper Lala Amarnath could not be persuaded by the Don (who feared the Indians would be greatly disadvantaged by wet wickets) to agree to have the pitches covered, and the Australians overwhelmed the opposition 4–0. It was against the Indians playing for an Australian XI before the Tests that Bradman posted his 100th first-class century, and it was in the Third Test at the MCG that he made a century in each innings of a Test for the first and only time in his career. In his book *Bradman: The Illustrated Biography*, Michael Page described this trip to Australia by the Indian team as "perhaps the happiest and most pleasant Test tour in the history of cricket". The Don's wife Jessie was hosted by Merchant when she stopped over in Bombay (now Mumbai) on her way to her husband's side when he took ill in England in 1934. Bradman is idolised in India, despite the fact that he never played there. In fact he set foot on Indian soil only once, when he was aboard a BOAC flight to London to report on the 1953 Ashes series for the *Daily Mail* newspaper. He'd instructed the airline to keep his flight a secret, as it was to make a brief refuelling stop in Calcutta. But BOAC, sensing a chance for some publicity, leaked it out and hordes of fans turned up at Dum Dum airport, as did cricket officials. Bradman faced the press patiently, but later sent a letter of protest to BOAC. Five years earlier, the Don was ill after playing in the oppressive heat of Colombo in the traditional stopover match on the way to England. After leaving Ceylon (now Sri Lanka), their ship, *Strathaird*, stopped in Bombay, but the Australians had heard rumours in Colombo of smallpox and even bubonic plague in India, and were reluctant to disembark. To the great disappointment of the Indians, only the manager, Keith Johnson, and one or two players were prepared to leave the ship at Ballard Pier. Bradman was nowhere to be seen, but the chanting of the crowd became so raucous that he was forced to appear at the deck rail and wave wildly back at them; but there was no question of him disembarking. The Don recorded (somewhat diplomatically) in his *Farewell to Cricket* only that he got out of bed to attend a small function at which (BCCI president) Anthony De Mello made a presentation to members of the team. "He made a speech (as did Peter Gupta and Vijay Merchant) to which hasty replies were made as the boat was about to leave."

Bradman received many invitations during and after his playing career to visit the subcontinent on his own terms but always declined. The Marxist Government of West Bengal considered erecting a statue of the Don alongside a memorial to Mahatma Gandhi in the heart of Calcutta but scrapped the plan when Bradman did not travel to India for the 1987 World Cup. Narendra Salve, the chairman of the Cup's organising committee, said: "It is difficult for me to explain the sentimental feelings of the people of India for Sir Donald. We in India look upon him not merely as a legend but something far beyond that." *Sportstar*, a mass magazine published in Chennai (formerly Madras), released a special edition to mark Bradman's 80th birthday on August 27, 1988. In an issue published on the Don's 90th birthday in 1998, Mumbai (Bombay) journalist Vasant Raiji wrote in an article entitled "The Unseen God": "Indians worship a multitude of gods. In Sir Donald Bradman they have their god of cricket. God is perfect. In the eyes of the Indians, Bradman is the perfect batsman. God is unseen. Indians have not seen Bradman play. God's ways are inscrutable. Indians cannot comprehend why, in spite of numerous pressing invitations, Bradman never came to India. Whatever happens is God's will. So if Bradman avoided India, it was Bradman's will. Disappointment, but no ill-feeling or rancour."

It was fitting that when the Don's final innings came to an end, the Australian Test side was in the country (in Mumbai) where he has more fans than the rest of the world. When told the news, coach John Buchanan said: "Let the spirit and the way he played the game live on." Captain Steve Waugh urged world cricket, beset by scandal, to "draw strength from Bradman's sportsmanly example". His team observed a minute's silence at their training session the next day. Great Indian batsman Sunil Gavaskar said: "To Indians, for most of whom cricket is a religion, Sir Donald Bradman was God, and there will be immense sadness at his passing away." On the first day of the Test the players from both teams wore black armbands. About 50 million people in India saw a television broadcast of the Adelaide memorial service a month later.

Ingham, Jack
English journalist who wrote of the Don in 1938: "It is strange, but, I think true, that all the time, day and night, somewhere in the world somebody is talking about Bradman."

Ink Group
Publisher (now part of John Sands) which produced a Bradman calendar for 2001 and 2002 with a photo and text about the Don on each page. Published in co-operation with the Bradman Museum. The 2002 calendar was sold out in the warehouse by November 2001.

Integrity
When asked by Ray Martin in the 1996 television interview how he would like to be remembered, the Don replied: "If I had to put it into one word: 'integrity'." During a conversation between journalist Frank Devine and the Bradmans in 1993, Jessie was speaking of the reputation for honesty in the Bowral district enjoyed by her husband's parents when he was a boy.
Jessie: "Don, do you remember the time your mother sent you to buy the biscuits and you couldn't help having a couple on the way home?"
Don: "Yes. She weighed them and sent me back to the store to complain of being short-weighted. So I did. The storekeeper made up the missing weight."
Jessie: "And it has stayed on his conscience to this day."

Intermediate Certificate
Examination passed by the Don at Bowral Intermediate High School in December 1922, when he was 14 years four months. The results were published in a local newspaper, the *Southern Mail*, on February 23, 1923. He gained A passes in Mathematics I and French and B passes in English, History, Mathematics II, Chemistry, Woodwork and Art.

I

Inverarity, (Robert) John MBE

Longtime West Australian and South Australian cricketer who lived two doors from the Don at no. 6 Holden Street, Kensington Park, in Adelaide from 1979 to 1988. John was mortified when Benji, his Cardigan Welsh corgi, wandered into the Bradmans' front yard one day in the early 1980s and made short work of several of the goldfish in their pond. But John's wife, Jane, said recently that the Don was good-humoured about it.

"Invincibles, The"

Nickname coined for the Don's team which toured England in 1948 after they captured a special place in cricket history by becoming the first Australian team to go through an Ashes tour undefeated. The team was Don Bradman (captain, SA), Lindsay Hassett (vice-captain, Vic), Sid Barnes (NSW), Bill Brown (Qld), Ron Hamence (SA), Neil Harvey (Vic), Ian Johnson (Vic), Bill Johnston (Vic), Ray Lindwall (NSW), Sam Loxton (Vic), Colin McCool (Qld), Keith Miller (NSW), Arthur Morris (NSW), Doug Ring (Vic), Ron Saggers (NSW), Don Tallon (Qld), and Ernie Toshack (NSW). The manager was Keith Johnson and the masseur Arthur James. The Australians arrived in England with thousands of food parcels and tins of meat donated by the people of Victoria and were warmly received wherever they went. In his 1950 autobiography *Farewell to Cricket*, the Don wrote: "In years to come, the 1948 tour will provide a topic of conversation amongst young and old. There will be arguments and counter-arguments as to whether it was the equal of earlier combinations. Nothing can alter the figures which will appear in black and white in the record books, but they cannot record the spirit which permeated the side, the courage and fighting qualities of the players, for these intangible things cannot be measured. They were on a very high plane."

But the "figures in black and white" were also on a "very high plane". The Invincibles played 31 first-class matches, winning 23 and drawing the remaining eight. Fifteen of their wins were by more than an innings, two were by 10 wickets, one by nine wickets, two by eight wickets and one by 409 runs. Their 721 runs in an innings in one day against Essex was a record which remains today. Seven members of the team racked up 1,000 runs and they scored 50 centuries against their opposing teams' seven. The tourists also drew a second-class game against Durham and won two others in Scotland. The Ashes series was won 4–0. Bradman played in 25 of the 34 games, having less rest than any other member of the team except Ian Johnson, who also made 25 appearances. Writing in his 1992 book *Captains of the Game*, former NSW captain and broadcaster Alan

McGilvray said of the Invincibles: "If the judgement were left to me, I would declare Bradman's 1948 side the best I have seen. It was my first tour of England as a broadcaster, so it all had a special adventure for me, I suppose, yet there was a mix to this side which made it as close to the perfect cricket team as I have experienced. Steadfastness in openers Arthur Morris and Sid Barnes, an emerging batting genius in nineteen-year-old Neil Harvey, a flamboyant and richly competitive all-rounder in Keith Miller, a lightning-quick wicketkeeper in Don Tallon, an extraordinary pace bowler in Ray Lindwall, a beguiling mix of pace and spin in Bill Johnston ... this team simply had it all. And, of course, there was Bradman himself, by now cricket's father figure, still commanding the adulation of English folk some eighteen years since he first captivated them with the brilliance of 1930."

The Don told Ray Martin in the 1996 television interview: "It was certainly the best Australian side that I played with, and it was not unreasonable to say that it was the best Australian side that was put together ... a very happy side. I think I felt like a grandfather, I had my 40th birthday on the tour ... the boys seemed very pleased to have me in charge. I had no worries with any of them on the tour. In previous tours I might have an argument with a young fella on how to play the game, but not in '48. They seemed happy to have me as the grandfather." Soon after the tour, the British Minister for State said: "No team has ever done so much to stimulate and to create good feeling." In 1998, on the 50th anniversary of the tour, a reception was held at Government House in Adelaide, followed by fundraising dinners in the same city then Melbourne and Brisbane. The Don attended the reception but passed on the dinners. In Brisbane the players and their wives were treated by ABC producer Lincoln Tyner to a preview screening of his documentary of the tour which was to be shown on television later in the year.

Invincibles, The

An ABC television documentary conceived and produced in Adelaide by Lincoln Tyner, originally shown on Tuesday, December 1, 1998 at 8.30pm, when it attracted nearly a million viewers Australia-wide. It has been repeated at least twice since. The 58-minute film features most of the surviving Invincibles in interviews with journalist Mike Coward, interspersed with footage of the 1948 tour. At the time of writing, sales of the video are approaching 30,000 copies, including about 9,000 of the boxed editions in which the film is packaged with Jack Egan's 1990 video, *Bradman*.

Also a book written by Peter Allen and published in 1998 by Allen & Kemsley in association with the Bradman Museum. The work includes the full match reports and scores originally published in the 1949 edition of *Wisden Cricketers' Almanack*. The publishers offered 48 copies of a leather-bound deluxe limited edition for $1,500 each. (At least two of these have since changed hands: one for $5,000 and another for $8,000.) A trade edition was distributed by the ABC at $49.95 rrp. The Bradman Museum receives royalties. Peter Allen's book and Lincoln Tyner's documentary were created independently of each other.

Ironmonger, Herbert ("Dainty")

Nicknamed "Dainty" because he was anything but, Ironmonger was a left-arm leg-spinner who started his first-class career in Queensland in 1909 but moved to Victoria in 1913–14. It was not until 1927–28, though, that he became a regular member of the Victorian side. He and the Don made their Test debuts in the same match the following summer: the first contest of the Ashes series at Brisbane's Exhibition Ground. In his 1946 book *Cricket Crisis*, Jack Fingleton wrote of a Sheffield Shield game in 1931–32 between New South Wales and Victoria at the SCG when Ironmonger took Bradman's wicket in the first innings for 23. The Don was not impressed by a newspaper claim overnight that Dainty had his measure. He said to his teammates before play the next morning: "It will be interesting to see what happens today." It would certainly have been interesting from Ironmonger's end, because the champion batsman flayed him from the first ball, hitting him all over the park with an array of drives and risky shots off his stumps before finally hoisting him over the fence. Bradman was eventually bowled by medium-pacer Lisle Nagel for 167.

In a charity match in the same season, Arthur Mailey, who by then had retired from the first-class game, was accorded the same treatment from the Don after a journalist reported that he had gone through the record books and found that the leg-spinner had taken Bradman's scalp on several occasions. But the treatment Ironmonger received from the Don in that game at the SCG did not discourage the 49-year-old. In the same season against the visiting South Africans he finished with the remarkable figures in the Tests of 31 wickets at 9.54. And Bradman lamented the fact that the Victorian never went to England. In his *Farewell to Cricket*, he wrote of Ironmonger: "Why he never went to England with an Australian team is a mystery to me. It is said that his action was doubtful, and he was not selected because of the fear that he would be 'no-balled' by English umpires. This can hardly be a reasonable excuse, seeing that the Australian umpires passed him. Anyway, in fairness to Ironmonger it should be pointed out that his peculiar delivery was caused by the loss of the first joint on the index finger of his left hand. This prevented him spinning the ball in an orthodox manner. I did not think his action questionable, and I feel sure he would have been a really outstanding success on an English tour." Bert Ironmonger died in 1971 at the age of 89.

"Is Don Bradman Still Alive?"

What Nelson Mandela asked Malcolm Fraser when they met in 1990 soon after Mandela emerged from 27 years' imprisonment, including 18 years on Robben Island. When Mandela came to Australia in September 2000, he recalled: "In the '30s and '40s, at least in our country, we regarded Sir Donald ... we were tempted to regard him ... as one of the divinities, so great he was and such an impact he made."

It Ain't Cricket

A play in which the Don made an appearance when it was staged by JC Williamson in Adelaide in 1933. The entertainment was written by Kerwin Maegraith and performed as a fundraiser for a testimonial for former South Australian and Test fast bowler Ernest Jones. The 16-page program for the event has a large photograph of Jones and a page of "sidelights" of his career, as well as a full-page synopsis of the play. A portrait of Bradman is accompanied by the text: "Don Bradman makes his first appearance as an actor in 'It Ain't Cricket'. He will beat the leg field in the second act and paste tennis balls at the audience and also at the gallery. He will hit a dozen to them and these will be autographed by himself and Ernest Jones." The Don corresponded with Maegraith into the 1960s.

"I Want to Know Everything"

What King George V said on hearing of the Don's critical condition with peritonitis in London in September 1934.

J

Jackson, Archibald Alexander

Had the Scottish-born Jackson lived longer, some observers believe the young man with a genius for timing and placement would have gone further as a batsman than even Bradman. His withdrawal from the New South Wales side to meet South Australia in a Sheffield Shield game in 1927–28 because of a boil on his knee provided the Don with his chance in first-class cricket. The 19-year-old Bradman was the nominal 12th man after being included in the squad for NSW's second shield game of the season only when the great Jack Gregory pulled out. He made the best of the opportunity at Adelaide Oval by scoring 118. Jackson, who like the Don was also a superb outfield, played first-grade cricket in Sydney as a 15-year-old and gained selection for his state at 17 in 1926–27. The following season, having been promoted to opener, he made 131 and 122 in a shield game against SA at the SCG.

The Don was at the other end on the third day of the Fourth Ashes Test in Adelaide in 1928–29 when Archie faced the first delivery after lunch, a new ball from Harold Larwood, and reached his hundred with a shot which, Bradman said later, was "the most beautiful square drive for four that I've ever seen in my life". Jackson went on to score 164, failing by one run to equal the record for an Australian on Test debut set by Charles Bannerman in the first-ever Test in 1877. But at 19 years 152 days, he became the youngest player to score a Test century, eclipsing the record set by Bradman a month before in Melbourne. Although Jackson helped the Don to a record fourth-wicket stand of 243 in the final Test of the 1930 series in England, he was rarely at his best in the Tests on the tour, no doubt feeling the effects of the illness which was to carry him off three years later. He became engaged to be married on his death-bed in hospital in Brisbane and died at the age of 23 from tuberculosis on February 16, 1933, the day that England regained the Ashes at the 'Gabba. The Don was a pall bearer at the funeral in Sydney.

Jackson-Nelson, Marjorie AC, CVO, MBE

Governor of South Australia who unveiled a statue of the Don near the eastern gates of Adelaide Oval on February 25, 2002 to mark the first anniversary of his death. Artist Robert Hannaford created the 2.5m statue, which depicts Bradman playing a straight drive, after a commission from Adelaide City Council in 1999.

James, Arthur

Australian masseur on the 1948 tour of England. He attended to players at any time of the night or day, but performed many other duties, notably opening the Don's many letters at the grounds and organising the mailing of replies.

Jardine, Douglas Robert

Born in Bombay in 1900 and educated at Oxford, Jardine was an austere character of iron will and inflexible self-discipline whose name will for ever be linked with Bodyline. As captain of England in the 1932–33 series in Australia, he instructed his fast bowlers, Harold Larwood, Bill Voce and Bill Bowes (and also Gubby Allen but he refused), to bowl short-pitched balls at the batsman's body with a ring of short-leg fielders and one or two men on the boundary in catching positions. There has since been much conjecture about when and by whom bodyline bowling was conceived, with no shortage of conflicting claims and counterclaims, but there can be no doubt the man who saw it through was Douglas Jardine, and he saw it through with an obsession unmatched in the history of international cricket. He and Larwood, his main strike weapon, always claimed that bodyline bowling, or "fast leg-theory", as they insisted on calling it, was not unlawful, and they were right. But their contention that the ploy was merely an extension of the leg-theory method of attack which has been a recognised tactic of the game since the late 19th century was refuted by the Don in his *Farewell to Cricket*. Jardine published a defence of his tactics in his book, *In Quest of the Ashes*, soon after the tour. But in rare praise of Bradman (and indeed of any Australian), he said in conversation years later with commentator John Arlott: "You know, we nearly didn't do it. The little man was bloody good."

Douglas Jardine played against the West Indians in England in 1933 (when he scored 127 at Old Trafford in the face of bodyline-type bowling from Constantine and Martindale) and captained the MCC in India in 1933–34, but thereafter he played very little first-class cricket. Just after Bill Woodfull's side arrived in England in 1934, he is reported to have said: "I have neither the intention nor the desire to play cricket against Australia this summer." In his 1992 book *Captains of the Game*, Alan McGilvray wrote of the time years later in England when he played golf with Jardine and asked him whether he had any regrets about what he had done in 1932–33. "Jardine drew himself to his full height and glared at me.

'None', he said. 'None whatsoever. I did what I had to do. I won the Ashes for my country, and if I offended people that's unfortunate. We had to prove we could defeat Bradman and we did.'" The Don's only contact with Jardine after Bodyline was a brief exchange when they were both working in the press box in England in 1953. When told of Harold Larwood's death in 1995, the Don paid him a tribute as "a fierce cricketing rival and a good friend", but when asked for his reaction after Jardine died in 1958, he had spoken just two words: "No comment."

Jarmers

A restaurant near the Don's home in Kensington Park, Adelaide, where he often entertained. On one occasion the management opened especially for their famous patron to host a luncheon for visiting MCC president Colin Ingleby-Mackenzie. Bradman had a preference for traditional food such as shepherd's pie and rice pudding but liked to wash it down with Henschke Hill of Grace shiraz.

Jeanes, W(illiam) H(enry) OBE

Then secretary of the Australian Board of Control who was manager of the Don's team on the 1938 tour of England. His OBE was announced during the tour. Jeanes was secretary of the South Australian Cricket Association before his appointment as secretary of the Australian Board.

"Jodrell Hall"

The country home of Sir Edwin and Lady Stockton where the Don and the other members of Bill Woodfull's touring side were entertained on the Sunday of the Fourth Test at Old Trafford in July 1930.

John Player's

Set of cigarette cards featuring 25 English players and several leading Australians, including the Don, issued in 1932. The cards were very popular with collectors in the '30s and '40s.

Johnson, Ian William CBE

A right-hand offspin bowler and useful batsman from Victoria, Johnson was capped for his state at 17 before joining the RAAF and flying Beaufighters in the south-west Pacific during the war. He made his international debut against New Zealand in Wellington in 1946 (a match which was not granted Test status until March 1948) and appeared in the Ashes series at home under the Don in 1946–47 and the series against India, again at home, the following summer. Of his first official Test against England at the 'Gabba in December 1946, Johnson was later to write: "He [Bradman] sat and talked with me for three-quarters of an hour because he didn't want me to be alone on the morning of my first Test. It was, I think, the most human thing I have encountered in sport." In the Second Test against the Old Enemy in Sydney, Johnson was virtually unplayable, taking 6/42 in 30.1 overs. He went to England with Bradman's great side of 1948 but his style of bowling, very slow through the air and relying on bounce and turn, was not generally suited by the softer wickets in the Old Dart, though he did have tour-best figures of 7/42 against Leicestershire.

He more than once made a valuable contribution with the bat, notably on the second day of a game against the MCC at Lord's when the skipper told his men to go for the runs, and Johnson, Miller and Lindwall hit 12 sixes between them, many of them well back into the crowd. And when the tourists were in danger of defeat in the match against Hampshire (having rested himself from the game, Bradman sent a motivational wire to stand-in skipper Lindsay Hassett from London), Ian was promoted in the order and played a match-saving dig. The Don was again absent when Johnson scored the first century of his career against Somerset. During the tour, Bradman recorded that Johnson, as a right-hand off-spin bowler, "… is a good example of one who intelligently combines the essential elements of flight, spin and accuracy". Summing up Ian's performance after the tour, he wrote: "Spinner who really turned the ball and had a beautiful control of flight. At his best on dry crumbling wickets – the wet ones made him too slow."

Ian Johnson became the first Australian captain to lead his country before West Indian, Indian and Pakistani crowds, and was only the fifth Australian to achieve the Test double of 1,000 runs and 100 wickets. He became a sports columnist and broadcaster, published several books, including *Cricket at the Crossroads* (dedicated to wife Lal) in 1957, and beat a field of 44 other candidates for the post of secretary of the Melbourne Cricket Club in April 1957, a job he held until 1983. He was awarded an MBE, OBE and a CBE. Ian attended the first two of three 50th-anniversary charity reunion dinners for the Invincibles during 1998 but then took ill and could not attend the third in Brisbane. Lincoln Tyner, the producer of the ABC television documentary *The Invincibles*, conducted a private preview screening of his then recently completed film in Brisbane for the players and their wives. Tyner said it was most satisfying for him to see them together watching it and to see how much they enjoyed it. "When I returned to Adelaide, I wrote to Ian and sent him a VHS copy of the documentary, hopefully to cheer him up. I received a typed and signed thankyou letter from him saying how much he enjoyed the film. It was dated 10 days before he died. After his passing I spoke to his widow and she said that the whole family gathered together to watch it and that Ian was beaming afterwards. It really meant a lot to me to know that I had given his spirits a lift during his final days. He was such a gentleman." Ian Johnson was 80 when he died in October 1998. He was the son of WJ (Bill) Johnson, who served with Bradman as a Test selector in the 1930s.

Johnson, Keith MBE

A New South Wales delegate to the Australian Board of Control who served as team manager on the Invincibles tour of England in 1948. In his *Farewell to Cricket*, the Don wrote: "Keith worked like a slave night and day. He never stopped answering the phone and writing letters." On the boat journey home he was presented by the players with a solid silver Georgian salver with their signatures. Keith Johnson was later made an honorary life member of the MCC.

Johnston, William Arras

A tall man who was a good-humoured character but a tough competitor, Johnston said he became a Test player only after selector and former Australian captain Jack Ryder advised him to change his bowling style and the Don agreed. "I was a slow left-armer when I started out, but Bradman convinced me I should try bowling fast. I thought that sounded like hard work, but I gave it a go and it helped me into the Test team." Johnston made his Test debut in the home series against India under the Don in 1947–48 and got the nod to tour England with his great side of 1948, when he was an invaluable link between Ray Lindwall and Keith Miller. His 27 wickets in the Tests (equal best with Lindwall) included a bag of 9/183 in 84 overs in Australia's victory at Trent Bridge, and he was the only member of the side to take 100 wickets on the tour.

In his *Farewell to Cricket*, the Don wrote of Johnston: "Clean-bowled some of the best, and throughout the tour was constantly getting good wickets when perhaps a little more glamour was attaching to his faster colleague, Lindwall ... With it all, a most amusing personality who saw the lighter side of everything he did." Of the Don as skipper, Johnston said: "Bradman was a very astute captain and he gave me advice on a number of occasions. But he would never answer your questions unless he was sure he had the right answer." Bill had the Don caught behind for 10 when playing for Lindsay Hassett's XI in the second innings of Bradman's testimonial game at the MCG in December 1948 and three months later bowled him for 30 in a Sheffield Shield game at

Adelaide Oval in the Don's final first-class innings. In life after cricket, Bill Johnston managed a beachfront highrise on Queensland's Gold Coast. Now 82, he is still resident in that part of the world.

Jones, Ernest

A fast bowler from South Australia who supposedly fired a ball through the beard of WG Grace in 1896 on the first of his three tours of England. The Don performed in a play written by Kerwin Maegraith and staged by JC Williamson as a fundraiser for a testimonial for Jones in Adelaide in 1933. In the play's second act, Bradman hit a dozen tennis balls (autographed by himself and Jones) into the audience. Ernie died in 1943, aged 74.

Jones, (Dr) Isaac

Australian physician in London who attended the Don when he had trouble with his back early in the tour of 1938.

Jones, Richard

State selector (later chairman of the SCG Trust) who was behind the letter dated October 5, 1926 from the secretary of the New South Wales Cricket Association to young Don Bradman (care of Alf Stephens, the president of the Bowral Town club) inviting him to a trial for promising country players at SCG no. 2 on October 11. The Don's style in the nets prompted Dick to suggest that he should play in Sydney club cricket, but the 18-year-old said that he could not afford to come to Sydney, and that "I'll have to go back to Bowral and play tennis." One of Jones's co-selectors, Harold Cranney, asked the lad to join his Central Cumberland club but later withdrew the offer because the club could not afford to pay his train fare to and from Sydney each week. But a few weeks later, Jones saw Bradman's ability in making 37 not out in a state trial match at the SCG and approached his St George club (of which Jones was a former captain) about making the Don an offer. He was signed up soon after.

Joseph, Betty

The Don and Jessie's housekeeper at their Holden Street, Kensington Park, home from 1989.

Joyce, Eileen Alannah

The Don was in the audience during his last tour of England when the Australian pianist collapsed on stage after performing in London's Albert Hall in August 1948.

K

Kelly, William Harvey
The team manager on the Don's first tour of England in 1930.

Kelly, Edward ("Ned")
The only Australian who is the subject of more biographies than the Don. Ned figures in 14 (including a recent A–Z) and the master batsman 12, although there are over a dozen other books with Bradman's name in the title.

Kemsley, James Frederick ("Jed")
Son of James Kemsley, co-editor and co-publisher of *Images of Bradman* and co-producer of *Farewell to Bradman* (and a former Bradman Museum director). James senior told *Southern Highland News* soon after the Don's passing that the Australian icon was an affable man who loved kids. "I've been involved in the Bradman Museum all the way along and there's one thing that stood out knowing him. When I was in Adelaide I called in to see him because I wanted to get some bats signed. I walked into his house with my eight-year-old son Jed, and Sir Donald asked him, 'Do you play?' and 'Do you bat or bowl?' Like all kids, Jed answered, 'I bat and bowl,' so Don proceeded to give him a batting lesson right there in his lounge room. I just stood there with the hairs on the back of my neck standing up. He did lots of things like that."

Kennedy, Joyce
Actress with whom the Don was photographed when the Australian team visited Elstree Studios in Hertfordshire near the end of the 1930 tour of England.

Kensington District Cricket Club
Adelaide club with which the Don played 46 innings in 37 games over eight seasons (all as captain) from 1935–36 to 1940–41 and in 1946–47 and 1947–48. He made 3,377 runs at an average of 84.43 with 14 hundreds. Bradman's most prolific season with the club was his first, 1935–36, when he scored 811 runs in 12 innings at 67.58, but his best average (excluding 1940–41, when he played only one innings of 212) was in his

last season, 1947–48, when he made 162 runs for only once out in four innings. Of the matches in which Bradman appeared, Kensington won 21, drew six and lost 10, but claimed only one premiership: ironically in 1945–46, when he did not play any grade cricket. The Don's top score, and his most famous innings, was his 303 (in 226 minutes), with 41 fours and a six, against Glenelg at Kensington Oval in November 1939, but probably his most remarkable innings was the 207 he scored in March 1947 in a semi-final against West Torrens at Adelaide Oval. On the first day, Torrens made 301. Halfway through the second afternoon when Kensington had lost 8/185 and needed 117 to win with only two "rabbits" to bat, many spectators left the ground with the Don still short of his century. But then the 38-year-old took the long handle to the attack and manipulated the strike to the extent that at one stage his partner, Peter Kitto, added six while his skipper put on 97, and in all contributed only nine of their stand of 117. Bradman hit 27 fours and a six. Chasing their second premiership on the trot, Kensington progressed to the final the following week against Sturt but, despite Bradman's 86 of 270, went down by six wickets.

The Don's only duck came in 1935–36, when he was bowled by Port Adelaide fast-medium Charlie Deveson in a semi-final which Port won by an innings. It was the fourth time that Deveson had dismissed Bradman (including twice in a Sheffield Shield match in 1930–31 when the Don was playing for New South Wales) but never did so again. Two bowlers dismissed Bradman twice in his career with Kensington: Colts' Alan Branstrom in March 1939 and Sturt's Harvey Hutton in the first match of the following season. Port Adelaide off-spinner Maurie Roberts once recalled being hammered by the Don for 30 and 22 off consecutive overs during his score of 188 in October 1939. He said the wider he bowled outside the off-stump, the more he was pulled and driven through the on-side. But Roberts gained some solace by being the last bowler to capture Bradman's wicket in grade cricket in January 1948.

The Don won Kensington's batting trophy five times and was a member of the committee from 1935 to 1959 and a delegate to the South Australian Cricket Association for over 20 years. He was made a life member of the Kensington District Cricket Club in 1961 and wrote the foreword for the club's history published in 2000. David Parkinson, a partner in the Adelaide firm Parkinson Blunden (now effectively run by his sons), which distributes cricket and other sporting equipment, has had a long association as a player then as an administrator (and now vice-patron) with Kensington. In a tribute to Bradman published in the club's annual report for 2000–01, Mr Parkinson wrote: "I was privileged to have known Sir

Donald personally for over fifty years; firstly as a 'wide-eyed' schoolboy, and then as a fellow committeeman and associate in later years. Although a very private man, Sir Donald was very approachable and, on request, would visit my business establishment in Norwood and personally sign Gray-Nicolls and Kookaburra bats, books and photographs, then willingly chat with my son Sam and me about many topics. You can imagine what a great thrill and honour these meetings were to Sam and me."

Kensington Park

Suburb of Adelaide where the Don and Jessie lived in the house they built at 2 Holden Street from 1935. Bradman stayed with his new employer Harry Hodgetts in his mansion in the same suburb for a few weeks in February–March 1934 before leaving for England to qualify residentially to play for South Australia in 1934–35.

Kippax, Alan Falconer

A stylish right-handed batsman who was the Don's captain in the New South Wales side, Kippax made his Test debut in the Ashes series at home in 1924–25 and toured England with Bradman in 1930 (when he averaged 54.83 in the Tests) and 1934 (when the 37-year-old was overlooked as vice-captain in favour of the 25-year-old Don). Kippax had been surprisingly omitted from the Ashes touring side in 1926 after averaging 112 in the Sheffield Shield competition the previous summer. Overall, his 61 shield appearances yielded 6,096 runs at 70.88. His career best was 315 not out against Queensland in 1927–28. In one match in 1928–29, against Victoria at the MCG, he scored 260 not out and added 307 for the last wicket with his final batsman, Hal Hooker, who made 62. Bradman shared in more century partnerships with Kippax (17) than with any other batsman.

Alan once wrote of Bradman: "If Don played for the West Indies they would be the leading cricketing country. If he played for New Zealand they would be the leading cricketing country. If he played for England they would be the leading cricketing country. If he played for South Africa they would be the leading cricket country." Of Kippax, the Don wrote in his autobiography: "This beautiful and stylish player was unlucky to emerge on the horizon of big cricket at a time when New South Wales had virtually an international side for its State XI. When his opportunity did come, Alan proved a real stalwart. In addition, his Trumperian style must have influenced for good vast numbers of young boys." When Bradman came out of retirement in February 1949 to play in a Kippax-Oldfield testimonial at the SCG under Arthur Morris, it was his last outing at his favourite ground and the first time in 14 years that he did not captain his side. He scored 53 in 65 minutes. Alan Kippax published a book, *Anti-Body-line*, and died in 1972, aged 75.

Kishenchand, Gogumal

Right-handed batsman and occasional leg-break bowler off whom the Don scored his 100th run in his 100th first-class century, in a game between an Australian XI and the Indians at the SCG on November 15, 1947. Bradman was on 99 when the last over before tea was due, and Indian captain Lala Amarnath threw the ball to Kishenchand, who had not bowled a ball so far on the tour. The Don pushed his second delivery to leg for a single to complete his century after 132 minutes. When film of the highlights was shown in England, the writer RC Robertson-Glasgow observed that "at that historic statistical moment, when Bradman was about to go from 99 to 100, there was the Indian bowler trying to deliver the ball with one hand and applaud with the other, a feat that is beyond the most enthusiastic practitioner."

Knight Bachelor

Title with which the Don was invested on March 15, 1949 by Governor-General William McKell in Queen's Hall, Parliament House, Melbourne. The honour had been announced on January 1 of the same year. He was knighted "in recognition of his services over many years as a cricketer and captain of the Australian Test team and for public services in several directions". Bradman is the only Australian to be knighted for services to cricket and was the first from any country to be so honoured mainly for performances on the cricket field rather than in the administration of the game. In the 1987 radio biography *Bradman: The Don Declares*, he told Norman May about receiving the honour: "I had gone to Melbourne to watch a match between South Australia and Victoria, and it was announced on the morning of January 1. I was in bed that morning when the South Australian boys came around to my bedroom to congratulate me, and they took a picture of me which was not very flattering, in my pyjamas." May commented that people have a choice whether or not they accept a knighthood, and he asked the Don for the reasons why he had accepted his. "That is true, yes they do have a choice, and I can recall when I was invited down to Government House and I was given the information that they wished to confer a knighthood upon me, I asked the question, 'Did I have to accept it,' and I can still see the look on the fellow's face when I asked

K

that question, which gave me to understand very smartly that I really didn't have any choice in the matter ... but this was an honour that I never sought nor dreamt about. If there had been nobody else to please but myself, I would've preferred to remain just plain Mister, and in many ways life would have been easier for me and my family in the future, I think, if I had, but it was an honour for the game of cricket, and in that context I accepted the responsibility of the title conferred by knighthood. I confess to feeling somewhat uncomfortable when close friends call me Sir Donald instead of just Don, but I've learnt to live with that. It has not changed the way I feel or the way I conduct my life. Of one thing I do feel very proud, and that is that few people have ever carried the title of lady as graciously as my wife has, and if ever a woman deserved to be called a lady, she did."

Kooyonga
Golf club in Adelaide where the Don won the A-grade medal at the age of 79 in 1988 with a 76 off the championship tees. For eight years from 1990 he played a round each Tuesday with Frank Zander, a retired pharmacist. Bradman also played four-ball on Saturdays. Kooyonga was one of the few places where he could find sanctuary and he enjoyed eating at the club where the staff were instructed not to single him out for special attention.

Kortlang, Harry Herbert Lorenz ("Bert")
When the Don told Kortlang, a friend, in early 1934 that he was considering an offer of employment from Adelaide stockbroker Harry Hodgetts, Kortlang on his own initiative went to see Harold Heydon, the secretary of the New South Wales Cricket Association. Kortlang told Heydon that Bradman was considering a move to another state and asked whether the association could do something to keep him in Sydney, and Heydon's response was: "The New South Wales Cricket Association has made Bradman what he is, and he can't afford to leave New South Wales." For the Don, this made up his mind, and, despite opposition from wife Jessie, he accepted Mr Hodgetts's offer of 600 pounds a year for a minimum of six years. Bert Kortlan was a much-travelled cricketer and a leading batsman for Victoria and Wellington, New Zealand, in 35 first-class games from 1909–10 to 1926–27. He died in Cottesloe, Western Australia, in 1961, aged 80.

L

Larwood, Harold MBE

From Australia's point of view, the one-time pit boy from the coalmines of Nottinghamshire and his ruthless captain, Douglas Jardine, were the villains of the turbulent Bodyline series in 1932–33, but when told in 1995 that Larwood had died, the Don said: "There was no personal animosity between us and we always remained good friends … and the fact that he made Australia his home showed his great love for this country." Though Larwood was booed around Australia for most of the summer when he bowled what he always insisted on calling "fast leg-theory", he was cheered from the field in the last Test of the series in Sydney after making a defiant 98 with the bat. He always objected to the term "bodyline": "It was maliciously coined by a cute Australian journalist for the express purpose of misleading. The mere use of the term 'body' was meant to damn me, and damn me it did." After returning home in 1933 Larwood refused a call from England's cricket establishment to apologise for his part in Bodyline and he never played for his country again, although a troubling leg injury sustained in Australia was a contributing factor. He once said of the Don: "Cricket fans of today have no idea how dynamic this little chap was." And on Bodyline he said: "There was only one man we were after – Bradman. There'll never be another like him. I've never seen such quick footwork."

In his final years there was no bitterness towards his treatment in either England or Australia. In fact, in an interview in 1994, when at 89 he was the oldest Test cricketer alive, he said cricket had been kind to him, taking him from the coal mines in England's Midlands as a 14-year-old to the grandest heights. He collected 2,000 pounds from his benefit match in Nottingham in 1935 and bought a tobacconist shop in Blackpool, where he had a visit from Jack Fingleton in 1948 when the former Australian Test batsman (who took many on the ribs from his host during Bodyline) accompanied the Don's tourists to England that year as a journalist. When Fingleton declined an offer of snuff, Larwood revealed that he always had some of the powdered tobacco in his pocket when he was bowling. "I often used to take a pinch of it on the field in Australia. It used to freshen me up. And it's much better for you than cigarettes."

L

Larwood and Bradman shook hands at their first meeting in 15 years at a farewell function for the Don in London at the end of the 1948 tour. Harold's emigration with wife Lois and their five daughters in 1950 to what had been enemy territory was encouraged by Fingleton. After former prime minister Ben Chifley died in 1951, Larwood discovered that "Chif" had paid half the Larwood family's accommodation costs when they arrived in Australia from his own pocket. Harold Larwood published two memoirs: *Bodyline* (1933) and *The Larwood Story* (1965, co-written by Kevin Perkins), and was awarded an MBE by British Prime Minister John Major in 1992. He was 90 when he died in Sydney in 1995. On Bradman's death, Enid Todd, one of Larwood's daughters, paid tribute to the man her father regarded as "utterly unique … there never was and never will be anyone like him again." Harold Larwood's name was unveiled on Australia's National Maritime Museum's Welcome Wall on March 25, 2001, the day of the Don's memorial service in Adelaide. There is a website (sanctioned by Harold's family) devoted to the Bodyline legend at www.haroldlarwood.com.

"Lascia Chio Pianga"
Aria from Handel's opera *Rinaldo*, which the Don's granddaughter Greta sang at the ceremony accompanying the scattering of his and wife Jessie's ashes at Bradman Oval on October 18, 2001.

Launceston
Where the Don played two first-class games on the NTCA ground, both on the way to Perth with the touring side to board the ship for England, in 1929–30 and 1937–38. He made 20 and 79 respectively, for an average of 49.50. The NTCA venue was the only first-class ground in Australia on which Bradman played that he did not register at least one century.

Laurenti, Mignon
Australian Broadcasting Commission (later Corporation) publicist who escorted legendary American mouth-organ player Larry Adler to the Don's Adelaide home for a visit when Adler was in Australia in 1957.

Laws
The Don summarised his philosophy on the laws of cricket at the end of his 1987 radio interview with Norman May: "I think the job of making and administering laws is one of extreme difficulty, and our thanks are due to those who've shouldered this responsibility so far. You should only make changes after deep consideration and, mostly, experimentation,

because it takes a long time to get the answer. And I think the public must understand and appreciate this, but the lawmakers themselves should give weight, in my opinion, to two things. Firstly, that any change must be acceptable from a playing point of view, and secondly, that it is devised to make cricket as attractive as possible for the spectators. The survival of cricket in the final analysis will rest on these two matters, that people will want to play the game and enjoy it, and that the public are prepared to come and watch."

Leak, Bill

Sydney artist and cartoonist who insists that his name is not William. He was commissioned by the Bradman Museum to paint a commemorative portrait of the Don in 1989 (when his subject was 81) to celebrate the opening of the first stage of the Bradman Museum. The work was hung in the Archibald Prize of that year and is now in the museum. A limited edition of 334 prints were signed by the artist and Sir Donald and some are still available from the museum. In 1991 Leak did another study, commissioned by the National Portrait Gallery in Canberra, where it is on display.

Lee, A(mos) J(ohn)

The Don's headmaster at Bowral Intermediate High School who admonished the 12-year-old Bradman at assembly for leaving his bat behind after scoring 115 not out in a game against Mittagong High School at Mittagong.

Lee, (Dr) John

Melbourne specialist practising in Harley Street who attended to Australian team members in England in 1934 and who diagnosed "an unusual appendix condition" when the Don took ill in a London hotel two days before the team was scheduled to leave for Australia. Dr Lee called in the Australian surgeon Sir Douglas Shields for a second opinion and they agreed that Sir Douglas should operate.

Leg Before Wicket

How the Don lost his wicket 27 times in 295 first-class dismissals and another 10 times in 267 second-class dismissals.

Leg-spin

Technique which the Don employed when he stepped up to the bowler's crease. He took plenty of wickets early in his career for Bowral on the coir

L

matting but said much later that in big cricket he was happy to "leave the bowling to those who knew what they were doing". Bradman's best performance in a Test was 1/8 against the West Indies at Adelaide Oval in 1930–31. His best figures in a first-class match were 3/35 against Cambridge University in 1930.

Leicestershire

English county which the tourists played in the second match of the 1934 tour when the Don, as Bill Woodfull's vice-captain, led an Australian side for the first time. Bradman had been out of sorts before leaving Australia and was still unwell when the team arrived in the Old Country. He asked skipper Bill Woodfull to be rested from the first game against Worcestershire, but Woodfull insisted he play to counter English press reports of his indifferent health. The Don made a quick-fire 206 but the effort took a heavy toll of him and he expected to be excused from the second match in Leicester, but Woodfull took time out himself and handed over the reins to his deputy, who made 65.

Leveson Gower, (Sir) H(enry) D(udley) G(resham)

The short, slight Englishman known as "Shrimp" had a long first-class career as a player with Surrey and was captain in his only three Tests – in South Africa in 1909–10 – but his name is indelibly linked with the popular annual cricket festival in the North Yorkshire resort town of Scarborough which he ran for nearly 50 years. Leveson Gower selected an English combination (Leveson Gower's XI) which played against the Australians during the festival in a match held traditionally as the last on the tourists' first-class program. In the 1930s and '40s, Shrimp's teams were so strong that the match was known in the Australian camp as "the Sixth Test". The Don played in the festival game in 1930, 1934 and 1948, scoring 96, 132 and 153 respectively. In 1938 he was sidelined with a fractured ankle sustained in the Oval Test a couple of weeks before.

Bradman ranked his 1934 innings, when he plundered 132 (including 102 in boundaries) in 90 minutes before lunch on the first day, as the equal of his memorable 160 in the Middlesex game at Lord's earlier in the tour as the most exciting he ever played in England. When he reached 112 in this innings at Scarborough, he notched up his 2,000 runs for the season. During the first of two games against Surrey in 1948, the Don and his men attended a dinner which coincided with Leveson Gower's 75th birthday. The Australian captain recorded that the septuagenarian "cut a beautiful cake made specially for the occasion". At the Oval after Bradman's last

Test appearance in England, Mr (as he was then) Leveson Gower joined England skipper Norman Yardley in paying a tribute to the Don. In the festival game a couple of weeks later, Bradman's final appearance in England, he scored 153 and bowled the last over of the match.

Lillee, Dennis Keith MBE

When asked by the ABC's Norman May in 1987 to nominate the best Australian fast bowler he had seen, the Don said it was hard to go past the man from Western Australia, although he considered there was very little between Lillee and Ray Lindwall. Both were named by him in his all-time best World XI, published by Roland Perry after the Don's death in the book *Bradman's Best*.

Limited-Overs Cricket

The one-day game was the theme of an article the Don wrote for *Wisden Cricketers' Almanack* in 1986. And the subject came up during Bradman's extensive interview with ABC radio the following year. When asked his opinion of the modern game, he told Norman May: "Limited-overs cricket is undoubtedly a product of the modern era, and it reflects the society in which we live. It provides what the people require, and that is entertainment. Of course it has its weaknesses, the biggest one being that you don't have to dismiss your opponent in order to win. All out for 200 beats none for 199! The result is a preponderance of defensive bowling and field placing, but conversely the batsmen are forced to take the initiative and to improvise in their batting. There's no room in limited-overs cricket for the boor who thinks occupancy of the crease and his own personal score are all that matters. You have a much younger viewing audience, people who have not been educated to watch a man bat all day for 80, or wait five days to get a result. People are happy to see an off drive played from outside the leg stump. I think the advent of television and cricket under lights are now important factors and are integral in the whole scene and, in my opinion, one-day matches are here to stay, and I must confess I like watching them, especially the night cricket with the white ball. Test cricket must, in my view, remain the pinnacle and the final true test of skill. It's a bit like comparing grand opera with pop music. They're different but there's room for both."

The Don did not mention the fact that it was he, as chairman of the Australian Board of Control, who introduced international one-day cricket to Australia when the first four days of an Ashes Test were washed out in Melbourne in January 1971 and the board was facing an enormous loss in gatetakings. The innovation was not popular with purists but the game drew a crowd of 46,000. As well as the financial consideration, Bradman saw the move as necessary to keep faith with the public. As for how the Don himself would have fared in the shorter version of the game, the question was put to four of his 1948 Invincibles by Kersi Meher-Homji for an article in Sydney's *Sun-Herald* on February 24, 2002. Bill Brown said: "Bradman was a champion in first-class and Test cricket and would have been a champion in one-day cricket. He would have been supreme as a batsman and one of the best as a fielder." Arthur Morris concurred: "Bradman was a fast scorer and had all the strokes. He was an excellent runner between the wickets, the best out-fielder I've seen and a tremendous thrower from the deep. I never saw him drop a catch. He would have been a natural one-day cricketer." Sam Loxton said: "Of course he would have been a world-beater in one-dayers. In fact, the 1948 Australian team would have been a wonderful one-day side with so many attacking batsmen and all-rounders – especially Keith Miller. Remember, we scored 721 runs in a day against Essex off 128 overs." Neil Harvey said: "Don was a freak and would have excelled in five-day, three-day or one-day cricket today. Beside being a brilliant, adventurous batsman, he was a marvellous cover fielder and a deep thinker."

Lindrum, Walter Albert OBE

When the legendary billiards player invited the Don to step up to the table at the Adelaide home of Bradman's boss, Harry Hodgetts, in July 1935, the master batsman started with a respectable break of 56. But when Lindrum replied with his customary century break, his 26-year-old opponent was not happy. Such was his competitive nature, the Don hated not being able to perform at Lindrum's level, so he had a billiards room built in his new home (a couple of blocks away from Hodgetts's mansion), and practised nearly every day for a year until he was able to make a break of 100.

Lindwall, Raymond Russell MBE

Known for his classical style (the England player and manager Plum Warner once likened it to "poetry"), Lindwall was one of Australia's truly great fast bowlers. He played his first of 61 Tests against New Zealand in Wellington in 1946 and his last, at the age of 38, against India in Calcutta in 1959–60. He was also a school athletics champion and represented Sydney club St George in rugby league. Lindwall first played under the Don in the First Ashes Test at the 'Gabba in 1946–47. After the 1948 tour of England, Bradman wrote of the "lovely, graceful rhythm in his action". At that time he rated Lindwall a very close second to (Australian paceman of the 1920s) Ted McDonald as the best fast bowler he had seen. "Here we have … smooth rhythm, splendid stamina and fighting spirit, magnificent control plus ability to swing the ball and vary the pace."

For his part, Lindwall said of his time playing under the Don: "I never heard him say a word of criticism about anyone else in the game, player or official, and I never heard him complain about an umpire's decision," and, "No one could have treated me better than Bradman and, after playing under him in nearly 20 Test matches, I still say the same about him." Many years after his retirement from the game, Ray Lindwall was asked about his most satisfying moment in Test cricket. "I suppose it was in the hotel after removing [England's] Trevor Bailey twice for no score in Melbourne [in 1958–59]," he said. "Bailey called the waiter over and ordered roast duck." Lindwall published an autobiography, *Flying Stumps*, in 1954, and a biography by John Ringwood, *Ray Lindwall: Cricket Legend*, was published in 1995. The Don named Lindwall in his World XI, published in 2001 in Roland Perry's book *Bradman's Best*. Ray Lindwall died in 1996 at the age of 74.

Listerine Face Mask
Mask handed out free to spectators at the First Bodyline Test at the SCG in December 1932. Having withdrawn from the Australian team because of illness, Bradman watched the game from the stand, but apparently it was not recorded whether or not he "donned" a mask.

"Little Fella, The"
A common honorific for the Don among his Invincibles of 1948.

Livingstone, (Rev. Canon) John Robert
Canon who conducted the thanksgiving service for the Don at Bowral's Church of St Simon and St Jude and then the memorial service which followed at Bradman Oval on March 28, 2001. At the church service, Canon Livingstone thanked God for the cricketer's talent, idealism and integrity which, he said, set an example for us all. But Sir Donald had moved on. Heaven was not "an upmarket version of Bradman Oval or the SCG".

Lord's
Historic ground in St John's Wood in north-west London where the Don played what he considered to be technically his best Test innings: a chanceless 254 on his first tour of England in 1930. Although he made several higher Test scores (including his highest-ever of 334 at Headingley in the very next Test), he considered the Lord's innings to be his best

L

because "every ball went exactly where I wanted it to go until the ball I got out". With Bradman 155 not out on Saturday evening, Neville Cardus wrote in the *Manchester Guardian* that the Australian had "knocked solemnity to smithereens" and had made Lord's appear "too big to cover". At the end of the game, cartoonist Tom Webster rendered a sketch of a batsman's back receding towards a pavilion gate, with the caption: "This is a picture treasured by every member of the English XI. It is Mr Bradman." The Don's score was then the highest by an Australian in a Test, the highest Test score against England and the highest score at Lord's by any touring batsman. The first two of these records were broken by Bradman himself less than a fortnight later in Leeds.

But Lord's was the scene of an equally memorable innings four years later in a game against Middlesex. The home side had made 258 and Australia in reply had lost both Woodfull and Ponsford for none. Having gone for a duck in the previous tour match (the fourth of four consecutive low scores), the Don was none too confident as he walked to the wicket, but after some early luck when an inswinger from Jim Smith shaved his off stump, everything clicked and he made his 100th run on the last ball of the day, his ton taking just 75 minutes, with 19 fours. In an account of the century in the press the next morning, William Pollock, who played in the match for the opposition (and was to help shape Bradman's 1938 biography, *My Cricketing Life*), wrote: "Never have I seen a masterpiece of batting more glorious than Don Bradman's 100. It was supreme, it was epic." The next day the Don went on to score 160 in an innings which Bradman himself wrote, "probably ranks as the most attractive of my career from a spectators' point of view". (The bat he used was auctioned in 1998 by Christie's to an Australian collector for $28,750.) On the second afternoon of the corresponding game against Middlesex in 1938, Bradman was on 30 and wanted only another 19 runs for a record aggregate by the end of May but declared 21 minutes before stumps to give Bill Edrich a chance to complete his 1,000, a feat he duly accomplished. His declaration was motivated by the gesture by the Hampshire captain, Lord Tennyson, on the last day of May in 1930 in not appealing against the light so that the Don could reach the same milestone.

Bradman's top score in eight Test innings at Lord's was his classic 254 in 1930, and he averaged 78.71 with two centuries and one fifty. It was during his 102 not out in the second innings of the Lord's Test of 1938 that Bradman passed Jack Hobbs's record of 3,636 runs in Ashes Tests. The England opener reached the mark in 71 innings but the Don needed only 44. Bradman's overall first-class average in 21 innings at Lord's (the most he played on any ground in England) was 79.47, with six hundreds (including two double hundreds) and three fifties. His top score was 278, against the MCC in 1938, three runs short of Bill Ponsford's record for an Australian on the ground four years earlier. He also took four catches. The only occasion on which the Don won the toss in nine Tests in England was at Lord's in the Second Test in 1948, when the wicket was green. It was probably the first time, Bradman wrote later, that a captain won the only toss he wanted to lose. But his side won by 409 runs. This 1948 match was the last of 14 consecutive Tests in which he made at least one fifty, a sequence which started with the Second Test at the SCG in 1936–37. His 89 in the second innings in 1948 was the closest the Don ever got to a Test century without achieving it (but Bradman said later that he actually made 90, claiming a single called a leg-bye had come off his bat). In making 98 against the MCC at Lord's earlier in this tour, he completed his 10th score of 50 or more in successive first-class innings. It was during his farewell appearance at headquarters three months later, in a match after the Tests against the Gentlemen of England, that the Don passed 2,000 runs for the tour, becoming the only player to achieve the feat on each of four tours of England. During a lunch break in the game, he was presented by the Earl of Gowrie, president of the MCC, with a cake to celebrate his 40th birthday.

Apart from the tours of 1953 and 1956 which he covered as a pressman for the *Daily Mail* newspaper, Bradman's only return visits to Lord's (and to England) were for the historic ICC conference on throwing in 1960 and for a charity dinner for the Lord's Taverners Fund in 1974, when he spent a day signing 900 menus. On both occasions he made the trip as a member of the Australian Board of Control. He declined several offers to become president of the MCC. The flags at the home of cricket were flying at half-mast soon after news of the Don's death on February 25, 2001.

Loseby Park
Ground at Bowral which was visited in February 1928 by a team of mainly St George players, including the Don, to open a new turf wicket. At a reception, Mayor Alf Stephens presented Bradman, who was in his first season of first-class cricket, with a gold watch and chain on behalf of Bowral citizens.

Low, David
School captain in the Newcastle, New South Wales, suburb of New Lambton who was pawing at his unruly hair at a school function when the Don, the honoured guest, pulled out his comb and flattened it for him.

L

Loxton, Samuel John Everett OBE

Loxton was an all-rounder who played some swashbuckling innings for Victoria and Australia. He made a sensational first-class debut in 1946–47 when he scored 232 not out against Queensland and then made 80 in his first Test the following summer under the Don against India at the MCG. In Australia's first innings in the historic Fourth Test at Headingley in 1948, Loxton hit an Ashes-record five sixes in a whirlwind innings of 93 when the Don's side was fighting to avoid defeat. His skipper later wrote that one of Sam's sixes, off a ball from Ken Cranston that sailed over the bowler's head and landed 20 rows back into the crowd, was the "most glorious six I ever saw hit". In the Test before at Old Trafford, Loxton and his captain were involved in a prank on the field which resulted in an unexpected wicket. In the Don's words: "I think he [Alec Bedser] would still have been batting (for I saw no way of shifting him) had not Loxton and I been associated in a piece of tomfoolery in the field. Purely in fun we both ran for a ball, went past it, and when the batsmen thought an opportunity had occurred to steal another run, Loxton recovered quickly and ran Bedser out. There was no intent on our part. It was just one of those things."

In the last first-class game of the tour, the festival match at Scarborough, Sam had to retire when he was just 27 short of a 1,000 runs for the tour when in trying to sweep he deflected the ball off the edge of his bat into his face, breaking his nose. In an assessment of Loxton after the tour, his captain wrote: "Did a magnificent job as utility player ... Extremely powerful driver and the best player of the lofted drive amongst the moderns ... could keep going for long spells – on occasions bowled really fast and worried the best batsmen. The most dangerous field in the team." Sam Loxton served as a state member of Parliament in Victoria for many years and now lives on Queensland's Gold Coast. He and the Don were good friends as teammates and also when they later served together as selectors. An essay he wrote for the Ironbark Legends book on Bradman was titled "My Mate George". Sam, who experienced great tragedy in his own family only months before, was very emotional when interviewed by ABC radio the day after the great man's death on February 25, 2001. He was one of several Invincibles and other players of the past who attended the memorial service in Adelaide. Now 83, Sam is in pretty good health aside from failing eyesight.

"Lulla and Grandpa"

Poem by an unknown author read by the Don's grandson, Tom Bradman, at Sir Donald's memorial service at Adelaide's St Peter's Cathedral.

Tom's father, John, found the poem among the Don's possessions just after his death.

Lynd, Robert

Irish essayist and critic who once said of the Don: "When Bradman came out of the pavilion with his bat, you could have guessed he was a man of genius even if you had never heard of him."

M

McAdam, (Dr) Francis Victor

Team manager on the Don's first trip away (to Adelaide and Melbourne) with the New South Wales Sheffield Shield side in December 1927. Dr McAdam was president of the Central Cumberland club in Sydney from 1925 to 1931 and a NSW delegate to the Australian Board of Control from 1926 to 1930. He was 46 when killed in a motor vehicle accident in Macquarie Street, Sydney, on September 10, 1934.

Macartney, Charles George

Great Australian batsman (nicknamed the "Governor-General") whose innings of 170 against England at the SCG in February 1921 inspired 12-year-old Bradman to play on the famous ground. A few months later in England, Macartney belted 345 in an astonishing 240 minutes against Nottinghamshire, for many years the record for the most runs scored in a day by any batsman in a first-class game. The Don played against the Governor-General at the SCG in a contest between a combined Country side and a City side at the end of the Country Week carnival in November 1926. Macartney scored 126 and Bradman an even 100. Around that time, Charlie wrote of the Don in the *Sydney Evening* News: "He is rather weak on the on-side ... and has a bad habit of walking away from the wicket when playing defensive strokes. The latter fault is a common hard-wicket player's error." A few months before, at Headingley, the 40-year-old Macartney became only the second man (after Australia's Victor Trumper at Old Trafford in 1902) from any country to make a century before lunch on the first day of a Test (the Don becoming the third at the same ground in 1930). Several years later, Charlie Macartney was moved to say of Bradman: "He is the supreme test for bowlers, and nothing yet devised by spin or swing, pace of slowness, seems to provide any unpleasant moment for him." Macartney was 72 when he died in Sydney in 1958.

McCabe, Stanley Joseph

But for the deeds of a man named Bradman, Stan McCabe would have been the most celebrated batsman of his era. The stylish right-handed bat and fastish-medium bowler was the baby of the team at 19 when he went to England as a teammate of the Don's in 1930. He had a successful tour, scoring over 1,000 runs and playing all the Tests. Success followed at home against the West Indies and South Africa. In Sheffield Shield matches for New South Wales in 1931–32 he had an average of 438! Bradman and McCabe were in a NSW team which toured north Queensland at the end of the 1930–31 season when the Don spent three weeks in hospital after spraining an ankle in a game at Rockhampton. He wrote later that he regretted not seeing an innings by Stan at Gympie when he hit 18 sixes in an innings of 173.

In the First Test of the Bodyline series in Sydney, a game Bradman missed because of illness (but watched from the stand), McCabe took block with his side 3/82 and hooked Larwood's first ball to the fence. He continued to attack while wickets were falling around him, but the Don said later he considered McCabe was lucky three times not to get out playing hook shots before finishing on 187 not out. Stan had a good tour of England in 1934 and went to South Africa (without the Don) as Victor Richardson's vice-captain in 1935–36, when he made 149 in the first Test and blasted 189 not out in the second. (On this tour, the Australians agreed to play a South African baseball team at baseball. When someone complimented Stan on hitting the ball three times into the outfield he replied: "How can you miss? They're all bloody full-tosses.")

McCabe was Bradman's vice-captain in the 1936–37 Ashes series at home when a newspaper suggested just before Christmas (after Australia lost the Second Test to be 2–0 down) that some of the Australians were not supporting their captain. McCabe released a statement the same day saying that the players were wholeheartedly behind their skipper, and the Don himself issued a disclaimer saying the non-success of his team was not due to any lack of effort or support for him as captain. Nevertheless, McCabe and three other players, Chuck Fleetwood-Smith, Leo O'Brien and Bill O'Reilly (all four Irish Catholics), were called before the board in Melbourne after the Third Test (won by Australia) in the second week of January. McCabe was again Bradman's 2IC in England in 1938, and in the opening Test of this tour at Trent Bridge played what was his greatest innings.

Chasing 8/658, Australia were struggling at 6/194 when McCabe tore into the bowling, making 232 (in even time) out of 300. For the last wicket, he and Chuck Fleetwood-Smith put on 77 in 28 minutes, of which Stan made 72. During this period Hammond had five men on the boundary. Bradman believed this innings, which saved the game for the visitors, was the best he ever saw. Writing in his *Farewell to Cricket* he said: "Towards the end, I could scarcely watch the play. My eyes were filled as I drank in the glory of his shots … Such cricket I shall never see again, nor shall I ever feel competent adequately to describe this elegant display." Stan McCabe captained NSW from 1936 to 1942 but trouble with his feet prevented his return to cricket after the war. Instead, he went into the sporting goods business. Later in life, McCabe suffered terribly from gout. When he was found dead at the base of a cliff behind his Sydney home in 1968 (aged 58), there was suspicion that he had committed suicide, but evidence suggests that he lost his footing when throwing a dead possum over the edge.

McCool, Colin Leslie

Victorian leg-spinning all-rounder who appeared in all five Tests against England in 1946–47 under the Don and in three of the five Tests against the Indians the following summer, again under Bradman. He toured with the 1948 Invincibles but although performing well in the county matches he did not play a Test, mainly because a callus on his spinning finger would break open and bleed when he had bowled about 15 overs. The Don wrote after the tour that McCool "was without doubt the unlucky member of the side". McCool was fielding in Bradman's testimonial game at the MCG in December 1948 when the Don was on 97 and skied the ball with a top edge when attempting to pull. McCool chased the ball towards the boundary and juggled it before finally spilling it and then kicking it, and the Don was able to run three, thereby bringing up his ton.

Bradman wrote in his *Farewell to Cricket* that he never asked – and never wanted to ask – the all-rounder whether or not he bungled the catch deliberately, but in *Bradman: The Don Declares*, a radio biography recorded by the ABC in 1987, he said that, despite "uncharitable" suggestions from others at the time, he didn't think for a moment that McCool dropped the ball on purpose. In fact he believed that Colin did extremely well to even reach the ball. In his 1961 book *Cricket is a Game*, McCool wrote of Bradman: "I might as well come straight out and admit that I liked the bloke. As far as I am concerned he was fair, just and very human." He also recounted in his book how he was still getting over his shock selection for the Australian team to tour South Africa in 1949–50 when he received a letter from his old skipper saying: "You are capable of making as many runs as anyone else in this side. Remember that, and make every post a winner." Colin McCool went to England in 1952 and had five successful seasons in League and county cricket. He died in Sydney in 1986 at the age of 69.

McCormick, Ernest Leslie

A tall, slim paceman from Victoria who ran in to bowl without moving his arms, McCormick first played for Australia on the tour of South Africa in 1935–36, when he took 15 wickets in the Tests at 27.86. Playing under the Don in the First Test of the Ashes series in Brisbane the following summer, he dismissed Worthington with the first ball of the match and soon after bowled Hammond for a duck, but then broke down in the match with lumbago after taking one more wicket. McCormick played in three of the remaining four Tests of the rubber but he was never to bowl again with such fire. He was the only fast bowler taken to England with Bradman's tourists in 1938 and, sensationally, in the first match of the tour, against Worcestershire, he was no-balled 19 times in his first three overs for overstepping the mark. Despite all manner of adjustment to his run-up, he could not get it right. McCormick never recovered from this setback and rarely displayed his hostile best during the tour. But in his autobiography, the Don wrote of Ernie: "This fellow had the sharpest wit and the keenest humour of any tourist I know. No matter what the situation, he invariably found a fitting remark to cause a smile." Ernie McCormick died in 1991, aged 85.

McDonald, Colin Campbell

A right-handed batsman from Victoria who opened for Australia in 47 Tests between 1951–52 and 1961. McDonald was in his second first-class season when the Don came out of retirement in March 1949 for a Sheffield Shield match between South Australia and Victoria at Adelaide Oval which doubled as a testimonial for Arthur Richardson. Both captains agreed in advance that regardless of who won the toss on the Friday morning, Victoria would bat first, thereby ensuring Bradman would bat for SA on the Saturday and pull a big crowd for Richardson. But the visitors were all out by tea, and then the SA top order fell quickly, so that the Don strode to the crease in fading light with 20 minutes left before stumps. An out-of-practice Bradman scratched and prodded for a while before hitting the ball down the throat of McDonald at backward square leg. "I didn't drop it deliberately," McDonald said later, "but thank goodness I did. The next morning there were 10,000 in the ground. It was the best catch I ever dropped."

McDonald, Edgar Arthur ("Ted")

Great Australian fast bowler from Victoria who played only 11 Tests for his country between January 1920 and November 1921 – before moving to England and playing League cricket then representing Lancashire in county cricket from 1924 to 1931, when he garnered 1,040 wickets.

M

McDonald played in the Ashes Test at the SCG in February 1921 at which the 12-year-old Don Bradman was present with his father George. Later that year in England, McDonald took 27 wickets in the Tests, at the time a record for an Australian in an Ashes series in England. Nine years later the Don had his middle stump uprooted by the 39-year-old for 9 in a tour match against Lancashire. In an earlier season with the county Ted had bowled 1,250 overs. Bradman recorded in his 1950 autobiography: "I am now ready to argue his place amongst the greatest of all fast bowlers. It was hard to visualise a more beautiful action which, coupled with splendid control and real pace, made him the most feared bowler in England at that time." In his 1987 interview with ABC radio, the Don rated both Dennis Lillee and Ray Lindwall slightly ahead of McDonald on the list of Australia's greatest pacemen. Ted McDonald was killed in Bolton, England, at the age of 46 in 1937 when he tried to stop passing traffic after crashing his car only to be run down by another one.

McGilvray, Alan David AM, MBE

The man who would be the consummate cricket broadcaster was two years younger than the Don and played against him in Sydney grade cricket before making his first-class debut for New South Wales against Victoria just before Christmas in 1933. McGilvray told journalist Peter FitzSimons 61 years later that when he walked out on the MCG in that match with Bradman to bat he couldn't help noticing that all 50,000 at the ground were on their feet and roaring. He was as nervous as hell, but felt he had to say something to show the occasion had not got the better of him. Turning to his celebrated partner, he said: "Fancy that, Braddles, isn't it nice how all these people have come out to see me bat." In reply, the Don said not a word, made not a gesture, but merely looked back at him with what McGilvray described as "an odd kind of look that I will never forget as long as I live", and walked on to the crease. McGilvray was out for 11 and Braddles went on to make 187 not out. For the ex-Sydney Grammar boy, it was a middling debut for what turned out to be a middling batting career. In the illustrious company of Bradman, Brown, Kippax and McCabe, it was always going to be a battle to cement a place in the side.

On ABC radio many years later McGilvray said that when the Don came to Sydney as captain of South Australia for a return shield game in 1935–36, his first season with his new state, he had scored 117 against his old state in Adelaide a couple of months before and followed with innings of 233, 357 and 31 against other states. It was rumoured that the maestro had set his cap on another big score but McGilvray, who was captaining

NSW in the absence of the leading players in South Africa, successfully executed a leg-side play when he had the Don caught second ball at fine leg for a duck. As Bradman walked from the wicket, McGilvray said to him: "Just dream about that 300 you were going to get, won't you." McGilvray said he "never saw a look of annoyance on a man's face as he looked at me". When Alan walked off the field at tea, he was confronted by a big man who said to him: "Look here, I drove 350 miles to see this fellow bat, and now you get him out early for none? Every time my wheel turns on the way back to Wagga, I'm gunna say, McGilvray, the * # ! *." But McGilvray felt conscious of what he had said to Bradman and soon after sought him out in the dressing room and apologised to him.

In Alan McGilvray's 1992 book *Captains of the Game*, his chapter on Bradman is titled "Two Eras of the Don". The first paragraph emphasises Bradman's competitiveness: "There was much about Don Bradman that was striking. The swiftness in his feet and hands, the quickness in his eye, the power in his wrists, and the capacity of his brain to co-ordinate all of them instantly and precisely. But from the time I first met him, when we were both young cricketers in the Sydney club competition, to me his most striking feature was the fact that he was never, never, beaten. It was reflected in everything he did. From a casual game of tennis to a Test match against the world's best, or a debate on cricket's laws at the highest level of administration, Bradman would fight, seemingly to the death, to have his will prevail. It was the single quality above all others that was the basis of his greatness, both as a player and a captain."

When McGilvray retired as a commentator in 1984, Bradman gave an interview as part of a tribute program to him on ABC radio. On Alan McGilvray's passing in 1996, the Don said: "Alan will be sadly missed by the cricket community throughout the world. He was a highly respected commentator who brought a new dimension to the broadcasting of cricket and did so with distinction over many decades."

McKay, (Dr) Douglas Gordon

Adelaide medical specialist who treated the Don's children, John and Shirley, in the 1930s and '40s. McKay was playing for South Australia when he caught and bowled Bradman in a Sheffield Shield game at the SCG in 1927–28.

McKell, (Sir) William John GCMG

Governor-general of Australia who invested the Don with his knighthood in Queen's Hall, Parliament House, Melbourne, on March 15, 1949.

M

McKeown, J

"Sole Manufacturers" of "the Don Bradman special cricket boot", endorsed by the Don in the 1930s ("You may be sure the Wonder Batsman wears the Cricket Boots obtainable anywhere!"). McKeown's made their fancy footwear in the Sydney suburb of Erskineville.

McMichael Super Range Portable 4 Radio

A gift presented to the Don when the Australians visited MGM Studios in Hollywood during the private tour of 1932.

Madame Tussaud's

Gallery in London where a wax figure of the Don was first displayed in 1934.

"Magnum Opus"

Murray Hedgcock, an Australian journalist who has worked in London for many years, told in a letter in 1986 of the time in 1974 when the Don was in town for a Lord's Taverners function. After a press lunch at the Hilton Hotel, a queue formed to secure Bradman's autograph. When Hedgcock introduced himself, he asked: "When are you going to write any more books, Sir Donald – or was *The Art of Cricket* your magnum opus?" The Don replied: "Magnum opus? I don't even know what that means." Hedgcock wrote that this "seemed a splendid, simple way of cutting into a touch of pretension on my part".

Mailey, Arthur Alfred

New South Wales and Test leg-spinner who made his first-class debut in 1913–14 and played his first Test in the Ashes series at home in 1920–21. In his *Farewell to Cricket*, the Don wrote: "Arthur Mailey had a vicious spin, far greater than Grimmett. He also had a 'wrong-un' which was far better concealed, but to obtain these things he had to sacrifice accuracy ... Mailey never cared how many runs were scored off his bowling so long as he captured wickets." In 1932, after his retirement from the game, Arthur organised a private cricket tour of North America by an Australian team under Victor Richardson which doubled as an extended honeymoon for the Don and new wife Jessie. The object of the tour was to help English expatriates promote cricket in Canada and the United States. It was sanctioned but not paid for by the Australian Board of Control. Mailey secured the necessary financial backing from the Canadian Pacific Railway Company but the support was conditional on the Don's presence in the team, and

Bradman agreed to go provided Jessie could accompany him. Jessie was the only player's wife on the tour. The Australians travelled 10,000 kilometres across and around North America, mostly by train. There were only 12 players in the team and the Don took the field in every one of the 51 second-class matches played over a period of 75 days.

Four months before the trip, in January 1932, Mailey and Bradman were in opposing sides in a charity match at Sydney's Callan Park Hospital. On the eve of the game, a statistician had revealed in a newspaper item that the spinner had taken the Don's wicket several times. After reading the item, the 46-year-old Mailey said to Test batsman Jack Fingleton over lunch: "They shouldn't write stuff like that," and sure enough, Bradman punished Mailey mercilessly from the very first ball, hitting him to all parts of the ground and even breaking windows in Darling Street on his way to a score of 143. But Arthur exacted revenge when he had the Don caught for 2 in another charity game the following summer a few kilometres up the road at Gladesville Hospital.

Mailey started his working life as a labourer and a plumber but became known as a wit, philosopher, cartoonist, painter (in oils) and journalist. He drew a famous caricature of the Don (adorned by his subject's signature) and covered Bradman's 1948 tour of England for the Sydney *Daily Telegraph*. His autobiography, *Ten for 66 and All That*, published in 1958, was inspired by his 10 wickets in an innings against Gloucestershire during the English tour of 1921. In a pen-portrait contributed to Jack Fingleton's 1949 book *Brightly Fades the Don*, Arthur Mailey wrote: "Bradman never made the mistake common to many, of thinking that personal popularity is more potent than success." And: "Bradman is an enigma, a paradox; an idol of millions, yet, with a few, the most unpopular cricketer I have ever met. People close to Bradman either like or dislike him, there is no halfway. To those who dislike him there is no compromise, no forgiveness, no tolerance. There are at least two reasons: jealousy and this great cricketer's independence." Arthur Mailey was 81 when he died in 1967.

Maloja

Ship on which the Don's wife Jessie travelled from Australia to England when he was seriously ill with peritonitis in 1934. She travelled overland from Sydney to Perth via Melbourne to join the P & O ship which had left Sydney a few days before. When in Melbourne she heard that her husband had died, but on telephoning London was relieved to hear there was no truth in the report and continued her journey.

M

Martin, Raymond George
Nine Network personality who conducted the Don's last major television interview (and the first on commercial TV), taped in April 1996 largely at Adelaide Oval and broadcast the following month. Martin was the Bradman family's choice of commentator for Nine's delayed telecast of the Adelaide memorial service on March 25, 2001.

Marylebone Cricket Club
The MCC was formed in 1787 by members of the White Conduit Club of Islington, based originally at a ground belonging to Thomas Lord on the northern fringes of London's West End but from 1814 based at the modern Lord's Cricket Ground in St John's Wood. Although only a private club, the MCC has always wielded immense authority – albeit largely unofficially – over the conduct and organisation of the game at national and international level, and it was only in the 1970s that many of the club's functions were devolved to more "official" bodies like the ICC and the TCCB. Within a year of its foundation the MCC had conducted the first major revision of the laws of the game, and it has been responsible since then for several further revisions. It remains today the chief authority on the laws, and they can only be changed if proposed amendments are approved by a two-thirds majority at a special meeting of the club.

The first England touring team to be selected and managed by the MCC was the side which visited Australia for the Ashes series of 1903–04. In his *Farewell to Cricket*, the Don wrote: "Eternal credit must go to the Marylebone Cricket Club for the painstaking watchfulness in preserving the best features of cricket, gradually altering the laws to keep pace with the game's changing technique; never giving way to any panic-stricken legislation." The club made the Don an honorary life member in 1958 and an honorary life vice-president in 1988. On three occasions he declined the MCC's offer of the presidency, because the distances would have "prevented me carrying out the duties well".

Mask of Fu Manchu, The
Movie in production when the Australian team visited the set at MGM Studios in Los Angeles during Arthur Mailey's tour of Canada and the US in 1932. The players were photographed with the stars of the film, Englishman Boris Karloff (a former wicketkeeper/batsman) and Myrna Loy. Also in the pic were two other British actors, Ronald Colman and C. Aubrey "Round the Corner" Smith, who captained England in his only Test.

Mathematics I and French

Subjects in which the Don gained A passes in the Intermediate Certificate in 1922. Mathematics was his favourite subject. He had B passes in his six other subjects, including Mathematics II.

Maxwell, James Edward

Cricket journalist who with Tony Squires provided the commentary for the ABC's live telecast of the Don's memorial service in Adelaide on March 25, 2001. Jim said recently that he had few dealings with the man himself, "other than his quick responses to my letters, or directing me to books 'which I am sure the ABC would have in their library' ". Jim takes up the story:
"I did a ninetieth-birthday special for ABC Radio with Bill McGowan, which is in our archives, and a three-minute audio obituary for ABC News which was played at the time of his demise, plus a live piece from my hotel in Mumbai at two thirty in the morning on the day after he died. Other than that my only meeting was probably in and out of the Gents at the SCG when he was a selector and I was a kid sitting in the MA Noble stand; he didn't go out of his way to visit commentary boxes. In his absence at the opening of the Bradman Museum in 1996 I was the MC and read Don's speech prior to Prime Minister John Howard's address to the multitude."

May, Norman Alfred Vale OAM

Former ABC broadcaster who interviewed the Don in 1987 for the seminal radio biography *Bradman: The Don Declares*. Of his subject, Norman recently said: "His recall of fact and information was just amazing. And I found him to be a very strong character; if he said he'd do something, he did it. He would not let you down ... But we agreed it was going to be about his cricket life, not his personal life. He said he'd got a lot of pleasure out of doing it, but he really did it for the Bicentennial. He owed it to Australia to tell his story – not as any special favour to me or the ABC, but just to the people of Australia. To tell his story in his own words, in his own way."

Norman conducted a short interview with the Don in 1979 for *The Greats of '48*, an ABC TV documentary (written and presented by May) made in conjunction with a reunion dinner in Sydney to mark the 30th anniversary of Bradman's Invincibles. Norman May started work with ABC Sport in 1957 as a 29-year-old "specialist trainee", and retired in 1984, although he has since worked on several assignments as a freelance for the ABC and for commercial networks. He had a very brief acting career (with a suitable haircut) as a radio commentator in the Kennedy Miller television miniseries *Bodyline*. May worked as a commentator on 11 Olympic Games starting

M

with Tokyo in 1964 and 11 Commonwealth Games starting with Perth in 1962. His cry of "Gold, Gold to Australia, Gold!" when calling the swimming on radio at the Moscow Olympics in 1980 is now etched into Australian sporting history. He has appeared at more than 500 fundraising functions for Olympic and Commonwealth games since 1963 and has received several awards and other honours from both movements in Australia. Now 76, Norman May lives at Bondi Beach in Sydney.

Melbourne Cricket Ground

The Don's most successful ground in Test cricket in Australia. He was the youngest man to score a Test century at the MCG when he made 112 (his first Test hundred) in the second innings of the Third Ashes Test in 1928–29. He had been dropped for the second match in Sydney, when as 12th man he substituted in the field for the injured Bill Ponsford. Of the ovation from the MCG crowd for Bradman when he reached his century, Harold Larwood told Jack Fingleton in 1948: "This was the greatest reception I have heard on any cricket field. The crowd cheered for five minutes. We couldn't go on with the game." In 17 innings in 11 Tests at the MCG, the Don racked up 1,671 runs at 128.54, with nine hundreds (including one double hundred) and three fifties. He made the fastest Test century of his career here, against the West Indies in 1930–31 when he scored 152 in 154 minutes (or 59 runs an hour), remarkably half of the dig being played on a sticky wicket. His top score in a Test at the MCG was 270 against England in 1936–37. The only occasion in his career that the Don registered a ton in each innings of a Test was in Melbourne when he made 132 and 127 not out against India in 1947–48. His only Test appearance at the MCG in which he was dismissed without scoring a hundred was in the Ashes series of 1946–47 when he made 79 and 49.

But it was also where he was dismissed for the only time for a duck first ball in a Test when he played on to Bill Bowes in the second match of the Bodyline series in front of a then world-record crowd of 63,993. In 45 innings in 29 first-class games at the MCG, the Don made 3,922 runs at 106, with 19 hundreds (including two double hundreds and one triple hundred) and eight fifties. He also held 14 catches. His highest score was 357 (out of a total of 569), in a Sheffield Shield game for South Australia against Victoria in 1935–36, his first season with his new state. The MCG was chosen for Bradman's testimonial game in the first week of December 1948 because of its capacity, and it was in this match that the Don scored his last first-class century, his 117th. And he took the last wicket in Lindsay Hassett's XI's second innings with the last ball he bowled in first-class cricket. Bradman considered there were factors working against cricketers at the MCG, namely a very hard pitch, stifling stillness on a hot day, and the swirling winds in the amphitheatre-like arena, but despite the drawbacks, the Don wrote that "somehow I liked batting in Melbourne … perhaps the wicket suited me". There was a notable exception though: when the wicket was wet. He claimed the MCG's sticky wicket was the world's worst.

Menzies, (The Rt Hon. Sir) Robert Gordon KT, AK, CH, QC

Longtime Australian prime minister and a great cricket fan who served in the 1940s as president of the Victorian Cricket Association. As Australia's attorney-general, he gave a speech at a dinner for the Don's tourists at Lord's in 1938. At the conclusion of a pen-portrait he contributed to Jack Fingleton's 1949 book *Brightly Fades the Don*, Menzies wrote: "As a pavilion lover of the greatest of all games, I have balanced up the Bradman Account, and hereby acknowledge that so long as my memory lasts I shall owe him that which I can never repay." In the 1950s the prime minister offered the Don the position of Australian high commissioner in London, but apparently the idea was vetoed by Sir Robert's Liberal Party colleagues, who considered the plumb diplomatic post should be reserved for politicians. Bradman came out of retirement to captain Menzies's Prime Minister's XI in February 1963. Of the occasion, Ray Robinson wrote in his 1975 book *On Top Down Under*: "It took all Sir Robert's eloquence to persuade Sir Donald to reappear at fifty-four as captain of the Prime Minister's XI against an English XI on Canberra's Manuka Oval. Knowing the 10,000 crowd wanted to see Bradman make runs, Brian Statham bowled with moderated menace. From a bottom corner of the bat a ball strayed between Bradman's boots. When it was heeled against the stumps bails fell. So did Statham's jaw." The Don had made 4 off five balls before he was dismissed going for his favourite pull shot.

Menzies, Roy

Jessie Menzies's older brother who was groomsman at his sister and the Don's wedding at Burwood in Sydney on April 30, 1932. The best man was the Don's brother, Victor.

Merchant, Vijay Madhavji

India's first great Test batsman, Merchant hosted the Don's wife Jessie when her boat stopped over in India on the way to her husband's side when he was seriously ill in London in 1934. Just a few months earlier, Merchant had represented his country against England in India's first home Test series. In a foreword to *Some Indian Cricketers*, a book by another Indian Test batsman, Rusi Modi, Bradman wrote of his affection for Merchant, whom he'd never met: "Such a kindness portrayed the man, and for that she and I remain eternally thankful." Vijay Merchant was named to captain his country in India's first series against Australia in 1947–48 but had to withdraw from the tour because of injury. The Don's side won the rubber 4–0. Merchant's first-class career average of 71.22 is second only to Bradman's.

Mick Simmons

Sydney retailer which the Don joined on February 1, 1929. The future of the real estate industry was looking decidedly shaky in the early stages of the Depression, and Bradman decided to leave Percy Westbrook's real estate business and accept the offer of a three-year contract with the sporting goods company. He accompanied the firm's travellers to sports stores in country towns and visited schools. At the end of the Don's record-breaking tour of England in 1930, Mick Simmons's publicity manager, Oscar Lawson, wanted to make the most of Bradman's success and so chartered a plane to fly him from Adelaide to Melbourne and then on to Goulburn. He was then chauffeured from Goulburn to Bowral and then Sydney by daredevil racing driver Norman ("Wizard") Smith. The Don's arrival ahead of the rest of the team in Melbourne and Sydney was seen by some as an attempt by him to steal the limelight.

"Mighty Don"

Song with words and music by Peggie Thorne, recorded by her in the late 1940s. The sheet music sold for two shillings.

Miller, Keith Ross ("Nugget") MBE

One of the game's greatest all-rounders, Miller was named after the celebrated aviators Keith and Ross Smith and served in World War II as a Mosquito pilot. He had debuted for Victoria as an 18-year-old in 1937–38 and after the war he played in the Services team in England, India and Australia. Strong performances at home against England (on his way to 141 in the Adelaide Test he resumed batting on the morning of the fourth day and hit the first ball of the day from Wright for six) and India earned him a bunk on the boat to England with the Don's great side of 1948. Described by Bradman as "one of the most volatile players of any age", the dashing Miller was an aggressive batsman with a penchant for big hitting but, perhaps paradoxically, never made runs just for the sake of it. In the middle of the run riot in the historic match against Essex in 1948 when the

Invincibles scored 721 in a day, Nugget was bowled first ball for a duck by Trevor Bailey. (One English cricket writer made the bizarre claim that Miller threw his wicket away in protest at his captain ordering him to put down his playing cards and go to the wicket. This would have been a little difficult seeing that the Don himself was in the middle at the time – and the delivery which uprooted Miller's off-stump was described by leading writer RC Robertson-Glasgow as "a very good ball".)

After the tour Bradman praised the bowling of his all-rounder but claimed he would have been a far better player had he showed more restraint in his batting. He said that Miller's limitations were caused mainly by his failure to concentrate. Nugget once claimed that supposed on-field clashes between himself and his captain had been blown out of all proportion, adding: "I'm a Bradman man and always will be." And: "Don has always set his men a perfect example so far as his demeanour on and off the field is concerned." When Keith was omitted from the side to tour South Africa in 1949–50 (a decision described by Jack Fingleton in his 1949 book *Brightly Fades the Don* as "the worst selecting blunder in Australia's cricketing history" – although Miller was dispatched as a late replacement and played an important part in the series), there were howls that the Don had overbowled him the previous year in England, but Bradman soon after refuted the claims with facts and figures in his autobiography. Keith Miller became a commentator and a journalist, published a book, *Cricket Crossfire*, and wrote several others in collaboration with Dick Whitington. Miller died aged 84 on October 11, 2004.

Minchin, (John) Eric

Australian landscape artist who founded the group of five Broken Hill painters known as the Brushmen of the Bush. The other four were Jack Absalom, Pro Hart, John Pickup and Hugh Schultz. Minchin was a boy of seven living in Kensington Park, Adelaide, when the Don and Jessie settled in the area in 1935. The Bradmans became friendly with Eric's parents and the four were regular bridge partners. The young Minchin caddied for the Don when he took up golf at the Mount Osmond club soon after arriving in Adelaide and continued to do so for several years leading up to the war. Eric Minchin was 66 when he died of a brain tumour in Broken Hill in 1994. He is survived by his widow, Roxanne (now a prominent landscape artist in her own right), and a son and a daughter.

Mitsubishi Sigma

Car which the Don owned in the 1980s. It was a rare indulgence when he bought a remote-control attachment for his garage in 1982.

Mittagong High School

The opposition when the Don recorded his first century when playing for Bowral Intermediate High School at Mittagong at the age of 12 in the summer of 1920–21. He scored 115 not out in his team's total of 156, but the next day at assembly was admonished by his headmaster for leaving a bat behind. In a second game against Mittagong in the same summer (the only other time he played for his school against another school), he scored 72 not out.

Monowai

Ship which brought Arthur Mailey's team of Australians home in 1932 after their 75-day tour of North America. The team stopped off in New Zealand for a planned one-day match against a representative Wellington side at the Basin Reserve. The local Bradman fans were disappointed when the game was washed out, but captains Victor Richardson and Stew Dempster agreed late that night at a dinner to play a two-hour exhibition match the next day before the *Monowai* set sail for Australia. However, the Don and Chuck Fleetwood-Smith, being unaware of the new arrangement, had planned a sightseeing tour with an early start for the next day. As a result, when the game started, the two players were conspicuous by their absence. Bradman was said to be astonished on returning in the afternoon to learn that cricket had been played, and, according to a contemporary report in Wellington's *Evening Post* newspaper, "more than a bit concerned" that the crowd had been deprived of the chance to see him bat.

Morris, Arthur Robert MBE

New South Wales opening batsman who became the first Australian to score two centuries in a Test in Australia when he made 122 and 124 not out under the Don in the fourth match of the Ashes series in Adelaide in 1946–47. He has the prodigious record of making six hundreds in his first 10 Tests against England. Morris played first-grade cricket with Sydney club St George (the Don's first club) as a 15-year-old and was only 18 when he became the first player from any country to score two centuries on his first-class debut, making 148 and 111 for his state against Queensland at the SCG in 1940–41. Morris confirmed his greatness during a second-wicket stand of 301 with Bradman which secured the historic win at Headingley in the Fourth Test in 1948, when the visitors had to score a record 404 in their second innings in 344 minutes. When the Don had a couple of escapes because, according to reports, he was having trouble detecting Denis Compton's wrong 'un, Morris declared at lunch that he would have to do something about it, and immediately after the break he hit the Brylcreem Boy out of the attack. Morris scored 182, Bradman 173 not out and Australia got the runs with 15 minutes to spare. Arthur said it had been his most satisfying innings.

In the following Test at the Oval, Morris's 196 in the first innings went largely unacknowledged in the publicity over his skipper's duck in his last Test. The Don was not aware at the time that he needed just 4 for an average of 100 but could still have achieved the ton by scoring 104 or 4 not out in the second innings had there been one. Ironically, it was largely Morris's great knock which delivered Australia an easy win without having to bat again. The left-hander finished the tour with an average in the Tests of 87, ahead of Barnes on 82.25 and Bradman with 72.57. His 290 against Gloucestershire on this tour was the highest of his career, and his average for all tour matches in 1948 was the highest of any player, except the Don in 1930, on his first trip to England. And Morris and Ernie Toshack were the only Australians to go through the tour without a duck against their names.

Of his teammates on the historic tour, Arthur told the *Sydney Morning Herald* in 1987: "They were great cricketers, good blokes and good mates. We were the despair of Don a few times." He said it was a great privilege to have played with Bradman. "I grew up in the 1930s and as a boy he was my idol as he was for so many tens of thousands of youngsters. To be able to play with him after the war in 1946 ... well, I just couldn't believe that I was there in the Australian team playing under Bradman." Of Morris, the Don wrote in his *Farewell to Cricket*: "I think Arthur, towards the close of the 1948 tour, was playing the finest cricket of any left-handed bat I've seen. He had that wonderful quality so noticeable in good players – plenty of time to make his shots. All strokes came alike – hooks, drives, cuts, glances. Powerful wrists and forearms ... Great team man; studious and intelligent observer." At the time of Bradman's retirement in 1949, when Morris had played Test cricket for only three years, the Don rated him the best left-handed Australian batsman since Clem Hill, another opener, who played around the turn of the century. On August 27, 1998, Arthur opened commemorative garden gates at Bowral to mark the Don's 90th birthday. Not surprisingly, he made it into his former Test skipper's World Best Team, published after the great man's death by Roland Perry in his book *Bradman's Best*. Now 82, Arthur Morris lives in Cessnock in NSW's Hunter Valley.

M

Moss Vale

As a 12-year-old near the end of 1920, the Don was scorer for the Bowral Town Cricket Club in a game in the Berrima District Competition against Moss Vale at Moss Vale when one of the men in the Bowral team did not turn up. Set by his captain to fill the breach, the "speck of a boy rigged out in short trousers" went in at the fall of the eighth wicket and, "wielding a man's-sized bat", scored 37 not out. In Bowral's second innings, at home the following Saturday, Bradman was sent in to open and at stumps was unbeaten on 29. He was not to play again for the senior Bowral team until near the end of the 1924–25 season but it was Moss Vale against which the Don played a memorable innings in the final of the competition at Moss Vale in 1925–26, when he was 17. His captain (and uncle) George Whatman won the toss, decided to bat and sent Bradman in to open with O. Pryor. The pair were together until just before stumps, when Pryor was dismissed for 52 and the Don was joined by his skipper. At the end of the day Bradman remained unbeaten on 80. The game resumed a week later, on the following Saturday, and at stumps on the second day Bradman was 279 and Whatman 119, the pair adding 323 in three and a half hours.

On the third day the Don was out for a district-record 300 (one suspects he threw his wicket away) and Whatman 227. The team's total was 672. Moss Vale were dismissed for 134 and 200, so Bowral won by an innings and 338 runs. The Don took four wickets for 39. The length of the match attracted interest in the Sydney newspapers. The *Sun* published a sarcastic piece and another paper ran a cartoon which depicted Bradman running up and down the wicket as an old man with a beard touching the ground and both he and Whatman in Heaven asking St Peter for directions to Moss Vale so they might finish the game. Play took place only from 2pm until 6pm but the match lasted five Saturday afternoons. The Don appeared for Bowral against Moss Vale in the final again the following season. Although he had played most of the season in the Sydney grade competition (and was on the verge of selection in the state side) he was eligible to play in the match because he had started the season with Bowral. This time he scored 320 not out and the opposition tried to have the rules changed so that a Sydney grade player would in future be ineligible to play in the competition.

Moss Vale Golf Club

Where Bowral solicitor Garry Barnsley approached the Don in 1983 for his support for a Bradman museum. The great man was non-committal at first but became formally interested after the Bradman Museum Trust was formed in 1987.

Moulton, Richard

Groundsman at Headingley who prepared the wickets on which the Don scored 334 in 1930 and 304 in 1934. Just before the Headingley Test in 1938 Dick Moulton told a reporter: "Don Bradman won't get three hundred this time." He said the outfield had not quite dried up after rain and there was still a little give in the pitch. The Australian skipper only scored 103 in a Test which he later wrote was the best in which he had played.

Mount Osmond

Golf club in Adelaide which the Don joined in the winter of 1935 to get his muscles back into condition for cricket after his long lay-off following his illness in England the previous year. He won the club championship a couple of months after joining. He also won the A-grade medal at Kooyonga in 1988 with a 76 off the championship tees at the age of 79.

Moustache

Adornment of the upper lip sported by the Don for several years in the 1980s. He received a letter from a concerned admirer who thought that for Bradman to grow a moustache would be like Mona Lisa having a beard, or Abraham Lincoln without one. Lady Bradman agreed. The Don got rid of it on October 7, 1987. Retired broadcaster Norman May said recently that when Bradman was approached in 1987 for an extended interview with the ABC for the approaching Bicentennial, the Don insisted he would do it on radio but not television because he was self-conscious about the mo', which he had grown after cutting his lip and then decided to keep. Bradman later said the moustache was a "mental aberration".

Moyes, Alban George ("Johnny") MBE

A former first-class player for South Australia and Victoria who became the Don's close confidant and greatest supporter. He wrote thousands of words on Bradman for newspapers and was his first biographer. Moyes was one of the three NSW selectors who asked Harold Heydon, the secretary of the New South Wales Cricket Association, to invite the young batsman from Bowral to attend a practice at the SCG on October 11, 1926. Three of the state's leading players soon to return from a tour of England had announced their retirement and another, the great Charlie Macartney, restricted his appearances to Sydney, so Moyes and the other newly appointed panelists, Dick Jones and Harold "Mudgee" Cranney, decided to search for talent and rebuild the state side with "youths of promise".

In his 1948 book *Bradman*, Moyes wrote of the arrival of the 17-year-old country boy at the nets: "Old-timers as well as stars of the day turned out … They saw a smallish lad, seemingly unperturbed and obviously the possessor of a superb eye. He didn't have the style of a Trumper, but, at the same time, those who expected and looked for crudities were relieved and delighted at their comparative absence. The youngster looked a batsman: his quick eye and speedy footwork were so palpable. There were possibilities here, though no one could have imagined what power was latent in the small frame. It was a severe trial, yet young Don faced it without any outward sign of nerves, in spite of the fact that he must have realised that he had come to the cross-roads of his career."

Moyes took a fatherly interest in the young Bradman after he moved from Bowral to Sydney to live in early 1928. His admiration of the boy and the man was defined by his introduction to his biography: "I opened the door and a lad said: 'Are you Mr Moyes? I'm Don Bradman!' Twelve years later I listened to this country lad make speeches in England that were surely among the finest ever made by a cricketer. I saw him lead Australia; make centuries by the dozen, but the picture that remains is that of the lad who said quietly: 'I'm Don Bradman.' His name will live as long as cricket is played, and his glory will never be blotted out." Johnny Moyes died in Sydney in 1963 at the age of 70.

Mt Gibraltar

Rock which overlooks the Don's boyhood home of Bowral.

Mulvaney, Richard

Cricket aficionado who is executive officer of the Bradman Foundation and director of the Bradman Museum. Richard has a Bachelor of Arts degree in Pre-history from the Australian National University and was curator of history at the Sovereign Hill Museum in Ballarat, Victoria, before taking up the post of curator with the Bradman Museum Trust in Bowral in 1989. On the day after the Don's passing on Sunday, February 25, 2001, he told AAP: "I believe he died peacefully in his sleep and his family were there not long after. He was suffering from pneumonia before Christmas and was hospitalised for a short period, went home before Christmas and was really trying to recover … Any cricket lover or, in fact, any Australian and in fact many people around the world will certainly mourn Sir Donald's passing."

In the eulogy at the memorial service at Bradman Oval, Mulvaney said that the Don often reminisced about Bowral, adding: "There is a special synergy with the world figure and this small country town." But he cautioned: "With his death we must not turn him into an icon or a religious figure. He was just a man." After the unveiling of the statue of the Don outside Bradman Museum on February 24, 2002, Richard said: "Bowral has now become the recognised place for people to pay their respects to Sir Donald, especially for the older generation, because it involves memories of their early life. The response to the statue has been wonderful and we couldn't have asked for a better pose, clearly demonstrating his lifelong service to the public." In July 2002, Richard handed over his curatorial duties to new curator David Wells to allow him to concentrate more on his managerial role. Richard Mulvaney and his family live in the former Bradman house at 20 Glebe Street, Bowral, opposite Bradman Oval and the Bradman Museum.

My Cricketing Life
A recounting by the Don of his life which was published by Stanley Paul in 1938, 189pp.

N

9

Number of Bradman's first-class appearances before he played in his first Test match, against England at Brisbane's Exhibition Ground from November 30, 1928, when he made 18 and 1.

19

Number of Tests the Don played in England. In 30 innings he scored 2,674 runs at 102.85, with 11 centuries, three fifties and two ducks. He also took five catches.

Also the number of Bradman's centuries in his 37 Ashes Tests: eight in Australia (including three double centuries) and 11 in England (including three double centuries and two triple centuries).

Also the number of matches in 29 wins in his 52 Tests in which the Don top-scored or equal top-scored for Australia.

Also the number of his centuries in 44 innings in 31 Sheffield Shield games for South Australia. The total included five double hundreds and one triple hundred. He also made eight fifties.

90

Number of the Don's innings in 73 first-class appearances in England other than Tests. He made 7,163 runs at 94.25, with 30 centuries (including seven double centuries), 21 fifties and two ducks. His highest score of 278 was made against the MCC at Lord's in 1938.

91

Number of catches taken by the Don in his 142 first-class games in Australia.

92

Number of first-class games the Don played in England. In 120 innings he made 9,837 runs at 96.44 with 41 centuries, 24 fifties and four ducks. He also took 40 catches. Of the 89 matches in which he batted, Bradman's side was beaten in only three.

93

Number of the Don's innings in grade cricket: 44 with St George, three with North Sydney and 46 with Kensington. He made 6,599 runs at 86.82, with 28 centuries. His best score was 303 for Kensington against Glenelg in 1939–40.

93.16

The Don's average in the first innings of all his first-class matches. Though he was equally successful in first and second innings, his average for first innings was down on second innings (100.84) because of the fewer not-outs.

93.65

The Don's average in first-class cricket other than Tests. He batted 258 times in 182 matches.

94.14

The Don's average in 23 innings in all matches for Bowral in 1925–26, his first full season with the club. He scored a record 234 during the season in a district competition game against Wingello at Bowral and upped the ante with 300 in the final against Moss Vale at Moss Vale. During the same season he took 51 wickets at 7.80 with his leg-breaks and held 26 catches.

94.46

The Don's average in his 218 innings in 142 first-class matches in Australia.

95.14

The Don's average in first-class cricket. He batted 338 times (with 43 not-outs) in 234 matches and made 28,067 runs, with 117 centuries (including 31 double centuries, five triple centuries and one quadruple century), 69 fifties and 16 ducks. Given a qualification of 20 innings, the next man on the list is India's Vijay Merchant, with 71.22, followed by another Indian, Ajay Sharma, on 67.80. The best Australians after the master are the opening partners and Bradman's teammates, Bill Ponsford (65.18) and Bill Woodfull (64.99). The highest point the Don's average reached was 98.04, halfway through the 1939–40 season. Bradman's first-class average was nearly five runs lower than his average in Tests only, but this is partly explained by the fact that in the shorter games he quite often threw his wicket away, and of course he played many more first-class games than Tests only.

96

Number of the Don's innings in his 62 Sheffield Shield matches: 52 in 31 games for New South Wales from 1927–28 to 1933–34, and 44 in 31 games for South Australia from 1935–36 to 1939–40 and 1946–47 to 1948–49. For NSW he scored 4,633 runs at 107.74, with 17 hundreds, 12 fifties and three ducks; and for SA, 4,293 runs at 112.97, with 19 hundreds, eight fifties and two ducks. Bradman's highest shield score for NSW was his then world-record 452 not out against Queensland at the SCG in 1929–30, and for SA, 357 against Victoria at the MCG in 1935–36.

96 Centimetres

The Don's chest measurement in the 1930s.

96.44

The Don's average in his 120 innings in 92 first-class games in England.

97.14

The Don's best average in an Ashes series in Australia, made in 1946–47. It improved on his 90.00 in 1936–37. His best in an Ashes series in England was 139.14, on his first tour in 1930.

98 Minutes

The Don's shortest time for reaching 100 in a Test: when he scored 167 in the third match of the 1931–32 series against South Africa at the MCG.

98.23

The Don's average in 50 innings in 33 Tests in Australia.

98.53

The Don's average in 69 innings in 41 first-class appearances for New South Wales.

98.66

The Don's average on his first tour of England in 1930, the highest to that point of any batsman (including Englishmen) in an English season. The previous best of 91.23 was registered by Irish-born Hampshire player Robert Poore in 1899. Bradman was to better his own mark with an average of 115.66 in 1938.

99.94

The Don's average in his 80 innings (including 10 not-outs) in 52 Tests. He racked up 6,996 runs with 29 centuries (including 10 double centuries and two triple centuries) and 13 fifties. When he walked to the wicket at the Oval in 1948 to a great ovation in Australia's first innings in the last Test of his career, he only needed to score four runs to finish with a century average. Instead, in what must be one of the all-time classic anticlimaxes in sport, he was bowled second ball for a duck. Immediately before that final failure, he was on 101.39. When asked by Ray Martin in the 1996 television interview: "And do you laugh now when you think, it's the most famous duck in cricket history?", the Don replied: "No, I don't laugh much about it, because I'm very sorry that I made a duck, and I would have been glad if I had only made those four runs so I could finish with an average of a hundred." But Bradman's average of 99.94 is nearly 40 runs better than the next best among past players. Given a qualification of 20 Test innings, the second batsman on the list is South Africa's Graeme Pollock with 60.97, followed by the West Indies' George Headley with 60.83 and England's Herbert Sutcliffe with 60.73. In 1983 the Australian Broadcasting Corporation adopted the four digits in the Don's Test average as its GPO box number in all state capitals and in Canberra and Darwin.

974

Number of runs made by the Don in the Tests on his first tour of England in 1930, still a record aggregate for any Test series. His seven innings in five matches produced scores of 8, 131, 254, 1, 334, 14 and 232, at an average of 139.14. Bradman's 334 at Headingley beat the world Test record of 325 set just three months before by Englishman Andy Sandham against the West Indies at Sabina Park, Kingston. The record for an Ashes Test had been held by Reg Foster, who made 287 for England on Test debut at the SCG in 1903–04. The Don also became the first Australian to score four centuries in a Test series, and the first man from any country to make three double centuries in a rubber.

9,342 Pounds

Amount on the cheque which the Don was handed after his testimonial game at the MCG in December 1948, made up of gatetakings of 7,484 pounds and 1,858 pounds from associated fundraising.

9,837

Runs scored by the Don in his 120 innings in 92 first-class appearances in England, including 2,674 in Tests. He averaged 96.44, with 41 centuries and 24 fifties.

9994

The GPO box number of the Australian Broadcasting Corporation in all Australian state capitals and in Canberra and Darwin. Lore has it that the adoption of the box number to commemorate Bradman's Test average was conceived by former ABC general manager Charles Moses, but this seems doubtful at best. The number was first used by the ABC when the Commission became the Corporation in 1983, 18 years after Sir Charles had retired, although he lived until 1988. Retired broadcaster Norman May said recently that he and his colleagues in ABC Sport understood that the box number was in fact the brainchild of Talbot Duckmanton, Moses' successor as general manager from 1965 to 1982.

$90,000

Australian equivalent of price paid for the Don's cap worn during the 1946–47 Ashes series when sold by Christie's in London in June 2003. At the time, it was the highest price paid at auction for an Australian Test cap. The buyer was an Australian collector based in London.

$94,000

Australian equivalent of price paid for the baggy green cap worn by Bradman during his first tour of England in 1930. The cap was sold at auction by Christie's in London in June 2004.

94,035

Total attendance at the Don's testimonial match at the MCG in the first week of December 1948. Gatetakings were 7,484 pounds. Bradman scored his 117th – and last – first-class century and the game finished in a tie.

Nagle, Lisle Ernest

Spin bowler who put on what the Don said in his autobiography was "possibly the grandest exhibition of medium-pace off-spin bowling I have ever seen" when he turned out for an Australian XI against the MCC at the MCG before the Ashes series in 1932–33. This game was the first time on the tour that Jardine unleashed the full force of his bodyline tactic, but Nagle finished with match figures of 8/32 from 10 overs. On the strength of this achievement the tall Victorian got the nod for the First Test in Sydney but performed moderately and was not to play for Australia again.

Nairana

The ship on which the Don travelled from Sydney to Launceston, Tasmania, with the Australian team on the first leg of the trip to England in 1930. It was the first time Bradman had been at sea, and he soon discovered that as a sailor he made a pretty good cricketer.

Nerves

When artist Bill Leak became jittery while doing preliminary sketches before painting the Don's portrait in 1989, he said to his subject: "Tell me Sir Donald, were you ever nervous as you walked out to the crease?" Bradman replied: "No, why would anybody ever be nervous about something they know they can do? Now, if you were to ask me to play something on the piano that I hadn't practised for a while, I would be nervous."

New South Wales

The Don recalled in *Farewell to Cricket* that after travelling from Bowral to Sydney as an 18-year-old with his father in October 1926 to attend a practice at the SCG at the invitation of the New South Wales Cricket Association, he "went to the nets quite confidently". His "practice" form attracted an offer from the Central Cumberland grade club (who later decided, however, that they could not afford to pay the Don's train fare from Bowral to Sydney and back each week), but more significantly he got the nod soon after to play in a trial game for an upcoming Sheffield Shield match against Queensland. The young Bradman's 37 not out in his first experience in a match on the SCG turf wicket was not good enough to win him a guernsey in the state side, but a 62 not out and four wickets in a trial in Goulburn soon after earned him the chance to represent Southern Zone in the annual Country Week carnival. His adequate performances (his highest score was 46) in several of the games on the unfamiliar turf wickets against the other country teams won him a place the following week in the Combined Country side to play a City team, which boasted in their ranks the great Charlie Macartney, whose brilliance in an Ashes Test at the SCG had inspired Bradman as a boy in the crowd six years before. Macartney scored 126 and the Don made an even 100.

Bradman returned to his local Berrima competition but a few weeks later was chosen to play for a NSW Second XI against Victoria at the SCG on New Year's Day, 1927. He top-scored for the locals in the first innings with 43 and made 8 in the second. Another promising player in the home side

N

was the 21-year-old Bill O'Reilly. During this season Bradman was making some good scores (though not outstanding scores, since he was still getting accustomed to turf wickets) in his first season with Sydney grade club St George, and there was some criticism of state selectors for leaving him out of the shield side. And despite impressive performances (including 130 not out in a total of 258 in the opening game of the season) with the club in the early part of the following summer, he did not find favour with NSW selectors when they settled on a combination to play Queensland on the first trip of the 1927–28 season. Bradman's name was again missing from the list a couple of weeks later when the squad to tour South Australia and Victoria was announced, but when two players, Hampden Love and the great Jack Gregory withdrew from the team, the Don and Albert Scanes got their seats on the train. It would be the first time the young Bradman had been outside his home state, but he was to make his first-ever appearance for a shield side in a second-class game in the NSW town of Broken Hill on the way to Adelaide.

Of the playing surface in the famous mining centre, the Don wrote: "There was not a blade of grass on the oval from one end to the other. The soil was a deep red colour, with dust in some parts a couple of inches thick." The concrete wicket was good but the bowler's approach was also concrete. Most of the NSW team played in sandshoes, but not having any with him, the Don played in his street shoes. He scored 46 but play was called off at 4pm when the ground was hit by a dust storm. Bradman managed to souvenir the ball as a memento of the game and it remained a cherished possession for many years. The Don was to be 12th man for the shield game in Adelaide but as fate would have it, Archie Jackson (who was a year younger than the 19-year-old from Bowral but had made his first-class debut the previous season), had to withdraw from the game because of a boil on his knee. History records that in his first innings in a first-class match, on December 17, 1927, the Don made 118. He was the 17th Australian batsman to make a century on his debut in first-class cricket. In the second innings, he scored 33 out of a total of 150 on a turning wicket against the might of the great Clarrie Grimmett, who finished with a bag for the innings of 8/57. Bradman was to play seven seasons with NSW, from 1927–28 to 1933–34. During this period, the state won the shield three times: in 1928–29, 1931–32 and 1932–33.

In early 1934, Harry Hodgetts, a member of the South Australian Cricket Association and a delegate to the Australian Board of Control, made the Don an offer of a position in his stockbroking business in Adelaide which it was proposed he would take up later that year on his return from the tour of England. He was guaranteed employment for six years with time off for cricket, enabling him to play the game as a sport and not for a living. Bradman's cricket-related contract with his three Sydney employers was about to expire and he wanted a career which had nothing to do with the game. He was reluctant to leave Sydney but the offer was seriously tempting. When the Don told a friend, Bert Kortlang (a much-travelled former first-class cricketer), that he was considering a move to South Australia, Kortlang went to see Harold Heydon, the secretary of the NSWCA. Kortlang told Heydon that Bradman was considering a move to another state and asked whether the association could do something to keep him in Sydney. Heydon's response was: "The New South Wales Cricket Association has made Bradman what he is, and he can't afford to leave New South Wales." For the Don this sealed the matter, and, despite opposition from Jessie, he accepted Mr Hodgetts's offer of 600 pounds a year.

In 52 innings in 31 Sheffield Shield matches for NSW, Bradman made 4,633 runs at 107.74, with 17 centuries (including five double centuries, one triple century and one quadruple century) and 12 fifties. He got out for a duck three times. His highest score was his then world first-class record of 452 not out, made against Queensland at the SCG in January 1930. The Don's most prolific season for NSW in shield cricket was his last, 1933–34, when his seven innings in five games produced scores of 200, 1, 76, 187 not out, 77 not out, 253 and 128, an aggregate of 922. His average of 184.40 also was his best in a shield season for the Blues. In all first-class cricket for NSW, Bradman batted 69 times in 41 appearances, racking up 5,813 runs at 98.53, with 21 centuries (including six double hundreds, one triple hundred and one quadruple hundred) and 17 fifties. His highest score was his 452 not out in 1929–30 and he made three ducks. He also took 17 catches. The Don's highest first-class aggregate in a season was in 1928–29, when he made 1,127 runs at 140.87, with five centuries (including his then SCG record of 340 not out against Victoria) and two fifties, but his best average was in 1933–34, when he compiled 1,036 runs at 148.00, with four centuries (including two double centuries) and three fifties. Bradman the bowler took 15 wickets for NSW at 47.46, his best figures 3/54.

In 14 innings in nine shield matches *against* NSW, he made 1,178 runs at 130.88, with five centuries. In all first-class cricket against NSW he batted 16 times in 10 matches and made 1,205 runs at 109.54, with five centuries. His highest score against his old state was 251 not out in a shield game at Adelaide Oval in 1939–40. A grandstand at the SCG was named in the Don's honour in 1973 and he was made a life member of the NSWCA in 1979. On February 2, 2000 he got the nod as captain of the Blues Living Legends.

New York Times, The

Newspaper which notably ran an editorial tribute to the Don soon after he was invested with his knighthood in March 1949. The respected broadsheet described Bradman as cricket's "unchallenged shining light", and declared: "We salute Sir Donald with admiration but without any regrets that we cannot match his title with a sports knight of our own. We like our kings uncrowned."

New Zealand

Country in which the Don wrote that he would always regret not playing. He missed selection (being named as a reserve batsman) in the Australian team which went to New Zealand at the end of the 1927–28 season (his first in first-class cricket), and a tour, for which it was intended Bradman would lead the Australians, scheduled for early 1940 was cancelled because of the war. He declined to make the trip across the Tasman with the Australian side in March 1946 because he had not fully recovered from the fibrositis which had forced his discharge from the Army in 1941. There were no Tests played on the 1927–28 tour, and the one international played in 1946, in Wellington, was not granted Test status until two years later. (There was not to be another trans-Tasman Test until 1973.) Bradman appeared in a first-class game for South Australia at Adelaide Oval in November 1937 against a team of New Zealanders who were on their way home by sea from a tour of England. He came very close to playing in New Zealand against a representative Wellington side at the Basin Reserve during a planned two-day stopover on the way home from the North American tour in 1932. The Don (with Jessie) and the rest of the team arrived (with 23 New Zealanders returning from the Los Angeles Olympics among fellow passengers) on the *Monowai* on September 18, a wet Sunday morning.

A big crowd thronged the wharf when the ship docked, and the Bradmans were escorted with difficulty through the mass of people to their car. Much to the disappointment of all concerned, the one-day match scheduled for the following day was washed out. But at a dinner that evening, the two captains, Victor Richardson and Stew Dempster, agreed to play a very short exhibition game, weather permitting, the following day before the Australians rejoined their ship, which was due to sail at 4pm. The match was to start at noon and finish at 2pm. A crowd of around 8,000 turned up at the ground the next day, but Don Bradman and Chuck Fleetwood-Smith didn't. The Bradmans were not aware of the late arrangements for the exhibition game when they left the dinner and had made plans for the following day which would have required a very early start. They and Fleetwood-Smith had arranged to hire a car and a driver for a "motor tour of the southern Wairarapa". The Don was said to be astonished on returning in the afternoon to learn that cricket had been played, and, according to a contemporary report in Wellington's *Evening Post* newspaper, "more than a bit concerned" that the crowd had been deprived of the chance to see him bat. Bradman turned down an offer at the end of the Ashes series in 1936–37 of 100 pounds a week plus fares for himself and Jessie to go to New Zealand to give two fifteen-minute talks a day on cricket.

Niagara

Royal Mail steamer on which the Don and new wife Jessie left on May 26, 1932 with an Australian team for an exhibition tour of Canada and the United States organised by Arthur Mailey. The young couple had tied the knot only four weeks before, and the trip served as an extended honeymoon. The Don spent the first three days of the trip in his bunk with the flu. The *Niagara* was sunk by a German mine off Auckland in 1940 and her cargo of gold was later retrieved in a famous salvage operation.

Nicholson, Robert

Lithgow coalminer who sang at Don and Jessie's wedding at St Paul's Church at Burwood, Sydney, on April 30, 1932. Jessie said later that the congregation was more excited about the singing than the wedding. The Don had asked Bob to do the honours after hearing him sing six months earlier at a dance at the Masonic Hall in Blackheath after the social match in which Bradman famously scored a century in 22 balls for a Blackheath side against a team from Lithgow. Nicholson, who bowled for the visitors in that game, had a rich baritone voice. He later won the Sydney Eisteddfod and went on to sing at the Metropolitan Opera House in New York.

Nimbalkar, Bhausahibe

Indian cricketer who was batting for Maharashtra against Kathiawar in a Ranji Trophy match in 1948–49 at Poona, a four-hour train ride from Bombay (now Mumbai), when the opposition team packed up during the tea break and left the ground. The problem was that Nimbalkar was on 443, moving ever closer to the Don's sacred first-class record of 452, and the Kathiawar players felt it would have been discourteous to allow the semi-divine's record to be broken. Nimbalkar: "It took me seven hours and 20 minutes, and there were 46 fours and one sixer. Sir Donald spoke on the wireless and told Kathiawar not to concede the match and to let me continue; to give me a chance to do it. But the Kathiawar players didn't come back from the tea break. They went to catch their train."

N

Northern District

Sydney grade club which approached the Don between seasons in 1927 to defect from the St George club.

North Sydney District Cricket Club

Grade club with which the Don played three innings in three first-grade games in October 1933. His three scores were 19 (against Waverley), 127 (in 90 minutes against Western Suburbs) and 62 (against Petersham), making a total of 208 runs at 69.33. His 1933–34 season in grade cricket was cut short by back trouble. He had been boarding with St George administrator and Board of Control member Frank Cush in the Sydney suburb of Rockdale (and playing with the St George club since 1926–27) until his marriage on April 30, 1932, when he and Jessie took up residence in McMahons Point, near the northern end of the then new Sydney Harbour Bridge. But because he left (with Jessie) soon after for North America and did not return until October, he was not qualified residentially for the North Sydney club for 1932–33, so he played that season with St George and signed up with North Sydney for the following summer. His transfer from St George to North Sydney occurred at about the same time that teammate and arch adversary Bill O'Reilly moved from North Sydney to St George.

"Not Very Imaginative"

How Sydney Deamer described the Don in an article in Sydney's *Daily Telegraph* in October 1946 after he interviewed him in Bradman's Adelaide office. Deamer added: "But he's no bore. If he does not laugh easily he can smile, and, without being affable, put a stranger at ease."

"Number One Piece"

A square of turf taken from just inside one of the creases of the SCG pitch early in 2000 when the pitch was removed as part of the refurbishment of the ground. It was handed by Sir Nicholas Shehadie, chairman of the Sydney Cricket and Sports Ground Trust, to Ian Craig, then chairman of the Bradman Museum, on March 21, 2001. The presentation was part of a special Bradman week leading up to his memorial service in Adelaide. Sir Nicholas said that the trust felt it most appropriate that the "Number One Piece" should go to the Bradman Museum because Sir Donald had always said the SCG was his favourite ground.

O

Once
Number of times the Don was out hit-wicket in his 295 dismissals in first-class cricket. In the First Test against India at the 'Gabba in 1947–48 he played so far back that his bat broke the wicket from behind. The bowler was the Indian captain, Lala Amarnath.

100
Average number of letters received each day by Bradman in his personal mail during the 1948 tour of England. The team overall got about 600 a day.

100 Pounds
The Don's fee for Arthur Mailey's 51-game, 10,000km tour of North America in 1932. He also got hotel and travel expenses for himself and new wife Jessie.

100.84
The Don's average in the second innings of all his first-class matches. Though he was equally successful in first and second innings, his average for the second was up on the first (93.16) because of the greater number of not-outs.

102
The Don's average on Arthur Mailey's tour of North America in 1932. In 51 games, he scored 3,779 runs, with a highest score of 260.

102.85
The Don's average in his 30 innings in 19 Tests against England in England.

104.60
The Don's average in 63 innings in 44 first-class games for South Australia.

107

Number of the Don's not-outs in his 669 innings in first- and second-class cricket.

107.74

The Don's average in 52 innings in 31 Sheffield Shield games for New South Wales.

109

Number of the Don's first-class games in Australia other than Tests. In 168 innings he scored 13,908 runs at 93.34, with 58 centuries, 35 fifties and seven ducks. He also took 64 catches.

109.40

The Don's average in 12 innings in district competition matches for Bowral in 1925–26. His average in 23 innings in all games during the season was 94.14.

110

The Don's score (run out) as an 18-year-old in his first innings in Sydney grade cricket, for St George against Petersham at Petersham Oval in November 1926. In making his century, he figured in a fifth-wicket partnership of 197 with Charlie Targett.

110.20

The Don's average in 96 innings in 62 matches in Sheffield Shield cricket for New South Wales and South Australia.

112.97

The Don's average in 44 innings in 31 Sheffield Shield games for South Australia.

115 Not Out

The Don's score (out of a team total of 156) when he posted his first-ever century, as a 12-year-old playing for Bowral Intermediate High School against Mittagong High School at Mittagong. He also took eight wickets in the game played on a concrete pitch covered with coir matting. The young Bradman was reprimanded the next day by his headmaster, Amos Lee, for leaving his bat behind. In a second match against Mittagong soon after, he made 72 not out.

115.66

The Don's average on the 1938 tour of England, a record for any batsman in an English season which still stands. It bettered the previous mark of 98.66 which he had set himself in 1930.

117

Number of first-class centuries scored by the Don: 76 in Australia and 41 in England. The total included 31 double centuries, five triple centuries and one score over 400. Bradman's first hundred was in his first-class debut – a Sheffield Shield match for New South Wales against South Australia at Adelaide Oval in December 1927 – and the last was in his testimonial match at the MCG in December 1948, a game which finished in a tie. Not surprisingly (because he played many more innings on an English tour than he did in an average summer in Australia), Bradman's three best seasons for hundreds were all in the Old Country: 13 in 26 innings in 1938, 11 in 31 innings in 1948, and 10 in 36 innings in 1930. (Interesting to note that despite his record-breaking scores in the Tests on his first tour in 1930, the Don's performances in the other matches were well below those of 1938 and 1948. But he attributed his run of relatively low scores in 1934 in the early tour games and in the first three Tests to indifferent health – understandably in view of what was to transpire a few weeks later.) The most centuries Bradman scored in an Australian season was eight, in 1947–48, which included four in six Test innings against India. He recorded seven hundreds in an Australian season three times: in 1928–29, 1931–32 and 1937–38, but he strung together a world record-equalling six consecutive centuries in a relatively short season in 1938–39. The Don's 100th ton came up in November 1947, before the Tests in a match between an Australian XI and the Indians at the SCG. He had the strike on 99 at the start of the last over before tea (bowled by Gogumal Kishenchand) and was careful with the first ball, but the second he played off his pads to the on-side. As Bradman and Keith Miller ran through for the single, a huge cheer engulfed the ground and the Indian players rushed to congratulate the Australian captain. Many thousands in the crowd sang repeatedly "For He's a Jolly Good Fellow". This century was the third of consecutive hundreds in his first three matches of the 1947–48 season, and he made another century in the First Test which followed. All told, Bradman played 338 first-class innings in 234 matches, so he posted a century about every third time he went in to bat, or in exactly every second game.

Also the Don's score in his first innings for South Australia in a Sheffield Shield game, against New South Wales in October 1935. It was one run less than his score in his first-class debut (for NSW) in 1927–28.

O

118

The Don's score in his first innings in first-class cricket, playing for New South Wales against South Australia in a Sheffield Shield game at Adelaide Oval on December 17, 1927.

120

Number of the Don's innings in 92 first-class matches in England. He scored a total of 9,837 runs at 96.44, with 41 hundreds (including 10 double hundreds and two triple hundreds), 24 fifties and four ducks. His highest score was his then world Test record of 334 at Headingley in July 1930.

121

Number of the Don's scores of 50 or over in his 218 innings in 142 first-class matches in Australia. Of the total of 121, he went on to make 100 or more 76 times.

124

The Don's Test number; that is, he was the 124th man to play Test cricket for Australia.

Also the number of times Bradman was caught by a fieldsman other than the bowler in his 295 first-class dismissals.

128

Number of innings in his 338 in first-class cricket in which the Don top-scored for his side.

128 Minutes

The average time it took Bradman to reach 100 in each of his 117 first-class centuries.

131

The most runs the Don scored before lunch in a Sheffield Shield game. On the third day of a match for New South Wales against Queensland at the SCG in 1933–34, he took his score from 122 to 253 in just 98 minutes before throwing his wicket away.

Also the number of catches taken by the Don in first-class cricket: 91 in 142 matches in Australia (including four as wicketkeeper) and 40 in 92 matches in England. He also executed one stumping (in Australia). Of his 32 catches in 52 Tests, 20 were in his 37 Tests against England. Bradman also took a catch when fielding as a substitute, in the Second Ashes Test at the SCG in 1928–29. He held 17 catches in 41 matches for New South Wales and 36 (including four as wicketkeeper, plus one stumping) in 44 matches for South Australia.

134 Minutes
The average length of each of the Don's completed innings over his first-class career.

135
The most runs the Don scored before lunch in a first-class game in Australia. On the second day of a match for South Australia against Tasmania at Adelaide Oval in 1935–36, he went from 127 to 262 before the main adjournment. On the first day, he had made 100 in 70 minutes. His 200 took 173 minutes and, incredibly, he needed only another 40 minutes to advance from 200 to 300, eventually throwing his wicket away when on 369.

137
Number of times the Don was caught by a fieldsman or the bowler in his 295 first-class dismissals.

139.14
The Don's average in the Tests on his first tour of England in 1930, easily the highest of his eight Ashes series. His next best was 108.50, in England eight years later. In 1930, Bradman's seven innings in five matches produced scores of 8, 131, 254, 1, 334, 14 and 232.

142
Number of the Don's first-class appearances in Australia. In 218 innings he made 18,230 runs at 94.46, with 76 hundreds, 45 fifties and 12 ducks. He also took 91 catches. Of his 142 matches in Australia, 33 were Tests, 41 were for New South Wales and 44 were for South Australia. The rest were matches for Australian XIs against touring sides, Test trial games and testimonials.

155 Minutes
Time taken by the Don for the fastest 200 of his first-class career: in his innings of 209 not out for South Australia against Western Australia at the WACA in 1939–40. At the time it was the fastest 200 by an Australian in Australia, only one minute slower than the quickest ever recorded here, by Frank Woolley for the MCC against Tasmania in 1911–12.

163 Minutes
The average length of each of the Don's completed innings in his 52 Tests.

164
Number of century partnerships in which the Don figured in his 338 innings in 234 first-class matches.

165 Minutes
The longest it took the Don to reach 50 in a first-class game: when he made 58 playing for an Australian XI against the MCC at the SCG in 1928–29.

168
Number of the Don's innings in his 109 first-class matches in Australia other than Tests. The total included 96 innings in Sheffield Shield: 52 for New South Wales and 44 for South Australia. He made 13,908 runs at 93.34, with 58 centuries (including 14 double centuries, three triple centuries and a quadruple century), 35 fifties and seven ducks. His highest score was the then world first-class record of 452 not out for NSW against Queensland in a shield game at the SCG in 1929–30.

172
The Don's score when he notched up his 100th first-class century, playing for an Australian XI against the Indians at the SCG in November 1947.

173
The Don's "average-per-century" in first-class cricket. Once he reached 100 (as he did 117 times), he added, on average, another 73 runs.

$173
What the Don was fined for speeding on Adelaide's grand prix circuit alongside Victoria Park racecourse on the way home from a game of golf at Kooyonga in April 1996.

174
The number of times the Don was caught in his 295 first-class dismissals: 124 times by a fieldsman, 37 times by the wicketkeeper and 13 times by the bowler.

182
Number of the Don's first-class appearances other than Tests: 109 in Australia (168 innings) and 73 in England (90 innings). He scored 21,071

runs at 93.65, with 88 hundreds, 56 fifties and nine ducks. His 99 catches included four for South Australia in Sheffield Shield matches as wicket-keeper. He also executed one stumping. Bradman's 182 matches included two in which he did not bat because of rain.

184.40

The Don's average for New South Wales in the 1933–34 Sheffield Shield season, the highest in the competition to that point. The left-handed Clem Hill of South Australia had the previous best of 152.25.

185

The Don's "average per century" in Test cricket. Once he reached 100 (as he did on 29 occasions), he added, on average, another 85 runs. His century average in Ashes Tests is 187.

186

Number of times the Don reached 50 in his 338 first-class innings (55.04%), on 117 occasions going on to make a century. By comparison, Victor Trumper had 63 more innings than Bradman but exceeded 50 only 129 times, going on to make 42 hundreds. The Don's longest sequence of consecutive scores over 50 was 10. It started with his 132 in the first innings of the Third Test against India at the MCG in January 1948 (when he also made a century in the second innings) and ended with 98 against the MCC at Lord's five months later. Bradman also had a sequence of 14 consecutive Tests (in which he batted) that he made at least one fifty, starting with the Second Ashes Test at the SCG in December 1936 and ending with the Second Test at Lord's in June 1948.

189

Number of wickets the Don took with his leg-spinners in 51 games on Arthur Mailey's 1932 tour of Canada and the US. In one match, in Victoria, Canada, he claimed six wickets in one eight-ball over, remarkably without a hat-trick.

1,318

The Don's aggregate in 23 innings in 1925–26 as a 17-year-old in his first season as a regular player for Bowral. He averaged 94.14 and his highest score was a district-record 300 (breaking his own record of 234 set earlier in the season) in the final against Moss Vale at Moss Vale in a match which lasted five Saturday afternoons. He also took 51 wickets at 7.80 and held 26

O

catches. In his 12 innings in competition matches during the season, Bradman made 985 runs at 109.40, took 35 wickets at 8.1 and claimed 16 catches.

1,690
The Don's first-class aggregate for the 1928–29 season, still a record and one which will probably never be broken.

O'Brien, Leo Patrick Joseph
O'Brien was a batsman from Victoria promoted to the Australian side as a replacement for the injured Bill Ponsford in the second of the Bodyline Tests at the MCG. He scored 10 and 11, losing his wicket in the second innings to a missile from Larwood which sent his stump cartwheeling. The gritty left-hander said later that some of the great paceman's deliveries were so fast he failed completely to see them. O'Brien was made 12th man for the controversial Third Test in Adelaide. He was the only other member of the team who witnessed the famous exchange in the Australian dressing room between his captain Bill Woodfull and England manager Pelham Warner, and it is O'Brien's version (told many years later to ABC radio) of what Woodfull said to Warner which is reported elsewhere in this book. O'Brien was dropped for the fourth match in Brisbane then recalled for the fifth, in Sydney, when he made 61 in the first innings in uncharacteristic style, slashing at Larwood and surviving three chances from him. He played two Tests in South Africa in 1935–36 and one Test against England in Australia the following summer. It was during this last series that O'Brien and three other Australians – Bill O'Reilly, Stan McCabe and Chuck Fleetwood-Smith – were carpeted by the Board of Control in Melbourne for a lack of discipline and not supporting the Don as skipper. Just before his death in March 1997 at the age of 89, O'Brien was Australia's oldest Test cricketer, a title which then passed to the Don. And the pair were the two last survivors of the Bodyline series.

Oldfield, William Albert Stanley ("Bert") MBE
The New South Wales and Australian wicketkeeper was at the centre of controversy on the Monday of the Bodyline Test in Adelaide when he was hit a sickening blow in the head trying to hook a legitimate bumper from Harold Larwood. Although Larwood was not blamed, the crowd was already furious after captain Bill Woodfull had been hit on the body on the Saturday, and it was feared someone would lead an invasion of the field. Oldfield had to be helped from the ground but said later that it was his own fault. The diminutive 'keeper played Test cricket from 1920 to 1937, tour-

ing England four times and South Africa twice and playing in seven home series, five against the Old Enemy. He retired from first-class cricket after being overlooked for Bradman's Ashes tour of 1938. The Don wrote of Bert Oldfield in his *Farewell to Cricket*: "There was about his work a polish far transcending that of all others ... Until his retirement, I could not do otherwise than class Oldfield as the finest wicket-keeper I had seen. Today I am inclined to hand that supremacy to Don Tallon. There can be little to choose between them." Of Bradman, Oldfield wrote: "An amazing chap is Don! Gifted as he is with attributes of greatness, he carried on in his quiet yet most determined way." Bert waxes lyrical about his former teammate's entry into Test cricket in footage used in Jack Egan's video, *Bradman*. The Kippax-Oldfield testimonial match in February 1949 (postponed from before the war) was the Don's penultimate first-class match and his last at the SCG. Bert Oldfield was 81 when he died in 1976.

Old Trafford

Though he liked playing on the Manchester ground, it was easily the Don's least successful Test arena anywhere. In his four innings in three Tests here (the Third Test in 1938 was washed out without a ball being bowled), he averaged just 27, his highest score being 30 not out in 1948 (his 50th Test) when he played the slowest first-class innings of his career at 14 runs an hour. But Bradman and Morris were defending grimly to save the game. Old Trafford was the only Test venue in England where the Don did not make a century in a Test, but he did have success on the ground in the games against Lancashire, with two centuries in eight innings. The first, 101 not out in 1938, was one of his best innings of the tour, making the fastest hundred of the year on the ground to that point by any player. The second was in 1948 in the Don's last appearance in Manchester, a benefit match for Lancashire and England batsman Cyril Washbrook, when he made 133 not out, 108 of them before lunch. In all first-class games at Old Trafford, Bradman made 470 runs at 58.75. He also took five catches.

Oliphant, (Sir) Marcus Laurence Elwin AC, KBE

Physicist and later governor of South Australia who, according to the *Sydney Morning Herald*, was not quite as popular as the Don in the 1940s. The first-ever item in the paper's "Column 8", on January 11, 1947 read: "Don Bradman, Test cricketer, can't remember the number of autographs he's signed – 'Must run into many thousands.' Marcus Oliphant, atom expert, can. He's never been asked for one."

O'Reilly, William Joseph ("Tiger") OBE

Born in the western New South Wales opal town of White Cliffs in 1905, Bill O'Reilly was a leading figure in the career of the Don and one of his two most trenchant critics. Bradman was always adamant that the tall, aggressive leg-spinner was the best bowler he had ever seen. O'Reilly reciprocated, claiming Bradman was "the greatest cricketer ever that I saw walk through a gate onto a cricket field". Tiger was a right-handed wrist spinner who bowled at close to medium pace yet delivered leg breaks, googlies, top spinners and occasional off-breaks with unerring accuracy. He did not gain a lot of spin but generated great pace and bounce. O'Reilly and Bradman first appeared in the same team when they played for a NSW Second XI against Victoria in a second-class game at the SCG on New Year's Day 1927. O'Reilly entered first-class cricket for NSW in the same season as the Don, 1927–28, but soon after was posted to the country in his job as a schoolteacher and did not gain selection in the national side until his return to Sydney over three years later, when picked for the Fourth Test against South Africa in Adelaide in 1931–32 (the match in which the Don ran out his last partner attempting the vital single off the last ball of an over when on 299).

O'Reilly and Bradman had famously first played against each other when they turned out for Wingello and Bowral respectively in the Berrima District Competition in January 1926, when the Don was 17 and O'Reilly 20. Tiger was a student at Sydney Teachers College and was on his way home to spend his summer holidays at home in Wingello. When the train stopped at Bowral, he was startled to hear someone on the platform yelling his name. He peered out the window to see the stationmaster telling him to get off the train because his home team wanted him to open the bowling against Bowral that afternoon. When O'Reilly protested that he had no cricket gear the stationmaster explained that Tiger's mother had sent it with the team. The Don had never met or seen the gangly spinner in action but was aware of his reputation, O'Reilly having routed Moss Vale in the competition final the previous season. And O'Reilly had been warned of Bradman's batting prowess but believed he had his measure, particularly with the ball darting high off the coir matting. Early in his innings Bradman was, in O'Reilly's words, "spilled twice off me under tragic circumstances in the slips" before going on to score 234 by close of play on the first day of the two-day match. To the end of his days, whenever O'Reilly spoke of his first on-field encounter with Bradman, he remembered the look in the 17-year-old's eyes as he arrived at the wicket. It was a look of supreme confidence which let the bowler know he was the master and was about to demonstrate it.

The Don always acknowledged that he was dropped twice in the slips off O'Reilly but denied the story later promoted by him that the slips fieldsman (the captain, Selby Jeffery) had failed to take the first catch because both his hands were occupied lighting his pipe, and had dropped the second chance because his vision was obscured by dense blue smoke emanating from his lungs. The Don later wrote that the tale "must be one of the best cricket jokes of all time". O'Reilly was to recount how he was so despondent during the week after being belted around the park by a 17-year-old that he seriously considered giving cricket away and going back to athletics with the Botany Harriers club in Sydney. But at Wingello (on the ground now known as Bill O'Reilly Oval) on the second day of the match, the following Saturday, he bowled the Don around his legs with the first ball of the day, and he thought, "By gee, this isn't a bad game after all; I'll stick at it." The personal relationship between the pair suffered during the 1930s and '40s for several reasons. The first was the omission of Clarrie Grimmett from the team for the series against England in Australia in 1936–37. O'Reilly and his spin twin had put the cleaners through the Springboks in South Africa the previous summer, and O'Reilly considered Grimmett's selection for the Ashes series a formality. Bradman, who had been appointed to the selection panel in September 1936 on the death of Charles Dolling (before being appointed captain), got the blame from O'Reilly, as he did more notably when Grimmett was left out of the side for the Ashes tour of 1938.

O'Reilly became particularly bitter when, in the first innings of the final Test at the Oval, England scored a mammoth 903 and he and Chuck Fleetwood-Smith were forced to bowl 85 and 87 overs respectively. Tiger's figures were 3/178 and Fleetwood-Smith's 1/298. O'Reilly was scarred by the experience and later told commentator and author Alan McGilvray how he would have loved to have had his "old mate" Grimmett at the other end to help. O'Reilly brooded over it for years, as did Grimmett for the rest of his life. The Don never revealed (at least publicly) his part in the selectors' decision to leave the 46-year-old Grimmett at home because he considered it a matter of honour that selection committees make group judgements and their discussions should be privy only to themselves. (In the radio interview with the ABC in 1987, Bradman defended the selectors' decision to take Frank Ward as the third slow bowler behind O'Reilly and Fleetwood-Smith, pointing out that the South Australian leggie's strike-rate in all matches on the tour was better even than O'Reilly's. But in his books *Farewell to Cricket* (1950) and *The Art of Cricket* (1958), the Don implied that he had in fact fought for Grimmett's inclusion in the earlier series at home.)

O

And there was the famous incident in 1936–37 after Bradman's side unexpectedly (because Gubby Allen's men had performed moderately in the lead-up games) lost the first two Tests against England. It was known that some Australian players resented Bradman's appointment over Victor Richardson, the longtime SA captain and skipper of the very successful Australian side which had toured South Africa the previous summer (and Bradman had also replaced Richardson as SA skipper when he was away with the touring side), but Richardson was not in the Test XI. Just before Christmas, Arthur Mailey claimed in a newspaper piece that some players in the Australian team were not supporting Bradman as skipper. Vice-captain Stan McCabe released a statement denying the claim, and the Don himself issued a statement defending his players. But in the second week of January, just after the Third Test at the MCG (won resoundingly by Australia), four members of the team – O'Reilly, McCabe, Chuck Fleetwood-Smith and Leo O'Brien – were summoned before the board for a dressing-down. As it happened, all four were Irish Catholics, and most cricket officials at the time were Masons, as was the Don for a few years in the early 1930s. But although Bradman had no knowledge of the hearing until it was over (the board decided to keep him in the dark to "protect" him), O'Reilly said many years later in taped reminiscences for the Australian Oral History Archive that he had never forgiven the Don for not attending the hearing. (Leo O'Brien liked to recall how Tiger went on the offensive at the meeting and gave the stunned board members such a withering blast that the proceedings broke up within minutes.) O'Reilly wrote about the event later in the first of his autobiographies, *Cricket Conquest* (his second was *Tiger*).

Bill O'Reilly was forced out of the game by a bad knee after the 1946 short tour of New Zealand and he became a print journalist. The Don notably took him to task in *Farewell to Cricket* over his "carping criticism" in an English newspaper of Australia's bowlers at the end of the first day of the Headingley Test in 1948. The forthright O'Reilly described Bradman's attack as "hopeless and meaningless" and branded Australia's out-cricket as "the worst of the tour". As it turned out, this was the match in which the Don's side went on to record a historic win by scoring 404 in 344 minutes in the fourth innings. Bill O'Reilly and Jack Fingleton were in the press box at the Oval when the Australian captain walked out to bat to a great reception and then three cheers from the England side around the wicket in his last Test. Almost 50 years later, English journalist Jim Swanton told Bradman's biographer, Charles Williams, that when the Don was bowled second ball, "I thought they [Fingleton and O'Reilly] were going to have a stroke – they were laughing so much." O'Reilly admitted to friends that he had laughed, but only at the incongruity of the occasion. In a letter to Williams in 1995, Bradman wrote: "O'Reilly nakedly exposes the disloyalty I had to endure during my early years as Australian captain, a disloyalty based on jealousy and religion."

But there was no sign of ill-feeling between the pair at Bradman Oval in Bowral in September 1976, when the two interacted cordially before O'Reilly bowled to Bradman (about two metres wide of the leg stump) to open the newly refurbished oval. Nor at the opening of a memorial to Clarrie Grimmett at Adelaide Oval in December 1988, when Tiger took the initiative in shaking hands with the Don. And Bradman approached O'Reilly to speak with him at the opening of the Bradman Pavilion in Bowral in October 1989. At an after-dinner speech in 1986, he said of the Don: "There's never been and never will be in my estimation a batsman so good as that fellow. I don't care how many you like to pour into one – all the Chappells, the Borders and so on. Forget them, they're just child's play compared with Bradman, and I've seen them all. The Yanks talk about Babe Ruth and all that. To hell with Babe Ruth. This boy was a modern miracle." But around the same time in an interview with ABC radio, although glowing again in his praise of Bradman as a batsman, O'Reilly said the Don was a "recluse", saying that "he was a man who had nothing really to contribute socially amongst any of the boys at all – and in fact, what's more, looking back now I don't think I ever really got to know Bradman, and I knew him longer than any other cricketer that has ever lived." But they were two entirely different personalities: O'Reilly was Irish, gregarious, bold, convivial, and the Don, reserved and circumspect. As for their respective abilities with bat and ball, Tiger said he believed that research would show that his record in the middle against the great batsman was "not lop-sided". In 15 seasons of Sydney first-grade cricket from 1931 to 1946, O'Reilly took an incredible 921 wickets for under 10 runs each, heading the averages 12 times. He published two tour books as well as his autobiographies and earned a reputation for no-holds-barred comment over many years as a cricket writer with the *Sydney Morning Herald*. Bill O'Reilly was confined to a wheelchair after having a leg amputated in May 1990 and died in Sydney in October 1992, aged 86, an unwavering champion of spin-bowling to the end.

Orford
Ship of the Orient Line which carried the Australians to England in 1934. The cricketers shared the boat with compatriot Davis Cup players Jack Crawford, Viv McGrath, Adrian Quist and Don Turnbull.

O

Orontes
Ship on which the Don and his team travelled to England in 1938, and also on which his Invincibles returned from England in 1948 .

"Our Bungalow of Dreams"
Dance tune composed by Charlie Newman and recorded by the Don for Columbia Records in 1930. He recorded another ditty, "An Old Fashioned Locket", in the same year for the same label.

"Our Don Bradman"
A "Snappy Fox Trot Song", recorded by Art Leonard and released before the Don's return from his triumphant tour of England in October 1930. Bradman told Ray Martin in the 1996 television interview that "it embarrassed me". The dedication on the sheet music reads: "Written in appreciation of his match-winning and record-breaking efforts." As a tune, the ditty written by prolific composer Jack O'Hagan puts subsequent songs about the Don in the shade.

Our Don Bradman
An anthology of writings about the Don edited by Philip Derriman and originally published in 1987 by Macmillan Australia. The selection of about 50 pieces were written between the 1920s and the mid-1980s. Forty per cent were taken from books and another 40 per cent from newspapers. A revised edition with about 20 new pieces was published by the ABC in 2001.

Oval, The
On arriving at south-east London's Kennington Oval early in the 1948 tour for the game against Surrey, the Don noted that workmen were painting the large gasometer green, "a big improvement on the previous colour scheme". In terms of average, the Oval was Bradman's second-most successful Test ground in England after Headingley, notwithstanding *that* duck in 1948 in the last Test appearance of his career, when he was bowled second ball by leg-spinner Eric Hollies. In Australia's first innings of this Test, the Don had walked to the wicket amidst continued applause from the standing crowd. When he arrived in the middle, England captain Norman Yardley called for three cheers from his players and then shook Bradman's hand. The Don wrote: "The reception had stirred my emotions very deeply and made me anxious – a dangerous state of mind for any batsman to be in. I played the first ball from Hollies though not sure I really saw it. The sec-

ond was a perfect length googly which deceived me. I just touched it with the inside edge of the bat and the off bail was dislodged." The crowd roared in disbelief and Bradman slowly retraced his steps to the pavilion and a sympathetic reception. Although acknowledging his emotional state as he faced those two balls, Bradman later dismissed Hollies's claim that he didn't see the ball which bowled him because he had tears in his eyes.

After the match, easily won by Australia, hundreds from the crowd ran onto the field in front of the pavilion to farewell the Don. Norman Yardley said: "In saying goodbye to Don we are saying goodbye to the greatest cricketer of all time. He is not only a great cricketer but a great sportsman, on and off the field. I hope this is not the last time we see Don Bradman in this country." In responding, the Don confirmed he had played his last Test match. Yardley then led the crowd and the players in three cheers and "For He's a Jolly Good Fellow". Ten years earlier at the Oval, the home side set several records on the ground in the last match of the series when they beat Bradman's side by a whopping innings and 579 runs after compiling 7 for 903 (declared). In this match, Len Hutton broke the Don's Ashes record of 334 when he made 364. Bradman was later critical of the pitch, which he believed heavily favoured batsmen. He was later to describe the match as "that nightmare game of 1938". Near the end of England's marathon innings, the Don put himself on to ease the burden on his exhausted attack but in his third over he fractured a bone in his ankle when he went over in a hole which had been worn by his bowlers. He had to be carried from the field and did not play in any of the remaining tour matches.

In his first Test appearance at the Oval, in 1930, Bradman made 232 (a Test record for the ground which he was to break four years later) during a record fourth-wicket stand with Archie Jackson of 243. He was given out caught behind by George Duckworth off Harold Larwood but the Don wrote later that he believed he was hard done by. At 438 minutes, this was his longest innings in his four tours of England, explained by a difficult sticky wicket on which Larwood and Hammond were able to make the ball fly. This was the match which Larwood was later to claim provided the inspiration for the "fast leg-theory" used in Australia in 1932–33. Though Bradman and Jackson received unanimous praise in the British press for their courage after they were hit repeatedly by Larwood bumpers, the Nottingham paceman said that on a couple of occasions he noticed the Don "flinching".

When Bradman was 164 in this innings of 232, he took his aggregate for the 1930 series to 906, improving on the record total for any Test series of 905 set by Wally Hammond in 1928–29 in Australia. Four years later the

O

Don and Bill Ponsford set up a decisive victory when they shared a second-wicket stand of 451 (in 316 minutes), a world Test record for any wicket which stood for 50 years – and Australia's 475 in a day was also a world record for a Test. Bradman's 244 (in 316 minutes and 272 balls) was his highest Test score at the Oval, and a Test record for the ground until Ponsford passed it the next morning, eventually making 266. The Don's four innings in four Tests at the Oval produced 553 runs, with two centuries (both double centuries) and one fifty, at an average of 138.25. It's worth noting that following his highly publicised failure in the Oval Test in 1948, he made scores in the remaining tour matches of 65, 150, 143, 153 and 123. In 12 innings in 11 first-class matches at the Oval, Bradman compiled 1,392 runs at 139.20, with six hundreds (including three double hundreds) and three fifties. He also took three catches.

Owens, Lillian

A niece of the Don's who sang "Home Sweet Home", one of her uncle's favourite songs, at the memorial service at Bradman Oval on March 28, 2001.

Oxford University

The opposition in 1930 when the Don scored his first six in a first-class match, hit off a no-ball in an innings of 32. This was the only six Bradman hit in an innings of under 50. The Bradman Museum Trust has awarded two scholarships to Oxford to two young Australian cricketers: Geoffrey Lovell in 1990 and Andrew Ridley in 1993.

P

Packer, Kerry Francis Bullmore

Media magnate whose grandfather, Robert Clyde Packer, controlled Associated Newspapers when the company's Sydney paper, the *Sun*, employed the Don as a journalist in the early 1930s. As a member of the Australian Cricket Board, Bradman served on the Emergency Committee which was set up in 1977 to deal with Kerry Packer's attempted takeover of big cricket when he signed up 66 of the world's leading players. Packer's "circus" ran concurrently with "establishment" cricket for two years until a peace deal was signed in 1979. Bradman refused many requests for interviews from commercial television over a period of 40 years but Packer wanted him so badly for his Nine Network that in March 1996 he went to Adelaide to persuade him. He told the celebrated octogenarian he could have anyone he wanted as interviewer and got him with an offer to pay the Bradman Museum $1.2 million. The interview was taped the following month and shown on May 29. Soon after the taping, the Don wrote to his biographer Roland Perry: "I agreed most reluctantly and it was a terrible ordeal for me, especially coming so soon after I had had this wretched stroke, but Ray Martin was wonderful to work with." A telethon held by Channel Nine in conjunction with the broadcast of the interview raised enough funds for the museum to be completed and opened on August 27, 1996, the Don's 88th birthday.

Parker, (Pipe Major) Rodney

Member of the Highlands Pipes and Drums who played the lament, "Farewell My Love", at the memorial service for the Don at Bradman Oval on March 28, 2001.

Parkinson, Michael CBE

Yorkshire television personality, author and cricket buff who wrote an introduction for Pavilion Books' 1985 edition of Jack Fingleton's book *Brightly Fades the Don*. In an article in the *National Times* in 1983, Parkinson told of the time, before he was born, when his father walked about 35 kilometres to see Bradman bat. The family believed he had a "slate loose", but his father, in retelling the story many times over the years, would say: "But I saw HIM bat and they didn't." But Michael also saw HIM bat, at Headingley in Leeds as a 12-year-old in 1948, when the maestro scored just 33 in the first innings. But he has said that his memory of the occasion is of the atmosphere at the ground and the response of the crowd to Bradman. He has also said that the two people he most regrets not being able to get on his talk show are Frank Sinatra and the Don. Michael Parkinson delivered the second Sir Donald Bradman Oration in Brisbane in December 2003.

Paterson, A(ndrew) B(arton) ("Banjo")

Celebrated bush balladist who "exchanged a few remarks" with the young Don in a Sydney sports store in 1929. In a radio talk, Banjo said of the encounter: "A couple of years ago I was in a sports depot in Sydney and a wiry sunburnt young bush chap came in and started looking over the goods. I've had so much to do with athletes I can generally pick a man fairly well, and I said to the salesman, 'That's a hard-looking young fellow and he's very light on his feet. I should say he's done some boxing or was accustomed to riding rough horses. They have to be pretty active for the game.' So the salesman laughed and said, 'No, you're a bit out. But he is a somebody all the same.' I said, 'Who is he?' 'Oh', he said, 'that's Don Bradman, this new boy wonder cricketer they have just discovered.'"

Payne, Iris

Girl who always came first in the Don's class at high school at Bowral. "Sooky" Turner generally came second and the Don was usually third.

Pearce, Geoffrey

Country traveller for a Sydney insurance company who became friendly with the Don and his father George in Bowral. When Bradman was made secretary of his employer Percy Westbrook's new real estate office in Sydney early in 1928, Mr Pearce offered the young Sheffield Shield star accommodation in his Sydney home in Concord West. (In an on-air phone call shortly after the Don's death in 2001, one of Mr Pearce's daughters, Heather, told ABC radio about how as a 14-year-old she had to vacate her bedroom and join her younger sisters to make way for the very shy 19-year-old when he moved in as a boarder. After, she was fond of telling people for many years that she had "slept in Don Bradman's bed".) The move to the city was a critical step for the Don in his ambition to make the Test side, as it cut out the long train trip from Bowral and back each Saturday for his grade matches with St George and also enabled him to practise on turf wickets during the week. He left the Pearce home in September 1928 and moved in with Frank Cush and his wife in the suburb of Rockdale to enable him to continue playing for St George after the residential rule was introduced. The former Pearce home at 232 Concord Road is a modest brick cottage near Yaralla Street, almost opposite Concord Library.

Peebles, Ian Alexander Ross

Slow bowler off whom the Don scored the first six of his first-class career, from a no-ball against Oxford University in 1930 before he was bowled soon after by Garland-Wells for 32. But two months later in the Test at Old Trafford the tall leg-spinner from Scotland had Bradman in all sorts of bother before claiming his scalp for 14. Of the Don, Peebles once wrote: "A fair impression of a typical Bradman innings may be gained by thinking of all the best strokes one has ever seen, all played in the course of an afternoon."

People

Newspaper which arranged a big farewell luncheon for the Don at London's Savoy Hotel after the tour of England in 1948. Bradman was presented with a replica of the famous Warwick Vase, a treasure discovered in 1770 by Sir William Hamilton in the ruins of Emperor Hadrian's villa near Rome. The replica, made of solid silver, was financed by the Bradman Fund, set up by the newspaper several weeks before and subscribed to by "cricket lovers of Britain".

Pepper, Cecil George

New South Wales all-rounder who hit what *Yorkshire Post* writer Jim Kilburn said was the biggest six he had ever seen. Playing for the Australian Services team in a 1945 match in the North Yorkshire seaside resort of Scarborough, Pepper dispatched one which cleared five-storey buildings outside the ground and landed in Trafalgar Square (no, not the one in London). In their book *Gods or Flannelled Fools*, Keith Miller and Dick Whitington (who both played in the game) related an incident involving Pepper and the Don in a match between South Australia and the Services team in Adelaide in 1945–46. Pepper was bowling to Bradman and appealed triumphantly when he rapped him on the pads. When umpire Jack Scott turned down the appeal, Pepper exclaimed: "What do you have to do, Jack?" The Don took a single off the last ball of the over, and when completing his run called to Scott: "Do we have to put up with this sort of thing?" Scott later told Pepper that in view of Bradman's complaint he would have to report the incident to the authorities. When the Board of Control demanded a written apology from Pepper he prepared one and

P

handed it to Keith Johnson, the manager of the Services team and a member of the board, but "in some way it became lost in transit".

In the meantime the Australian team to tour New Zealand was picked, and when Pepper's name was not on the list he accepted an offer to play in the Lancashire League in England. When the board asked Pepper for another apology, he asked journalist and Services teammate Whitington whether he thought he should comply. Whitington replied: "That all depends upon whether you want to play for Australia again or not, Cecil." Pepper decided that if his word wasn't good enough for the board he would not send another apology.

In a discussion of the evolution of bowling in *Farewell to Cricket*, the Don wrote that "Pepper made the ball turn from the off by some unique method of delivery which even now remains a mystery to me." Cec Pepper made thousands of runs and took hundreds of wickets in England and later became a first-class umpire. He died in Littleborough, Lancashire, in 1993, aged 76.

Perfect Ten, A

An exhibition at the Bradman Museum which honours the top performers in 10 world sports, opened by the then governor-general, Sir William Deane, on August 27, 2000, the Don's 92nd birthday. After the opening there was a birthday lunch for invited guests, the highlight of which was the cutting of a cake shaped like a cricket bat and topped with a ball and a baggy green cap. The Don was represented at the opening by son John and grandson Tom. Featured with Bradman in the exhibition are Carl Lewis, Dawn Fraser, Muhammad Ali, Rod Laver, Jack Nicklaus, Pele, Nadia Comaneci, Michael Jordan and John Eales. The exhibition includes a 20-minute film which starts on the hour and the half-hour.

Peritonitis

Serious condition with which Bradman fell gravely ill in London on September 24, 1934, two days before the tourists left for Australia. Peritonitis is inflammation of the peritoneum, the two-layered membrane which lines the abominal cavity and covers the stomach, intestines and other abdominal organs. In Bradman, it occurred as the result of appendicitis. He was operated on by expatriate Australian surgeon Douglas Shields, and the Don's wife Jessie made the trip from Australia to be at his side. At one point he was close to death but recovered after a long convalescence in Europe and Australia. He had not felt well in the weeks before leaving for England (and had even considered withdrawing from the team) but doctors could not pinpoint the problem. His indifferent health was reflected in a run of poor performances in the first half of the tour but, paradoxically, he returned to his brilliant best in the weeks leading up to his collapse.

Perry, Roland

Author of the 1995 book *The Don: A Biography of Sir Donald Bradman*, published by Pan Macmillan, 645pp. Perry, whose earlier books covered a range of subjects outside cricket, interviewed Bradman for the work and quoted him at length. He is the author also of *Bradman's Best: Sir Donald Bradman's Selection of the Best Team in Cricket History*, a book devoted to a selection by the Don of his all-time best world side; and *Bradman's Best Ashes Teams*, which features portraits of each member of the Don's best sides chosen from all Australian and England Test players over the last 125 years. Both books were published by Random House Australia. Roland Perry has also written biographies of Steve Waugh and Shane Warne.

Pickard Cup

Cup won by the young Don's Bowral A side when they beat Moss Vale A in the final of the Berrima District Competition in 1926–27.

"Pie Jesu" (Blessed Jesus)

Duet from Andrew Lloyd Webber's *Requiem* sung by the Don's grand-daughter Greta and friend Emily Roxburgh at the memorial service at St Peter's Cathedral in Adelaide. In his last years Sir Donald enjoyed playing the piano score of Lloyd Webber's *Phantom of the Opera*.

Platypus

Animal whose image was replaced by that of the Don on the Australian 20-cent coin. Approved by Prime Minister John Howard in March 2001, the Bradman design represented the first change to the face of the 20-cent coin since it was introduced when decimal currency began in 1966. The new coin features an action shot of Bradman, ringed by his name and the years of his life, 1908 to 2001. The platypus will be restored at some time in the future and both designs will circulate simultaneously.

Politics

The Don said in his *Farewell to Cricket* that when the ship neared Australia on the team's return from England in 1948, he received a cable asking whether it was true that he had decided to enter Australian politics.

P

"Although I had not indicated any interest in such a proposal, the matter evidently received prominence in the Australian press and on the wireless. I had not been consulted by anybody and had expressed no views. Yet such is the force of 'rumour' that the matter gave rise to a question in Parliament." Bradman was sceptical about Liberal and Labor politicians alike, including iconic Liberals such as long-serving South Australian Premier Sir Thomas Playford, whom he called "Uncle Tom". In a letter in the 1960s to good friend Rohan Rivett, the Don wrote: "My suspicious nature still doesn't make me believe that either political party is 'well meaning'." He told Ray Martin in the 1996 television interview that nothing would ever have persuaded him to go into politics. "I was asked by the Labor Party, I was asked by the Liberal Party if I would accept nomination for a particular seat, and in most cases I said no, politics doesn't appeal to me. I just didn't like it, politics and the lifestyle doesn't appeal to me."

Ponsford, William Harold MBE

A master of spin bowling, the hard-hitting Victorian and Australian opener scored heavily in two tours of England with the Don in 1930 and 1934. In two consecutive Tests in 1934, Ponsford and Bradman added 839 runs in 645 minutes. Ponsford is the only player to compile centuries in each of his first and last two Tests, and until Brian Lara equalled the feat in April 2004 was the only batsman to make two first-class scores of 400 or more. The second of these, when he broke his own world record with 437 on December 17, 1927, was registered on the same day that the Don scored 118 in his debut first-class appearance playing for New South Wales against South Australia in a Sheffield Shield game at Adelaide Oval. Ponsford's record performance, achieved for Victoria against Queensland in a shield game at the MCG, was bettered by the Don's unbeaten 452 for NSW against Queensland at the SCG in 1929–30. As well as his two scores over 400, Ponsford achieved another two feats not managed by the Don: he made more than 1,000 runs in a month in Australia (in December 1927) and accrued 1,000 runs from four consecutive innings.

As 12th man, Bradman had to field for England's entire innings of 636 after Bill had a bone in his hand broken by a ball from Harold Larwood in the first innings of the Second Test at the SCG in 1928–29. Ponsford and Bradman figured in three notable Test partnerships. The first was a stand of 229 for the second wicket against the West Indies at Brisbane's Exhibition Ground in 1930–31. The second and third were both in England in 1934. At Headingley the sturdy right-hander scored 181 when he and Bradman added 388 in 330 minutes for the fourth wicket after a batting collapse. Then, at the

Oval in Ponsford's last Test, the pair put on 451 for the second wicket in only 315 minutes, a partnership which remains an Australian record. In the Tests on this tour Ponsford and the Don dwarfed their teammates. The opener headed the averages with 569 at 94.83 but Bradman made more runs. Bill Ponsford figured in 22 first-class century partnerships with Bill Woodfull, and in 43 shield games scored 5,413 runs at 84.57. Of the Don, he once said: "The reason is very simple. Don sees the ball about two yards sooner than any of the rest of us." In an interview in 1980, Bill told journalist Michael Davie that "Bill Woodfull never forgave him [Bradman] for a couple of things." But in Davie's words: "I was too cowardly to ask the key question." Bill Ponsford was 90 when he died in Kyneton, Victoria, in 1991.

Pope, Roland James ("Doc")

A great lover of cricket who travelled at his own expense with Australian teams to England and elsewhere several times from 1921. He took medical supplies, as well as books and other items – in fact he had almost every conceivable object that players might want. And he was a great comfort to the Don in 1930 when he told him that people usually grow out of sea-sickness after 20 years. Pope was famous for the amount of luggage he carried. On the trip to Canada and the US in 1932, manager Arthur Mailey restricted him to 36 bags. At home it was his custom to send boxes of fruit into the dressing rooms at the SCG. Pope was a cricketer himself, having represented New South Wales in two matches and then playing one Test, the second match of the 1884–85 series against England in Melbourne, when most of the original Australian team refused to play because of a dispute over match payments. Batting in the middle order, he failed in both innings. Pope also played first-class cricket for Scotland. He died in Sydney in 1952, aged 88.

Publicity

The Don spent the first 40 years of his life making certain of his immortality but spent much of the rest of his life trying to live with the uniqueness of his mortality. In a 1971 letter written to good friend Rohan Rivett, Bradman said: "In my moments of triumph (if any) in the modest arena I have trodden, I have sought seclusion and peace – not publicity. But hate it as I might, publicity seems to be my lot. Perhaps my reward will come posthumously for I guess historians will assess whether I faithfully served mankind." He became obsessive about his privacy later in life, often railing against the intrusiveness of a forever burgeoning media. His distrust of the media, despite a one-time association with it, bordered on contempt. In

1989, Bradman wrote to a journalist: "I am glad you recall my saying that my dislike of publicity has increased. Since then, it has increased still further. No doubt you find my desire to live a private life free from publicity incompatible with your occupation but, having done more than a fair thing for over 50 years, at age 81, I am determined as far as possible to resist further encroachments on my private life." When the Don told biographer Roland Perry in 1995 that "I can't get to the corner without someone approaching me," Perry asked him if he ever regretted his fame. The Don replied: "Yes, often. I wish I never had it." And the following year he told Ray Martin: "I've spoken to a lot of people, but not publicly. I don't like publicity of any kind, never have done. And I like it less as I get older."

Public Schools Club
Club in Piccadilly, London, where the Cricket Writers Club held a dinner for the Don and his men soon after arriving in England in 1948. Bradman believed that of all functions he attended during his career, this one stands out for the wit of the speeches. Speakers included club chairman EW (Jim) Swanton, Canon Gillingham and Sir Norman Birkett, and the special guest was Prince Philip, the Duke of Edinburgh. The Don drew laughter when he suggested in his speech that England selectors should consider the Duke for selection in their side as an off-spinner. The BBC held back their nine o'clock news on the night of the dinner to allow the British public to hear Bradman's speech in full.

Q

Queen's Hotel

The Leeds hotel where the Don famously retired to his room and a pot of tea after scoring 309 not out on the first day of the Third Test at Headingley on July 11, 1930.

Queensland

State against which the Don made his highest first-class score of 452 not out, then a world record, playing for New South Wales in a Sheffield Shield game at the SCG in January 1930. The epic knock took just 415 minutes, compared with 621 minutes taken by previous record-holder Bill Ponsford for his 437 playing for Victoria, also against Queensland, in a shield game at the MCG in 1927–28. And the two occasions in shield cricket when Bradman scored a hundred in each innings were both against Queensland: for NSW at the Exhibition Ground in 1928–29 and for South Australia at the 'Gabba in 1937–38. He made centuries in five consecutive innings against the northern state in 1937–39. But Queensland was also the opposition when the Don was dismissed first ball for the first time in his first-class career at the SCG in 1927–28 by slow bowler Frank Gough, and it was in Brisbane that he was cleaned up for another duck by Aboriginal speedster Eddie Gilbert in 1931–32. In his 23 innings in 16 shield matches against Queensland, Bradman made 2,837 runs at 141.85, with 13 centuries. In all first-class cricket against Queensland, he batted 25 times in 17 appearances for 2,957 runs at 140.80, with 13 centuries. The Don played second-class matches in country Queensland with an Alan Kippax XI in 1931, a tour cut short for Bradman when he sprained an ankle during a game in Rockhampton and spent 18 days in hospital.

Quickest, the Brightest and the Best, The: Bradman's Fabulous Century

Thirteen-page booklet which gives an account of the social match in which the Don famously scored a century off 22 balls at Blackheath in the Blue Mountains of New South Wales on November 2, 1931. The booklet was written by John Boyd, a talented all-round sportsman who

Q

played in the game in Bradman's Blackheath side as a 17-year-old, and published in February 1985 for the Blackheath Village and School Centenary celebrations. Boyd was inspired to research and write an accurate account of the occasion "after reading yet another garbled report of the Bradman match" in a Sydney newspaper around 1975. A foreword in the booklet was written by Jack Burrows, then president of Blackheath Bowling Club.

R

RAAF

When the Don enlisted in the Royal Australian Air Force in June 1940 there was a surplus of manpower over aircraft and training facilities, so he was placed on the reserve. But Army authorities saw an opportunity to use Bradman and offered him a transfer (and a commission) as a physical training instructor. He accepted and was posted to the Army's School of Physical and Recreational Training at Frankston, Victoria.

Radford, Robert Michael AM

Cricket administrator who served on the board of the Bradman Museum Trust then the Bradman Foundation from 1987 to 1998, including a period as chairman from 1993 to 1997. Bob Radford was passionate about the Bradman Museum and was actively engaged in fundraising for the project. The second stage opened during his tenure as chairman in 1996. Bob Radford was assistant secretary of the New South Wales Cricket Association from 1970 to 1976 and secretary then executive director from 1976 to 1995. When the Don dubbed him the best cricket administrator in Australia "before lunch", he was joking about Bob's reputation for imbibing at lunchtime. The relationship between Bradman and Radford started in the early '70s and they corresponded regularly over the years. Garry Barnsley, who served as deputy chairman under Radford before succeeding him at the helm, said recently of Bob: "Despite his cultivated image as a lovable rogue and merciless executioner of a triple gin and tonic, Bob was a very shrewd operator who knew the value of networking long before that word was coined. I had the privilege of looking on as he put his circle of contacts to work: cricket administrators, players, media, celebrities, business people. He could play the role of urbane diplomat just as well as the role of knock-about 'good bloke'." Bob Radford received his AM in 1992 and died at his Sydney home in February 2004, aged 60.

Remembering Bradman

Book edited by Margaret Geddes, published in hardback in December 2002 by Penguin Group (Australia), 488pp. Publicity from Penguin's website:

R

"Despite all the words written about him, Sir Donald Bradman has long been something of an enigma. A prisoner of his own fame, he valued his privacy more than anything else, yet as a point of honour answered every letter he received. Drawing on interviews with many of The Don's friends, work and cricketing colleagues, Margaret Geddes builds up a remarkable and refreshingly human picture of Don Bradman and gives the first real insight into the private world of this great Australian."

Rhodes, Wilfred

Legendary England left-arm slow bowler from Yorkshire who once told Len Hutton: "I bowled against all the great players from 1900 to 1930 – Hobbs, Trumper, WG Grace, Ranji and many more – but Don Bradman was the greatest player whom I bowled against."

Rice Pudding

The Don's favourite dessert.

Richardson, Arthur John

All-rounder from South Australia who played nine Tests (all against England) in the mid-1920s and later served as an umpire and a coach. It was for a Sheffield Shield match in March 1949 between SA and Victoria at Adelaide Oval which doubled as a testimonial for Richardson that the Don came out of retirement to play what turned out to be his final first-class game. The match started on a Friday and both captains agreed in advance that regardless of who won the toss, Victoria would bat first, thereby ensuring Bradman would bat for SA on the Saturday and pull a big crowd for Richardson. But the visitors were all out by tea on the first day, and then the SA top order fell quickly, so that the Don strode to the crease in fading light with 20 minutes left before stumps. An out-of-practice Bradman scratched and prodded for a short while before hitting the ball down the throat of Colin McDonald at backward square leg. "I didn't drop it deliberately," McDonald said later, "but thank goodness I did. The next day there were 10,000 at the ground. It was the best catch I ever dropped." Arthur Richardson died in Adelaide in 1973, aged 85.

Richardson, Victor York

A grandfather of cricket's three Chappell brothers, Richardson was an accomplished all-round sportsman and a longtime captain of South Australia. He was a forcing right-handed batsman and a top-notch fielder who just failed to secure a permanent place at Test level. Richardson was vice-captain to Bill Woodfull in England in 1930 (claiming after the tour that Australia could have won the Test series without Bradman but not without Grimmett) and skippered the team on Arthur Mailey's tour of Canada and the US in 1932, which served as an extended honeymoon for the Don and new wife Jessie. He played all the Bodyline Tests, performing respectably until the last match when he went for a pair. Richardson skippered the touring side to South Africa in 1935–36, a trip Bradman was forced to miss because doctors feared it would be too arduous for him even more than a year after his serious illness in England.

Though unorthodox as a captain, the cheerful Richardson was popular with players, and there was some resentment from team members when the Don was appointed leader for the Ashes series at home the following summer. (Bradman had also taken over from Victor as SA skipper while the touring side was away.) But the 42-year-old's form was not good enough to earn him a place in the side. The policy at the time was for the Test side to be chosen by the selectors and referred to the board, who then appointed the captain. Richardson played only a couple of first-class matches in 1936–37 before giving the game away. He became a highly regarded radio commentator with the ABC, especially in partnership with former England captain Arthur Gilligan. Victor Richardson was in no doubt about his admiration of Bradman the cricketer, once saying: "Don Bradman is the only batsman I would have offered 100 runs every time he came in to bat against my team on the understanding that he threw his wicket away when he reached his century." Richardson's memory is honoured by the gates at Adelaide Oval which bear his name. He died in 1969, aged 75.

Ridings, Philip Lovett AO

All-rounder who debuted for South Australia in 1937–38 and captained the state from 1945 to 1957. He led the side in the Don's final first-class appearance (the only time that Bradman turned out for the state when he was not captain): a Sheffield Shield game against Victoria in March 1949 which doubled as a testimonial for Arthur Richardson. But it was as an administrator that Ridings made his greatest mark, when he worked with the Don for several years at both state and national level. He was a state selector from 1949 to 1979 and filled in for Bradman when he took time off as Test selector in 1952–54, before serving on the panel again from 1971 (when the Don stood down) until 1984, all but the first year as chairman. He was president of the South Australian Cricket Association from 1972 until 1987 and chairman of the Australian Cricket Board from 1980 to 1983, remaining on the board as an SA delegate until 1991. He also managed many Australian tours. Phil and his wife Joan became close friends of the Don and Jessie. Phil Ridings died in 1998, aged 80.

Ring, Douglas Thomas

Tasmanian-born Ring was a right-arm leg-spin bowler and useful batsman who made his first-class debut in 1938–39 for Victoria at the age of 19 and played his first Test against India in 1947–48 under the Don. He secured a berth on the boat to England with the Invincibles in 1948 but played only one Test, the last at the Oval. Of Ring's performance during that tour, Bradman wrote: "Bowled consistently well, always better than his figures indicated … Normally, he was a light-hearted cricketer who liked having a bit of a go … His spirits remained high under all circumstances." Of the Don, Ring said: "Playing with Bradman was one of the greatest privileges of my life. He was always a good bloke to us [the Invincibles] … As a batsman he had this amazing capacity to concentrate. That's why he made so many runs. It was an amazing experience to see Bradman in full flight with the bat. There would be balls going everywhere, like bullets. That little man! When he was on song he was very hard to bowl to." Ring played at home against the West Indies in 1951–52 and South Africa the following summer and returned to England in 1953, again appearing in one Test. Doug Ring survived a heart attack at a dinner to launch *The Bradman Albums* in Adelaide in 1987 and died in Melbourne in June 2003, aged 84.

Rivett, Rohan Deakin

Australian journalist, author and editor with whom the Don had a close friendship for more than 20 years from the 1950s. A feature by Christine Wallace in the *Weekend Australian Magazine* on February 28–29, 2004, covered the release by the National Library of Australia to public view of 115 letters written by Bradman to Rivett. The letters were contained in Rivett's papers, which were donated to the NLA in 1989 by his widow, Nan, who added the correspondence in 1998. The NLA opened the letters to scholarly use. The Bradman letters begin on May 5, 1953, with a note to Rivett in his capacity as editor-in-chief of the Adelaide tabloid the *News*, accepting Rivett's offer to cover Australia's 1953 Ashes tour for the paper. But most of the correspondence runs from the early 1960s to the '70s, after Rivett moved to Zurich for two years and then to Melbourne for the rest of his life. Rohan Rivett was nine years Bradman's junior – tall, affable, son of a knighted academic, and grandson of Alfred Deakin. He came to the editorship of the *News* in 1951 via Wesley College, Melbourne University, Oxford, the AIF – including three years as a POW on the Burma–Thailand railway – and Melbourne's *Herald*. Bradman's letters to Rivett are a virtual diary of his life, its joys, work and worries. Jessie Bradman was the love of his life but the Don made no secret of his soft spot for Nan. The Bradmans occasionally made the trip from Adelaide to Melbourne to visit the Rivetts and vice versa. The correspondence between Bradman and Rivett ended with a letter from the Don to Nan after her husband's shock death on October 5, 1977, from a heart attack at the age of 60.

Robertson, (Dr) Allen

Born in 1867 of humble origins, unmarried, and intolerant of rude language, Allen Robertson had played cricket for Melbourne University and was a noted Collins Street surgeon when serving as chairman of the Australian Board of Control during the Bodyline Series in 1932–33. After the explosive Third Test in Adelaide, he wrote to board secretary Bill Jeanes: "I would go so far as to cancel the next Test game and all the Test games for the next ten or twelve years, but of course I am only one of a number." A proposal to cancel the rest of the tour was defeated 8–5, mainly through the opposition of Queensland and NSW delegates, whose states stood to lose good revenue at a time when the Depression was biting hard. Robertson was not long into a second term at the helm when four Test players – Chuck Fleetwood-Smith, Stan McCabe, Leo O'Brien and Bill O'Reilly – were carpeted by the board in the rooms of the Victorian Cricket Association just after the home side had won the Third Ashes Test in early January, 1937. The meeting had been convened by the board just before Christmas in the wake of Australia's loss to England in the second match in Sydney, which gave the visitors a 2–0 lead in the series. In his book *Cricket Conquest*, O'Reilly described how Dr Robertson opened the hearing by reading to the players a long screed alleging that some members of the team were not completely loyal to the Don as their captain, that some were drinking too much and that others were neglecting their fitness. But the chairman told the four there were no charges against them, and the men were puzzled that the whole team had not been called. Allen Robertson had a third stint as chairman in 1948–51. He died in 1955.

Robertson-Glasgow, R(aymond) C(harles) ("Crusoe")

Oxford University and Somerset fast bowler who became one of the most respected writers on the game. He penned thousands of words on the Don, but part of an oft-quoted tribute in the 1949 edition of *Wisden Cricketers' Almanack* read: "He was, as near as a man batting may be, the flawless engine. Poetry and murder lived in him together. He would slice the bowling to ribbons, then dance without pity on the corpse." He also wrote: "Stripped to the truth, he was a solitary man with a solitary aim." When Bradman scored his 100th century against the Indians in Sydney in November 1947, Robertson-Glasgow saw highlights of the film in England. "At that historic statistical moment," he observed, "when Bradman was about to go from 99 to 100, there was the Indian bowler trying to deliver the ball with one hand and applaud with the other, a feat that is beyond the most enthusiastic practitioner." The following year, when the Don's Test career came to a close, "Crusoe" said: "So must ancient Italy have felt when she heard of the death of Hannibal." Robertson-Glasgow had the first of several nervous breakdowns at the age of 21 and committed suicide in 1965 when he was 63.

Robins, R(obert) W(alter) V(ivian)

England leg-spinner who bamboozled Bradman with a googly when the Don was on 131 in the second innings of the First Test at Trent Bridge in 1930, probably the only time Bradman was bowled not offering a stroke. Robins and Bradman became good friends and each later became godfather to one of the other's children. When the Don broke his ankle in the last Test of the series in 1938, he rested for a couple of weeks at Robins's home in Burnham, Essex. As the Australian Board of Control's liaison officer for the 1948 tour, Robins organised a game of golf for the Don's men at the Burnham Beeches Club a couple of days after their arrival in the Old Country. Of Bradman, Walter Robins once said: "I have known him for many, many years, and no-one I can think of has equalled him as a player, as a thinker or as a citizen. He's an astonishing man." In retirement the longtime Middlesex captain served as an England selector and manager of a tour to the West Indies. In the 1950s, the Don gave his godchild, Walter's son Richard, the cap he wore on the 1948 tour. The baggy green was on loan to the Bradman Museum for three years before its sale to an Australian buyer in June 2003 for a record $425,000. Walter Robins died in 1968, aged 62.

Robinson, Raymond John

In the chapter on the Don in his classic 1975 book *On Top Down Under*, about Australia's Test captains, Robinson wrote of Bradman's propensity to capitalise on his fame: "Those who said he was chasing money were inaccurate. He was overhauling it." Robinson was a subeditor with the Melbourne *Herald* in December 1932 when the term "bodyline bowling" was used for the first time in the press in a piece on the First Test by the paper's Hugh Buggy, who was echoing the phrase, "on the body line", used earlier in the tour by Jack Worrall in the Melbourne weekly, the *Australasian*. Robinson became a regular companion to Australian Test teams abroad and his journalism was published around the world. His association with Pelham Warner's (London) *Cricketer* magazine lasted 54 years.

But though greatly respected by publishers (and writers) in England, press proprietors in his own country largely snubbed him, preferring to use his services as a subeditor. *On Top Down Under*, one of his seven books, won the British Cricket Society's Silver Jubilee Literary Award in 1976. Robinson updated it for a Cassell Australia paperback edition in 1980 and it was fully revised and updated by Gideon Haigh for Wakefield Press in 1996. Soon after Ray Robinson died in Sydney in 1982, the Don described him in a tribute in Australia's *Cricketer* magazine as a "dedicated cricket lover and writer fit to compare with the best". He wrote: "I think his book *On Top Down Under* ... was his finest work and no cricket library could be complete without it. Ray lived as he wrote: honestly, modestly, [and] sincerely respected a confidence. It was a privilege to have known him."

Rockhampton, Queensland

Where the Don badly sprained his right ankle when attempting a run-out very early in a match on a Queensland tour with an Alan Kippax XI in 1931. The resulting spell of 18 days in Rockhampton Hospital provided a welcome rest, but he missed seeing a knock of 173 by Stan McCabe in Gympie which included 18 sixes.

Rotary

Service organisation of which the Don was a member. He attended weekly meetings of the Adelaide Rotary Club in the 1950s and '60s.

Roxburgh, Emily

Singer and a good friend of the Don's granddaughter Greta Bradman who joined her in the duet "Pie Jesu" ("Blessed Jesus"), from Andrew Lloyd Webber's *Requiem*, at Sir Donald's memorial service at St Peter's Cathedral in Adelaide.

Royal

The Don's typewriter in the 1930s. He bought a new machine from the manufacturer in London in 1938.

R

Running Between Wickets
The Don's key fitness regime.

Run Out
How the Don lost his wicket four times in his 295 first-class dismissals. The first three run-outs were in 1928–29 and 1929–30 (twice) but the fourth was not until 1939–40. His first was in Adelaide against England in his first Test series and the other three were in Sheffield Shield matches. One of Bradman's 10 run-outs in 267 dismissals in second-class cricket was when he went for 1 in a promotional game in Cootamundra at the end of the 1927–28 season, the only time he played in the town of his birth.

Ruth, George Herman ("Babe")
Legendary American baseballer whom the Don met on July 20, 1932 in Ruth's private box at Yankee Stadium in New York when the Australians went to see a game between the New York Yankees and the Chicago White Sox during the tour of North America. According to a New York newspaper, Ruth sat "resplendent in a brown sports coat, white-striped trousers, buckskin shoes and white cap – the true nabob". The Babe, who was not playing in the game because of an injury, was surprised to find that Bradman was so slight of stature but said: "Us little fellows can hit 'em harder than the big ones." The Don later recalled: "I had the utmost difficulty explaining cricket to him, and still hear the bewilderment in his slow American drawl as he said: 'You mean to tell me you don't have to run when you hit the ball?'" Ruth was interested to know what impressed Bradman about baseball. The Don replied: "In two hours or so the match is finished. Each batter comes up four or five times. Each afternoon's play stands on its own. Yes, cricket could learn a lot from baseball. There is more snap and dash to baseball." An account of the meeting between the two batting legends written by Ric Sissons for his book about the 1932 tour appeared in the anthology *Carlton and United Breweries Best Australian Sports Writing and Photography*, published in 1996 by Heinemann. An edited extract appeared in the *Australian* newspaper in January 1997.

Ryder, John
The right-handed batsman and longtime captain of Victoria was the Don's first Test skipper, in the Ashes series in Australia in 1928–29, when England carved up the home side 4–1. When asked how Bradman batted, his skipper replied: "He belts the hell out of every ball he can reach." In that series, Ryder himself was the highest-scoring Australian with 492 runs at 54.66,

but surprisingly, particularly since he was one of the selectors, he did not get a berth on the ship to England in 1930. Bradman played in a testimonial for Ryder at the MCG in November 1930, scoring 73 and 29 for Bill Woodfull's Australia side against Ryder's Rest of Australia, on both occasions being dismissed by Arthur Mailey. Jack Ryder led an unofficial team to India in 1935 and worked with the Don as a national selector from 1946 until 1970. He died just a few days after leading the parade of old Australian Test players at the Centenary Test celebrations in Melbourne in 1977.

S

6

Number of ducks registered by the Don in 63 Test innings against England, or 9.52%, a high proportion.

Also the number of sixes he hit in his 80 Tests innings: five against England and one against India.

Also the number of times the Don made 300 or more in a first-class innings. The total included one score of over 400. Of his five triple centuries, three were in Australia and two in England, the latter being both in Tests. He came tantalisingly close to 300 in a Test in Australia when he finished on 299 in the Fourth Test against South Africa at Adelaide Oval in 1931–32, running his last partner out when going for the vital single on the last ball of an over.

Also the number of double hundreds in the Don's 21 centuries in 69 innings in 41 first-class appearances for New South Wales. He also scored one triple century and one quadruple century.

Also the number of double hundreds in his 25 centuries in 63 innings in 44 first-class games for South Australia. He also made two triple centuries.

Also the number of times in Bradman's 295 first-class dismissals that he was out in the nineties: four times in Australia (97, 92, 91, 97) and twice in England (96, 98). None of these innings was in a Test.

Also the number of tour matches in England in 1934 in which Bradman as tour vice-captain skippered the Australians when Bill Woodfull took time out. The Don did not register a century in any of these games. His highest score was 65 (twice) and his aggregate for the six matches was 299 at 49.83.

7

Number of times the Don was dismissed for a duck in his 80 innings in 52 Tests, or 8.75%. The first man to send him packing for nought was Herman Griffith, playing for the West Indies in the Fifth Test at the SCG in 1930–31. Having claimed Bradman's scalp for 4 earlier in the series, the belligerent Griffith was later fond of calling him his "rabbit". The first and only man to dismiss the Don first ball in a Test was Bill Bowes, in the first innings of the Second Bodyline Test at the MCG.

Also the number of times the Don averaged over 100 in his 14 full seasons in Australia.

Also the number which was hung on a nail at Lord's during the Second Test in 1930 because the scoreboard could not cope with Australia's 700 runs. This was the innings in which the Don scored his chanceless 254 in 320 minutes in a performance he rated as technically his best ever.

16

Number of the Don's ducks in his 338 innings in first-class cricket, including seven in 80 innings in Tests. Of the 16 ducks, 12 were in 218 innings in Australia (including five in 50 Test innings) and four were in 120 innings in England (two in 30 Test innings). Of the 16 dismissals, he went first ball six times and second ball three times. Bradman's first duck in Australia was when he was bowled first ball by leg-spinner Frank Gough in the 19-year-old Don's third first-class match, for New South Wales against Queensland in a Sheffield Shield game at the SCG in January 1928. In *Farewell to Cricket*, Bradman wrote of his faux pas: "Instead of the ball coming slowly and turning as I anticipated, it went straight through and fast, taking with it my middle stump. Since that day I have never made up my mind what to do with the ball before it was bowled." The first time the Don went for a duck in England was against Cambridge University in the third tour match in 1934, when he was bowled by off-spinner Jack Davies with the fourth ball he faced.

17

Number of centuries in the Don's 52 innings in 31 Sheffield Shield games for New South Wales. The total included five double centuries, one triple century and one quadruple century. He also made 12 fifties.

Also the number of fifties in the Don's 69 innings in 41 first-class appearances for New South Wales. By comparison he scored 21 centuries.

Also the number of catches he held for New South Wales in first-class matches.

61.06

What the Don would have averaged in his first-class career had he been compelled to retire at 100 in all his innings.

62

Number of Sheffield Shield matches played by the Don: 31 for New South Wales from 1927–28 to 1933–34, and 31 for South Australia from 1935–36 to 1939–40 and 1946–47 to 1948–49. In 96 innings he racked up 8,926 runs at 110.20, with 36 hundreds, 20 fifties and five ducks. He took 38 catches.

63

Number of times the Don batted in his 37 Tests against England. He scored 5,028 runs at 89.78, with 19 centuries (including six double centuries and two triple centuries), 12 fifties and six ducks. His highest score was his world Test record of 334 at Headingley in 1930.

Also the number of the Don's innings in 44 first-class matches for South Australia. He made 5,753 runs at 104.60, with 25 centuries (including six double centuries and two triple centuries), 12 fifties and three ducks. His highest score was 369 against Tasmania at Adelaide Oval in 1935–36.

63 Per Cent

The greatest proportion of his side's score in an innings which the Don achieved in first-class cricket. Playing for South Australia against Victoria in a Sheffield Shield game at the MCG in 1935–36, he made 357 in SA's total of 569.

65

Number of scores of 50 or more made by the Don in 120 innings in 92 first-class games in England. Of this total, 41 were centuries.

67.04

The Don's average in his 55 innings in 32 first-class matches against MCC and England touring teams in Australia.

69

Number of the Don's innings in his 41 first-class appearances for New South Wales. He scored 5,813 runs at 98.53, with 21 centuries (including six double centuries, one triple century and one quadruple century), 17 fifties and three ducks. His highest score was his then world first-class record of 452 not out made against Queensland in a Sheffield Shield match at the SCG in January 1930.

Also the number of fifties Bradman made in his 338 innings in 234 first-class matches. By comparison, he made 117 hundreds.

70 Minutes

The Don's shortest time for reaching a first-class hundred: when he scored 369 for South Australia against Tasmania at Adelaide Oval in 1935–36.

73

Number of the Don's first-class appearances in England other than Tests. He batted 90 times and scored 7,163 runs at 94.25, with 30 centuries, 21 fifties and two ducks. He also held 35 catches.

74

Number of the Don's 117 first-class centuries which were chanceless. Twenty others were chanceless as far as 100.

74.79

What Bradman would have averaged in his 80 Test innings if he'd been out to the first chance he offered.

76

Number of centuries the Don scored in 218 innings in 142 appearances in first-class cricket in Australia. The total included 21 double centuries, three triple centuries and one quadruple century. He also made 45 fifties.

77.92

What Bradman would have averaged in his 338 first-class innings had he been out to the first chance he offered.

78

Number of occasions on which the Don was bowled in his 295 first-class dismissals.

78.46

The Don's average in his 33 innings in 18 Tests against England in Australia.

669

Number of innings the Don played in first- and second-class cricket. He had 338 first-class innings and 331 second-class innings, the latter largely made up of 93 innings in grade cricket with St George, North Sydney and Kensington; 51 innings on the exhibition tour of North America in 1932; and charity and social matches. He made 50,731 runs at 90.27, with 211 hundreds, including 41 double hundreds, eight triple hundreds and one score over 400. The highest score of Bradman's career was 452 not out, which was also his best first-class score. His highest second-class score was 320 not out.

S

702

Entry number in the registry of St Paul's Anglican Church in Burwood, Sydney, when Don and Jessie were married on April 30, 1932.

721

Number of runs scored by the Don's Invincibles on the opening day of the match against Essex at Southend in 1948. Bradman's contribution was 187 in 124 minutes. The total, a world record for one day of a first-class match, represented a run-rate of more than two a minute.

$750

What two mint-condition mono Bradman trade cards produced by the Morrow biscuit company fetched at auction in Brisbane in 1999.

6,259

The Don's aggregate in his 84 innings in 54 first-class matches against all touring teams in Australia at an average of 82.35. He made 25 centuries.

6,599

Number of runs the Don scored in 93 innings in grade cricket: 3,014 for St George, 208 for North Sydney and 3,377 for Kensington. His average was 86.82 and he made 28 centuries.

6,996

The Don's aggregate in his 80 innings in 52 Tests at an average of 99.94. Four runs in his last innings at the Oval in 1948 would have given him an average of 100. His 29 centuries included 10 double centuries and two triple centuries. He made 5,028 runs in 63 innings in 37 matches at 89.79 against England; 715 runs in six innings in five matches at 178.75 against India; 806 runs in five innings in five matches at 201.50 against South Africa; and 447 runs in six innings in five matches at 74.50 against the West Indies. Bradman scored 4,322 Test runs in Australia and 2,674 in England. His aggregate stood as a record for an Australian until passed by Greg Chappell in his last Test (in his 151st innings) against Pakistan in 1983–84.

6996 Appeal

An appeal conducted by the State Library of South Australia in conjunction with the Adelaide *Advertiser* newspaper to raise funds for the "Bradman Collection": an array of bats, balls, apparel, stumps, artworks, clippings, photographs, mementos and ornaments. Its foundation is personal cricket memorabilia donated by the Don himself. The appeal, and the library's Bradman website, www.bradman.sa.com.au (now www.slsa.sa.gov.au/bradman/index.htm), were launched by then South Australian premier John Olsen at the library on June 19, 1997. Mr Olsen announced that his government would donate $500,000 towards a permanent Bradman exhibition (later established as "Bradman the Legend") and promised to match public donations to the 6996 Appeal dollar for dollar. The "Bradman Collection" was opened in January 1998.

7,163

Number of runs the Don scored in 90 innings in his 73 first-class matches in England other than Tests. He averaged 94.25, with 30 centuries and 21 fifties.

7,484 Pounds

The gatetakings at the Don's testimonial match at the MCG in December 1948. Along with donations from collection boxes at the gates and proceeds from other functions, Bradman pocketed 9,342 pounds.

$74,000

What Melbourne collector Sir Donald Trescowthick paid at a 1998 Christie's auction for the world's then only life-size sculpture of Bradman. The bronze figure of the great batsman playing a cover drive, produced by a process invented by NASA, weighs in at 160kg.

Also the Australian equivalent of the price paid at Christie's in London for a bat used by Bradman in several matches on the 1930 tour of England, including his innings of 232 in the Fifth Test at the Oval and 205 not out against Kent. It bears an inscription in the Don's handwriting and signed off "To my friend DL Comb". It is also signed on the reverse with "Don Bradman, Private", the mark he put on all his cricket kit.

Saggers, Ronald Arthur

Saggers went to England in 1948 as the Don's second-string wicketkeeper under Don Tallon and played in one Test, the historic fourth match at Headingley, after Tallon withdrew with an injured finger. He showed he could bat by rattling up a century in the game against Essex when the Australians made 721 in a day. Bradman wrote of Saggers after the tour: "Had not quite the speed or agility of Tallon but could always be relied on for a solid performance. A most polished and unostentatious player." In the newsreel footage of the Don saying his farewell to Norman Yardley on the Tilbury pier in 1948, Saggers is conspicuous in the centre of the frame, to the left of his skipper. Ron was New South Wales captain in two matches in 1947–48 and retired from first-class cricket after touring South Africa in 1949–50 as Australia's frontline 'keeper. He died in 1987 at the age of 69.

Sandham, Andrew

Opening batsman from Surrey whose short-lived world-record Test score was eclipsed by the Don's 334 at Headingley in 1930. Sandham's 325 (in a total of 849) at Sabina Park, Jamaica, three months earlier was the first triple century in Test cricket and surpassed the previous world mark set by another Englishman, Reg Foster, who made 287 in his Test debut at the SCG in 1903–4. Andy Sandham was 91 when he died in 1982.

S. A. Rubber Mills Ltd

Company whose board the Don joined in the mid-1940s.

Saunders, Ernest

Melbourne masseur who greatly relieved the Don's muscle pain when his fibrositis returned with a vengeance in March 1945.

SAVE

Acronym for Some Australians Have Ethics, a self-styled anonymous group of businesspeople who paid $16,000 for five letters written by the Don to former Australian cricket captain Greg Chappell when they were auctioned by Christie's in July 2001. The letters were presented on the group's behalf by 12-year-old cricketer Tim Wilson to the Bradman Foundation's executive officer, Richard Mulvaney, at a lunch at the Melbourne Cricket Club on August 27, 2001, Bradman's birthday. SAVE funds causes and campaigns from cancer research to securing national heirlooms and building bathroom amenities for families with disabled children.

Scarborough

Seaside resort in North Yorkshire where the Don played an innings in the last game of the 1934 tour which he considered was the equal of his great 160 against Middlesex at Lord's three months earlier as the most exciting he ever played in England. Against a top-flight attack in the festival match against Leveson Gower's XI, he went in after the fall of Bill Brown's wicket soon after the start of play and was back in the shed before lunch, having made 132. Bradman missed the corresponding game in Scarborough in 1938 after fracturing an ankle in the Test at the Oval, but it was in the festival match in 1948 that he played his last game in England, when he gave his wicket away after scoring 153 in 190 minutes, his third century in successive innings. His final game of the 1948 tour, and his last in the UK, was a second-class fixture against Scotland in Aberdeen, when he made yet another hundred.

Scheeren, Henricus Hilary ("Ricky")
Then nine-year-old Canberra Grammar student and polio victim who was photographed securing Bradman's autograph in February 1963 at Manuka Oval in Canberra when the Don came out of retirement to captain Robert Menzies's Prime Minister's XI against the touring MCC side.

Scholz, Eliza Ellen ("Granny")
The first person to get the Don out! She was the midwife who delivered the new boy at her house at 89 Adams Street, Cootamundra, on August 27, 1908. She once said: "Don was always a good boy, and a bonny baby. He was a sturdy little chap."

"Scone Theory"
What the Australian players called England's method of bowling short-pitched balls to a packed leg-side field in Australia in 1932–33 before the term bodyline became entrenched in the cricket lexicon. The word "scone" was then fashionable slang for the head.

"Secret Sixteen, The"
A nickname coined by an English journalist for Bill Woodfull's Australians in the early stages of the 1934 tour on the eve of the first Test series between the two countries since Bodyline. The Australian players, of whom the Don was vice-captain, were under instructions not to talk to the press. The nickname was a play on the title of a 1931 crime film, *The Secret Six*.

Seitz, (John) Arnold CMG
Then president of the Victorian Cricket Association whose CMG was announced on the same day as the Don's knighthood: January 1, 1949.

Selector
The Don was first appointed to the Australian Test Match Selection Committee in September 1936 on the death of Charles Dolling, from South Australia, and served as one of three selectors until he resigned in 1952 when his son, John, contracted polio. He was re-elected to the committee in 1954 and remained a member until 1971. Bradman was on the state

panel in SA from 1935 to 1970. He wrote about the duties of a selector in his *Farewell to Cricket*: "A Selector's job is interesting, sometimes exasperating, occasionally heartbreaking. For a captain to sit on a committee which leaves one of your trusted colleagues out of an Australian team, because in their collective judgement he must give way to a better player, is not a pleasant experience. Thank goodness most cricketers understand full well that only eleven can be chosen, though occasionally a Selector finds an unfortunate repercussion from a disgruntled player. Favouritism is a luxury no Selector can afford. Sentiment must not cloud his judgement, for his job is to try and select the best possible team." And: "In most cases the men chosen for Selection Committees have had wide experience and possess a good knowledge of the game. I have always found them to be scrupulously impartial and anxious to carry out their duties in a manner befitting the trust reposed in them. Criticism of selections is inevitable and proper. Again, it is a matter of opinion. I have not found any Selector who expressed hostility towards his critics unless they become personal. Selectors are constantly blamed for failures, but seldom congratulated on the success of their judgement or foresight." The Don also wrote of his experiences as a selector in his 1958 book *The Art of Cricket*.

Self-Confidence

The Don wrote that he always had confidence in his ability when he walked to the wicket but, as he told journalist Frank Devine, his assuredness off the park was another matter. When Devine interviewed Bradman during an aborted attempt to write a biography, his subject made (in Devine's words) "an extraordinary statement". He said: "In all my life, I have never had self-confidence in anything I did off the cricket field." In his column in the *Australian* newspaper on August 27, 1998, the Don's 90th birthday, Devine described the statement as "a revelation that fills in interstices in the record of Bradman's magnificent 90 years". He suggests it may have been the reason the Don refused invitations to become president of the MCC and governor of South Australia. "The iron will Bradman exercised in overcoming lack of self-confidence and succeeding at everything he undertook, from marriage to public speaking to social mingling to business, is a marvel of courage sustained."

Sheffield Shield

Australia's first-class competition played between the states. It became known as the Pura Milk Cup in 1999–2000 and is now the Pura Cup. The shield was donated by the third Earl of Sheffield, a leading patron of English cricket, in gratitude to Australians who hosted his tour of 1891–92. Only three states – New South Wales, Victoria and South Australia – contested the competition for the shield from its inception in 1892–93 until 1926–27, when Queensland joined. Western Australia won the trophy in their first season in the competition in 1947–48, and Tasmania were admitted in 1977–78. The Don turned out for two states in the Sheffield Shield: NSW for seven seasons from 1927–28 to 1933–34 and SA for eight seasons from 1935–36 to 1939–40 and 1946–47 to 1948–49. For NSW he played 52 innings in 31 games, scoring 4,633 runs at 107.74, with 17 centuries (including five double centuries, one triple century and one quadruple century) and 12 fifties. His highest score was his then world first-class record of 452 not out against Queensland at the SCG in January 1930. He made three ducks.

For SA, Bradman batted 44 times in 31 appearances, compiling 4,293 runs at 112.97, with 19 centuries (including five double centuries and one triple century) and eight fifties. His highest score was 357 against Victoria at the MCG on New Year's Day 1936. He made two ducks. He was captain in every one of his shield games for SA except his last, when he played under Phil Ridings against Victoria (in a match which doubled as a testimonial for Arthur Richardson) in March 1949. Overall, in 96 innings in 62 shield matches, the Don amassed 8,926 runs at 110.20, with 36 centuries (including 10 double centuries, two triple centuries and one quadruple century) and 20 fifties. He got out for a duck five times and took 38 catches. Bradman's most prolific season in the shield was 1939–40, when he made 1,062 runs for SA at 133.50, but his best average was in 1933–34, his last with NSW, when he scored 922 runs at 184.40. The Don was in a shield-winning combination on five occasions: three times with NSW (1928–29, 1931–32 and 1932–33) and twice with SA (1935–36 and 1938–39). A review carried out in the 1980s of the Bradman era showed that in shield cricket, attendances were twice as large on days when the Don was batting or likely to bat than on other days. The NSWCA made a profit of more than 3,000 pounds in Bradman's last season in Sydney and lost the same amount the next season after he had moved to Adelaide.

Shepherd Street, Bowral

Where the Bradman family lived in a weatherboard cottage at no. 52 from 1911 until 1924, when they moved around the corner to a house built by George at 20 Glebe Street, opposite Glebe Park, now Bradman Oval. It was at the back of the cottage in Shepherd Street, on the corner of Holly Street, where the Don played his now famous game throwing a golf ball at the 45cm-high circular brick stand beneath an 800-gallon (3,600-litre) water tank and trying to hit the ball on the rebound with a cricket stump.

And he honed his fielding skills in a nearby paddock by throwing a golf ball at a rounded fence rail and catching it on the rebound. The tank was demolished many years ago when town water came to Bowral, but the house, a private residence, is in excellent condition. The front fence bears a sign identifying it as the Don's former home.

Shields, (Sir) Douglas

Melbourne surgeon under whose care the Don was placed after badly tearing a thigh muscle while fielding in the Headingley Test of 1934. Bradman spent three weeks in Sir Douglas's Park Lane Nursing Home then stayed for a few days at the surgeon's home at Farnham Common. A few weeks later Sir Douglas was called in for consultation by Dr John Lee when the Don became ill in the team hotel in London on the eve of the tourists' departure for Australia. The medicos agreed that their patient had appendicitis and Sir Douglas operated on Bradman soon after in the nursing home. When news spread of the 26-year-old's critical condition, the surgeon was inundated with offers of blood if the Don needed a transfusion. "The telephone is ringing day and night," he said. "A constant stream of callers and innumerable flowers are arriving." Sir Douglas was to operate also on Australian bowler Ernie Toshack's knee cartilage near the end of the 1948 tour.

Shooting Rabbits

What the Don and his older brother Victor were doing during a stay of a few days with his parents in Bowral when the team to tour England in 1930 was announced on radio.

Shortbridge, (Captain) FW

Pilot who served with the Royal Air Force during Word War I and joined Charles Kingsford Smith's Australian National Airways when it was formed in 1929. Shortbridge flew the Don in his *Southern Cloud* from Adelaide to Melbourne then onto Goulburn (for a rousing welcome home at Bowral) en route to Sydney in October 1930 after his record-breaking tour of England. It was the first time Bradman had flown. He was chauffeured by daredevil racing driver Norman ("Wizard") Smith on the final leg of the trip from Goulburn to Sydney via Bowral. The Don's employer, the sports retailer Mick Simmons, wanted him back in Melbourne and Sydney as soon as possible to maximise the benefit of the publicity, so they arranged for him to fly from Adelaide after travelling from Perth with the rest of the team by rail.

Shortbridge and his famous passenger were two hours late arriving at Essendon because the pilot had trouble finding it, but the plane was rushed by hundreds of people when it landed. Bradman was welcomed by former Australian Test captain Warwick Armstrong, who stressed that the credit for regaining the Ashes belonged not just to the 22-year-old star but to all members of the side. The Don's arrival in Melbourne and Sydney before the remainder of the team was accompanied by a blaze of publicity and, together with the presentation to Bradman of a red Chevrolet Roadster sports car by General Motors, created the impression that the young champion was attempting to steal the limelight. Shortbridge's plane with his six passengers and another crew member was to vanish in March 1931 on a flight from Sydney to Melbourne. The wreckage of the three-engine Fokker was found 27 years later in remote country near Cabramurra in the Snowy Mountains.

Sightboards

The Don was critical of the practice of not providing sightboards for batsmen at both ends of the ground in England. At Lord's, the Oval and Trent Bridge there was a board at one end only, and at Headingley none at all. This was in contrast to the practice in Australia, where no first-class games were played without sightboards at both ends.

Simpson, David

Photographer who snapped a 1977 portrait of Bradman at home standing in front of his familiar oil painting. The photo was printed by the photographer in an edition of only five in the mid-1990s, 47.5cm x 47cm.

"Sir Don"

Song penned and recorded by John Williamson in 1996 to coincide with an appeal to raise funds for the Bradman Museum. It was the Don's favourite. Williamson wrote the ditty after his grandmother (referred to in the song as Aunty Duckie) told him how she had once danced with the Don. Said Williamson: "He liked the song. I think it was because it was about him being an ordinary bloke underneath. He was the ultimate true-blue quiet achiever." John performed his tune at the memorial service in Adelaide.

Sir Donald Bradman: A Biography

Renowned work by Irving Rosenwater, published by Batsford in 1978. In his book, Rosenwater wrote: "His temperament marked him as a man apart. In a confrontation with a bowler, there was never any doubt in Bradman's mind who was the master." On the Don's critics, he said: "The school of

Bradman-baiting grew almost into an industry as Bradman's career advanced, in Australia at any rate. The early triumphs, so vociferously hailed, served only to put him on a pedestal from which it was a temptation to seek, even if in vain, to depose him. Much of the criticism of Bradman in his career was irresponsible, even if honestly expressed. But on the other hand there were many, especially Test cricketers who had the highest credentials to talk – and many were as often proved wrong as right."

Also a short biography with a few photographs written by Anthony Davis and published in 1960 by Cassell, 122pp.

Sir Donald Bradman: Australian Legend

Twenty-eight-page booklet published by Australia Post in 1997 in conjunction with the issue of the Bradman "Australian Legend" stamps, the first bearing the likeness of a living Australian. The booklet was written by Colin Fraser and designed by Ian Kerr.

Sir Donald Bradman Commemorative Coins

Special series of three legal-tender coins authorised by Australia's Commonwealth Treasury in celebration of the life and achievements of the Don. They were minted and inspected by the Royal Australian Mint and the Perth Mint. The three coins in the series – a bi-metal coin, a silver coin and a bronze coin – were issued at the end of March 2001 at $380.00, $55.00 and $12.95 respectively. The bi-metal and silver coins were housed in a green leatherette presentation box accompanied by a certificate of authenticity and all three feature images of Bradman at the batting crease. The coins were also available as a set in a limited issue of no more than 5,000 at $447.95 a set. Royalties benefit the Bradman Museum.

Sir Donald Bradman Drive

The name of the main Adelaide thoroughfare from the international airport to the CBD which was known until January 1, 2001 as Burbridge Road. When the Don gave his consent to City of West Torrens Council for the name-change in 1998, the family failed to anticipate that businesses on Burbridge Road would have geographical grounds to change their names by replacing the word "Burbridge" with "Bradman". There was a squabble between the Bradman Foundation and a restaurant formerly called Luciano's when the eatery registered the new name, Bradman Café Restaurant. Another to come under notice was Tiles on Burbridge, which registered the name Tiles on Bradman, but they tweaked it to Tiles on Bradman Drive after a letter from the Bradman lawyers. The controversy over a sex shop changing its name to Erotica on Bradman was, according to the manager, "a storm in a teacup". It was all a "joke cooked up by a newspaper" designed to generate publicity for the shop and sell papers.

But the Bradman camp did not see the funny side. Sir Donald's son, John, visited the Mayor of the City of West Torrens, the Hon. John Trainer, to express the family's displeasure, and the Don himself wrote to Mr Trainer asking that the renaming of the road be abandoned. The mayor also received letters from many Bradman supporters and came under intense pressure from an Adelaide radio station. But the council was advised that if it were to revert to the original name it would be liable to legal action by businesses to recover costs of over $100,000 for stationery, advertising, directories, etc. So bearing in mind the potential cost to ratepayers, the council in September 2000 voted to proceed as planned. But after the decision, Mr Trainer appealed to the Bradman Foundation to use commonsense: "Surely there is a reasonable compromise where businesses can refer to their address." A "reasonable compromise" was achieved in the case of the restaurant when the owner, Lyn Mounsey, and the foundation settled on Café on Bradman Drive, but Ms Mounsey had to sell the business when she became seriously ill just as an agreement was reached. The restaurant was subsequently known as Bico's.

Sir Donald Bradman Oration

The Sir Donald Bradman Oration was established by the Australian Cricket Board (now Cricket Australia) in 2000 to honour the contribution of Sir Donald Bradman as a player, leader and administrator. The event also recognises the role that cricket has played in shaping the Australian culture and way of life. The occasion provides a platform for a prominent national or international figure to reflect on Sir Donald's career, and on cricket's place in their own lives and the life of the nation. The Honourable John Howard delivered the inaugural oration in Melbourne on August 17, 2000 in his capacity as the prime minister of Australia. The Don declined to make the trip from Adelaide but in a statement read out by his son John before Mr Howard's address, he wrote: "Little did my parents dream that on August 27th, 1908, their newborn son would have an oration named after him and delivered by the Prime Minister. On their behalf I thank the Australian Cricket Board for the idea and our most distinguished citizen for so generously giving of his time to deliver the address. There was no radio or TV in may days as a toddler but somehow I developed a love of cricket which has stayed with me for nearly 90 years. My father never made a century in his life but always wore a gold medal on his watch chain for some bowling feat. Whilst my mother was preparing the evening meal

S

I persuaded him to bowl to me in the backyard. In those humble days I was taught the rudiments of the game which consumed so much of my later life. As my days on earth draw rapidly to a close I am proud to have set an example of all that is best in our noble game. My father took me to see a Test match in Sydney in 1921 and I was so impressed I told him I would never be happy until I played there. Today the Bradman Museum stands in Bowral where I played in my youth and I hope it will forever stand as a monument to our game. Despite recent sad developments cricket will survive and remain our most noblest game and I shall always remain proud of the part I played in its history and development."

A second Sir Donald Oration was delivered by British journalist, author and broadcaster Michael Parkinson in Brisbane on December 18, 2003. In a media release issued just before the event, Cricket Australia chief executive officer James Sutherland said that the oration, jointly hosted by Cricket Australia and Queensland Cricket, would continue to acknowledge the game's traditional values. "This year's event will continue to acknowledge Bradman's legacy as part of a broader celebration of Australian cricket, highlighting the efforts of those committed to upholding the laws, traditions and values of the game. Cricket's appeal extends to much further than the success of our national sides, and it's important we continue to recognise, strengthen, and protect the spirit of the game." An excerpt from Michael's address: "There is a certain irony in me being invited to give a speech in the name of Sir Donald Bradman in that he was one of two men I most wanted to interview but never did. Never got close. Never even met him. The other one who got away was Frank Sinatra but at least I was introduced to that great man … But why was he [Sir Donald] top of my list? Because he dominated a game more than any player before or since. Because he gave a nation pride and status. Because he was one of the first great superstars of sport and because, for all his celebrity, he remained a private and elusive figure. What more does an interviewer want? No player embodied the principles of the game more than Sir Donald Bradman. There has been no more ardent custodian of the game's traditions. So anyone making a speech bearing his name needs to be aware of the standards he set and to investigate if they are being tampered with. And that is what we will attempt to do tonight …"

Sir Donald Bradman Trophy

The centrepiece of a proposal by the company CricketWorld for a perpetual trophy to be awarded each year (on the Don's birthday, August 27) to the World Champion Test Cricket nation. The suggested annual title, based on results over the previous three years, would supplement the ICC Test

Series Championship, which is calculated on results of the previous five years. The luminaries of CricketWorld claim their proposed points system is more realistic than the ICC's version, which is based on a method formulated by *Wisden Cricket Monthly*. There has been support for the initiative, though mainly from past players. Former Cricket Australia chairman Denis Rogers said before his retirement that he thought the idea had "much merit". Details of the scheme are at www.cricketworld.com.au.

Sissons, Ric(hard) Ian

Australian author who published a book about Arthur Mailey's goodwill tour of North America by an Australian team in 1932. Sissons's account in his book of the meeting between the Don and legendary baseballer Babe Ruth at Yankee Stadium appeared in the anthology *Carlton and United Breweries Best Australian Sports Writing and Photography*, published in 1996 by Heinemann.

Six

The size of the Don's cricket boots.

Sixes

The Don was not a great hitter of sixes, because he generally liked to keep the ball on the ground. The first he ever hit in a first-class match, off a no-ball from Ian Peebles in his innings of 32 against Oxford University in 1930, was his only six in a first-class innings of under 50. Most of his other 44 sixes were scored late in his innings, usually after he had hit a century or double century and was not too concerned about getting out. Only six of Bradman's 45 sixes were in Tests: five against England and one against India. His first, in the Adelaide Bodyline Test in 1932–33 (off Verity), was also his first in a first-class game in Australia. His first in a Test in England was in 1934, when he hit two in his innings of 304 at Headingley.

Sledging

Disease of modern cricket which the Don held in contempt. In the 1996 television interview with Ray Martin, he said: "If a fellow attempted it under me, I would have given him one warning and if he repeated it I would have made sure he was not selected again."

Smith, (Sir) C(harley) Aubrey

British stage and film actor who was 69 when he led the Hollywood team against Arthur Mailey's Australian tourists in 1932. Smith had the distinc-

S

tion of captaining England in his only Test appearance, against South Africa in Port Elizabeth in 1888–89.

Smith, Norman ("Wizard")

Daredevil driver who chauffeured the Don the 200 kilometres from Goulburn to Sydney in 1930 when Bradman's employer Mick Simmons arranged for him to fly on ahead of the team from Adelaide to Melbourne and then Goulburn and travel (via Bowral) the rest of the way by road.

Smith's Weekly

Sydney magazine, launched in 1919 by Robert Packer, Joynton Smith and Claude McKay, which carried a paragraph about the Don in 1921 when he was 13, his first mention in the press. His mother Emily clipped the item, which referred to the boy as a "crack bat", and kept it in an exercise book which became the repository for newspaper reports of her son's deeds in the middle.

Sobers, (Sir) Garfield St Aubrun ("Garry")

Great West Indian all-rounder whose innings of 254 at the MCG in January 1972 as captain of a World XI was the best batting performance the Don said he had seen in Australia, and second only to Stan McCabe's 232 at Trent Bridge in 1938. The World XI tour was organised as a stand-in after the Board of Control, under Bradman as chairman, cancelled the scheduled 1971–72 tour by South Africa because of fears over apartheid demonstrations after protests during the Springbok rugby tour of Australia in 1971. The Don believed that Sobers was the best all-round cricketer he had seen and, not surprisingly, included him in his best World XI, published soon after Bradman's death in 2001. In a poll conducted by Wisden in 2000 to choose the top five cricketers of the century, Sobers came in second behind the Don, being nominated by 90 of the 100 panellists. In his 1987 radio interview with the ABC's Norman May, the Don waxed lyrical about a shot from Sobers at Adelaide Oval when, off the back foot, he hit a bumper from Alan Davidson for six halfway up the mound under the scoreboard. Sobers was born in Bridgetown, Barbados, in 1936 with five fingers instead of four on each hand. The extra two were removed in boyhood. Bradman wrote a foreword to Sobers's 1989 book *Sobers: Twenty Years at the Top,* and on the Don's death, Sobers said: "We often talked about the game and I found him very knowledgeable and sympathetic to young players. I learned a lot from listening to him."

South Africa

The Don got off to a flying start against South Africa in Australia in 1931–32 when he scored a hundred then a double hundred in two games for New South Wales against Jock Cameron's tourists. In five innings in the five Tests, Bradman made 806 runs, with four centuries (including two double hundreds). His highest score was 299 not out (his best score in a Test in Australia) in the fourth match at Adelaide Oval, when he ran out his last partner, Hugh Thurlow, going for the vital single on the last ball of an over. The Don's average of 201.50 is the best in a five-Test series by any batsman against any other country (and the next best is his 178.75 against India in 1947–48). In the last Test of the rubber, at the MCG, Bradman injured his ankle when jumping down from a bench in the dressing room as the players were leaving to go onto the field. He did not bat in the match but fielded in South Africa's second innings.

When the Australians toured South Africa in 1935–36, the Don stayed at home because his doctors considered the tour would be too arduous for him even more than a year after his serious illness in England, but he did play a relatively short season for South Australia in the same summer. Bradman was offered 1,000 pounds a week plus fares for himself and his family ("the best offer I ever received") in the 1930s to travel to South Africa to conduct coaching clinics and give talks. As chairman, the Don recommended to the Australian Board of Control that the 1971–72 tour by South Africa be cancelled because of expected protests over apartheid after the recent demonstrations in Australia against the Springbok rugby team. He organised a substitute tour by a Rest of the World team led by Garry Sobers which produced a "rainbow" side (including three South Africans) and some riveting cricket. On his way back from London in 1974, Bradman stopped over in South Africa to visit an old friend, Jack Cheetham (who captained the touring side in Australia in 1952–53), and while in the country took the opportunity to call on Prime Minister Balthazar Vorster to discuss the cricketing impasse with his country over apartheid. The postal authority in South Africa issued stamps in honour of the Don known as the "South African Collection".

Southampton

Where the Don brought up 1,000 runs in England by the end of May in 1930 (the first touring batsman to do so) and repeated the dose in 1938. In 1930, he had 954 on the board when the tourists went to Southampton to play Hampshire, so he needed to make 46. The opening day of the match was the last day of the month, and Hampshire won the toss and batted, but they were all out before tea, and Bill Woodfull sent Bradman in to open

S

with Archie Jackson so he could reach the milestone. He had only just made the vital runs when rain ended play for the day. He resumed the next day and went on to score 191. In 1938, the weather again threatened to spoil the party but after achieving his goal, the Don went on to make 145 not out. Bradman and his men had arrived at Southampton about six weeks before on the *Orontes* for the start of the tour.

South Australia

When the Don accepted stockbroker and Board of Control member Harry Hodgetts's offer in early 1934 of a minimum six-year contract of employment in his Adelaide office, Bradman went to the city of churches to stay with Hodgetts in his Kensington Park mansion for a few weeks before leaving for England so as to qualify residentially to play for South Australia in the 1934–35 season. But Bradman was not to make the permanent move from Sydney until Anzac Day 1935, having come face-to-face with his Maker at the end of the tour in England and then resting up for three months on his return to Australia at the property of wife Jessie's parents at Mittagong, near Bowral. Soon after arriving in Adelaide, the Bradmans built the two-storey red-brick house at 2 Holden Street, Kensington Park (a couple of blocks from the Hodgetts residence), which was to be their home for the next 60-odd years. In the winter of 1935 the Don played golf on a regular basis to get his muscles back into condition for cricket. A couple of months after joining the Mount Osmond club he won the club championship. His first cricket after the lay-off was for his local district club Kensington in October, and soon after (having been appointed captain in the absence of Victor Richardson, who was skipper of the Test side in South Africa) turned out for the first time for South Australia in a contest against an MCC team on their way to New Zealand. Bradman's contribution was 15 and 50, but in his next match, a Sheffield Shield game against his old state, New South Wales, he scored 117, though, he was to write later, it was a struggle: "The muscles refused to co-ordinate, and my score was a high percentage of singles."

But by the time of his next game, against Queensland, his form had returned and he made a brilliant 233 against an attack which included the controversial paceman Eddie Gilbert. The Don's scores for SA for the remainder of the season were 357, 31, 0, 1 and 369. His side went through the summer undefeated in shield matches and won the trophy for the first time in nine years. His 369 (in 253 minutes) in a game against Tasmania after the shield season had ended broke Clem Hill's record for the highest score at Adelaide Oval and the best-ever for SA. The Don's third-wicket stand of 356 with Ron Hamence (who made 121 on first-class debut) was a record for the state. In 1938–39, the skipper's 801 runs (including five consecutive centuries) at 160.20 in six shield games helped SA lift the trophy once again. Bradman's most prolific season in all first-class games for SA was 1939–40, when he compiled 1,448 runs in eight matches at 144.80. Three of his five centuries in that season were double hundreds. The Don played a total of 10 seasons with his second state: from 1935–36 to 1940–41 and from 1945–46 to 1948–49, although there were no shield games played in 1940–41 or 1945–46. His last appearance was at Adelaide Oval in March 1949, when he scored 30 (under the captaincy of Phil Ridings) in a shield game against Victoria which doubled as a testimonial for SA coach and former Test player Arthur Richardson.

In 44 innings in 31 Sheffield Shield appearances, the Don scored 4,293 runs at 112.97, with 19 centuries (including five double centuries and one triple century, and hundreds in five consecutive innings against Queensland and four straight against NSW), eight fifties and two ducks. His highest score was 357 against Victoria at the MCG in 1935–36. In all first-class cricket for SA, Bradman had 63 innings in 44 appearances, racking up 5,753 runs at 104.60, with 25 centuries (including six double centuries and two triple centuries), 12 fifties and three ducks. His highest score was his record 369 against Tasmania in 1935–36. He also took 36 catches. The SACA presented the Don with a drinks cabinet (he took umbrage at its being called a bar) when he scored his 100th first-class century in Sydney in 1947. In 20 innings in 11 shield matches *against* SA, Bradman made 1,269 runs at 63.45, with 4 centuries. His highest score was 258 at Adelaide Oval in 1930–31. He played no first-class games against SA other than shield cricket.

In an obituary in the SACA's newsletter, *Long Boundary*, in March 2001, editor (and museum curator) Bernard Whimpress wrote: "Don Bradman might have been born in Cootamundra, grown up in Bowral, and played more first-class innings on the SCG than anywhere else, but his closest and longest connections with cricket have been at Adelaide Oval in the city where he has lived and worked since February 1934 … After his playing days ended he attended 1,713 South Australian Cricket Association meetings at the ground, spent innumerable hours behind the practice nets as SA cricketers went through their paces; and watched thousands of days play from the leather armchairs in the Committee Lounge at the back of the George Giffen Stand. For South Australia Sir Donald served as State selector between 1935 and 1970; member of the Cricket Committee from 1938–65; member of the Ground and Finance Committee from 1943–86; treasurer 1949–50; vice-president 1950–65; State coach 1957–58; and president 1965–73. For

Australia he was a national selector between 1936 and 1971; SA delegate to the Board of Control 1945–80; and twice chairman of the Board of Control, 1960–63 and 1969–72." In a tribute in the same edition of the newsletter, SACA chief executive Mike Deare wrote: "We all knew it would happen some day but somehow Sir Donald Bradman seemed as though he could live forever. The man who has, without dispute, contributed more to the status and wellbeing of cricket throughout the world than any other, has left us. South Australians will be forever grateful for his decision to make Adelaide his home and that of his family. He has left us a wonderful legacy and the South Australian Cricket Association will always have the honour of having had this man as part of our rich history, as a player and a President."

Southend

Where the Don's Australians scored a world first-class record of 721 in a day in a tour match against Essex early in the 1948 tour. The captain's contribution was 187 in 124 minutes, the fastest innings of his first-class career at 90 runs an hour.

Southern Cloud

The aircraft (a sister plane to Charles Kingsford-Smith's *Southern Cross*) in which the Don was flown by Captain FW Shortbridge from Adelaide to Melbourne and then on to Goulburn on his return from England in 1930.

Speeches

In his *Farewell to Cricket*, the Don wrote of his arrival in England for the tour of 1948: "I wonder if the public gave any thought to what happened behind the scenes. For instance, did they think I never contemplated having to make a speech at the Savoy before over 400 distinguished guests? Did they imagine I just got up and spoke ad lib? If so, they were wrong. People do that sort of thing occasionally, but mostly in story books. I knew when I left Australia what the future held in store and for weeks in advance I worried about each and every function. Would I make an unholy mess of my speech – say the wrong thing – repeat myself? That may not happen to accomplished speakers. I make no claim in that direction and would prefer to face almost any ordeal on this earth than make a speech. But having accepted the responsibility of Australian XI Captain, I knew what it entailed, and was prepared to face the facts. Hence I made little jottings at all sorts of queer hours and places, hoping they might be useful somewhere or other and in the end I think I have no reason to be ashamed of my efforts."

Retired ABC broadcaster Norman May (who interviewed the Don for the seminal radio biography in 1987) said recently: "As a speaker, Bradman couldn't ad lib. If he had to make a speech, he'd have to type it all out and rehearse it, and go through and read it all out then memorise it. That's how he did all his speeches, and he made a lot speeches in public, and they were all done that way – so just imagine the amount of work he would do just to make a speech." When Bradman was working on a speech for a testimonial dinner in the early 1970s, he said in a letter to friend Rohan Rivett: "If only I could speak like you, with your flair and confidence. But somehow my inferiority complex reaches its zenith in speeches."

Spencer, Claude
Sydney businessman who acted as intermediary when the Don was offered a contract in August 1931 to play for the Accrington club in England's Lancashire League. Spencer had been a teammate of the Don's in the Bohemians side which toured country NSW in 1928 under the management of former Test spinner Arthur Mailey.

Sphinx
Of which the Don's "sort of cynical grin" reminded South African fast bowler Alexander ("Sandy") Bell when he played in Australia in 1931–32. Bell bowled to Bradman in seven matches on the tour, often for hours on end, but all to no avail.

Sportstar
Mass-circulating magazine published in Madras (now Chennai), India, which released a special edition to mark the Don's 80th birthday on August 27, 1988.

Squash
Game which the Don took up for mental relaxation and to keep fit in winter soon after moving permanently from Sydney to Adelaide in 1935. Such was his progress that in 1939 he made it to the final of the South Australian Championship, where he met Davis Cup player Don Turnbull. Bradman lost the first two sets 0–9 and 4–9 and was down 1–5 in the third before coming back to win it 10–8 and then racing through the fourth set 9–3 to level the match at 2–2. In the deciding set, Turnbull was up 7–2 but again the Don came back from the dead to take it 10–8. Bradman was exhausted after the hour-long battle and – remembering tennis coach Harry

S

Hopman's advice when the Don took up the game not to play for more than 30 minutes – never played competitive squash again.

Squires, Anthony

Journalist and television personality who with Jim Maxwell provided the commentary for the ABC's live telecast of the Don's memorial service in Adelaide on March 25, 2001.

Stance

The Don's stance and backlift puzzled many. His grip brought the bat down between his feet rather than behind his right toe. The bat face was closed rather than square, so it offered a clearer view of the stumps. When he picked it up, it rose towards slips rather than straight back. In his book *The Art of Cricket*, Bradman wrote: "I was never conscious of my backlift and I did not take any particular notice where the bat went until I saw movie shots of me in action. Then it was clear my initial bat movement almost invariably was towards the slips. This was accentuated by my grip and stance and perhaps it should have been straighter, but to me, anyway, the important thing was where the bat went on the down swing."

Jack Fingleton wrote in his 1946 book *Cricket Crisis*: "His batting stance was unique. His bat touched the ground between his feet, not behind them, like every other batsman and photograph I have seen. He stood perfectly still as the bowler approached: the end of his bat did not act as an escape conductor for energy with that nervous tap, tap, tap on the pitch so common to most batsmen as the bowler ran to deliver the ball. Bradman at the wickets was completely at ease and at rest until the ball began its apologetic advance towards him."

The Don's backlift has been the focus of research into his "unorthodox" batting technique carried out by scientists at John Moores University in Liverpool, England, at the instigation of coach Tony Shillinglaw. Three-dimensional computer images show that a Bradman-like backlift gives the batsman a fraction longer to play the ball – and automatically puts the batsman on his toes. Former Australian captain Greg Chappell has also taken a special interest in the Don's backlift, and has become convinced that it had a lot to do with his phenomenal success. "Basically, Bradman didn't lift the bat at all – he levered it up ... the bat virtually weighed nothing because it was pointing straight up ... Once he'd levered the bat up, Bradman's hands were in the middle of his body, and his balance was perfect. The reason he's the best player ever is that he was the best-balanced player ever."

Star, **The**

English newspaper which carried the famous headline "HE'S OUT", when the Don was dismissed after scoring his world Test-record 334 at Headingley in 1930.

State Library of South Australia

Library in Adelaide which houses the "Bradman Collection", an exhibition of material gathered by or presented to the Don throughout his playing career. Located in the Institute Building on North Terrace, the exhibition is open seven days a week and entry is free. Fans anywhere in the world can see the collection on the State Library's website, the Bradman Digital Library, at www.slsa.sa.gov.au/bradman/index.html.

Statham, (John) Brian CBE

Fluid England paceman who dismissed the Don for 4 when the 54-year-old came out of retirement to captain a Prime Minister's XI against an MCC side in Canberra in February 1963.

Stephens, Alfred

Bowral businessman who closely followed the Don's fortunes and more than once travelled to England to see him play. Two-year-old Donald's father George went to work for Stephens as a carpenter when he moved his wife and five children to Bowral in 1911. Stephens was the owner of a joinery shop which he had inherited from a father of the same name. Alf junior became the most powerful man in Bowral. He was president of the local cricket association from 1926 to '46 and often captain of the Bowral Town Cricket Club, a longtime alderman and mayor, and was influential in all matters commercial. The young Bradman had batting practice on the concrete pitch at Stephens's home. When the New South Wales Cricket Association wrote to the Don in October 1926 asking him attend a trial at the SCG, they did not know his address, so they sent the letter to him care of Alf Stephens in Boolwey Street, Bowral. The letter was signed by the NSWCA secretary, Harold Heydon. Stephens officiated at the farewell for the Don at Bowral's Empire Theatre in March 1930 before the 21-year-old left for his first tour of England.

St George District Cricket Club

Sydney club with which the Don played first-grade from 1926–27 to 1932–33. In his seven seasons with the club he scored 3,014 runs in 44 innings at 91.33 (an average which still stands as a club record), with 13 centuries. Six of his hundreds were made on the trot: two in 1931–32 and then four in 1932–33. Bradman's highest score was 246, made against Randwick in 1931–32. This was his most prolific season with the club, compiling 785 runs in eight innings at 112.14, but his best average was in the season before, when he made 215 runs for only once out in three innings. In his first appearance for St George, against Petersham at Petersham Oval during the Country Week carnival in November 1926, he was run-out for 110. A few weeks earlier Bradman had been asked by the New South Wales Cricket Association to attend a practice for promising country players at the SCG. The state selectors at the trial were Dick Jones (of St George), Harold "Mudgee" Cranney (Central Cumberland) and AG "Johnny" Moyes (Bradman's first biographer). Moyes's report read: "Bradman possesses an excellent defence and should make many runs when he masters turf wickets." (The Don was to tell his publisher, Tom Thompson, many years later that Moyes's comments were what inspired him to leave Bowral. He was "ready for big cricket".)

Cranney was sufficiently impressed to ask the 18-year-old to join Central Cumberland, but when the Don accepted, the club decided they could not afford the second-class train fare of nine shillings and fivepence for the trip from Bowral to Sydney and back each week. But not long after, he played his first game on the SCG when chosen for a trial match for the NSW side to play Queensland. He did not make the state side but showed enough ability in scoring 37 not out for Dick Jones to approach his club, St George, and Bradman was signed up soon after. He had to rise at 5am for the excursion to the city each Saturday for the whole of the 1926–27 season and for part of the next. A bigger drawback than the travel, though, was the fact that he could not practise on turf wickets during the week. But in early 1928, when Bradman's employer, Percy Westbrook, offered him a transfer to Sydney to run a new branch office, he was invited to board at the West Concord home of Geoffrey Pearce, an insurance traveller who was a friend of his father George's. In September 1928, when the residency rule was introduced, he transferred across town to Rockdale to live with longtime St George administrator and (later) Board of Control member Frank Cush (who had a hand in the young Bradman joining the club).

After the Don and Jessie married in April 1932 they took up residency in the North Sydney district at McMahons Point before they left for the tour of North America, but he was tied to St George for 1932–33 because, under the residency rules, he had not lived in the area long enough to qualify for North Sydney. St George members were told officially at the AGM on July 5, 1933, that Bradman had signed with the North Sydney Club for the following summer. Coincidentally, Bill O'Reilly transferred from the North Sydney club to St George soon after the Don's move from St George to North Sydney. Bradman was the first player from St George to play Test cricket, and he and Alan Fairfax were the first players from the club to tour England. Other Test teammates of Bradman's to play for the Hurstville-based club were Ray Lindwall and Arthur Morris. The St George District Cricket Club held a memorial service for their celebrated son in the Booth-Saunders Pavilion at Hurstville Oval on March 3, 2001. Bradman's publisher Tom Thompson claims the leading men of the club had an important but largely overlooked role in teaching the Don about business, cricket administration and the values of the game. When Thompson asked Bradman during his final years what he saw as the most important stepping stone in his career, he replied: "Look at the record. I learnt everything at St George."

St Jude Street
Street in Bowral which runs alongside the Bradman Museum, on the opposite side of Bradman Oval and Glebe Park to Glebe Street.

Stockbroking
The business which the Don moved from Sydney to Adelaide to learn in 1935 after an offer from leading South Australian broker and Board of Control member Harry Hodgetts. When his boss declared himself bankrupt (leading to a conviction soon after for fraud) in June 1945, Bradman took over the business in his own name. In a 1983 article in the *Australian* newspaper, journalist and publisher Max Harris wrote: "His colleagues, both in the world of stockbroking and company directorships, are unanimous in their description of his business psychology and aptitudes. There was shrewdness, speed of assessment, and instinctual wariness, and a total lack of high-flying inclinations. In consequence, stockbrokers have told me, he was the ideal man to handle portfolios for people who wanted safe and secure returns. Bradman was never associated with the wild mineral booms and busts in his territory." The Don retired from the business in 1954 after "a serious warning" from his doctor.

In November 2001, the *Weekend Australian Magazine* published an article by David Nason alleging the Don was complicit in Hodgetts's fraudulent dealings in 1945. Nason also claimed that Bradman received special treatment from the official receiver and the Adelaide Stock Exchange in being allowed to take over the business in the Grenfell Street premises complete with Hodgetts's client list without the approval of creditors. The article provides an insight into Hodgetts's opinion of Bradman in the wake of the affair from Adelaide lawyer Trevor McFarlane,

S

who said that he was visiting the dying Hodgetts in an Adelaide hospice on New Year's Day 1949 when the news came through on radio of the Don's knighthood. "Hodgetts didn't take very kindly to that. He thought it was most inappropriate."

Frank Devine, writing in his column in the *Australian* five days after Nason's story, cited a conversation Devine had had with Bradman on the subject in 1993 and pronounced him innocent on all counts. The day before Devine's column, on November 21, the Bradman family and the Bradman Foundation issued a statement expressing disappointment at the publication of the *Weekend Australian Magazine*'s story, and also another negative article about the Don by the same journalist in a daily edition of the paper the day before, which they said "had caused a considerable amount of distress and sadness amongst members of the family and the Foundation". John Bradman said: "My dad was a decent person and scrupulously honest. He was a man who made an enormous contribution to the welfare of the community. It is unfair that the material has been published when my dad is not able to defend himself."

St Paul's Cathedral

Cathedral in London, miraculously spared from German bombing during World War II, where the Don and tour manager Keith Johnson attended the Silver Jubilee in 1948 to commemorate the wedding anniversary of the King and Queen. Of the occasion, Bradman wrote in his autobiography: "No matter to what age I may live, I shall always remember the conclusion of the service and the playing of 'God Save the King' in which the Cathedral Grand Organ and the trumpets of the Heralders joined to produce music of indescribable beauty. It made one's heart swell with pride."

St Paul's Church

Anglican church in Burwood, Sydney, where Don Bradman and Jessie Menzies were married on Saturday, April 30, 1932. The best man was the Don's brother, Vic, and the groomsman was Jessie's older brother, Roy. Jessie's younger sisters, Lily and Jean, were the bridesmaids. The Rev. Canon ES Hughes, then a vice-president of the Victorian Cricket Association, made the trip from Melbourne to officiate. Of the wedding, the Sydney *Sunday Sun* of May 1 reported: "Don Bradman faced his great moment like a sportsman. Despite the presence of the police, who good-humoredly attempted to keep the pathways clear, hundreds of women and children continually broke through the barriers. Hero-worship seemed to develop into a positive frenzy, to be close to both bride and bridegroom. The church itself, which was beautifully decorated with pink flowers and greenery, was filled to its uttermost limit, and that poor harassed verger hurried hither and thither continually exhorting visitors and guests to 'remain seated and not stand upon the seats'. From early afternoon crowds had thronged the church approaches, eager to make certain of a good position, but it was dark by the time the wedding party arrived, so many were doomed to disappointment."

St Peter's Cathedral

Anglican church near Adelaide Oval in which a public memorial service for the Don was held on Sunday, March 25, 2001, four weeks after his passing. The moderator for the service, which was broadcast live on ABC television and shown later the same night on the Nine Network, was the Most Rev. Ian George, the Anglican Archbishop of Adelaide. Speakers included the Don's son, John; granddaughter, Greta; grandson, Tom; leading commentator and former Australian Test captain Richie Benaud; then governor-general Sir William Deane; and a good friend, Jill Gauvin. The public were able to watch the service on large television screens at Adelaide Oval and the SCG. A public memorial service was also held in St Peter's for Lady Jessie Bradman on September 28, 1997.

Strathaird

The ship on which the Don and his team, later to become known as the Invincibles, travelled to England in 1948. When the ship docked in Bombay (now Mumbai) for a few hours, Bradman was ill and wanted to rest in his cabin, but eventually came on deck to wave to a crowd of university students on the wharf who had been clamouring for an appearance by their idol.

St Simon and St Jude, Church of

Anglican church in Bowral attended by the Bradman family and where the Don did duty as a choirboy during World War I. A thanksgiving service was conducted by the Rev. Canon John Livingstone at the church, in Bendooley Street opposite Bowral Public School, for the Don on March 28, 2001. The congregation of 400 included former Test captains Ian Craig (then chairman of the Bradman Foundation) and Mark Taylor, and a daughter of Bodyline bowler Harold Larwood. Kamahl, a friend of the Bradman family, sang the Lord's Prayer. Afterwards, about 300 people attended a memorial service at Bradman Oval.

S

Stumped

How the Don lost his wicket 11 times in 295 first-class dismissals and another 10 times in 267 dismissals in second-class matches.

Sun-Palmer Team

A team made up of Sydney schoolboys which the Don coached in 1933 as part of his contract of employment with the Sydney *Sun* newspaper and FJ Palmer & Sons.

Suva

Where Arthur Mailey's touring party of 1932 stopped off on the way to North America for a scheduled match which was called off because of rain.

Sydney Cricket Ground

Where the Don had his initial taste of first-class cricket as a spectator. His father, George, who had been employed briefly on the construction of a bicycle track at the SCG in 1896, made the trip from Bowral 25 years later, in February 1921, with his 12-year-old son to see the first two days of the Fifth Test against England. The experience, memorable for a blazing 170 by Australia's Charlie Macartney, played a big part in the Don's decision to make cricket his number one sport (over tennis). At one point during the match he said to his father: "I shall never be satisfied until I play on this ground." In October 1926, when he was 18, Bradman was invited by the New South Wales Cricket Association to attend an all-day trial at the SCG for promising country players. The state selectors at the nets were Dick Jones (of St George), Harold "Mudgee" Cranney (Central Cumberland) and AG "Johnny" Moyes (Bradman's first biographer). Moyes's report read: "Bradman possesses an excellent defence and should make many runs when he masters turf wickets." (The Don was to tell his publisher, Tom Thompson, many years later that Moyes's report was what inspired him to leave Bowral. He was "ready for big cricket".) Bradman made his first appearance in a match on the SCG soon after the nets when he scored 37 not out in a trial game for NSW, but his initial first-class match on the ground was not until January 1928, in a Sheffield Shield contest against Queensland, when he was bowled first ball by leg-spinner Frank Gough.

Bradman played 12 innings in eight Tests at the SCG, compiling 703 runs at 58.58. He made his first Test century here against South Africa in 1931–32, but did not score another until his double hundred against England in 1946–47. He also scored three fifties and took six catches. His average is the lowest of the five venues at which he played Test cricket in

Australia, although he batted only three times in Tests at Brisbane's Exhibition Ground for his second-lowest average of 80.67. It was at the SCG that Bradman was dismissed for his first duck in a Test when bowled by Herman Griffith in the fifth match of the 1930–31 series against the West Indies. And it was also at the SCG that he was struck for the only time during the Bodyline series when he took one on the arm as he drew away to cut a rising ball from Larwood during his innings of 71. Though his centuries at the SCG were few and far between in Tests, the Don made more hundreds here in first-class cricket overall than anywhere else, though he also played more innings here than on any other ground. In 47 appearances he batted 78 times for 6,230 runs at 90.28, with 22 centuries (including seven double centuries, one triple century and one quadruple century) and 18 fifties. He also held 32 catches.

The SCG was the scene of Bradman's highest first-class score of 452 not out, then a world record, in a shield game against Queensland in January 1930, and also his 100th first-class century (172), playing for an Australian XI against the Indians in 1947–48. The Don wrote in his 1950 autobiography *Farewell to Cricket* that when he played a ball from the occasional leg-spinner Gogumal Kishenchand to mid-on for a single to bring up his century of centuries, it was the most exhilarating moment of his career. His last appearance in a game at the ground was before a crowd of 41,575 in a testimonial match for Alan Kippax and Bert Oldfield (which had been postponed from before the war) in February 1949 when, although he had not played or practised since his own testimonial two months before in Melbourne, he performed adequately with 53 in 65 minutes. The Don believed the SCG was the best ground in the world on which to play. He liked its dimensions, turf and soft light, and he cherished its memories, once referring to it as "the ground I loved so well". The Sir Donald Bradman Stand was opened in 1974, when the legendary batsman, then 65 but still a member of the Australian Cricket Board, made an appearance for the occasion and entertained the crowd by walking out to the middle and playing a phantom drive in his business suit.

Sykes

Just before playing for Bowral against Moss Vale in the final of the Berrima District Competition in 1925–26, when the Don was 17, his mother promised him a new bat if he made a hundred. He not only scored a hundred but made 300! The bat he chose was a Sykes, the brand which was to bear his signature throughout his career. Bradman was photographed on a visit to the English home of William Sykes during the tour of 1934.

T

2

Number of times in his first-class career that the Don was twice dismissed in a match for single figures: the first time when he was tried as an opener and made only 5 and 2 for New South Wales against South Australia in a Sheffield Shield game in Adelaide in 1928–29, and the second time when he scored 0 and 6 batting at no. 3 for SA against Victoria in Adelaide in 1940–41 (not a shield game).

Also the number of Test wickets taken by the Don (at an average of 36.00). He dismissed Ivan Barrow of the West Indies lbw in the First Test of the 1930–31 series at Adelaide Oval and bowled Wally Hammond in the Third Test of the Bodyline series in 1932–33, also at Adelaide Oval. In all first-class matches, Bradman took 36 wickets at 37.97. His best performance was 3/35 playing for an Australian XI against Cambridge University in 1930.

3

Number of Tests (from 24) which he lost as captain, all three against England (two in Australia and one in England). He drew six: five against England and one against India.

Also the number of ducks in his 52 innings in 31 Sheffield Shield games for New South Wales.

10

Number of the Don's not-outs in his 80 innings in 52 Tests.

Also the number of double hundreds in his 29 Test centuries. Seven were in Australia and three in England. He also scored two triple centuries, both in England.

Also the number of times Bradman made three or more first-class hundreds in successive innings. Only one such occasion was in Tests, when he scored 132, 127 not out and 201 in the third and fourth matches against India in Australia in 1947–48. Three other great batsmen, WG Grace, Jack Hobbs and Bill Ponsford, could only manage the feat five times in their first-class careers.

Also the number of double hundreds in the Don's 41 centuries in England. He also scored two triple hundreds.

Also the number of not-outs in 69 innings in 41 first-class games for New South Wales.

10 Shillings a Day
What the Don was paid (plus expenses) for playing in a Sheffield Shield match in the early 1930s.

12
Number of times (in 14 full seasons) the Don exceeded 1,000 runs in a season in Australia. His highest aggregate was 1,690 in 1928–29.

Also the number of fifties he scored in 52 innings in 31 Sheffield Shield games for New South Wales. By comparison he made 17 hundreds.

Also the number of fifties in 63 innings in 44 first-class games for South Australia. By comparison he scored 25 centuries.

13
Score which the Don made most often other than nought in his 80 Test innings. He made a duck seven times and scored 13 three times.

Also the number of times he was caught and bowled in his 295 first-class dismissals.

Also the most number of consecutive innings that Bradman played in first-class cricket without making a hundred. His "horror stretch" started with a score of 77 in his only innings against Surrey on May 31, 1934 and ended with 6 not out in his second innings against Derbyshire 43 days later. Included in the drought were his 36 and 13 in the Second Test at Lord's ("Verity's match") and 30 in the Third Test at Old Trafford.

Also the number of centuries scored by the Don on the 1938 tour of England, a record for any touring batsman. Australia's Victor Trumper made 11 in 1902 and Bradman himself was to notch up 11 on his last tour in 1948. In 1938 the Don batted 26 times, so he chalked up a ton every second time he walked to the wicket.

Also the number of English counties against which the Don scored a century. They were Essex, Hampshire (2), Kent, Lancashire (2), Leicestershire, Middlesex, Nottinghamshire, Somerset (2), Surrey (4), Sussex, Warwickshire, Worcestershire (4), and Yorkshire. In other tour matches he made hundreds against Cambridge University, England XI, Gentlemen of England (2), Leveson Gower's XI (2), MCC and South of England.

Also the number of scores of 200 or more he made in 96 innings in 62 Sheffield Shield games: seven for New South Wales and six for South Australia. Three of them were in consecutive shield innings against

Queensland: two for NSW in 1933–34 and one for SA in 1935–36. In the third of these innings, when he made 233 at Adelaide Oval, his time of 168 minutes in reaching 200 was the shortest-ever in shield cricket, beating his own record of 172 minutes for NSW against Victoria in 1932–33. Bradman's total of 13 scores over 200 included two triple centuries (one for each state) and one quadruple century (for NSW). He racked up 23 shield scores of between 100 and 199 (10 and 13).

20

Number of runs scored by the Northern California All Stars team of 15 men in their first innings in a match against the touring Australians in San Francisco in 1932. Ten runs of the total were scored by one batsman and there were three sundries. The Don held three catches and was involved in four run-outs.

21

Number of centuries scored by the Don in 69 innings in 41 first-class games for New South Wales. The total included six double centuries, one triple century and one quadruple century. He also made 17 fifties.

Also the number of double hundreds in Bradman's 76 first-class centuries in Australia. He also scored three triple hundreds and one score over 400. He made a Test double hundred on every Australian ground on which Tests were played and at least one against each of the six first-class states.

Also the lowest score the Don never made in a first-class match. Other scores under 100 which he never made in his first-class career were 34, 41, 45, 46, 60, 69, 70, 72, 74, 75, 80, 83, 93, 94, 95 and 99.

Also the number of lines which Bradman was given in the 1939 edition of *Who's Who*, only eight fewer than Hitler and 17 more than Stalin.

23

Number of first-class wins by the Don's Invincibles in England in 1948. They played 31 matches and drew the remaining eight. Fifteen of the 23 wins were by at least an innings. They also won two second-class games in Scotland and drew another second-class fixture against Durham.

24

Number of Tests in the Don's 52 appearances in which he top-scored for Australia.

Also the number of fifties he scored in his 120 innings in 92 first-class appearances in England, 17 fewer than his centuries.

Also the number of his Test appearances as captain: 19 against England and five against India. Against the Old Enemy he won 11, lost three and drew five, and against India he had four wins and a draw.

25

Number of centuries the Don made in 63 innings in 44 first-class games for South Australia. The total included six double centuries and two triple centuries. He also recorded 12 fifties.

25 Pounds

The Don's fee for a Test match in Australia in the early 1930s.

25.47 Per Cent

Proportion of the Don's runs in his first-class career to the total runs (excluding extras) scored by the sides for which he was playing. His highest percentage was in Sheffield Shield cricket for South Australia: 30.14.

26

Number of grounds on which the Don batted in England. He made at least one century on 18 of them, a double-century on six of them, and a score of at least 50 on 23.

Also the number of ducks recorded by the Don's Invincibles in their 31 first-class matches in England in 1948, compared with 82 scores of nought made against them.

26 Minutes

The shortest time it took the Don to go from 50 to 100 in a first-class game: during his innings of 140 against Yorkshire at Bramall Lane, Sheffield, in 1934.

26.03 Per Cent

Proportion of the Don's runs in Test matches to the total runs (excluding extras) scored by the Australian sides for which he played. His best series based on this criterion was the one against South Africa in Australia in 1931–32, when his percentage was 38.25. His best against England was in the 1930 series in England: 35.50.

27

Number of times in his 338 first-class innings that the Don scored 200 or more in a day.

Also the number of occasions on which he was out lbw in his 295 first-class dismissals.

28

Number of centuries the Don made in grade cricket: 13 in 44 innings for St George, one in three innings for North Sydney and 14 in 46 innings for Kensington. His highest score was 303 for Kensington against Glenelg at Kensington in 1939–40.

28 Minutes

The longest it took the Don to get off the mark in a first-class game: in the second innings of the Third Test at Old Trafford in 1948 when he and Arthur Morris were defending grimly to save the match. Bradman scored 30 not out and the match was drawn, which meant that Australia retained the Ashes. The Don's second-longest wait was 18 minutes in a tour match against Somerset in 1930.

29

Number of centuries the Don scored in his 80 innings in 52 Tests: 18 in Australia and 11 in England. He made hundreds on nine different grounds, and on eight grounds in Tests against England. When he scored his first hundred, 112 in the Third Ashes Test at the MCG in 1928–29, he was, at 20 years 129 days, the youngest man to score a Test century. The total of 29 included two triple centuries, 10 double centuries and another six scores over 150. He was the first player to notch up a century in four consecutive Tests: in the last match of the 1928–29 series in Australia and the first three in England in 1930. He recorded 19 hundreds against England (in 37 matches, 63 innings), four against India (5, 6), four against South Africa (5, 5), and two against the West Indies (5, 6). Bradman's 19 tons against England included two triple centuries, six double centuries and three scores over 150. Of his 29 centuries, 14 were scored as captain (from 1936–37). He made a hundred (including his two triple centuries) in each of the four Tests he played at Headingley, and his most successful ground in Australia was the MCG, where he registered nine centuries in 11 Tests, including the only occasion in his career when he made a hundred in both innings of a Test, against India in 1947–48. His highest score of 334, registered at Headingley in July 1930, broke the world Test record of 325 set by Englishman Andy Sandham against the West Indies in Jamaica just three months earlier. The record in Ashes Tests had stood since 1903–04, when Reg Foster (the only man to captain England in both cricket and football) scored 287 at the SCG in his first Test. Bradman's world mark was eclipsed by England's Wally Hammond when he blasted 336 not out in 318 minutes against New Zealand at Eden Park, Auckland, on the way home after the Bodyline series. The Don's Ashes record fell to Len Hutton when he made his 364 in 13 hours 17 minutes at the Oval in 1938.

Also the Don's score (not out) when at the age of 12 he opened for Bowral at Glebe Park in the second innings of his first-ever game for the senior side, on the second Saturday of a match against Moss Vale in 1920–21. He had made 37 not out the previous Saturday at Moss Vale when he was acting as scorer and was sent in at no. 10 when a regular member of the side failed to turn up.

30

Number of the Don's innings in 19 Tests in England. He made 2,674 runs at 102.85, with 11 centuries (including three double centuries and two triple centuries), three fifties and two ducks. His highest score, and his highest Test score, was his world-record 334 at Headingley in 1930.

Also the number of innings in his 80 in Tests in which Bradman top-scored for Australia.

30 Minutes

The Don's fastest time for reaching 50 in a first-class match: in his innings of 238 for New South Wales against Victoria in a Sheffield Shield match at the SCG in 1932–33.

31

Number of the Don's scores of 50 or more in his 63 innings in 37 Tests against England. He made 100 or more 19 times.

Also the number of Bradman's Sheffield Shield appearances for New South Wales. In 52 innings he made 4,633 runs at 107.74, with 17 centuries, 12 fifties and three ducks.

Also the number of shield appearances for South Australia. In 44 innings he scored 4,293 runs at 112.97, with 19 centuries, eight fifties and two ducks.

Also the number of double hundreds in his 117 centuries in first-class cricket. Of the 31, 21 were in Australia and 10 in England. He also scored five triple hundreds (three in Australia, two in England) and one quadruple

T

hundred (in Australia). In Test cricket, Bradman made at least one score of 200 or more on eight different grounds.

Also the number of first-class matches played by the Don's Invincibles in England in 1948. They won 23 (15 by an innings) and drew eight, the best record of any touring team in the Old Dart. They also played three second-class fixtures, winning two in Scotland and drawing the other against Durham.

32

Number of the Don's first-class appearances against MCC and England touring teams in Australia. In 55 innings he scored 3,352 runs at 67.04, with 11 centuries.

Also the number of catches taken by the Don in his 52 Tests: 27 in Australia (15 against England) and five in England.

33

Number of the Don's Test appearances in Australia. In 50 innings he made 4,322 runs at 98.23, with 18 hundreds, 10 fifties and five ducks. He also held 27 catches.

Also the number of innings in Bradman's 18 Tests against England in Australia. He made 2,354 runs at 78.46, with eight centuries (including three double centuries), nine fifties and four ducks. His highest score was 270 in the Third Test at the MCG in 1936–37.

34.61 Per Cent

Proportion of the Don's centuries to innings played in all first-class cricket, 117 in 338. His percentage in Australia was 34.86 (76 in 218) and in England, 34.16 (41 in 120).

36

Number of centuries the Don scored in Sheffield Shield cricket: 17 in 52 innings in 31 games for New South Wales and 19 in 44 innings in 31 games for South Australia. Of the 36, 10 were double hundreds (five for NSW, five for SA), two were triple hundreds (one each) and one a quadruple hundred (NSW). He also made 20 fifties: 12 for NSW and eight for SA.

Also the number of wickets Bradman took in first-class cricket at 37.97. The total included two Test wickets at 36.00.

36 Runs an Hour

The Don's average rate of scoring in his 80 Test innings.

36.24 Per Cent

Proportion of the Don's Test centuries to innings played, 29 in 80. In Australia it was 36.00 (18 in 50) and in England, 36.67 (11 in 30).

37

Number of Tests the Don played against England: 19 in England and 18 in Australia. In 63 innings he amassed 5,028 runs at an average of 89.79, with 19 hundreds, 12 fifties and six ducks. He also held 20 catches.

Also the number of Bradman's scores of 200 or more in his 338 first-class innings. The total included six scores over 300.

Also the Don's score (not out) in his first game of senior cricket (in 1920–21) when, at the age of 12, he was acting as Bowral's scorer for a match at Moss Vale and was sent in at the fall of the eighth wicket after one of the men failed to turn up. The young Don had to use a man's bat ("almost as tall as I"), and after his innings teammate Sid Cupitt gave the boy one of his old bats, from which his father, George, cut three inches at the bottom.

Also the number of times he was caught by the wicketkeeper in his 295 first-class dismissals.

38

Number of catches the Don took in his 62 Sheffield Shield games for New South Wales and South Australia.

211

Number of centuries scored by the Don in all his recorded matches. The total included 41 double centuries, eight triple centuries and one quadruple century. Of the 211 tons, 117 were at first-class level, including 29 in Tests.

214 Minutes

The quickest the Don reached 200 in a Test: in his world-record innings of 334 at Headingley in 1930.

218

Number of the Don's innings in 142 first-class appearances in Australia. He scored a total of 18,230 runs at 94.46, with 76 centuries (including 21 double centuries, three triple centuries and one quadruple century), 45 fifties and 12 ducks. His best score was his then world-record 452 not out for New South Wales against Queensland in a Sheffield Shield game at the SCG in January 1930.

223

The most the Don scored in a day in a Test in Australia: against the West Indies at the Exhibition Ground, Brisbane, in 1930–31, when he was missed in the slips when 4. His innings of 223 was then a record for an Australian in a home Test.

230

Number of first-class games in which the Don batted. He made 234 appearances but did not bat in four of them: two because of rain (both in England), and two because of injury (one in Australia, one in England).

232

The Don's score when he played his longest innings in England: in the Fifth Test at the Oval in 1930. It occupied 438 minutes. His longest innings in all Tests, 458 minutes, was when he made 270 in the Third Test against England at the MCG in 1936–37.

234

Number of all first-class appearances by the Don: 142 in Australia (218 innings) and 92 in England (120 innings). The total included 52 Tests (33 in Australia and 19 in England), 41 matches (including 31 Sheffield Shield games) for New South Wales, 44 (including 31 shield games) for South Australia, and 73 in England other than Tests. The remaining 24 appearances were largely games for Australian and state XIs against touring sides, Test trial matches and testimonials. He scored 28,067 runs at 95.14, with 117 hundreds (including 31 double hundreds, five triple hundreds and one quadruple hundred), 69 fifties and 16 ducks. He took 36 wickets at 37.97 and held 131 catches, including four in two shield matches with SA as wicketkeeper, also executing one stumping. His 234 matches included four in which he did not bat: two because of rain (both in England) and two because of injury (one in Australia, one in England).

243

Number of times in his 338 first-class innings that the Don batted in his usual position of no. 3. The next most common position was no. 4, in which he batted on 39 occasions. He opened the innings nine times, the last occasion in 1933–34. Bradman never put himself in first when he was captain. In 1927–28, his first-season, he never batted higher than no. 6. In Tests, he batted at no. 3 in 56 of his 80 innings. The Don never opened in a Test.

246

The Don's highest score for his first Sydney grade club, St George, made against Randwick in 1931–32.

253 Minutes

The longest time it took the Don to reach a first-class hundred: on his way to 144 not out in the second innings of the First Test at Trent Bridge in 1938.

258

Number of innings played by the Don in 182 first-class matches other than Tests: 168 in 109 games in Australia and 90 in 73 games in England. His aggregate was 21,071 runs at 93.65, with 88 hundreds (including 21 double hundreds, three triple hundreds and one quadruple hundred), 56 fifties and nine ducks.

260

The Don's highest score on Arthur Mailey's exhibition tour of Canada and the US in 1932. It was made on a matting pitch laid over grass in the grounds of a Toronto prison. Bradman played in all 51 games on the tour over 75 days between June and September.

295

The number of innings the Don took to reach his 100 hundreds in first-class cricket, against the Indians at the SCG in 1947–48. He remains the only Australian to record a century of centuries, though several Englishmen have achieved the feat, as well as New Zealand's Glenn Turner, who was the next non-Englishman after Bradman to do it, and Pakistan's Zaheer Abbas and the West Indies' Viv Richards. But the Don is the only man to reach the milestone who did not play English county cricket, and his 100 centuries in 295 innings is the quickest recorded.

300

Number of centuries scored by the sides for which the Don played in his first-class career. He batted in 230 matches and contributed 117 of the 300 centuries.

Also the Don's score as a 17-year-old when he opened for Bowral against Moss Vale at Moss Vale in the final of the local competition in 1925–26. The score broke Bradman's own district record of 234 (made in one afternoon) set earlier in the season against Wingello (and Bill O'Reilly) at

Bowral. In a final that lasted five Saturday afternoons, skipper George Whatman (the Don's uncle) scored 227 and the visitors won by an innings and 338 runs.

303

The Don's highest score in grade cricket, made for his Adelaide club Kensington against Glenelg at Kensington Oval in 1939–40.

320 Not Out

The Don's highest score in second-class cricket, made for Bowral against Moss Vale at Moss Vale in the final of the Berrima competition in 1926–27. It broke his own district record of 300 set in the final the previous summer against the same opposition. According to a contemporary newspaper account of the innings, "Never before has the Moss Vale bowling received such an unmerciful flogging; good and bad were treated alike, the balls whizzing to every part of the field, and only those who attempted to stop them know how much ginger was behind them. His experience in Sydney first-class cricket his season has made a marked improvement in Bradman's play, and he gave one of the most exhilarating displays one could wish to see."

331

Number of innings played by the Don in second-class cricket. He made 22,664 runs at 84.80, with 94 centuries. His best score was his district-record 320 not out for Bowral against Moss Vale in the final of the Berrima competition in 1926–27.

334

The Don's highest Test score, made in the Third Test at Headingley in July 1930 on his first tour of England. It beat the Ashes record of 287 set by Englishman Reg Foster at the SCG in 1903–04 (on Test debut), and also eclipsed the world record set by another Englishman, Andy Sandham, against the West Indies at Sabina Park, Kingston, in April 1930. Joining his captain Bill Woodfull eight minutes after the start of play on the first day after Archie Jackson was dismissed for 1, Bradman made 105 before lunch, 115 between lunch and tea, and 89 in the final session. With his score 138, he reached 1,000 runs in only 13 innings in seven Test matches. His double-century in 214 minutes remained the fastest in a Test for over 50 years. When the Don returned to the pavilion at the end of the day unbeaten on 309, he said to Woodfull: "I am sorry I was slow today Bill, but I've had a bit of practice and will chase them tomorrow." When he was caught behind by George Duckworth off Maurice Tate the next morning, the British newspaper the *Star* produced a poster with the famous headline: "HE'S OUT". Australian-born soap magnate Arthur Whitelaw sent the Don a cheque soon after for 1,000 pounds "as a token of my admiration". The mammoth innings was Bradman's highest first-class score on his four tours of England.

338

Number of innings played by the Don in 234 first-class matches: 218 in Australia and 120 in England. He was dismissed 295 times, 193 in Australia and 102 in England. Of his 338 turns at the crease, 230 were first innings (141 in Australia, 89 in England), and 108 were second innings (77 in Australia, 31 in England). His busiest season in Australia was 1928–29, when he batted 24 times, and his most active in England was his first in 1930, when he batted 36 times. Bradman's 338 innings included 80 in Test cricket and 96 in Sheffield Shield matches. His aggregate was 28,067 runs at 95.14, with 117 hundreds (including 31 double hundreds, five triple hundreds and one quadruple hundred), 69 fifties and 16 ducks. In four of his matches (three in England and one in Australia) he did not bat, twice because of rain and twice because of injury.

357

The Don's highest score in 44 innings in 31 Sheffield Shield games for South Australia, recorded in 1935–36 (his first season with the state) against Victoria in Melbourne. It was the highest score of Bradman's career at the MCG but, incredibly, it was not enough to win the game for SA.

369

The Don's highest score in 63 innings in 44 first-class matches for South Australia, made against Tasmania at the end of the 1935–36 season. The huge knock, a record score for a first-class match at Adelaide Oval and the highest-ever for SA, took Bradman just 233 minutes. His first hundred occupied 70 minutes; his second, 103 minutes; and his third, an incredible 40 minutes. The quickest fifty took 19 minutes and the slowest, 47 minutes. He threw his wicket away when he dollied a catch back to the bowler, Townley. This was the last of Bradman's six first-class scores over 300, four of them in Australia and two in England. His 46 fours (he also hit four sixes) was his equal second-best in a first-class game. The Don and Ron Hamence (who made 121 in his first-class debut) shared in an SA record third-wicket stand of 356.

396

The Don's aggregate in his least prolific Test series, not surprisingly the Bodyline series against England in Australia in 1932–33. But it was the best of the Australians in that rubber, as was his lowest-ever average for a series of 56.57.

2,020

The Don's aggregate for 27 first-class innings at 84.16 in England in 1934. He scored seven centuries and six fifties. Both his aggregate and his average were the lowest of his four tours.

2,354

Number of runs made by the Don in 33 innings in 18 Tests against England in Australia at an average of 78.46. He compiled eight centuries and nine fifties.

2,428

The Don's aggregate for 31 first-class innings at 89.92 in England in 1948. He made 11 centuries and eight fifties. Both his aggregate and his average were the second-lowest of his four tours.

2,429

The Don's aggregate in 26 first-class innings at 115.66 in England in 1938. His 13 hundreds was a record by an Australian in an English season and included three double hundreds. He also made five fifties. His average was the best, and his aggregate the second-best, of his four tours.

2,586

Number of fours scored by the Don in 338 first-class innings, making up 10,344 runs of his aggregate of 28,067 (36.86%). By comparison, he hit only 46 sixes.

2,674

Number of runs the Don made in 30 innings in 19 Tests in England at an average of 102.85. He racked up 11 centuries and three fifties.

2,960

The Don's aggregate in 36 first-class innings at 98.66 in England in 1930, a record total by an Australian in one season. At 21 years 318 days, Bradman was also the youngest batsman, including Englishmen, to score

2,000 runs in an English season. His 2,000th run came up with a four off
the last ball of the first day when he made 309 in a day on the way to a then
Test-record 334 at Headingley. His tour total included 10 centuries and
five fifties. The Don's aggregate in 1930 remained the highest of his four
tours, but he bettered his average and made more centuries (in 10 fewer
innings) in 1938.

3,352
The Don's aggregate in his 55 innings in 32 first-class matches against
MCC and England touring teams in Australia at an average of 67.04. His
highest score was 270 in the Third Test at the MCG in 1936–37. He made
11 centuries, including three double centuries (all three in Tests).

3,779
The Don's aggregate on Arthur Mailey's 1932 tour of North America. In
51 second-class games, he averaged 102, with a highest score of 260.

13,908
Number of runs the Don made in his 109 first-class matches in Australia
other than Tests. In 168 innings he averaged 93.34, with 58 hundreds and
35 fifties.

21,071
The number of runs accumulated by the Don in his first-class career other
than Tests. He had 258 innings in 182 appearances at an average of 93.65.
The total included 8,926 runs in 96 innings in 62 Sheffield Shield games at
110.20. In all first-class matches for New South Wales and South Australia
he scored 5,813 at 98.53 and 5,753 at 104.60 respectively. Of his total of
21,071 runs, 13,908 were made in Australia and 7,163 in England.

22,664
Number of runs scored by the Don in second-class matches. He batted 331
times with 64 not-outs and averaged 84.88, with 94 hundreds.

28,067
The number of runs accumulated by the Don in his first-class career of 338
innings in 234 matches at an average of 95.14. The total includes 6,996
runs in 80 innings in 52 Tests at 99.94, and 8,926 runs in 96 innings in 62
Sheffield Shield games at 110.20. In all first-class matches for New South
Wales and South Australia he scored 5,813 at 98.53 and 5,753 at 104.60

respectively. Of the total of 28,067, 18,230 were made in Australia and 9,837 in England. Bradman's best aggregate for a season in Australia was 1,690 in 1928–29, a record for an Australian summer, but his best average was in 1938–39 (the season he made six consecutive hundreds), when he finished at 153.16. His highest total in England was in 1930, when he amassed 2,960 runs (a record for an Australian in England) at 98.66, but his best average was in 1938, when he made 2,429 runs at 115.66.

$28,750

What an Australian collector paid at a Christie's auction in 1998 for the bat used by the Don in his epic innings of 160 against Middlesex at Lord's in 1934.

$34,500

Price paid in October 2003 for a bat used by the Don in the 1946–47 Ashes series in Australia. It was sold at auction in Bowral by Lawson Menzies to a Brisbane dealer who onsold it to a client in Queensland.

350,534

The attendance for the Third Ashes Test at the MCG on January 1, 2, 4, 5, 6 and 7, 1937, to that point a record number of spectators for any cricket match. The Don's Australians went into the contest 2–0 down but the skipper's chanceless 270 in the second innings steered the home side to an easy victory and so laid the foundation for a historic comeback when Australia won the last two Tests (Bradman contributing 212 and 169) to take the series 3–2 and so retain the urn. It was the first time any country had won a rubber after losing the first two matches. The attendance of 943,000 for the series was also a record.

2FC

ABC station on which the Don made his first radio broadcast, on January 10, 1930, when he and other New South Wales players thanked their supporters.

2UE

Sydney radio station which was one of three organisations in Australia to make the Don a joint offer of employment in late 1931. The offer was to counter a bid by the Lancashire League club Accrington to lure him to England with the offer of a lucrative player's contract. He gave talks on the station each weeknight at 8 o'clock, "together with Uncle Lionel and the Listerine Serenaders".

Table Tennis

Sport which the Don took up as a 16-year-old in 1925 (when he was a very good tennis player) with a view to breaking the dominance of local champion Oscar Bunt, who was four months older than Bradman. In a tournament that year in Bowral, the Don was eliminated in an early round and Bunt went on to take the title. Soon after, in a social get-together between the two boys' clubs at Kangaloon, just outside Bowral, Bradman and Bunt played each other twice and shared the honours with a win apiece.

Tails

What the Don called for the toss very successfully in the tour games in England in 1938. But with the law of averages in mind, he called heads for the four Tests (there was no toss for the washed-out match at Old Trafford) and lost every one. In 1948, he decided to call heads for both the Tests and the minor fixtures, and in the big matches lost all but one.

"Take Your Hats Off to Bradman"

A song recorded in 1930.

Tallon, Donald

The lightning-quick wicketkeeper from Queensland made his first-class debut in 1933–34 and may have been unlucky not to tour England with the Don's side in 1938. He made his first Test appearance in New Zealand in 1946 and appeared in all 10 Tests under Bradman in the home series against England and India before going to England with the Don's great side of 1948. The Australian skipper later waxed lyrical about a catch of Tallon's in the Test at Lord's: "Toshack bowled a full toss wide of the off-stump. Washbrook swung fiercely to try and square cut it for four, but in his attempt to hit it extremely hard, was a fraction late and just touched the ball. Miraculously Tallon got his gloves under what to him was practically a yorker. I cannot remember a similar catch. Wicket-keepers are not expected to perform miracles." In the next Test at Old Trafford, Tallon took "one of the grandest low and wide right-hand catches ever seen in Test cricket". Bradman gave second-string 'keeper Ron Saggers his chance in the big time at Headingley when Tallon had a suspect finger, but the number one custodian was back in the Test side at the Oval, when he took a somersaulting catch off Lindwall to dismiss Hutton of which his skipper said: "No greater catch has been seen behind the wickets."

In an assessment of Don Tallon's performance in England, the Don wrote in *Farewell to Cricket*: "Performed some astonishing feats behind the stumps. Taking his performance as a whole, I rated his wicket-keeping better than that of any predecessor." He said that Tallon's effort with the bat playing in the Don's side in Bradman's testimonial game at the MCG a few weeks after the team's return to Australia was the best innings he had seen Tallon play. With his side needing 403 to win and losing the seventh wicket for 210, the 'keeper-cum-batsman began to stroke the ball with exquisite timing and defied Hassett's bowlers to the end, reeling off 146 in 123 minutes, with 17 fours. The match finished in a tie. Of the Don, Tallon said in 1969: "The greatest thrill of my cricket career was to be a member of Bradman's 1948 side to England. As captain, he gave me great encouragement and support. As a batsman I've never seen a player like him. His shot-making was incredible. I've never seen anyone who gets into position so quickly to play his shots. Another amazing thing was the power of his shots for such a small man. I thought I could hit the ball pretty hard until I saw Bradman play. His placement is another thing. He picked holes in the field and just belted the ball to the fence." The Don considered Tallon was the best custodian he ever saw, so not surprisingly gave him the nod in *Bradman's Best*, a world team selected by Bradman and published soon after his death. Don Tallon died in 1984 at the age of 68.

Tasmania

The island state did not enter the Sheffield Shield competition until 1977–78 but the Don played five innings in five first-class matches (one for South Australia and four for Australian XIs before leaving for England) against the Apple Isle for 751 runs at 150.20, with three centuries. His highest score was 369 at Adelaide Oval in 1935–36, the innings in which he reached 100 in 70 minutes, the fastest of his first-class career, on the second morning adding 135 before lunch.

Tate, Maurice William

A great bowler for England who made three trips to Australia and played in two Ashes series at home. His 38 wickets in the 1924–25 series down under was unprecedented for a medium-pacer. In film of a Test in the 1928–29 series in Australia, Tate is seen hitching up the tie around his waist after every delivery. During that series, Bradman's first, he suggested to the Don he would need to play with a straighter bat to get runs in England. Eighteen months later, in the Test at Headingley, Tate all but bowled Bradman with his first ball to him, but then the Don proceeded to hit him all around the ground on his way to his record 334. England's wicketkeeper George Duckworth said to the bowler: "Say, Maurice, you said in Australia that you'd get Don out in England. What about trying?" Tate replied: "You'd better try yourself, Ducky, I've had enough." There was some small consolation when Tate and his 'keeper combined to eventually claim Bradman's wicket on the second morning. Maurice Tate toured Australia with Douglas Jardine's side in 1932–33 but was bitterly opposed to his captain's new form of "leg theory", and he was doubly upset because under his captain's plan, there was no place in the Tests for a bowler of his type. In his autobiography, the Don rated Tate on a par with Alec Bedser as the best England medium-pacers he faced. Although he said Bedser troubled him more than Tate, he made special mention of the latter's "beautiful shoulder action". Maurice Tait was 60 when he died in 1956.

Tauber, Richard
Austrian-born tenor whom the Don heard sing in Queen's Hall in London in 1938. Tauber later became a British citizen.

Taylor, John Morris
Johnny Taylor was an attacking right-handed batsman and spectacular fieldsman from New South Wales who played 10 Tests between 1920 and 1926. A boyhood hero of the Don's, he played in the Ashes Test at the SCG in February 1921 which the 12-year-old saw with his father. Taylor was one of three leading NSW players whose retirement after the English tour of 1926 moved the new state selectors to invite the 17-year-old Bradman and other promising country players to Sydney to trial with a view to rebuilding the side.

Taylor, Mark Anthony AO
Former Australian Test captain from New South Wales who equalled the Don's record Test score for an Australian of 334 against Pakistan in Peshawar in October 1998. In a letter to Taylor dated the 16th of the following month, the Don wrote: "Might I take this opportunity to congratulate you on your wonderful batting performance overseas during which you equalled my 334. It was extremely generous of you to declare when our scores were level. It was a most sportsmanlike act when you could so easily have gone on to get the record. Your recognition in the interest of the team will never be forgotten." On Bradman's passing Taylor said: "Sir Donald is certainly the greatest Australian I have met. Fifty years after playing his final Test match, he was still revered around the world, and held in incredible esteem. As a cricketer, the world has known no equal. He was the true symbol of fine sportsmanship, the benchmark that

all young cricketers aspired to. His innings may have closed but his legacy will live forever in the hearts of millions of Australians."

Tea

The Don's favourite beverage. In his book *With the 1930 Australians*, Geoffrey Tebbutt noted: "The tea that Bradman drinks is the most extraordinary concoction! Nobody but himself, he says, can brew tea as he likes it … When I saw him fill his cup a third full of milk, add a depth of half an inch or so of tea from the pot, and go filling the rest of it with hot water, I thought he had an attack of absent-mindedness. No! That is the way he likes it. Imagine if he'd drunk full-strength tea!"

Tebbutt, Geoffrey

Melbourne *Herald* journalist whose book *With the 1930 Australians* did much to foster the belief that the Don was aloof. In his account of the tour, Tebbutt wrote about the time that Bradman made his Ashes-record 309 not out on the first day of the Headingley Test and on returning to the team hotel chose to retire to his room and "play the phonograph" rather than celebrate with other members of the team. Tebbutt also noted that when the 21-year-old received a cheque for 1,000 pounds for his efforts from an Australian-born industrialist, Arthur Whitelaw, he did not share the spoils with his teammates, or even shout them a drink. While recognising the Don's "supreme skill", Tebbutt expressed the hope that "he will become, on and off the field, a little more human".

Technique

The Don's unorthodox technique was something of a talking point among the England players during his first Test series, the Ashes rubber in Australia in 1928–29. The great medium-pacer Maurice Tate told him: "You'll have to learn to play with a straighter bat before you come to England." But history records that it was Tate (and his compatriots) who learned a lesson a little over a year later. Also in 1928–29, Percy Fender wrote: "One of the most curious mixtures of good and bad batting I have ever seen … He makes a mistake, then makes it again and again: he does not correct it, or look as if he were trying to do so. He seems to live for the exuberance of the moment." The Don was to make 252 not out early in the 1930 tour against Fender's Surrey side. In 1934, Pelham Warner wrote: "A purist might argue that Bradman's bat was not straight, but ordinary rules do not govern a player who, perhaps, is the greatest batting genius … It is strikingly apparent how absolutely still Bradman stands until the ball is halfway down the pitch.

Then follows a lightning movement of his feet and the bat, and the ball crashes into the crowd." Arthur Morris summed up his old skipper at the crease thus: "Good eyesight, great reflexes, quick to move, good footwork and wonderful hand-to-eye coordination." The man himself had the last word in *The Art of Cricket*: "Better to hit the ball with an apparently unorthodox style than to miss it with a correct one." And hit it he did.

"Teddy"

The family dog, a terrier, when the Bradmans lived at 52 Shepherd Street, Bowral.

Temora Rural Museum

Museum in the Riverina district of New South Wales where visitors can inspect "Bradman Cottage", the house in which the Don lived at Yeo Yeo, near Cootamundra, until he was two years and nine months old.

Tendulkar, Sachin Ramesh

Celebrated Indian batsman whose aggressive style most reminded the Don of his own. In the 1996 interview with Ray Martin, he said: "I asked my wife to come at look at him ... now I never saw myself play, but I feel that this fellow is playing much the same as I used to play, and she looked at him on the television and said, 'Yes, there is a similarity between the two.' ... I can't explain in detail. To me it's his compactness, his technique, his stroke production, it all seemed to gel as far as I was concerned ... that was how I felt." Of this ultimate tribute, Tendulkar told Sanjay Rajan of *Sportstar* magazine in India in 1998: "I was really thrilled when I got to know that Sir Don said my game was close to his. I think we were on a tour then. I really have no words to express the feeling." Tendulkar is the son of the late Ramesh Achyut Tendulkar, a Bombay college professor who had no interest in sport, let alone cricket, before the youngest of his four children became a living legend in the most obsessed of cricket countries. As a 14-year-old, Sachin was named as a reserve player in Bombay's squad in the Ranji Trophy. In February 1988, when still 14, he made 326 in a world-record unbroken stand for a schoolboy tournament of 664 with 16-year-old Vinod Kambli. Tendulkar made his first-class debut in December 1988 at the age of 15 years seven months, when he scored a century for Bombay against Gujarat. In November 1989, as a 16-year-old, he became the youngest Indian Test player ever.

Tendulkar had a private audience with the Don at his Adelaide home on his host's 90th birthday, just before attending a celebratory fundraising dinner at the Adelaide Convention Centre. He said meeting Bradman was a lifelong dream. He was awoken at 6am to be told the sad news the day the Don's death was announced and said later: "I'm sure the whole world, not only the cricketing world … will miss him badly." The next day, the first day of a Test against Australia in Mumbai, the players of both teams wore black armbands – all on the left arm except Tendulkar, who wore his on the right. Tendulkar was the only current player – and the only Indian – to be included in Bradman's all-time World XI, revealed in Roland Perry's book *Bradman's Best*. When the book was launched in August 2001, Tendulkar said: "After Sir Don bats and before Garry Sobers. What else can you ask for? All I can say is that it is a great honour. There are a lot of great names missing in that list, and my name was considered. I'm on top of the world." Three months later, the 28-year-old passed his idol and became the youngest cricketer (and just the second Indian) to score 7,000 Test runs during his innings of 155 on the opening day of the first Test against South Africa at Bloemfontein. When a single took him to 6,997, one run ahead of the Don, Tendulkar became 21st on the list of Test cricket's highest run-scorers. At the end of June 2004, Tendulkar had amassed 9,470 Test runs at 57.39, with 33 hundreds and 37 fifties.

Tennis

Tennis was only one of several sports the Don played when going to school but in the summer of 1923–24, when he was 15, he played tennis exclusively – a preference no doubt influenced by the fact that one of his mother's brothers, George Whatman, owned a court. He concentrated on tennis again the following summer until near the end of the season when he turned to cricket with the senior Bowral team, with whom he'd acted as scorer and occasional player as a 12- and 13-year-old. He played as a regular member of the cricket team through 1925–26 and his big scores attracted the attention of the New South Wales Cricket Association, who invited him to trial at the SCG in October 1926. When after the nets an official told him he should consider coming to Sydney to play, the 18-year-old said he couldn't afford the train fare (of nine shillings and fivepence) from Bowral to Sydney and back each week, lamenting: "I'll have to go back to Bowral and play tennis."

The problem seemed to be solved when the Central Cumberland Club invited Bradman to join them, but soon after they decided they couldn't manage the fare. But St George official and NSW selector Dick Jones liked the look of the Don in scoring 37 in a trial game at the SCG between NSW Probables and Possibles and he was soon after signed up by the Hurstville club. Having continued his tennis, the Don was selected to represent his Southern region in Sydney in both Tennis Country Week and Cricket Country Week. He was told by his boss, Percy Westbrook, that he could have time off for one or the other, but not both. His place in Sydney grade cricket now secure, the choice was not difficult. But the Don was to take the court regularly against top Australian tennis players during the 1930s, and in 1934 the great Jack Crawford ranked the celebrated cricketer just behind the world's top 10 players. And Bradman beat a Davis Cup team member, Don Turnbull, in the final of the South Australian Amateur Squash Championship in 1939.

Thomas, David Kenneth
Artist whose portrait of Bradman adorns a framed Slazenger bat sold by ESP Direct from July 2001. Two hundred and sixty of the bats were signed by the Don in 1997 and stored by the Bradman Foundation at Bowral. Each piece was accompanied by a Certificate of Authenticity and endorsed by the foundation. They were offered at $5,700 each. Thomas's portrait of former House of Representatives speaker Leo McLeay hangs in Parliament House, Canberra.

Thompson, Tom
Sydney author, playwright and publisher whose company, Editions Tom Thompson (ETT), reprinted the Don's autobiography, *Farewell to Cricket*, as an Imprint paperback in 1994 and (as ETT Imprint) followed three years later with a revised version (with substantial corrections to the original 1950 Hodder text) in a larger C format. Thompson's ETT Imprint also published a new version of the Don's coaching manual, *The Art of Cricket*, firstly in book form (1998) then as a CD-ROM (2000). The book version contains a new preface by Richie Benaud as well as many photos not in the original 1958 edition. The CD utilises Bradman's original demonstration films, interviews and footage of his Test career to create the world's first personalised electronic cricket coaching manual. The Don shows and talks about all aspects of the game from batting, bowling and fielding through to the roles of the captain and the umpire. In conjunction with the books and CD, Thompson's company also offers a range of Bradman memorabilia, including First Day Covers in the "Australian Legend" collection, coins, posters, videos and signed limited-edition copies of the book version of *The Art of Cricket* with an accompanying Bradman Test cap.

These products, as well as *Farewell to Cricket* and the CD-ROM of *The Art of Cricket*, are available on the website, www.bradmancopyrightmaterials.com.au. The publication of Bradman's works in electronic form is a joint venture with the Sydney Cricket Ground Trust. ETT Imprint also publishes classic and contemporary Australian works by Judith Wright, Arthur Upfield, Christina Stead, and many others. Tom Thompson was at the centre of controversy early in 2001 when it was revealed that he planned to sell the National Library a collection of 30 letters written to him by the Don between 1994 and 1998. The collection is part of Thompson's literary archive of 300 folders which he offered to the library through his agent, Paul Feain, in July 2000. After considering the objections of the Bradman family and the Bradman Foundation to the sale and public exhibition of the letters, the library returned the entire archive to Thompson on the basis of "breach of confidentiality".

Thomson, A(rthur) A(lexander) MBE

In his own foreword to *The Art of Cricket*, the Don wrote of "the great pleasure of meeting and dining at the Savage Club with that distinguished author, orator and cricket lover, A.A. Thomson". He then quoted Thomson's philosophy on the game: "There are several ways of looking at the game of cricket; first, and probably best, it is a game played for enjoyment. It is an art, rich in the expression of subtle technical skills, where grace and strength may be magically blended. It is a long picturesque romance, as rich in comedy and character as *Don Quixote* or *Pickwick Papers*. It is also a fascinating form of controversy. It is a spectacle, it is drama, it is good fun. It is undoubtedly an art; an art that can give pleasure to those who practise it and to those who watch."

Thorn, Frank Leslie Oliver

Victorian bowler who had the Don caught by Chuck Fleetwood-Smith at square leg for 5 in Adelaide in South Australia's last Sheffield Shield game of the 1938–39 season when Bradman was attempting to set a world-record seven consecutive first-class centuries. In his previous six innings (in six games) the Don had scored 118, 143, 225, 107, 186 and 135 not out. The first ton was made in a Melbourne Cricket Club centenary match and the next five in shield games. The only other man to score six straight hundreds to that point was England's Charles Fry in 1901, but South Africa's Mike Procter has since done it also (in 1970–71). Frank Thorn died in Papua New Guinea on war service in 1942, aged 29.

Thurlow, Hugh Motley ("Pud")

Fast bowler who in his only Test innings was batting with the Don when he was run out by him for 0. Thurlow was last man in when he joined

Bradman in Australia's first innings in the Fourth Test against South Africa at Adelaide Oval in 1931–32. The master batsman was on 298 when he got one away to the leg side and the pair ran one, but the Don called for an impossible second, sent Thurlow back, and the hapless Queenslander was easily run out. Bradman finished on 299 not out.

"Tiger and the Don, The"

A song written and recorded by Australian Ted Egan, who as a five-year-old witnessed the Don's 270 in the Ashes Test at the MCG in January 1937. He saw "Tiger" O'Reilly bowl just after World War II and described him as "devastating".

Tilbury

Port in Essex on the north bank of the Thames, 32km east of London, where the Don's touring side docked and departed from in London in 1948.

Tindill, Eric William Thomas

A Kiwi who represented his country at both cricket and rugby, Tindill filled in for the visitors in a two-hour exhibition game in Wellington in 1932 when Arthur Mailey's team of Australians stopped over on their way home from the goodwill tour of North America. The game had been arranged at the eleventh hour the previous night at a dinner by captains Victor Richardson and Stew Dempster (mainly to give the locals a chance to see Bradman bat) after rain had caused a planned match the previous day to be abandoned without any play possible. But the Don (with wife Jessie) and Chuck Fleetwood-Smith had made their own plans for a sight-seeing tour the next day (with an early start), and were unaware when they left the dinner that a two-hour exhibition match was to be played from noon the following afternoon. The crowd of about 8,000 at the Basin Reserve were none too happy about Bradman's no-show, and neither were the Wellington players. Because the Australians were two men short, 21-year-old Eric Tindill (who kept wicket) and another Wellington player, Ken James, made up the numbers for Richardson's side. But despite the Don's absence the spectators were treated to some scintillating batting from the Australians, particularly Stan McCabe who scored a quick-fire 78 not out, before the visitors rushed off to the wharf to catch their ship.

Tindill was to meet Bradman five years later when the New Zealand team played a match against South Australia on the way home from their 1937 tour of England. Eric and his new wife were allowed to leave the Old Dart ahead of the team, he going to Adelaide and his bride going home to New

T

Zealand. When he arrived in the city of churches Eric called on the Don in a sporting goods shop. "He was very welcoming and I enjoyed the few minutes' talking to him." In the match, the Don was 11 overnight after the first day, and long queues of fans formed at the Adelaide Oval gates the next morning to see the master batsman flay the Kiwis. Bradman had been in the nets well before play started, and to the New Zealanders' consternation, was "belting it all around the field". But in the first over of the day, by paceman Jack Cowie, the SA captain edged the first ball of the over that he faced and it carried through to Tindill. Eric recalls his part in the Don's downfall with pride: "It was an obvious nick." Eric Tindill is a fit 94-year-old still living in Wellington. Until March 2003 he was working part-time for the South Wellington branch of the Returned Servicemen's Association. He is the oldest living All Black and probably the oldest Kiwi Test cricketer. As well as playing both cricket and rugby for his country, he later umpired in Test cricket and refereed in Test rugby, surely a unique achievement in world sport.

Toby Jugs
Jugs fashioned in the mid-1930s with images of the Don's face.

Tom Mack Cup
Cup won by the young Don's Bowral A side when they beat Moss Vale A in the final of the Berrima District Competition in 1925–26.

Toose, Harold
Harry Toose was 89 and still living in Moss Vale when he was invited to the opening of the first stage of the Bradman Museum in 1989. Toose's team took more than one fearful hiding from the Bradman bat in the mid-1920s. He said in 1989 that the young Don was "a very steady chap with no wild habits". Bradman twice scored 300 or more against the hapless men, yet Toose's recollection was that none of them considered him then as other than a pretty hot bush cricketer. The possibilty of his going on to great things simply did not enter their heads.

Toronto, Canada
Where the Don made his highest score of 260 (in the grounds of a prison on a matting pitch laid over grass) on Arthur Mailey's 1932 tour of North America.

Toshack, Ernest Raymond Herbert

The man nicknamed by teammate Keith Miller "the Black Prince" was a New South Wales left-arm medium-pacer who could be unplayable if there was anything in the wicket. He took 6/18 (in the match) in his first Test, in 1946 under Bill Brown in Wellington against New Zealand, claimed 3/17 and 6/82 under the Don at the 'Gabba against England in 1946–47 (when he twice sent the great Wally Hammond packing) and, again playing under Bradman, returned figures of 5/2 and 6/29 on a glue-pot at the 'Gabba the next season against India. In the match against the Indians he twisted a knee when he slipped on the wet ground and had to leave the field. The injury proved troublesome and Toshack had to pass a medical test before boarding the ship for England in 1948. On this tour he took 50 wickets in all matches, including 11 Test wickets, and scored 51 Test runs for once out, figuring in some comical last-wicket stands with Bill Johnston. Toshack gave what the Don considered was his best bowl-ing performance of the tour in an early game against the MCC at Lord's, when he kept one end going for three hours and finished with 6/51, in the process getting the scalp of Denis Compton after an entertaining battle with the Brylcreem Boy. Ernie broke down late in the tour in the match against Lancashire and had to have an operation on his knee before returning to Australia.

Toshack told Sydney writer Kersi Meher-Homji in an interview for a *Wisden Cricket Monthly* article in July 1995: "Bradman advised me to get operated on in England because it would be free. I would have had to pay myself in Australia, he told me. By a coincidence I had the same sur-geon [Sir Douglas Shields] who had operated on Bradman for appendici-tis on a previous tour." Ernie Toshack and Arthur Morris were the only Australians to go through the tour without a duck next to their names. The Don wrote of Toshack after the tour: "A player unique in every way. I cannot remember another of the same type … He worried and got out all the best bats, was amazingly accurate and must have turned in fine figures had not his cartilage given way." Not having recovered from his operation, Toshack was the only one of the Invincibles not to play in the Don's testimonial game at the MCG a couple of months after the team returned to Australia. When asked by Kersi for his opinion of Bradman, Toshack said: "I couldn't speak too highly of him. He was a great captain and you couldn't find a nicer chap. He treated everyone alike and enjoyed a good joke." After a fall in the mid-1980s, Ernie had a steel plate with 14 screws inserted in his left leg, prompting a radiologist to later exclaim: "There is more iron in your leg than in the Sydney Harbour

T

Bridge!" Ernie Toshack died in Sydney in May 2003 from the effects of pneumonia. He was 88.

Toss

In the minor games in England in 1938, the Don was very successful calling tails but in the Tests he called heads and lost every one. In the Tests in 1948 he again called heads and lost four of the five. In his interview with ABC radio in 1987, Norman May asked Bradman if he favoured retaining the system of tossing for innings or did he think that after the first Test of each series, the teams could alternate having the right to bat first. The Don's reply: "I very strongly maintain that we should stick to the system of tossing for every game. If this was not so, the way would be open to insinuations that the pitch had been specifically prepared to suit one side, a claim which can be rejected today when nobody knows in advance which side will bat first. And it would also be an inducement to influence a selection committee. Supposing one side was leading in the series; there would be a great temptation for the leaders to pack their next team with batsmen and play for a draw. Now both these things would be bad for the image of the game, so please let us stick to tossing for every match."

Trent Bridge

The Nottingham ground was the scene of the Don's first Test on his first tour of England in 1930, when he made 8 and 131. His century was the first by an Australian in a Test match at Nottingham and he was the fourth Australian to make a hundred in his first Test against England in England. In eight innings in four Tests here he compiled 526 runs at 75.14, with three centuries and a fifty. His highest score was 144 not out in the eventful First Test of 1938, when four Englishmen scored centuries in the home side's first innings, the first time four batsmen from either side had done so in an Ashes Test. One of them was opener Charles Barnett, who was the closest that any England batsman had come to scoring a hundred before lunch on the first day of a Test. At the break he was on 98, and got his ton off the first ball after the adjournment. This was the Test in which Stan McCabe played his legendary innings of 232 in the first innings in even time, a performance his captain always considered was the best he had seen. Bradman's 144 in the second innings of this match was his slowest-ever Test century. He took 253 minutes to reach 100 and his innings occupied 365 minutes. At one point he suffered the indignity of a slow-hand-clap, but his performance saved the game for Australia.

After Australia's win in the Test here four years earlier, the crowd surging onto the field obscured the boundary rope and the Don, racing off the ground to reach the sanctity of the dressing room, caught his foot in the rope and took a tumble. Because of the injury he had to use a runner in the next tour match and withdraw from the following one. In the 1948 Test, the crowd booed Bradman's team, especially Keith Miller, off the field at the end of a session after the flamboyant all-rounder struck Len Hutton on the arm with a short-pitched ball barely more than waist level. The president of the Notts County Club apologised to Australia's captain for the behaviour of the crowd and on the next day of play an official ticked off the Nottingham public over the public address. The Don made 138 in the first innings of this match but his duck in the second innings was his first in a Test in England. It came in his 23rd Test innings in the Old Country. Bradman believed that Australia won this Test because he lost the toss. "It enabled our speed bowlers to break through quickly while there was still life in the pitch." In 11 innings in six first-class appearances at Trent Bridge, Bradman made 812 runs at 81.20, with four centuries and three fifties. His highest score on the ground was his Test-highest 144 in 1938 (when he broke Jack Hobbs's record of 12 tons in Ashes Tests), but he was dismissed for the same score in the second innings of the county game on the same tour. When he got to 98 during this innings against Nottinghamshire, the Don completed 20,000 runs in 243 first-class innings (the next quickest to the landmark being England's Kumar Ranjitsinhji in 401 innings), and when he was on 120, he reached 2,000 runs for the season. In all matches at Trent Bridge, he took two catches.

Trescowthick, (Sir) Donald Henry AC KBE CLJ

Melbourne collector who paid $74,000 at a Christie's auction in 1998 for the (then) world's only life-size sculpture of Bradman. The bronze figure of the master batsman playing a cover drive was produced by a process invented by NASA and weighs in at 160kg.

Trueman, Frederick Sewards OBE

Though he acknowledged that Harold Larwood and Frank Tyson were faster, the Don rated Trueman, the quintessential Yorkshireman, as the best paceman for England he had seen: "His run to the wicket and his delivery action were a model for anyone." Against Australia at the Oval in 1964, "Fiery" Fred became the first bowler from any country to achieve 300 Test wickets, and he held the record at 307 until it was eclipsed by West Indian off-spinner Lance Gibbs in 1975–76.

T

Turnbull, Donald

Davis Cup player and winner with Adrian Quist of the 1936 and '37 Australian Doubles title who was beaten by the Don in the final of the 1939 South Australian Squash Championship. Turnbull won the first two games and had match point in the third but Bradman came back to level at 2–2. In the fifth game, Turnbull again held match point (at 8–5) but once more his opponent fought back to take the deciding game 10–8. The Don took up squash soon after moving from New South Wales to SA in 1935 to provide relaxation away from cricket.

Turner, Glenn Maitland

Right-handed opening batsman from New Zealand who at one time was the only non-Englishman apart from the Don to score 100 hundreds in first-class cricket. The milestone has since been reached also by Zaheer Abbas and Viv Richards, but Bradman remains the only man to achieve the feat without playing in English county cricket. Turner was also the only non-Englishman apart from Bradman to make 1,000 runs in England in May until Zimbabwean Graeme Hick achieved the same feat before he was qualified for England.

"Two Eras of The Don"

A chapter in Alan McGilvray's 1992 book *Captains of the Game* (as told to Norman Tasker, published by the ABC). The title of the chapter is a reference to the pre-war Bradman and the post-war Bradman. McGilvray's opening paragraph summed up his impression of the great batsman: "There was much about Don Bradman that was striking. The swiftness in his feet and hands, the quickness of his eye, the power in his wrists, and the capacity of his brain to co-ordinate all of them instantly and precisely. But from the time I first met him, when we were both young cricketers in the Sydney club competition, to me his most striking feature was the fact that he was never, never, beaten. It was reflected in everything he did. From a casual game of tennis to a Test match against the world's best, or a debate on cricket's laws at the highest level of administration, Bradman would fight, seemingly to the death, to have his will prevail. It was the single quality above all others that was the basis of his greatness, both as a player and a captain."

U

Umpires

Although he later wrote of being wrongly given out, the Don made it a rule as a player never to question an umpire's decision. He ranked England's Frank Chester as the greatest umpire he played under. Bradman's opinion was based partly on Chester's "miraculous judgement" in the First Test at Trent Bridge in 1938 when he correctly gave him out caught behind by Les Ames off Reg Sinfield. Frank Chester was a promising batsman with Worcestershire who took to umpiring when his playing career was cut short by the loss of an arm in World War I. He officiated in many of the matches on the Don's four tours of England. Of the Australian run-machine, Chester once said: "I left the Lord's Test in 1930, after watching Bradman, firmly convinced that he was the greatest batsman of all time."

The umpire rated by the Don as the best in Australia between the Wars was George Hele, who stood with George Borwick in each of the five Bodyline Tests in 1932–33. Hele said after the explosive Third Test in Adelaide that had the incidents which so enraged the crowd happened in Melbourne, many of the angry spectators would have jumped the fence. Bradman himself passed the test of the New South Wales Cricket Umpires Association on August 1, 1933. The occasion was marked by a cartoon in a newspaper by former Test bowler Arthur Mailey. The Don told the ABC's Norman May in 1987 that "I never had the slightest intention of becoming an umpire. It was just that I realised the necessity for me as an international player to have a thorough understanding of the laws." But he tried out his knowledge when he officiated with then South Australian premier Tom Playford in a match between the Chamber of Manufacturers and Trades Hall at Adelaide Oval in 1949.

"Uncanny Feeling, An"

How the Don described the experience of talking to members of his family in Australia from Liverpool, England, on the newly established radio-telephone link on May 26, 1930.

V

Verity, Hedley

England slow bowler who claimed 14 Australian scalps for 80 runs – six of them in the last hour on a wet wicket on the third day of the Lord's Test in 1934. He dismissed the Don in both innings – for 36 and 13. The resounding victory for England, in what became known as "Verity's match", was the home side's first win over Australia in a Test at Lord's since 1896. Despite getting the measure of Bradman in this match, Verity was later to deny claims by some that the Don could not bat on a wet or sticky wicket: "Bradman was a great batsman on any wicket." The orthodox left-arm spinner from Yorkshire had taken the Don's wicket three times in Australia on the Bodyline tour in 1932–33 – twice in the Tests. Bradman's first six in a Test, and his first in a first-class game in Australia, was at the expense of Verity in the controversial Bodyline match in Adelaide, but Hedley caught-and-bowled him with his next ball. Former England captain Charles Fry described the shot played by the Don when he was bowled by Verity for 82 in the Second Test at the SCG in 1936–37 as "the worst stroke in the history of cricket". In county cricket Hedley Verity twice took all 10 wickets in an innings (on the second occasion conceding just 10 runs), and in the last game of his career, in 1939, claimed 7/9 against Sussex at Hove. He shares with Australia's Clarrie Grimmett the distinction of taking Bradman's wicket more times than any other bowler: 10 times each. Of Verity's 10 dismissals of the Don, eight were in Tests. He died as a POW in Italy in 1943, aged 38.

Victoria

State which tried to woo the Don from New South Wales in 1929–30. It was against Victoria that Bradman posted his highest score in Sheffield Shield cricket for South Australia when he made 357 at the MCG in 1935–36, his first season with his new state. It was also against Victoria that he played the last match of his first-class career, when he turned out for SA in a shield game at Adelaide Oval in March 1949 which doubled as a testimonial for SA coach and former Test player Arthur Richardson. He made 30 in the first innings but did not get a chance to improve on that score after twisting his ankle (the same one he had broken 11 years before) when he stepped on a sunken water tap in the field. In 39 innings in 26 shield matches against Victoria, the Don scored 3,642 runs at 113.81, with 14 centuries. His best score was his 357 for SA in 1935–36 but his 340 not out for NSW against Victoria in 1928–29 was then a record for the SCG. In all first-class matches against Victoria he batted 41 times in 27 matches, compiling 3,648 runs at 107.29, with 14 centuries.

Also the Canadian city near Vancouver where in a match on the 1932 tour of North America the Don took six wickets in one eight-ball over – without getting a hat-trick!

Voce, William

The big paceman was a left-arm bowling partner of Harold Larwood's, both at Nottinghamshire and, famously, for England in the Bodyline series of 1932–33. Bill Voce was involved with the Don in the most controversial incident of the 1946–47 Ashes series at the 'Gabba in Brisbane. When the Australian skipper was on 28, Voce bowled him a yorker. Bradman attempted to chop down on top of the ball to play it wide of the slips but instead it flew to Ikin at second slip. Voce's appeal for a catch was turned down by umpire George Borwick, who ruled it a bump ball. Many of the England players thought it was a catch, but the broadcasters agreed with the umpire, and the newspaper writers were divided. (Square-leg umpire Jack Scott agreed with Borwick in an article after the series that it was a bump ball.) The incident took on major proportions when Bradman went on to score 187 but as it turned out it did not make a difference to the result, because Australia won by an innings and 332 runs. Bill Voce died in 1984, aged 74.

W

WACA

Perth did not host Test cricket until 1970 but the Don played eight innings in six first-class appearances at the WACA ground between 1929–30 and 1947–48, compiling 643 runs at 91.86, with four centuries, including one double hundred. He also took two catches. His top score was 209 not out for South Australia against Western Australia in 1939–40.

Wakley, B(ertram) J(oseph)

Author of *Bradman the Great*, the definitive record of the Don's achievements in first-class cricket, originally published by Nicholas Kaye in London in 1959. A second edition was published in 1999 by Mainstream Publishing of Edinburgh. Having started the book for "my own spare-time amusement", Wakley worked from the scorebooks of Australian scorer Bill Ferguson, the sources of the MCC library, county cricket club records, the files of many newspapers in England and Australia, and several other books on cricket, most notably *Wisden Cricketers' Almanack*. BJ Wakley was born in 1917 to a Scottish mother and an English father and educated at Oxford before serving during the war in the Mediterranean. He was called to the bar in 1948 and specialised in divorce work. A keen cricketer, Wakley opened the batting for the Wimbledon club and once took all 10 wickets with his slow-medium bowling. He wrote a history of the club which was published in 1954. It was his misfortune that the only time he saw Bradman, at Hove in 1934, the Don scored only 19 of the 83 runs added to the score while he was at the crease, the lowest proportion of his career. Bertram Wakley was a judge in south-eastern England from 1973 to 1992 and also published *Classic Centuries*, in 1964. He died in October 2001, aged 84.

Wales

Where the Australians traditionally played a first-class tour game against the county side of Glamorgan in the seaport of Swansea. The Don appeared in the match in 1930 and 1938, scoring 58 and 19 not out, and 17.

Walker, Charles William

South Australian wicketkeeper who toured England with the Don in 1930 as Bert Oldfield's back-up custodian and in 1938 as deputy to Ben Barnett. Walker broke a finger in a Sheffield Shield game at the SCG in January 1938, requiring Bradman, his captain, to take over as 'keeper on a day on which the temperature reached over 110 degrees (43 degrees celsius) and hot westerly winds carried smoke from country bushfires over the ground. He executed a stumping in the first innings and took three catches in the second. The Don was to stand in for Walker again a year later almost to the day, once more for SA against NSW at the SCG, and again in sweltering heat. This was the match in which Bradman scored his sixth century in six innings, five of them in shield games. Charlie Walker was 33 when killed in action in Germany in 1942.

Wall, Thomas Welbourne ("Tim")

Fast bowler from South Australia who was an Australian teammate of the Don's from 1929 to 1934. Bradman considered that he was the best bowler that he ever faced while the ball was new. Wall was one of only eight bowlers to dismiss Bradman five times or more in the great man's first-class career. In a memorable performance for his state against New South Wales in a Sheffield Shield match at the SCG in 1932–33, Wall took all 10 wickets for 36 runs, a feat never before achieved in shield cricket. The Don top-scored for NSW with 56 out of a total of 113. Opener Jack Fingleton made 43, but the next-highest scorer was Bill O'Reilly with 4. Six batsmen, including Bill Brown and Stan McCabe, went for ducks. In later years Tim and his family became good friends of the Don and Jessie's. Tim's wife, Ev, accompanied the couple as the Don's assistant when he travelled to England to write on the 1953 Ashes series for London's *Daily Mail* and the Adelaide *News*. Tim Wall died in 1981, aged 76.

Ward, Francis Anthony

A South Australian leg-spinner of the 1930s who bowled in tandem for his state with the legendary Clarrie Grimmett. Having had a good season in 1935–36 during Grimmett's absence in South Africa, Ward got the nod at the start of the 1936–37 season for the Rest of Australia team (captained by the Don) in a testimonial for Warren Bardsley and Jack Gregory against Victor Richardson's Australian team which had returned triumphantly from South Africa a few months before. Bradman was at his best with 212 out of a score of 385, but Ward was outstanding with a bag of 12/227, overshadowing Grimmett's 7/228 for the Australians. The Rest won the match by six wickets. Ward continued his good form with 10 wickets for SA against the MCC (a match from which the Don stood down because of the death of his two-day-old son, Ross) and when the side for the First Ashes Test was announced, Ward learned he was to make his debut for Australia.

His selection (by a committee of three which included captain Bradman) at the expense of the 44-year-old Grimmett caused an uproar. Particularly put out was "the Gnome's" leg-break partner, Bill O'Reilly, with whom Clarrie had formed the spearhead of Australia's attack since 1931–32. In the First Test at the 'Gabba, Frank Ward answered his critics with 2/138 and 6/102, but performed moderately in the second and third matches and was dropped from the remaining two. But Grimmett was not re-instated. And when the party to tour England in 1938 was picked, and again Ward was chosen ahead of Grimmett, the outcry was even louder. In England, Ward bowled very well in the minor games, with tour figures of 92 wickets at 19.27 (capturing his scalps at an average of every 33 balls), but played in only one Test: the first at Trent Bridge when he finished with 0/142 in England's innings of 8/658 dec. Frank Ward died in 1974, aged 65.

Warne, Shane Keith

Of the celebrated Australian leg-spinner, the Don said in his 1996 interview with Ray Martin: "I think he's the best thing that has happened to the game of cricket for many, many, years, because the epitome of the game of cricket is a top batsman playing against a great third-finger leg-spinner … that's the best cricket you could possibly see." Soon after Bradman's death Warne said: "Myself and Sachin met him on his 90th birthday and we had a great day. Driving up in the car we were both very, very nervous. We asked him a few questions and it was just a great couple of hours, something I'll treasure forever. It's a sad day for everybody. Not just sportsmen but for all Australians. Sir Don has been such a great icon for Australia and for cricket." When Warne scored 63 with the bat in his 100th Test in South Africa in March 2002, he became only the fourth man to achieve the double of 2,000 runs and 400 wickets. In July 2004, Warne drew level with Sri Lankan spinner Muttiah Muralitharan as leading world Test wicket-taker.

Warner, (Sir) Pelham Francis ("Plum")

The former England captain and longtime administrator was once referred to by eminent British jurist and cricket aficionado Sir Norman Birkett as "that repository of all cricketing knowledge and wisdom", but is remembered by Australians as the target of the famous rebuke from the home side's captain, Bill Woodfull, on January 14, 1933 at Adelaide Oval during the Third Test of the Bodyline series: "Mr Warner, there are two teams out there on the field, and one is playing cricket and the other's not. That's all I'll have to say. Good afternoon." Woodfull had just been dismissed soon after being hit a bad blow over the heart by a short-pitched delivery from Harold Larwood to an orthodox field and then two overs later having to evade another of Larwood's bumpers which was bowled to a bodyline field. Warner, as co-manager of the touring team, went to the home side's dressing room to enquire about Woodfull's condition.

(Interestingly, Warner had himself protested a few months before in England about Bill Bowes bowling short-pitched balls with five men on the on-side in a county game. Writing in the London *Morning Post* on August 22, 1932, he said: "Now that is not bowling; indeed it is not cricket." But two years earlier, just after the Don's 334 at Headingley, Warner wrote in the same newspaper: "England must evolve a new type of bowler and develop fresh ideas and strange tactics to curb his almost uncanny skill.")

Warner was furious when the ticking-off from Woodfull appeared in the press, and blamed Jack Fingleton, a full-time journalist who was playing in the game, for the leak. Fingleton denied the charge and many years later alleged in a book that the source of the leak was the Don. In a quote in a biography of Bradman published in 1983, two years after Fingleton's death, the Don called the claim "a lie". In a pen portrait contributed to Fingleton's 1949 book *Brightly Fades the Don*, Warner was otherwise full of praise for Bradman but criticised him for his part in the omission of Clarrie Grimmett from the touring team to England in 1938. During Bradman's final appearance at Lord's, a match against the Gentlemen of England in August 1948, the Australian captain was presented with a cake and a copy of Plum Warner's book, *Lord's*, on the occasion of his 40th birthday.

Warwick Vase

A replica of which was presented to the Don at a farewell function at London's Savoy Hotel hosted by *People* newspaper at the end of the 1948 tour. The original vase was discovered in 1770 by Sir William Hamilton in the ruins of Emperor Hadrian's villa near Rome. The replica, made of solid silver, was financed by the Bradman Fund, set up by the newspaper several weeks before and subscribed to by "cricket lovers of Britain".

Waterman's

Exclusive pen shop in Montreal outside which the Don and new wife Jessie were photographed during the 1932 goodwill tour of Canada and the US. A few days later, the team were guests of Frank D. Waterman at a banquet at the Waldorf Astoria Hotel in New York.

Waugh, Stephen Rodger AO

Former test captain and leading Australian batsman who has the utmost respect for the Don and is in awe of his achievements. In "Privileges in the Shadow", an essay he contributed to the Ironbark Legends book on Bradman, he concluded: "In my favourite dream I have a vantage point high on the Hill at a packed Sydney Cricket Ground and I am watching Don Bradman, one of the world's greatest ever sportsmen, carve into an English attack. It is a mild summer's day and the operators in the old scoreboard are working overtime as Bradman cruises to another dazzling century and hundreds of Stetsons are thrown into the air in tribute to the maestro. This is as good as it gets." When told of the great man's death, Waugh's team was in Mumbai preparing for a Test. "By playing cricket we're showing him the necessary respect and I'm sure that's what his family wants also. Everyone loved Sir Donald Bradman in Australia. He united the country in times of need after the Second World War. Obviously he was a great player and an inspiration to millions of people, including myself. I was lucky enough to have a meeting with him one-on-one 12 months ago for about an hour and a half. It was a great time. It went too quick. I couldn't ask enough questions … He knew the game back to front and was very humble about his achievements. That is what struck me about him."

Weekes, (Sir) Everton De Courcy KCMG OBE

With (Sir) Clyde Walcott and (Sir) Frank Worrell, Weekes was one of the famous "three Ws" from the West Indies. An extremely aggressive right-hander with a wide range of shots on both sides of the wicket, he was rated by the Don as the best batsman ever to represent the Windies. In the last match of his first Test series, against England in 1947–48, Weekes scored a century, and then in his next series, against India the following season, he made consecutive hundreds in his four Test innings (including two in the same Test). He missed a fifth only when run out for 90. In England in 1950 his seven tour tons included a triple century and four double centuries. Weekes was not at his best in Australia in 1951–52 when badly hampered by a leg injury, but at home against India in 1952–53 he averaged 102.28 in the Tests with three hundreds. In New Zealand in 1955–56 he scored six centuries in eight first-class matches, including three in consecutive innings in the first three Tests. On hearing of the Don's passing, he said he was "a very fine gentleman with a great love for and understanding of the game". Everton Weekes attended the memorial service in Adelaide.

Weerakoon, Bradman

Senior Sri Lankan government official whose father, the head of the Colombo Port Police, went on board the Australians' ship and secured the Don's autograph when the Ashes-winning team docked in Colombo on the way home on October 30, 1930. After gaining the prized signature, Mr Weerakoon senior went to a nursing home where his wife was expecting a baby. When he found that a boy had been born when he was away getting Bradman's autograph, he immediately named him after his hero.

Weet-Bix ®

In August 1998, Sanitarium Health Food Company ® issued a set of 16 Weet-Bix ® series cards to mark the Don's 90th birthday. The series, titled "Sir Donald Bradman AC: Greatest Hits", depicts the great batsman at various stages of his career. The cards were:

1. FIRST CENTURY
2. FIRST TRIPLE CENTURY
3. FIRST 1st GRADE CENTURY
4. 1st SHEFFIED SHIELD CENTURY
5. FIRST TEST CENTURY
6. WORLD RECORD
7. MOST TECHNICALLY SATISFYING INNINGS
8. RECORD TRIPLE CENTURY AT LEEDS
9. THE BODYLINE SERIES
10. BACK TO BACK SUCCESS
11. SOUTH AUSTRALIAN TEAM MEMBER
12. THE LAST TOUR OF ENGLAND, PRE-WAR
13. 100th FIRST CLASS CENTURY
14. LAST ENGLISH TOUR
15. TESTIMONIAL CENTURY
16. BATTING BRILLIANCE

Sanitarium ran out of the cards in January 1999 but had a system whereby collectors could send in cards to swap for others they needed to complete the set. Sanitarium Health Food Company ® and Weet-Bix ® are registered trade marks of the Australian Health & Nutrition Association Limited.

Weissel, Eric

Brilliant five-eighth from the Riverina area of New South Wales who played eight rugby league Tests for Australia between 1928 and '32. Also a good cricketer, he took a magnificent catch to dismiss the Don in a match in the annual Country Week carnival in Sydney in November 1926 when they were playing for regional country sides.

Wellington

Where the Don almost played in New Zealand in 1932, when Arthur Mailey's team of Australians stopped over on their way home from the goodwill tour of North America. There were many disappointed Wellingtonians when a one-day exhibition game planned for Monday, September 19 at the Basin Reserve was washed out without a ball being bowled. But late that night at a dinner the captains, Victor Richardson and Stew Dempster, desperate to give the locals a chance to see Bradman bat, agreed to play a two-hour match the next day from noon until 2pm, allowing the Australians time to get to the wharf before their ship sailed at 4pm. But the Don (with wife Jessie) and Chuck Fleetwood-Smith had made their own plans for a sightseeing tour of Wairarapa the next day (with an early start), and left the dinner before the match was arranged. The crowd of about 8,000 at the Basin Reserve were none too happy when Bradman failed to show, and neither was the Wellington team. Two of their players made up the numbers for Vic Richardson's side and there was consolation for the crowd when the Australians made 155 for 4 wickets in 70 minutes, Stan McCabe reeling off a quick-fire 78 not out, before the visitors rushed off to the wharf to catch their ship.

West Bengal

Government in India which planned to erect a statue of the Don alongside a memorial to Mahatma Gandhi in the heart of Calcutta but had a change of heart when Bradman decided not to travel to India for the 1987 World Cup.

Westbrook, Percival

Bowral real estate agent who employed the Don as a clerk in his office when he left school at 14 in 1922. As well as keeping the books, the young man learned to drive so he could show properties to clients. Westbrook installed Bradman as secretary of his Sydney office when he opened a branch in the city early in 1928. In his speech at the farewell function at Bowral's Empire Theatre on the eve of his first tour to England in 1930, Bradman said: "After leaving school I spent five years with Mr Westbrook before going to Sydney. Everything lay in his hands, but at great inconvenience he let me go to Sydney. It was due to him that I got my chance in big cricket." Westbrook later said of the Don: "He is worthy of all the praise lavished upon him, and no one need fear its effect on his character, as he remains today the same frank, open boy he was years ago."

Western Australia

Western Australia entered the Sheffield Shield competition in 1947–48 (when they won it), the Don's last full season in Australia, but he did not play in a shield match against WA. He did, however, play six other first-class matches against the state (three for South Australia, and three for Australia touring teams before boarding the ship for England) between 1929–30 and 1947–48, when he batted seven times for 731 runs at 121.83, with five centuries. His highest score was 209 not out for SA at the WACA in 1939–40, when he reached 200 in 155 minutes, the fastest double hundred of his first-class career.

West Indies

When a team from the Caribbean under George Grant toured Australia in 1930–31, it was the first time the two countries had met. In terms of average, the Test series against the West Indies was the third-least successful of the 11 in which the Don played, and easily the leanest of the three series he played against countries other than England. In his six Test innings he made scores of 4, 25, 223, 152, 43 and 0, for an average of 74.50 (by comparison, he averaged 201.50 against South Africa in 1931–32 and 178.75 against India in 1947–48). The duck in the second innings of the Fifth Test at the hands of paceman Herman Griffith (who had dismissed him in the first innings of the first match for 4) was Bradman's first in a Test. Earlier in the series he had another first – as a bowler. When he trapped wicket-keeper Ivan Barrow lbw for 27 in the second innings of the First Test in Adelaide, it was the first of the Don's only two wickets in Test cricket.

Whatman

Maiden name of the Don's mother, Emily. The move of the Bradman family from Yeo Yeo in the Cootamundra district to Bowral in 1911 was a return home for Mrs Bradman, whose family had been resident in nearby Mittagong since the beginning of white settlement. Emily's brother, George, was the Don's captain with the Bowral Town cricket side in the 1920s, and another brother, Dick, was also a regular member of the team. Gordon Whatman, a grandson of another brother, Mark, is now in his early 80s and lives in Glebe Street, Bowral, two doors from where the Don lived from 1924 to 1928.

Whatman, Gordon Lewis

A second cousin of the Don's son John who was president of the local cricket association in 1972 when he decided that Bradman Oval was in need of a makeover. He persuaded then Bowral Municipal Council to part with the necessary funds and saw the project through. And on the day of the opening on September 4, 1976, he provided the ball (one of his spares) which Bill O'Reilly bowled (about two metres wide of the leg stump) to the Don. As one of the several officials who had accompanied the pair to the middle, he fielded his own ball behind the wicket. In September 1975, when the refurbishment of the ground was in progress, Gordon submitted a proposal to the council to replace the old brick and sandstone dressing sheds and wooden seats with a new pavilion (incorporating a cricket museum) to supplement the new oval. This time the council said that part of the funds had to be raised by the two local cricket clubs. But Gordon's enthusiasm was not shared by the clubs and the project stalled. Eventually the campaign was taken up in 1983 by local solicitor Garry Barnsley. With the announcement of a grant from the New South Wales Bicentennial Council in 1985, a committee of Wingecarribee Shire Council was formed to oversee the project, with Barnsley in the chair and Sydney barrister Bruce Collins a notable contributor. A fundraising drive led to the formation of the Bradman Museum Trust in 1987 and later the building of the Bradman Pavilion (which housed a temporary museum) and the Bradman Museum. When the pavilion was completed in 1989, Gordon was invited by then trust chairman Bruce Collins to join him on the balcony. Gordon told Bruce that he was "overwhelmed" by the new pavilion – and that it was "a dream come true". He had kept the ball which was bowled by O'Reilly to Bradman at home (in Glebe Street, opposite the oval) for some time before having it mounted and donating it to the museum, where it remains on display. Of the Don, Gordon said: "Over the years we did have contact, not regularly, but we did talk. He was an average, quiet person, one you could talk to. He was one of those people who never acted above you. He was always on your level, you could talk to him quite comfortably." In June 2004, Dulcie and Gordon Whatman received letters of congratulation from a host of luminaries, including the Queen, Governor-General Michael Jeffery, Prime Minister John Howard and NSW Premier Bob Carr, on the occasion of their diamond wedding anniversary.

Whitelaw, A(rthur) E(dward)

Expatriate Australian soap magnate in England who sent the Don a cheque for 1,000 pounds sterling (worth around $60,000 today), "as a token of my admiration", after his world-record Test score of 334 at Headingley in 1930. Whitelaw also sent each of Bradman's teammates an ash tray. Australian Test player Jack Fingleton (who was not on the tour) was later to criticise the Don for not sharing the proceeds with his teammates or at least shouting drinks.

Whitington, R(ichard) S(mallpeice)

Dick Whitington was a journalist and a South Australian opening batsman who played for the Australian Services team against South Australia at Adelaide Oval in December–January, 1945–46. The Don agreed to play for SA in the match "purely as a gesture to try and get sport started again after the war". It was only his second game after a five-year lay-off because of illness and the war, and, despite being unfit and out of practice, scored a chanceless 112 at a run a minute. But Whitington wrote in a newspaper article during the match: "I have seen today the ghost of a once-great cricketer." Dick Whitington later published several books on the game, including *Time of the Tiger: The Bill O'Reilly Story*. He died in Sydney in 1984, aged 71.

Williams, Charles

Welshman who wrote the biography *Bradman: An Australian Hero*, published in London in 1996 by Little, Brown. Lord Williams of Elvel is a banker who was made a life peer in 1985 and became Labour's deputy leader in the House of Lords in 1989. He was a solid middle-order bat for Oxford University for three years in the 1950s, including one year as captain when he succeeded Colin Cowdrey (who was later to introduce him to the Don), and played six seasons with Essex. The idea for the book came from another Labour life peer, Lord Willis, in 1992, just after the publication of Williams's biography of Charles de Gaulle, a work now widely regarded as the definitive study of the French general and politician. Williams explains in a prologue how Willis walked up to him in a bar in the House of Lords and said: "I have got the subject for your next book." When Willis revealed it to be Bradman, Williams replied that "either he had gone mad or had been in the bar longer than I had". But Willis argued that Bradman was as much in the heroic mould, although in a different context, as was de Gaulle, "and since I was in the business of heroes – and a former cricketer – this was a natural book for me to write."

After preliminary research on Bradman in England, he made his first trip to Australia in January 1995, when he enjoyed a four-hour session with his subject in his Adelaide home. Lord Williams told Murray Hedgcock, an Australian journalist in London: "Much has been written about Bradman as a cricketer, but nobody, as far as I know, has written the story of his life as an Australian. I have tried to show how his cricketing genius became a focus for Australian aspirations during a particularly important period of history." And he told the *Sydney Morning Herald*'s Tony Stephens: "The Depression hit Australia harder than it hit the UK or the United States. The Mother Country was arrogant and imperialist, telling her dominion what to do. Morale was low in Australia – that is why Don became such a hero." In his book, Williams makes much of the sectarian divide between Catholics and Protestants before the war but he said that the Don "felt strongly about it".

Wilson, Timothy

Twelve-year-old cricketer who said it was "a once-in-a-lifetime opportunity" when asked by a group of businesspeople calling themselves SAVE (Some Australians Have Ethics) to present to the Bradman Foundation on August 27, 2001 (the Don's birthday) five letters written by Bradman to former Australian captain Greg Chappell which the group had bought anonymously at auction for $19,000 a few weeks before. Tim handed over the letters to the foundation's executive officer, Richard Mulvaney, at a lunch at the Melbourne Cricket Club.

"Wimbledon Throat"

An ailment which afflicted the Don and several of his teammates at the time of the Third Test at Old Trafford in early July, 1934, which was (most unusually for Manchester) played in heatwave conditions. Alan Kippax was ruled unfit to play and Bradman and Arthur Chipperfield went to the wicket directly from their sick beds and thence back again for observation. It was feared at one point that the men had diphtheria. Bill Brown (who had a touch of the bug himself) said recently that he remembers it well, though he could not recall why it was called Wimbledon Throat. But apparently the high temperatures affected most of England in June–July 1934. According to Audrey Snell, assistant librarian at the Wimbledon Lawn Tennis Museum: "Wimbledon fortnight in 1934 was 25 June to 7 July. It was terribly hot that year and the dust and dryness was said to be the cause of Wimbledon Throat. The infection was by no means confined to Wimbledon but it seemed worse than anywhere else."

Wine

Contrary to common belief, the Don was not a teetotaller after his playing days. He was a moderate drinker who enjoyed wine with his food and also had the occasional brandy, and even a Scotch. In his 1975 book

On Top Down Under, Ray Robinson wrote: "Relaxation was a state which I know he appreciated in mellower years in life when, without over-indulgence, the ex-abstainer became an authority on the red wines of South Australia." But in 1994, when the parents of children at a Catholic school in Melbourne asked Bradman as one of various celebrities to donate a bottle of wine to be auctioned for the school, he declined. In a letter of reply he said it wouldn't be fitting for him to contribute, because he didn't think children should be associated with alcohol. The auction raised more than $5,000 for the school. The highest price paid was $200 – for the Don's letter.

Wingello

Small town a few kilometres south of Bowral which fielded a team in the Berrima District Competition. It was against Wingello that 17-year-old Bradman played a famous innings of 234 in 1925–26, his first full season as a member of the Bowral side. The Wingello attack included the outstanding leg-spinner Bill O'Reilly, at the time a 20-year-old student at Sydney Teachers College at home for the summer holidays. Bradman was dropped twice in the slips off the great leggie before finishing the day on 234, his last 50 including 4 sixes and 6 fours. But O'Reilly bowled the Don with the first ball of the second day, a week later, at Wingello on the ground now known as Bill O'Reilly Oval.

Wisden

The 1948 edition of *Wisden Cricketers' Almanack* claimed that, royalty apart, the Don was the best-known person in England with the possible exception of Winston Churchill. Bradman wrote only two major articles for the cricket bible: the first in 1939, and the second in 1986. The theme of both was the need for cricket to adapt to the quickening tempo of modern life. In the second piece, he was several years ahead of the game when he advocated the use of television replays for some decisions in limited-overs cricket. When Wisden in 2000 voted Bradman the Cricketer of the Century, the Don said in a statement: "I am very honoured to be recognised by Wisden in this way. I am very pleased that Jack Hobbs was also chosen, as he was one of my boyhood heroes." As the clear winner of the poll to decide the top five players of the century, Bradman was the only man chosen by each of the 100 panellists. When the Don passed away on February 25, 2001, Wisden delayed their 2001 *Cricketers' Almanack* so it could go to press with a comprehensive updated chapter on the master batsman.

Wisden on Bradman

Book edited by Graeme Wright and published in Australia by Hardie Grant Books of Melbourne, 301pp. It was released as a 90th Birthday Edition in hardback in August 1998 at $32.85, then in paperback in August 1999 at $17.95. The work boasts all the Don's first-class scores as well as essays and match reports in "Wisden's idiosyncratic, time-encapsulating style".

Withersfield

Hamlet of about 200 people in Suffolk, England, which the Don visited during the 1930 tour in search of his forefathers. Bradman's grandfather, Charles, was living in the area when he emigrated to Australia in 1852 to escape the harsh agricultural recession. In a letter of reply in the 1980s to researcher Nigel Ward, the Don wrote: "On the question of my ancestry, I must confess to having little knowledge. Some people claim my forebears came from Withersfield but I have no proof of that. I believe I did pay a visit there in 1930 to see an old lady who claimed relationship, but it was never proved. There are many people who have made claims of this sort, but I found the claims to be false." But Ward's research over the next 10 years was to prove that most of Bradman's ancestors had lived in Withersfield after moving from Bradenham in Norfolk. He discovered that Sir Donald's great-great-grandparents, John and Susanna, had married in St Mary's Church, Withersfield, in 1769. Their second son, John, married Anne Hiner in the same church in 1795. Their son, also John Bradman, married Lucy Rowlinson there in 1838. The Don accepted an invitation in the 1990s from the local cricket club – which then played in the Haverhill midweek league and in division three of the Suffolk league on Sundays – to become an honorary member. At the time of his death, Bradman was honorary vice-president and a registered player. The village pub, the White Horse, has a 1930s Bradman bat, and, as club headquarters, is official home to the Sir Donald Bradman Trophy, awarded annually to the club's best player.

Woodfull, William Maldon OBE

Known variously as "Old Steadfast", "the Unbowlable" and "Wormkiller", Bill Woodfull was a longtime right-handed opening partner of Bill Ponsford's for both Victoria and Australia, the pair notching up more than 20 century partnerships in first-class cricket, 18 of them for the first wicket. Woodfull toured England in 1926, 1930 and 1934, the last two occasions as captain, and appeared in two Ashes series at home: in 1928–29 and, as skipper, in the Bodyline series of 1932–33. He also captained the winning side in home series against the West Indies in 1930–31 and South Africa in 1931–32. In all, Woodfull led the Australian side in 25 of his 35 Tests, winning back the Ashes in 1930 and 1934. His words to England manager Plum Warner in the home side's dressing room during the Third Bodyline Test in Adelaide soon after being hit by a Larwood bouncer are etched in Australian folklore: "Mr Warner, there are two teams out there on the field, and one is playing cricket and the other's not. That's all I'll have to say. Good afternoon." (Incensed when Woodfull's comments were published in the Australian press, Warner attributed the leak to Jack Fingleton, a member of the Australian team in Adelaide and a career journalist. But Fingleton claimed in a book published in 1978 that the Don was the culprit, and said he had always been dirty on him for not clearing him by owning up. Two years after Fingleton's death, in a quote in a 1983 biography, Bradman called Fingleton's allegation "a lie". But Fingleton notably also wrote that "Warner himself had the cheek to think such a sensational story would not leak out.")

Though he deplored Jardine's intimidatory tactics, the Australian captain maintained his standards throughout the rubber and refused to retaliate. Bill Woodfull combined with the Don in seven second-wicket century partnerships in Tests, the best of them 274 against South Africa at the MCG in 1931–32 and 231 at Lord's in 1930. Bradman made 124 and 225 playing for Woodfull's XI in a Test trial at the SCG in December 1929. Woodfull once said the Don was worth three batsmen, and on another occasion summed him up in just three words: "He's a freak." But in an interview in 1980, Bill Ponsford told journalist Michael Davie that "Bill Woodfull never forgave him [Bradman] for a couple of things." In Davie's own words: "I was too cowardly to ask the key question," but he speculated the first "thing" may have had to do with the leaking of Woodfull's exchange with Warner. Apparently the Australian captain was not happy that his barb became public (though not nearly as upset as his target) and may have known, or believed, the Don to be the leaker. The second sticking point may have been Bradman's sudden withdrawal because of illness the day before the First Test in Sydney, won resoundingly by England despite the great knock by McCabe. The Don was very run-down after the gruelling tour of North America and had just been through a dispute with the Australian Board over his contract to write for the press, but Woodfull may have expected his star batsman to steel himself in the interest of the team. Bill Woodfull was a mathematics teacher who became headmaster of Melbourne High School. He retired to Tweed Heads on the north coast of New South Wales and died of a heart attack in 1965 at the age of 67 while playing golf.

Wooldridge, Ian

Of the 77 players missing from the official Test Centenary celebrations in London in 1980, 14 were Englishmen and another 14 were Australians, but the *Daily Mail* cricket writer singled out the Don for criticism because he did not make the trip. In a piece on August 27, 1980, Bradman's 72nd birthday, Wooldridge wrote: "The Don is averse to sharing anything, lime-light not excluded," and conjured up an analogy with "Patton's lust for glory". But the Don did not travel to England for the occasion because of the ill-health of his wife, Jessie, who had survived open-heart surgery a few years before and had suffered periodic relapses since. In 1983, writing in the *Mail* of a new Bradman biography, Wooldridge praised the great man's qualities as a batsman but, in a reference to when the Don received a gift of 1,000 pounds from an Australian industrialist in 1930 after his 334 at Leeds and did not shout his teammates, he wrote: "In short, he was shockingly mean."

Woolley, Frank Edward

Great England all-rounder who made his Test debut in the match in which Australia's Warren Bardsley became the first player from any country to score a hundred in each innings of a Test: at the Oval in 1909. Woolley did not consider the Don worthy of a place in a World XI he chose in his book, because of doubt about Bradman's ability on sticky wickets.

Worcester

Beautiful ground (with, in the Don's words, "the architectural gem of a cathedral in the background") in the loop of the Severn River where Bradman scored three double centuries and a century against Worcestershire on his four tours of England. His average here of 201.75 was his best of any ground on which he made a total of more than 500 runs. He was the youngest player to score a double ton in England when he made 236 in 1930 in his first innings in England. The Don wanted to sit out the corresponding game in 1934, traditionally the first match of the tour, because he felt too ill to play, but captain Bill Woodfull urged him to give it a go for the sake of the team: "They [the English media] are saying you are a sick man and won't be a force on the tour. And so psychologically I want you to play in this match and I want you to do well; that is to under-cut what the press are saying." Bradman played and made 206 at a run a minute (with one chance), recalling later that "it took a heavy toll on me". But he rated his chanceless 258 in 293 minutes, with a five and 33 fours, four years later as the best of his three double hundreds. Later on that tour he was presented with a Royal Worcester Vase by the Royal Worcester Porcelain Works to commemorate his three consecutive double centuries.

Words from the Don
Compact disc which contains excerpts from speeches given by Bradman to the Australian Cricket Society in 1973; the Lord's Taverners at the Hilton Hotel, London, in May 1974; the Adelaide Rotary Club in September 1974; the South Australian Cricket Association umpires dinner in March 1977; and at a South Australian Cricket Association dinner commemorating Sir Donald's 80th birthday in August 1988. Published by the Bradman Collection in association with the State Library of South Australia.

World Confederation of Sport
Body which voted the Don one of the Top Ten sports figures of the 20th century.

World Series Cricket
The Don served on the Australian Board's Emergency Committee which was set up in 1977 to deal with Kerry Packer's revolution when the media magnate signed up 66 of the game's leading players. But Bradman at the time was notably silent (at least in public) on the breakaway movement, as he was also a few years later when the sanctity of Test cricket was threatened by the rebels who went to South Africa in droves. There were murmurings that it was because the Don himself was the prototype of the contemporary professional cricketer and he therefore had empathy with those seeking radical change. But Bradman resented the charge, as was evidenced in 1989 when he wrote testily in a letter: "With respect, may I point out that I was not a professional cricketer or a cricket mercenary. I was always a genuine amateur in the true sense of the word in that I earned my livelihood from a civilian occupation divorced from cricket as far as I could make it." For two years there were two forms of cricket being played, one under WSC and the other under the ACB, until the rift was healed with a compromise deal signed by the protagonists in April 1979. But the game had been changed forever.

Wrestling
One of the many sports at which the Don was more than a dab hand. There is a photo of him in *Images of Bradman* with a headlock on then New South Wales amateur champion Jim Deakin. The Don believed that wrestling was good for his fitness by strengthening his shoulder and arm muscles.

Wright, Douglas Vivian Parson

A leg-spinner from Kent, Wright was an integral part of the England team from 1938 until 1951. He suffered badly at the hands of Stan McCabe during his great innings of 232 (out of 300) at Trent Bridge in 1938, at one point McCabe taking 44 off three of his overs. During the Adelaide Test in 1946–47, Keith Miller hit the first ball of the day, a no-ball from Wright, over the fence for six. In the last Test of that series at the SCG, Wright's seven wickets gave England a first-innings lead but the Don's side went on to win the match by five wickets. Fred Trueman, the England paceman of the 1960s, wrote in his 1977 book *Ball of Fire*: "It was said Australia had helped pick the England team for years. The classic case was when Don Bradman went on about Doug Wright being the finest leg-spin bowler he had ever played against. They kept picking Doug and Bradman kept knocking double centuries off him." Doug Wright died in 1998 at the age of 84.

Wyatt, Robert Elliott Storey

Opening and middle-order batsman who replaced Percy Chapman as captain of England (his side having been demoralised by the Don's record performances) for the Ashes-deciding last Test in 1930 at the Oval. He was Douglas Jardine's vice-captain in the Bodyline series and the losing skipper when Bill Woodfull's side regained the urn in England in 1934. Wyatt lost two more series as captain against the West Indies and South Africa before touring Australia in 1936–37 under Gubby Allen. Bob Wyatt published the widely acclaimed *The Ins and Outs of Cricket* and served as chairman of England selectors. He died in 1995, aged 93.

X

X-ray
Which revealed a slight fracture of the bone after the Don went over on an ankle when bowling in the gruelling Test at the Oval in 1938. The mishap put paid to Bradman's cricket for the rest of the tour, and also prevented him from keeping an appointment in London for a game of squash with world champion Amr Bey.

Y

Yardley, Norman Walter Dransfield

Yardley was a right-handed batsman and a right-arm medium-pace bowler who as England captain at the Oval in 1948 shook the Don's hand and called for three cheers for him from his team before Bradman took guard in the final Test of his career. After the match, won convincingly by the Invincibles to give them a 4–0 victory in the series, Yardley again called for three cheers for Bradman and his men from the balcony of the pavilion. The Yorkshire all-rounder played his first Test in 1938 against South Africa and was wounded in the Western Desert during World War II. He was Wally Hammond's vice-captain on the Ashes tour of Australia in 1946–47, when he dismissed the Don in three consecutive Test innings. Yardley took over as England skipper for the last Test of the rubber when the disenchanted Hammond's fibrositis forced him to withdraw. Australia won the series 3–0. Norman Yardley was North of England squash champion on five occasions and was also a good hockey and rugby player. He served as chairman of England Test selectors and became a popular BBC radio broadcaster. Yardley's regard for the Don was beyond question: "For me, it is an honour and a pleasure to have played against him." Norman Yardley was 74 when he died in 1989.

Yeo Yeo (pronounced Yo Yo)

Former small railway settlement (now virtually non-existent) 25 kilometres north of Cootamundra where the Don's father, George, had a wool and wheat farm. The family had moved from nearby Jindalee to Yeo Yeo when George bought the property from James Raymond on April 25, 1907. Emily and George's fifth child, and second son, was born at the house of midwife Eliza Scholz in Cootamundra on August 27, 1908 and taken home after two-and-a-half days. Almost three years later the family moved from Yeo Yeo to the cooler climate of Bowral to benefit the health of the Don's mother. The property was sold to Charles Tibble on May 26, 1911. In the 1970s, the then owner, Bob Caldwell, offered the cottage where the Don had spent his infancy to Cootamundra Shire Council with a view to the building being dismantled and re-erected as a museum. Committees were set up to consider the matter but the council did not take up the offer. Mr

Caldwell then approached the Temora Historical Society, which gladly accepted, and the society dismantled and moved the cottage to the Temora Rural Museum in 1980.

Yorkshire County Cricket Club

Club of which the Don was made a life member (the first time a non-Englishman had been so honoured) in recognition of his achievement in scoring a century – including 334 in 1930 and 304 in 1934 – in each of his four Test appearances at Headingley in Leeds. He received the honour at a presentation during a lunch interval at the festival match at Scarborough in 1948, the last first-class game of the tour. The Don was later accorded the same honour by Manchester and Lancashire CCC, and by Hampshire CCC. Bradman wrote in 1948 that he believed Yorkshire crowds were the most knowledgeable in England, and that the best crowd in Yorkshire was the one at Bramall Lane in Sheffield. (Yorkshireman Len Hutton was later to claim in his book *Fifty Years of Cricket* that Bramall Lane spectators had no equal for lively wit.)

Z

Zander, Frank
Retired pharmacist who was the Don's regular golf partner on Tuesdays at the Kooyonga club in Adelaide for eight years from 1990.

Zanetti, Paul
Freelance artist whose cartoon of God asking the Don for his autograph on his arrival in Heaven appeared in many newspapers in Australia soon after his passing on February 25, 2001.

Bibliography

The following sources were of great assistance in research for
The A–Z of Bradman:

Books

Bradman, Don, *Don Bradman's Book.* Hutchinson, 1930.

Bradman, Sir Donald, *The Art of Cricket.* Hodder & Stoughton, 1958, rev ed 1969.

Bradman, Sir Donald, *Farewell to Cricket.* Pavilion Books, 1988 (originally pub by Hodder & Stoughton, 1950).

Cotter, Gerry, *The Ashes Captains.* Century Hutchinson Australia, 1989.

Coward, Mike (ed.), *Sir Donald Bradman A.C.* Pan Macmillan Australia, 1998. Essays by Bannon, John; Cavalier, Rodney; Gough, John; Parish, Bob; Raiji, Vasant; Waugh, Steve.

Derriman, Philip (ed.), *Our Don Bradman.* Macmillan Australia, 1987.

Docker, Edward Wybergh, *Bradman and the Bodyline Series.* Angus & Robertson (UK), 1978.

Ferguson, WH, *Mr Cricket – An Autobiography of Fergie.* Nicholas Kay Limited, 1957.

Fingleton, Jack, *Cricket Crisis.* Cassell, 1946.

Fingleton, Jack, *Brightly Fades the Don.* Pavilion Books, 1985 (originally pub by Collins, 1949).

Franks, Warwick (ed.), *Wisden Cricketers' Almanack Australia.* Hardie Grant Books, 2003.

Fraser, Colin, *Sir Donald Bradman, Australian Legend.* Australia Post, 1997.

Frindall, Bill (ed.), *The Wisden Book of Test Cricket 1876–77 to 1977–78.* Macdonald and Jane's, 1978.

Frith, David, *Bodyline Autopsy.* ABC Books, 2003.

Geddes, Margaret (ed.), *Remembering Bradman.* Penguin Group Australia, 2002.

Hutchins, Brett, *Don Bradman: Challenging the Myth.* Cambridge University Press, 2002.

Inglis, Ken, *This is the ABC.* ABC Books, 1983.

Jervis, James, *A History of the Berrima District.* Berrima County Council, 1962.

McGilvray, Alan & Tasker, Norman, *Captains of the Game.* ABC, 1992.

Martin-Jenkins, Christopher, *The Complete Who's Who of Test Cricketers.* Rigby (in Australia), 1980, rev 1981 (originally pub in Great Britain by Orbis, 1980).

Morris, Barry (coll.), *Bradman: What They Said About Him.* ABC, 1994.

Moyes, AG, *Bradman*. Angus & Robertson, 1948.

Powell, Gareth, *Australian Motoring Guide*. Random House, 1995.

Robinson, Ray & Haigh, Gideon, *On Top Down Under*. Wakefield Press, 1996.

Rundell, Michael, *The Dictionary of Cricket*. Guild Publishing, 1985.

Sando, Geoff & Whimpress, Bernard, *Grass Roots*. SACA, 1997.

Smith, Ric, *The ABC Guide to Australian Test Cricketers*. ABC, 1993.

Wakley, BJ, *Bradman the Great*. Mainstream, 1999 (originally pub by Nicholas Kaye, 1959).

Williams, Charles, *Bradman: An Australian Hero*. Little, Brown, 1996.

Newspapers

(Adelaide) *Advertiser*
Jory, Rex
Shiell, Alan
Uncredited

Age
Debelle, Penelope

Australian
Blair, Tim
Chulow, Martin
Conn, Malcolm
Coward, Mike
Crawford, Barclay
Devine, Frank
Debelle, Penelope
Este, Jonathan
Gould, Shane
Haigh, Gideon
Hedgcock, Murray
Kogoy, Peter
Krupka, Peter
Leak, Bill
McGarry, Andrew
Nason, David
Plane, Terry
Reid, Michael
Shedden, Iain

Sissons, Ric
Wallace, Christine
Wilson, Ashleigh

(Sydney) *Daily Telegraph*
Connolly, Steve
Kershler, Ray
Lalor, Peter
Morgan, Peter
Perry, Roland

Southern Highland News
Jefferson, Andrew
Walsh, Gerard

Southern Mail
Uncredited

Sun-Herald
Benns, Matthew
Meher-Homji, Kersi

Sydney Morning Herald
AAP
Allen, Peter
Brown, Malcolm
Coward, Mike
Davie, Michael

Davis, Charles
Debelle, Penelope
Dennis, Anthony
Derriman, Philip
Engel, Matthew
FitzSimons, Peter
Glendinning, Lee
Growden, Greg
Hinds, Richard
Huxley, John
McKernan, Michael
Mann, Simon
Masters, Roy
Meacham, Steve
Meher-Homji, Kersi

Ramsey, Alan
Ray, Mark
Richards, George
Robertson-Glasgow, RC
Stephens, Tony
Thompson, Tom
Verghis, Sharon
Wilkins, Phil

(London) *Times*
Woodcock, John

Wairarapa Times-Age
Wyatt, Andrew

Magazines

Boundary
Radford, Bob

Cricket Talk
Ezekiel, Gulu
Laurie, Rob

Outlook
Ezekiel, Gulu

Sportstar
Amarnath, Lala
Rajan, Sanjay

Weekend Australian Magazine
Wallace, Christine

Wirrimbirra
Maslin, Ron

Wisden Cricket Monthly
Meher-Homji, Kersi

Radio

Bradman: The Don Declares,
ABC radio interviews with
Norman May (1987).

Television/Video

Bradman, ABC television interview
with Jack Egan (1990).

87 Not Out, Nine Network television
interview with Ray Martin (1996).

Websites

www-aus.cricket.org

www.bradmancopyrightmaterials.com.au

www.cricketworld.com.au

www.cricinfo.com

www.cricket.com

www.go4cricket.com

www.indya.com

www.jasreview.com

www.news.com.au

www.334notout.com

www.thepavilion.com.au

www.penguin.com.au

www.treloars.com